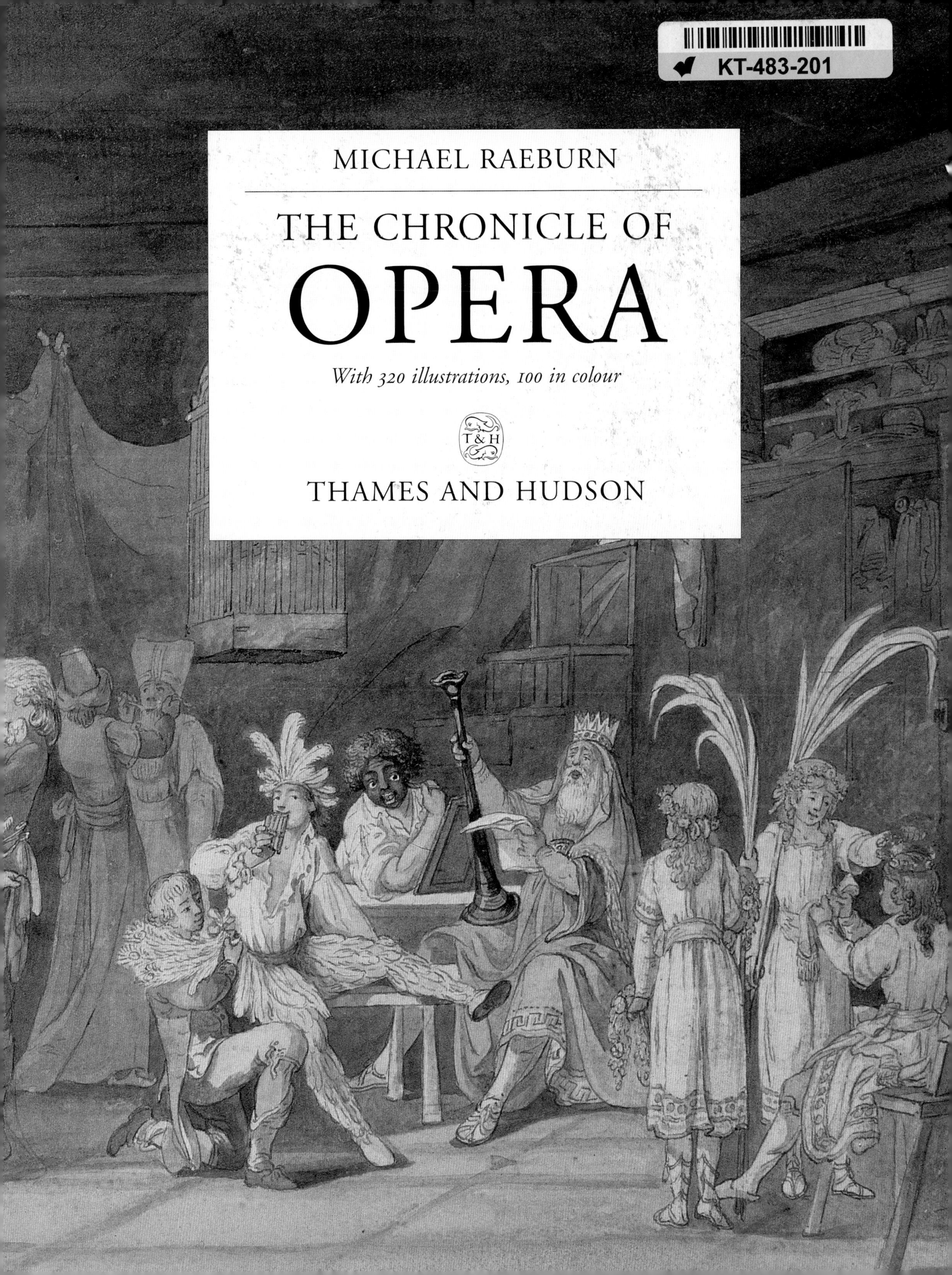

MICHAEL RAEBURN

# THE CHRONICLE OF OPERA

*With 320 illustrations, 100 in colour*

THAMES AND HUDSON

Half title: The principal opera houses in the USA in 1914.
Frontispiece: Singers dressing for *Die Zauberflöte*, 1794.

# ACKNOWLEDGMENTS

My first debt is to the many musicians who through their performances in the opera house or on record have made it possible for me to undertake such a wide-ranging book about opera; with them must be associated the family and friends who first encouraged me to listen to opera and who helped me to become acquainted with unfamiliar works, particularly Dora Raeburn, Christopher Raeburn, Erik Smith, the late John Culshaw and H. C. Robbins Landon. My publishers, Thames and Hudson, have been exceptionally helpful and I would like to thank everyone there who has been involved. The music and reference librarians of Hammersmith Central Library, the librarian of the London Library and the staff of the Performing Arts Library and the Westminster Music Library were unfailingly helpful. For assistance and support given while the book was in preparation I am especially grateful to Christine and Anthony Baker, Roger Chubb, Julia Engelhardt, Margaret Fisher and Bob Hughes, Jane L. Poole, Christina Raeburn, Sam Raeburn, John Richardson, Nick Thorner and Ann Hoenigswald, Russell Wilkinson and Eileen Guggenheim and, above all, Marilyn McCully, who read the text as it was written and whose encouragement and helpful criticism have been invaluable.

# DATES

For the sake of consistency, all dates are given according to the Gregorian calendar with years running from 1 January to 31 December. Old-style English (to 1752) and Russian (to 1918) dates commonly given according to the Julian calendar have been converted. 'Carnival' is sometimes used to indicate an approximate time of year during the seventeenth century. In principle the carnival opera season lasted from Epiphany (6 January) to Lent (generally starting in February), but dates varied from place to place, and in Venice the season began as early as October, often making precise dating impossible.



British Library Cataloguing-in-Publication Data
A catalogue record for this book is available from the British Library

ISBN 0-500-01867-7

Printed and bound in Singapore by C. S. Graphics

# CONTENTS

# Introduction

A CHRONICLE presents events in sequence as they occur, and there is a risk that as a result too simple a story will emerge. In the case of opera, this approach could be quite misleading: the milestones – premières of new operas, singers' débuts, openings of new theatres – mark beginnings, and their significance can only emerge in the light of subsequent developments. Although we generally think of the composer as the 'author' of an opera, music is only one of several elements that go to make up the on-stage performance, and every new production, indeed every performance, is itself an event, a new re-creation of the work. Furthermore, the composition, performance and reception of an opera are not simple matters, for opera is fraught with contradictions: between the words and the music; between tragedy and comedy; between the composer's intentions and their realization by the performers; in the function of an opera audience, which takes part in a social performance that has often rivalled the performance on stage; and between the demands of 'authenticity' and the need for creative interpretation in performing older works.

'Music first, then the words' was the title of a little eighteenth-century satire on the composition of an opera, set to music by Antonio Salieri (and later adapted by Richard Strauss for his *Capriccio*). In opera's earliest days the reverse was the case: the 'recitative style' was developed at the end of the sixteenth century specifically to clarify the musical setting of words in a natural dramatic context, and as opera developed it was the libretto on which theorists and reformers first lavished their attention. Composers – and singers – could be too wilful and needed to be reined in, so that music could resume its proper function as the 'handmaid of poetry'. *Opera seria*, the highly formalized style of operatic composition that was dominant for over a century, creates serious problems for modern audiences not only because the formality of the dramatic presentation is now wholly alien, but also because it was a genre that relied for its effect on the ritualized performance of themes and texts familiar to audiences. The libretti of Apostolo Zeno or Pietro Metastasio were variations on an extremely limited range of plots and subjects, and each one was set again and again by different composers.

However, the power of music, which the earliest composers wanted to demonstrate, was stronger than they could have imagined; whether the words are well or badly written, the internal drama of an opera progresses through its music. Librettists have learned to accept this situation. W. H. Auden wrote that 'the verbal text of an opera is to be judged not by the literary quality or lack of it which it may have when read but by its success or failure in exciting the musical imagination of the composer.' Christopher Hassall (who wrote the libretto for Walton's *Troilus and Cressida*) went further. He pointed out that it is at the moments when a character exits or makes an entrance that a librettist 'has the best chance of insuring that the story, both what has just gone before and what is immediately to come, is transparently clear...Since one should never rely on words being heard, the physical

*Pages 6–7*
Performance of Lully's *Armide* in 1761 in the opera house of the Académie Royale de Musique in the Palais-Royal, Paris. The opera had been written in 1686, but Lully remained the most important operatic composer in Paris long after his death, and the sets and costumes are in the modern rococo style. The audience, engaged in their own lively performance, are in intimate proximity to the musicians.

Orchestra in the eighteenth-century opera house in Drottningholm Castle, Sweden – where performances follow original conditions as far as is practicable – preparing for a performance of Haydn's *L'infedeltà delusa*.

movement of a character in opera has about it an especial eloquence – it is indeed…the special "language" in which the writer conceives his libretto…This action will be followed by the ideal critic for a libretto – the spectator who catches nothing of the text but has his eyes open.' Should an opera, then, be sung in the language of the audience? Are surtitles valuable, or do they distract from the special language of librettist and composer? There is no simple answer to these questions.

The earliest operas were narratives based on classical myth or ancient history. Their original intention, in their function as court entertainment, was to provide a moral lesson – and often an obsequious allegorical compliment – for a royal patron. Public opera needed more obvious attractions, and in Venice, where the first public theatres for opera opened in the 1630s, comic characters and a pronounced strain of sensuality were soon introduced. Moralists took strong exception to this, and the strict form of *opera seria* confined itself largely to political themes which illustrated royal clemency, justice and benevolence as a response to illicit passion, jealousy, treachery and lust for power.

Comedy, however, could not be kept out of the opera house, and the practice began (starting in Naples at the beginning of the eighteenth century) of performing a comic *intermezzo* in one or more parts between the acts of a serious opera. These were generally based on the stock figures of the *commedia dell'arte*: sentimental lovers, young servants, ridiculous old men, bragging captains and the mischief-making Harlequin. One of these works, Pergolesi's *La serva padrona* of 1733, has remained in the standard operatic repertory. In France where the *tragédie-lyrique* shared many of the features of *opera seria*, comic episodes were not interspersed, but parodies of each new tragedy would be performed in the popular theatres at the annual Paris fairs, with Harlequin taking on the hero's role. In England, where the taste for Italian opera matched that for Palladian architecture, operatic conventions were lampooned in the political satire *The Beggar's Opera*, in which various ballads and popular airs were strung together to accompany the plot. The development of comic opera as a sophisticated genre – of which Mozart's *Le nozze di Figaro* must be the undisputed masterpiece – was indebted to each of these traditions, but simpler kinds of musical comedy coexisted with works designed for the opera house, often leaving little trace other than a record of their performance. However, popular genres continued to flourish throughout the nineteenth and twentieth centuries: the *zarzuela* in Spain; the *opéra-bouffe* and *opérette* in France; the *operette* or *singspiel* in Germany; and light operas and musical comedies in Britain and America. Records of their performances appear only rarely in this book, unless the works have become a regular part of the opera-house repertory or have a special bearing on contemporary operatic history. It is impossible to make a precise delineation of 'opera', particularly when the varied forms of twentieth-century music-theatre have to be accommodated, but, as a rule of thumb, only works written for trained operatic voices have been

Three Venetian paintings showing performances of an *opera seria* (above) and a comic *intermezzo* (top left), and the audience leaving the opera house.

included. At the same time, space has not allowed the documentation of the phenomenon of 'crossover' – nothing new, though the Three Tenors' concerts have outdone even P. T. Barnum.

The performance of an opera depends, principally, on the singers. Prima donna – the principal female singer in an opera – has acquired a secondary meaning, and countless books of operatic anecdotes have been published that account for the origin of this usage. Although such compilations are generally repetitious and unilluminating, they can occasionally provide surprising insights. In his memoirs Otto Klemperer tells a story that says a great deal about the relationship between singer, conductor and the opera itself: Gustav Mahler was finding it impossible to get the tenor Erik Schmedes (who, like many tenors, had started his career as a baritone) to understand the role of Tristan. Klemperer asked his assistant, Bruno Walter, to explain to him its inner meaning, that it was 'about day and night, about Schopenhauer's philosophy etc. Walter did his best to put all this to Schmedes, but it was no use at all. The next orchestral rehearsal with Tristan showed no change in the singer's attitude. Mahler conducted, suddenly stopped the music and said: "Herr Schmedes, before the love potion you are a baritone, after the potion you are a tenor." That did it, and immediately everything worked.'

The fascination of such stories lies in the fact that singers are generally quite ordinary people, but the operatic voice is such an extraordinary gift that it sets them apart, creates an aura around their physical presence, especially when they are on stage. No amount of study and practice will produce a voice which is not there to start with. The physical appearance of opera singers has often been the target of satire, for while there have been – there still are – beautiful and handsome opera singers, vocal abilities are not necessarily matched by a singer's looks (and the reverse can also be true). But appearance is forgotten if the singer possesses that mysterious, sensuous gift of a voice. Opera singers had adoring fans long before there were film-stars or sporting heroes, and their magnetic effect on audiences, and often on composers too, is an important thread that runs through the chronicle of opera (Wayne Koestenbaum's remarkable book *The Queen's Throat: Opera, Homosexuality and the Mystery of Desire* explores many of the recesses of this subject).

On occasion, of course, the magic might wear thin, or perhaps a singer might stray into a rival's territory, and then the insurance of a claque was required. Singers (and composers) would pay a section of the audience to applaud their performances noisily, and also to show their disapproval at performances by their rivals. The disastrous premières of several famous operas – such as Rossini's *Il barbiere di Siviglia*, Verdi's *La traviata*, Puccini's *Madama Butterfly* – were due, at least in part, to the activities of these organized groups: playing away could be more hazardous than playing at home. In Milan, Paris, Vienna and elsewhere the claque would extort protection money, and singers making their début in any of these cities could expect a visit

A photographic montage of celebrated opera singers dating from 1915, when the Victor Talking Machine Company was the leading producer of operatic recordings.

from the semi-official head of the claque (as well as from impostors claiming this position) before their first appearance.

The earliest operas were court entertainments, and records of operatic premières show that royal birthdays and special events continued to be occasions for special performances well into the nineteenth century. For members of the audience, appearance at these functions was part of the constant jostling for position that life at court entailed. When the first public opera houses opened in Venice, not only were other entertainments, such as gambling, available, but there were opportunities for amorous encounters, and the theatre was also a place to see and be seen. Accounts of early operatic performances suggest that the audience paid scant attention to what was happening on stage or in the orchestra. The auditorium remained lit during the performance until the beginning of the twentieth century (though by then lights were beginning to be dimmed), and the social performance could be at least as important as the musical and theatrical one.

A delightful chapter in Dumas's operatic novel of revenge *The Count of Monte-Cristo* describes an evening at the Paris Opéra during a performance of Meyerbeer's *Robert le diable*. The bass Nicolas Levasseur (returning after a long illness) was singing the Mephistophelian part of Bertram, which he had created, while the great tenor Mario, Knight of Candia, played the title role, so the year must be around 1840. 'The curtain rose, as usual, with the auditorium practically empty. It is still a fashionable custom in Paris to arrive at the performance after the performance has started: as a result, during the first act those who have arrived are not occupied with watching or listening to the piece but in watching the audience come in and hearing the noise of the doors and of their conversation.' The progress of the performance on stage, punctuated by intervals in which social visits are paid to ladies in their *loges*, provides a time-frame for the continuing dialogue of the chapter; in the second interval the Count is asked what he thinks of the music. 'What music?' is his reply.

A scene from Peter Sellars's production of Handel's *Orlando* set at the Cape Canaveral Space Center, which was staged at the PepsiCo Summerfare Festival in Purchase, N.Y., in 1983.

Sixty years later, when the Moravian tenor Leo Slezak first appeared at Covent Garden, there had been little change. The brief opera season was part of the social calendar, so attendance was expected, but seats in the boxes and the stalls were all sold on subscription, and their occupants would not arrive until the end of the first act. 'They would meet in the first interval, when the ladies could show off their dresses and jewellery, sit through the second act so as to be able to meet again in the second interval, and leave as soon as Act III had begun. Only the holders of cheap tickets, who had actually come for the music, would see the performance through from beginning to end...Very few of the subscribers actually know how the opera ends.' Meyerbeer's operas were the ideal works to accompany the social performance, since they consist of a succession of visually and musically spectacular tableaux with striking climaxes, rather than a coherent ebb and flow of complex musical development; it is perhaps a sign of more attentive audiences that his operas, once the mainstay of the world's opera houses, are so seldom performed today. Not that the social imperative has disappeared from opera-going: opera seasons and summer festivals have become fixtures on the corporate entertainment calendar as important as art museum benefits or sporting championships.

Pleasing the audience while remaining faithful to the composer's intentions is one of the opera director's great dilemmas. There have been some composers – Berlioz is perhaps the most striking example – who were so discouraged by the contemporary operatic climate that some of their works were conceived as 'operas of the imagination', never intended for performance on stage, while others, like Wagner, composed operas which so tax the resources of singers that a perfect performance is virtually unattainable. At the opposite extreme, problems of interpretation can be caused by attractive works that seem flawed because their composers, who were less high-minded, exploited musical effects and pandered to the demands of self-promoting singers in order to win easy approval from their audiences.

There is, in any case, something faintly absurd about striving for absolute 'authenticity' in the musical performance, when the literary or political context of the libretto is lost beyond recall, the social and acoustic circumstances cannot be reproduced, and the staging and lighting – which caused the destruction by fire of so many opera theatres – would never be permitted. Nevertheless, it is true that opera has survived the centuries as a musical rather than a literary or dramatic form, and the music, whether by Monteverdi or Mozart, Wagner or Berg, has to be mediated for modern performance conditions. The latitude that should be permitted to the music director, the singers and the stage director is not subject to easy or clear-cut rules. Operas have survived, or have been successfully revived, because they appealed to the taste of the time, and Wagner's revisions of Gluck, Mahler's 'retouching' of Mozart or Vincent d'Indy's performing versions of Monteverdi and Lully, which would be unacceptable to modern ears, brought those works to life for audiences of their periods.

Now, perhaps, the comprehensive catalogue of recordings may help to establish standards, although disputes about style are never likely to be resolved. It is, of course, in its recorded form that opera reaches its widest audience, and it is possible to create operas of the imagination in the studio without having to confront all the most intractable problems presented by a live production in the opera house. Recordings also enable listeners to become far more familiar with both the music and libretto than was possible in the past, even when home music-making was a regular activity. The available repertory is much wider, and the performances, in general, may have far fewer faults, but nothing can compensate for the absence of the singers themselves. There is no way to reproduce the eloquence of that physical gesture implied by the librettist and composer which can only be understood when it is seen as well as heard.

It is the role of the stage director to ensure that the experience of live opera communicates the essence of the work to the audience. In a way his task is comparable to the baroque composer preparing to make the twentieth, or thirtieth, or sixtieth setting of one of Metastasio's libretti – *L'Olimpiade* perhaps or *Artaserse*; many members of the audience will be familiar not only with the work, but with several other interpretations, and his own efforts will be judged by the ways in which his version differs from these and offers innovative and surprising insights. Although free interpretations are nothing new – there was a celebrated series of productions under Klemperer at the Kroll Theater in Berlin in 1927–31 which included a realist *Fliegende Holländer* and a modern-dress *Falstaff* – the latitude and variety of approaches to opera production is a more recent phenomenon. They can frequently be unsuccessful, but sometimes the idea of setting *Rigoletto* in Al Capone's Chicago (Jonathan Miller) or Handel's *Orlando* at a space control centre (Peter Sellars) can capture the essence of an opera which in the one case has become overfamiliar, and in the other belongs to a genre which, to be acceptable to a modern audience, must be transformed in some way.

Opera, like myth, is the sum of its contradictions. It is about the power of music to restore what has been lost, even if it perishes again as soon as we try to grasp it; the power to transform the banal and the absurd into the transcendental. E. T. A. Hoffmann described the perfect opera as one 'whose music stems directly from the poetry, as its inescapable creation...Is not music the secret language of a distant spirit world, whose wondrous tones are echoed in our souls and waken a higher, more intense life? All the passions battle with one another in bright and shining armour, and are overwhelmed in an inexpressible longing, which fills our hearts.'

Placido Domingo as Hoffmann and Agnes Baltsa as Giulietta in John Schlesinger's Covent Garden production of Offenbach's *Les Contes d'Hoffmann* in 1985.

1

# 1589–1761

# BAROQUE OPERA

*Opera began as a bold intellectual experiment, an attempt to enhance the effect of dramatic verse with the emotional power of music and to create a modern equivalent for the great works of ancient classical drama. To focus attention on the text, a new 'recitative' style was developed, and this was adopted and transformed by Claudio Monteverdi into the first operatic masterpieces. Within a few decades public opera houses had opened, showcase 'arias' for idolized singers, particularly the* castrati*, overshadowed the dramatic language of recitative, and the social antics of the opera-going public had begun.*

*While a French style of opera and ballet flourished at the court of Louis XIV, a German composer, George Frideric Handel, made London the leading centre of Italian opera, writing a series of brilliant and enduring works for this artificial world.*

A performance of Jean-Baptiste Lully's *Alceste* at Versailles in 1674. The orchestra was divided into two parts to allow King Louis XIV an uninterrupted view of the stage.

# Baroque Opera

MUSICAL THEATRE was not invented at the end of the sixteenth century. Liturgical and secular dramas with music as an important element had been performed since the early middle ages and continued to be performed outside Italy after the birth of opera, but the earliest composers of opera in Florence did have a fundamentally new conception, for which they also found a new form and a new style of music. They were inspired by the model of classical Greek tragedy, and many of the features that went to make up the conventional structure of opera over the centuries were derived from this original model: the use of a chorus that both partakes in the action and comments on it; the inclusion of dramatic dance; and the combination in the individual roles of direct speech with reflective soliloquies, which gave rise to the alternation of recitative and aria. Polyphony had been a characteristic of Renaissance music, but in order to convey full dramatic impact, the words of the characters required monodic setting, and this meant the evolution of a new vocal style.

The reconstruction of Greek tragedy was a creative rather than an archaeological enterprise, and the nature and power of music itself was as important as the concept of drama. It was for this reason that the earliest operas took for their subject matter myths in which the power of music is an important element: *Dafne* is about the transformation of the nymph Daphne by Apollo, god of music, while in *Orfeo*, music is used to tame the spirits of the underworld. The most striking difference from ancient drama, however, is the moderation of the tragic material. In the ancient myth, not only does Orpheus lose Euridice when he is unable to resist turning to look at her – an action which will result in her having to remain in Hades – but afterwards he shuns all women and, as a punishment from Dionysus, is torn apart by Bacchantes. Peri's *Euridice*, however, ends with general rejoicing as Orpheus successfully brings Euridice back from the underworld. Even in Monteverdi's *Orfeo* the horror of the ancient story is toned down: Orpheus, leading Euridice out of Hades, turns, believing he hears the pursuing Furies. As he gazes on her beautiful eyes, she is taken away from him by the spirits. He mourns her death, singing to the woods and mountains with only Echo to respond to him, but Apollo takes pity on him and invites him to Heaven, where he sees Euridice's eyes among the stars.

In the earliest years of opera, several related forms were developed: in Rome, the sacred drama, or oratorio; and in Venice, the madrigal opera, in which the action was mimed while the story unfolded through a succession of polyphonic madrigals. The earliest oratorio, by Emilio de' Cavalieri, was not what we would understand by the term today, but a work intended for stage performance with a sacred subject and allegorical characters, employing the new monodic style; other operas on sacred themes followed during the seventeenth century. Madrigal operas, on the other hand, were soon eclipsed by the dramatic force of staged opera in which each character was sung by an individual singer. Both Rome and Venice were, however, important in developing the operatic form. Venice played the more obvious role, with the development of opera in public theatres, which encouraged the elaboration of plots, the development of comedy, a strong vein of sensuality, the featuring of individual singers with music composed to highlight their virtuosity, and the evolution of the opera house as a stage for social as well as a musical and dramatic performance.

Design for one of the *intermedi* in *La pellegrina*, staged in Florence in 1589, in which the new style of monody developed by Bardi's camerata was first tried out. Bernardo Buontalenti's drawing shows the figure of Necessity seated above the three Fates.

A rehearsal in London for Alessandro Scarlatti's opera *Pirro e Demetrio*, which was first produced there in 1709. The English soprano Katharine Tofts stands in the foreground with the *castrato* Nicolini in full-bottomed wig beside the harpsichordist.

In Rome, the new form received great encouragement after the Florentine Maffeo Barberini was elected pope as Urban VIII in 1623. His cardinal-nephews built an opera-theatre in their palazzo, and the operas put on there drew on a wider range of subject matter for their libretti, including pastoral and epic themes. When Urban died, the Barberinis, who were accused of financial misappropriation on a massive scale, fled for a time to France, and (with their former employee Giulio Mazzarino) were responsible for the introduction of Italian opera to the French court. There was later a reconciliation, and it was through the Barberinis that Christina, Queen of Sweden, who had given up her throne to join the Catholic church and in 1655 moved to Rome, discovered opera. She became a tireless enthusiast and had her own private opera, where she employed the young Alessandro Scarlatti. She was the moving spirit behind the opening of Rome's first public opera house, but her most lasting achievement was the foundation of the Accademia Reale, a group of intellectuals who used to meet in the gardens of her Roman palace and later formed the Arcadian academy. They set themselves the task of reforming the excesses of Venetian opera by prescribing the ideal libretti to be set to music. Their principles (as embodied in the many libretti of Apostolo Zeno, written between 1695 and the early 1730s) led to the strict form of baroque *opera seria*. They wanted opera to be concerned only with the 'noble passions', honour, duty and glory, rather than love. Consequently, historical subjects were far more fitting than mythological plots, and the number of characters was reduced in order to intensify the psychological force of the drama. Particular attention was paid to the form of the aria: it had to be in two stanzas, with the first repeated after the second, so that the music was in ABA form with a contrasting middle section and the reprise of the first allowing the singer scope for ornamentation. The poetry and music of each aria was designed to express one – or at most two – specific emotions, and a whole series of musical conventions was developed to indicate love, jealousy, anger, courage, despair, resignation or hope. The Arcadians' zeal for reform created a structure that all too soon became fossilized; Handel was one of the few composers whose music was able to transcend all these conventions.

Rome's other contribution to opera at this period arose from the papal ban on female singers on stage, which contributed to the extraordinary domination of *castrato* singers in both female and male roles. Pope Innocent XI went so far as to forbid women to be taught to sing: this is said to have been due to the beauty of a favourite singer of Queen Christina's, Angelica Giorgini, whose pursuers included a cardinal. The Pope ordered Angelica to be locked up in a convent, but she managed to escape and lived under the ex-queen's protection in her palace. Indeed, it was on hearing of the attempted rape of the singer by a dissolute abbé who was also a member of her household that Queen Christina suffered a fatal stroke. La Giorgini went on to become the mistress of the Viceroy of Naples, who did much to establish the operatic tradition of that city.

# 1589<br>1634 The New Art

*The efforts of the members of the Florentine camerata to replace Renaissance polyphony with music based on a single vocal line led to a new form of musical drama with the words sung in a declamatory style following the natural rhythms of speech. Opera swiftly reached maturity in the works of Monteverdi, in which the music serves to carry forward the dramatic plot, define the characters and express their emotions with intensity and great beauty.*

**DATES**

**1598**
On death of Fedor I Boris Godunov seizes the Russian throne; he dies in 1605

**1600**
Shakespeare's *Hamlet*

**1603**
Death of Queen Elizabeth I of England, who is succeeded by James VI of Scotland as James I

**1605**
Publication of first part of Cervantes' *Don Quixote* (second part 1615)

**1616**
Deaths of Shakespeare and Cervantes

**1618**
Start of Thirty Years' War throughout Germany

**1620**
Pilgrim Fathers leave for North America on the *Mayflower*

**1589** *May* ***La pellegrina*** (Bargagli) was performed with six *intermedi* devised by Count Giovanni de' Bardi and directed by Emilio de' Cavalieri (with music by Marenzio, Caccini, Malvezzi and others) for the marriage of Ferdinando de' Medici and Christine of Lorraine in Florence. The overall theme is the power of music over gods and men, and the musical style anticipates the first operas.

**1597** Performance of the *commedia dell'arte* 'madrigal opera' ***L'amfiparnasso*** (Vecchi) in Venice. It was composed in 1594, probably to words by the composer himself, who wrote: 'Life is my model, and in life the grave and the pleasant alternate and intermingle all the time. This is why I invent characters who appear on an imaginary stage and develop actions that can only be followed by the sense of hearing.'

**1597–8** *Carnival* Première of ***Dafne*** (Peri/Rinuccini), composed in 1594, in the palace of Jacopo Corsi in Florence. Most of the music of this and of Caccini's setting of the text (which may have been used in August 1600) is lost.

**1598** Publication of ***La pazzia senile*** (Banchieri/composer) in Venice. Since the parts for the individual characters are set as madrigals, the work was presumably mimed by masked *commedia dell'arte* characters.

**1600** *February* Performance of ***Rappresentatione di anima, e di corpo*** (Cavalieri/Manni?), at the oratory of the Chiesa Nuova, Rome. Although composed in the new style, the work contains very little recitative and consists largely of ensembles, choruses and dances.
*6 October* Première of ***Euridice*** (Peri/Rinuccini) at the Pitti Palace, for the marriage of Maria de' Medici and Henri IV of France. The title role was sung by Peri himself, but some of the settings of the text were by Caccini, who would otherwise not have allowed his pupils to take part in the performance.

**1602** *5 December* Première of ***Euridice*** (Caccini/Rinuccini) in the Salone Antonio de' Medici of the Pitti Palace, Florence. The opera was written in 1600 using the same libretto as for Peri's opera.

**1607** *22 February* Carnival première of ***La favola d'Orfeo*** (Monteverdi/Striggio) at the Accademia degl'Invaghiti, Mantua; two further performances were given shortly afterwards in the theatre at the Ducal Palace. Parts of the opera were sung in the composer's birthplace, Cremona, the same year (10 August) and there were performances around 1610 in Turin, Florence and Milan. At the première the title role was sung by Giovanni Gualberto.

LA DAFNE
D'OTTAVIO
RINVCCINI
Rappresentata alla Sereniss. GRAN DVCHESSA
DI TOSCANA
Dal Signor Iacopo Corsi.
IN FIRENZE
APPRESSO GIORGIO MARESCOTTI.
M D C.
Con Licenza de' Superiori.

Title page of Rinuccini's libretto for *Dafne*, set by Peri, Caccini and Gagliano.

Design by Bernardo Buontalenti for the musician Arion in the fifth *intermedio* in *La pellegrina*, also believed to be a portrait of the composer Jacopo Peri.

Design by Alfonso Parigi for the scene in *La regina Sant'Orsola* (1624) where the appearance of St Michael in the heavens scatters Lucifer and his devils. Spectacular apparitions and transformations were an integral part of the *intermedi* performed between the acts of spoken plays, and they quickly became an important element in opera.

**1608** *February* ***Dafne*** (Gagliano/Rinuccini) performed in the Ducal Palace, Mantua, to entertain guests who had arrived for the wedding of Francesco Gonzaga, originally planned to take place before mid-February but postponed. It was Gagliano's first opera, a resetting of the libretto used by Peri (see 1597–8).
*28 May* Première of ***Arianna*** (Monteverdi/Rinuccini) at the Ducal Palace, Mantua, for the marriage of Francesco Gonzaga and Margaret (Margherita) of Savoy; the first of numerous treatments of the myth of Ariadne's abandonment by Theseus and rescue by Bacchus. Of the music only the four-section 'Lamento d'Arianna' has survived, a wonderfully expressive piece which started the tradition of operatic laments. The festivities also included (4 June) a performance of ***Il ballo delle ingrate*** (Monteverdi/Rinuccini), a work influenced by the *ballets de cour* Monteverdi had seen in Flanders in 1590.

**1614** *27 January* Performance at the Archbishop's Palace, Salzburg, of an Italian opera – the first known performance of an opera outside Italy.

**1624–5** *Carnival* ***Il combattimento di Tancredi e Clorinda*** (Monteverdi/after Tasso) given in the Palazzo Dandolo, Venice, as a *madrigale con gesto*, in which the story is narrated and the two characters sing their own words within the narration. This was Monteverdi's first dramatic work for Venice, where he had taken the post of director of music at San Marco in 1613 after being summarily dismissed from the court at Mantua. To express the conflict between love and war he adopted what he called the *stile concitato*, in which the same note is articulated in quick repetition, breaking the regular established rhythm.
*6 October* ***La regina Sant'Orsola*** (Gagliano/Salvadori) performed in the Uffizi, Florence. The preface claimed that 'as in this theatre under the auspices of the most serene grand dukes the usage of the ancient dramas of Greece was revived, so today in the same place may there be a new field, of treating with more use and delight, leaving the vain stories of Gentiles, true and sacred Christian actions'.

**1625** *3 February* Première of ***La liberazione di Ruggiero dall'isola d'Alcina*** (Francesca Caccini/Saracinelli) at the Villa Poggio Imperiale,

In Stuart masques, the solemn action of the principal performance was contrasted with comic figures in the 'anti-masque', and the performance would culminate in dances in which the court audience would join. The principal action was carried forward in mimed dance rather than through the recitative of opera. The designs for Sir William Davenant's masque *Britannia triumphans* (1638) were by Inigo Jones, whose set shows a view of London with old St Paul's Cathedral in the distance.

Florence, on the occasion of a visit by Wladislaw Sigismund, Prince of Poland, to the Grand Duchess of Tuscany. The earliest example of an *opera ballo*, and the first opera written by a woman composer, it is also one of the first operas (preceded only by Gagliano's ***Il Medoro*** [1619], of which the music is lost) to be based on an episode from Ariosto's *Orlando furioso*, a rich source of opera libretti for several centuries, with its stories of chivalrous knights and the spells of the wicked enchantress Alcina.

**1627** *23 April* Première of ***Daphne*** (Schütz/Opitz) at Schloss Hartenfels bei Torgau for the marriage of Georg, Landgrave of Hesse-Darmstadt, and Sophia Eleonora, Princess of Saxony. The first German opera (score lost). The text, by one of the foremost German poets of the age, was partly translated from Rinuccini's libretto.
***La finta pazza Licori*** (Monteverdi/Strozzi), the first comic opera, was written. The planned performance in Mantua never took place, and neither text nor music survives.

**1631–2** Première of ***Sant'Alessio*** (Landi/Rospigliosi), the first opera to be performed in Cardinal Barberini's theatre, Rome. The production was designed by Bernini.

**1633** *30 January* Première of ***Erminia sul Giordano*** (Michelangelo Rossi/Rospigliosi after Tasso) in Cardinal Barberini's theatre, Rome. Rossi himself sang the role of Apollo.

Plan of the Teatro di SS. Giovanni e Paolo, Venice's second public opera house, where Monteverdi's *L'incoronazione di Poppea* had its first performance in 1642. The combination of a horseshoe-shaped auditorium, a deep stage allowing scenic perspectives, and extensive public rooms was replicated in opera houses into the twentieth century.

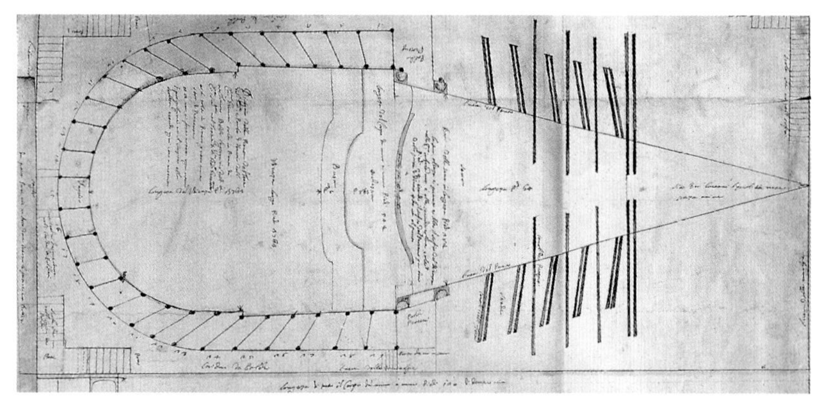

## The Florentine camerata

Opera was the outcome of the new vocal style that evolved as an attempt was made to re-create ancient drama. The elements of this new style were discussed and developed among musicians and intellectuals in Florence, particularly in the circle (camerata) around Giovanni de' Bardi, Count of Vernio, and his protégé Vincenzo Galilei. In 1581 Galilei published his *Dialogo della musica antica e della moderna*, advocating monody on the model of ancient Greek music rather than polyphony, and – although few of his own compositions have survived – his principles are exemplified in the compositions of Giulio Caccini, which employ both the *stile recitativo* or declamatory style, in which the rhythm of the vocal part closely follows speech patterns, and the *stile rappresentativo*, where the music itself serves both to set the scene and describe the action. Another group with similar aims, which included the composers Jacopo Peri and Emilio de' Cavalieri and the poet Ottavio Rinuccini – some members overlapped with those in Bardi's camerata – was centred around Jacopo Corsi, in whose Florentine palace Peri's *Dafne*, the first opera, was performed. The composer aimed to steer a course between the 'slow and suspended movements of song' and 'the swift and rapid movements of speech', and wrote: 'having in mind those inflections and actions that serve us in our grief, in our joy, and in similar states, I caused the bass to move in time to these, either more or less, following the passions.'

## Monteverdi

Claudio Monteverdi was the first great opera composer, and the existence of opera in the form in which we know it would be inconceivable without his contribution. His predecessors had produced works that were practical demonstrations of their theories but lacked any strong sense of theatrical effect or musical direction; with Monteverdi's operas, written between 1607 and 1643, poetry, music and theatre immediately achieved a synthesis that was only rarely equalled by later composers.

The composer had entered the service of the Duke of Mantua around 1592 as a string player, and in that year he published his third book of madrigals, in all of which his music serves to underline the emotional force of the poetic texts. Duke Vincenzo had attended the celebrations at which Peri's *Euridice* had been performed in 1600, and it is possible that Monteverdi had accompanied him, or had attended performances of other early operas, although it was not until 1607 that the Duke commissioned him to write his own work in the genre. *La favola d'Orfeo* takes as its subject the same Greek myth that had been used by Caccini and Peri, but the musical quality of the recitative gains from a more melodious treatment, while the richness of Monteverdi's harmony and instrumental colour are used to give a powerful shape to the individual numbers and to the dramatic shape of the work as a whole. Of his next opera, *Arianna*, only the heroine's celebrated Lament survives.

In 1613 Monteverdi accepted the post of director of music at San Marco, Venice, and not until the 1620s did he undertake further dramatic compositions, a *madrigale con gesto*, *Il combattimento di Tancredi e Clorinda*, based on an episode from Tasso's *Gerusalemme liberata* (which over the centuries was to provide a fertile source for opera librettists) and a comic opera, *La finta pazza Licori*, the music for which is lost, written for Mantua. However, the opening of the first public opera house in 1637 evidently encouraged the seventy-year-old composer to return to opera; in the years until his death *Arianna* was revived and he wrote four new operas, *Il ritorno di Ulisse in patria*, *L'incoronazione di Poppea*, and two more that are lost.

Portrait of Claudio Monteverdi, around 1640.

LAMENTO
D'ARIANA
DEL SIGNOR
CLAVDIO MONTEVERDE
MAESTRO DI CAPELLA
Della Serenissima Republica.
*Et con due Lettere Amorose in genere Rapresentatiuo.*
CON PRIVILEGIO.
STAMPA DEL GARDANO
IN VENETIA MDCXXIII.
*Appresso Bartolomeo Magni.* A

Title page of Ariadne's Lament, the most celebrated – and only surviving – scene from Monteverdi's *Arianna*. It is a piece of extraordinary emotional intensity, beginning with the line 'Let me die', then tenderly remembering Theseus, then bursting into an angry denunciation of him, and finally, at the end of the fourth section of the piece, reiterating the first despairing phrase.

**1635**
**1646**

# Opera in Venice

*The earliest operas had been court entertainments, generally forming part of the celebrations of a dynastic marriage or other great event, and for centuries they continued to serve this function. However, in the Republic of Venice public theatres were opened where operas could be performed. Within a short time Venice had become the leading operatic centre in Italy, and the nature of opera was transformed in response to its new audience.*

**DATES**

**1642**
Beginning of English Civil War

**1643**
Death of Louis XIII of France, succeeded by his five-year-old son as Louis XIV, although Cardinal Mazarin is effectively regent

**1644**
Publication of Descartes's *Principia philosophiae*

Scenes of battle, fire and destruction were among the most spectacular scenic effects in baroque opera. The burning of the city in Cavalli's *L'Hipermestra* was designed by Ferdinando Tacca, architect of the Teatro della Pergola in Florence, where the opera was first performed in 1658. Cavalli was described at the time as 'the first composer in Italy, particularly in the dramatic style'.

**1637** *Carnival* ***L'Andromeda*** (Manelli/Ferrari), with sensational transformation scenes and other production effects, was the first opera to be performed in a public theatre, at the Teatro San Cassiano, Venice. The music is lost, since – as was generally the case with commercial opera houses – only the libretto was printed. Maddalena Manelli, the composer's wife, sang the prologue and title role, one of the first women to appear on the operatic stage, but the other female roles (including that of Venus) were sung by *castrati.*
*12 February* First performance of ***Chi soffre speri*** (Mazzocchi and Marazzoli/Rospigliosi) at Palazzo Barberini, Rome, one of the earliest comic operas. When it was performed again two years later, the guests present included Giulio Mazzarino (soon to be Cardinal Mazarin) and John Milton.

**1639** *January* Opening of the Teatro SS. Giovanni e Paolo, Venice's second public opera house, with a performance of ***Delia*** (Sacrati/Strozzi).
*24 January* Première of ***Le nozze di Teti e di Peleo*** (Cavalli/Persiani) at San Cassiano, Venice; the first of Cavalli's thirty operas and the earliest Venetian opera of which the music survives.

**1640** The third Venetian opera house, San Moisè, opened with a performance of Monteverdi's ***Arianna.***
Première of ***Il ritorno di Ulisse in patria*** (Monteverdi/Badoaro) at

SS. Giovanni e Paolo, Venice. The opera had great popular appeal, with lavish spectacle and strongly characterized music that goes from Penelope's lament following the prologue, to comedy for the gluttonous suitor Irus and intense drama as Ulysses confronts the other suitors. Badoaro wrote a new libretto on the same subject for Sacrati a few years later, explaining that Monteverdi's opera could not be revived 'because the great master has gone to sound the music of the angels before God.'

**1641** *Carnival* Première of ***La Didone*** (Cavalli/Busenello) at San Cassiano, Venice; the archetypal *melodramma decorativo*, a form characterized by the lavishness of cast and scenery and the complications of intrigues in the plot.

**1642** *26 December [?]* Première of ***L'incoronazione di Poppea*** (Monteverdi/Busenello) at SS. Giovanni e Paolo, Venice. The first Venetian opera based on a historical subject, it was played throughout Carnival 1643 and revived at the same theatre in 1646. It is Monteverdi's operatic masterpiece, in which characterizations (including the comic character of Poppea's nurse) are sharply drawn, while the action relies on dramatic rather than spectacular effects. Busenello's libretto, which contrasts the pedantic stoicism of Seneca, the sensuality of Nero and the ambition of Poppea, has been convincingly interpreted as representing the decadence of Rome in contrast to the vigour of the Venetian republic, although Monteverdi was more interested in the moral, human, dimension than any political message.

**1643** *Autumn* Première of ***L'Egisto*** (Cavalli/Faustini) at San Cassiano, Venice. This was the composer's seventh opera, but the first written in a new style: recitative, interspersed with short arias, continues to play a major role, but the chorus is eliminated. It was performed soon after the Venice production in Rome, Genoa, Paris, Florence, Bologna and, possibly, Naples.
*29 November* Death of Monteverdi.

**1644** *Carnival* Première of ***L'Ormindo*** (Cavalli/Faustini) at San Cassiano, Venice, which has a celebrated lament in the prison scene. Première of ***Seelewig*** (Staden/Harsdörffer) in Nürnberg; the earliest surviving German opera, described as a 'sacred pastoral'.

**1645** *February* The first opera performed publicly in Paris was probably ***La finta pazza*** (Sacrati/Strozzi) designed by Giacomo Torelli and with ballets inserted at the end of each act; its première was in 1641 in Venice for the opening of the Teatro Novissimo, the city's fourth opera house.

> *'This night, having with my Lord Bruce taken our places before, we went to the Opera where comedies and other plays are represented in recitative music by the most excellent musicians vocal and instrumental...taken together it is one of the most magnificent and expensive diversions the wit of men can invent.'*
>
> *John Evelyn, Venice, 1645*

Set for Paolo Sacrati's *Il Bellerofonte*, first performed in Venice in 1641. Sacrati was one of the pioneers of public opera, but, as with Manelli, the music of his operas is known only from a few surviving fragments. The design, which shows Venice's Piazza San Marco in the background, is by Giacomo Torelli, the outstanding scenic artist of the early years of opera, who worked in Venice and designed the earliest Italian operas in Paris.

## The first public opera houses

In 1636 two musicians, Francesco Manelli and Benedetto Ferrari, arrived in Venice from Rome and rented the newly renovated Teatro di San Cassiano, where they were given permission to put on opera during the following carnival season. Their first production was their own *Andromeda*, but they soon made contact with Monteverdi, and when they took several productions on tour to Bologna in 1640 and 1641, they included his *Ritorno di Ulisse in patria*. Opera was taken up by the principal intellectual and political group in the city, the Accademia degli Incogniti, and their emphasis on the importance of the present moment (since they questioned the immortality of the soul), a factor which gave rise to the city's tradition of libertinism, accounts for the sensuality of many Venetian operas, in which philosophy is often opposed – and defeated – by love. Gian Francesco Busenello, one of the leading members of the Accademia, wrote libretti for both Monteverdi and Cavalli, which also courted popular appeal with lavish productions, roles for star singers, and the inclusion of comic as well as serious characters. The success of the new musical and dramatic form was such that ten opera houses opened in Venice before the end of the century, and over 350 different operas were performed in the city before 1700, while Venetian opera companies also introduced public opera to Florence, Naples and other cities of Italy.

# 1647 / 1677

# Italian Opera Reaches Paris

*Francesco Cavalli had taken on Monteverdi's mantle as the leading composer of opera and was the natural choice to write an opera to celebrate the wedding of Louis XIV. By the mid-century Italian operas were included in court festivities across Europe, from Germany and Austria to Spain, while France and Commonwealth England began to devise new operatic forms in their native languages.*

**DATES**

**1648**
Thirty Years' War concluded by the Peace of Westphalia

**1649**
English Civil War ends in defeat for King Charles I, who is tried and executed

**1654**
Abdication of Queen Christina of Sweden, and her conversion to Catholicism

**1658**
Leopold I of Austria elected Holy Roman Emperor

**1660**
Restoration of Charles II as English king

**1661**
On the death of Cardinal Mazarin, Louis XIV begins his personal reign

**1647** *2 March* Première of ***L'Orfeo*** (Luigi Rossi/Buti) at the Palais-Royal, Paris. The performance of this, the first Italian opera to be written for Paris, was organized by Cardinal Mazarin, whose secretary Benedetti brought singers, including two *castrati*, from Rome and Florence. The production was by Torelli, and the work ran for six hours and included many digressions, among them ballets for owls, tortoises and snails.

**1649** *5 January* Première of ***Il Giasone*** (Cavalli/Cicognini) at San Cassiano, Venice, the composer's most popular opera, performed throughout Italy over the next quarter century. In his later operas Cavalli reduced the length of recitative and introduced longer arias and dramatic duets, with music that is sensual, witty and often highly descriptive.

**1650** *October* Cavalli's ***La Didone*** (see 1641) was performed in Naples (in a pavilion in the grounds of the viceregal palace) by the Venetian travelling opera company 'I Febi Armonici'. Further performances by the troupe the following year included two more Cavalli operas (***Il Giasone*** and ***L'Egisto***) and Monteverdi's ***L'incoronazione di Poppea***. Venice was to provide the main operatic fare for Naples throughout the seventeenth century – the first extant opera by a Neapolitan composer was a setting of ***L'Orontea*** by Cirillo in 1654.

**1651** *28 November* Première of ***La Calisto*** (Cavalli/Faustini) at the Teatro San Apollinare, Venice's sixth opera house. This was one of four operas the composer wrote in 1651 and has become familiar through modern revivals.

**1652** ***La Gara*** (unknown composer/Vincina) with sets by Giovanni Burnacini was the first grand Italian opera to be performed at the Viennese court.

**1653** The Teatro San Bartolomeo, Naples, was reconstructed and within a year or so was established as an opera house.

**1656** *19 February* Première of ***L'Orontea*** (Cesti/Cicognini) at the Hofsaal, Innsbruck. The composer's first opera, it has the characteristically Venetian theme of the defeat of philosophy by love. Cesti became one of Cavalli's chief rivals, tailoring his music to allow singers to display their virtuosity in set-piece arias. He left Venice in 1652, to pursue his career at the Habsburg courts in Innsbruck and Vienna, where he was able to write for a much larger orchestra than that available to him at home.
*September* Première of ***The Siege of Rhodes*** (Locke, Lawes et al./Davenant) at Rutland House, London: 'Made a Representation by the Art of Perspective in Scenes, And the Story sung in Recitative Musick'. This was the first public performance in England to use Italian-style movable scenery, designed by Inigo Jones's pupil John Webb.

Queen Semiramis marching to war, in one of the scenes from Cesti's *Il pomo d'oro*, an incredibly lavish work designed by Ludovico Burnacini for the festivities surrounding the coronation of Emperor Leopold I in 1666. The opera was performed three times a week for a whole year.

A cloud scene in Legrenzi's opera *Germanico sul Reno* performed in 1675 at the Teatro San Salvatore, Venice, with the machinery used to create the effects. It was one of four of the composer's operas staged there in 1675–6.

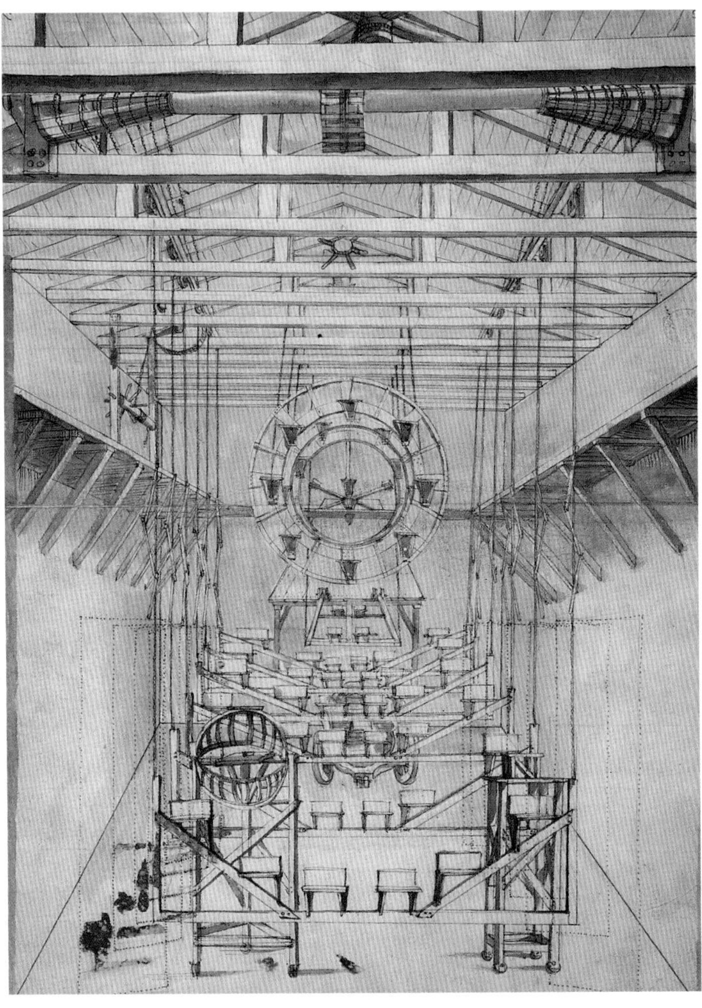

**1657** *5 February* Première of the comic opera ***La Tancia, ovvero Il potestà di Colognole*** (Melani/Moniglia) to inaugurate the Teatro della Pergola, Florence, as an opera house. The opera was later repeated in Florence and performed in Pisa, Bologna and other cities.
*13 February* Première of ***L'Oronte*** (Kerll/Alcaini) to inaugurate the first Munich opera house – which survived until 1802. One of the first German composers to write Italian opera, Kerll had all his dramatic works staged at the Munich court.
Première of ***La Dori, ovvero La schiava fedele*** (Cesti/Apolloni) at the Hofsaal, Innsbruck, one of the most successful operas of the seventeenth century.

**1658** *12 June* Première of ***L'Hipermestra*** (Cavalli/Moniglia) at the Teatro della Pergola, Florence, a spectacular opera commissioned by Cardinal Giovanni de' Medici to celebrate the birth of the Infante of Spain.

**1660** *22 November* Performance of ***Xerse*** (Cavalli/Minato), for the wedding of Louis XIV and Maria Theresia of Austria in the Grande Galerie du Louvre. ***Ercole amante*** had been commissioned from the composer for the wedding, but because of problems with the new Salle des Machines and the illness of Cardinal Mazarin the organizers fell back on the earlier opera, premièred in Venice in January 1655, adding ballet music by Jean-Baptiste Lully, an Italian who had joined the royal household as a kitchen boy in 1646.
*5 December* Première of ***Celos aun del aire matan*** (Hidalgo/Calderón), the first Spanish opera, based on the legend of the jealousy of Cephalus and Procris, at the Buen Retiro Palace, Madrid. Hidalgo continued to write dramatic works for the Spanish court until the 1670s, but the Spanish *zarzuela* with spoken dialogue always remained outside the mainstream of operatic development.

**1662** *7 February* Première of ***Ercole amante*** (Cavalli/Buti) to inaugurate the Salle des Machines at the Tuileries, Paris, in a production designed by Vigarani and Torelli. Cavalli had reluctantly accepted the commission, which entailed going to Paris to see the opera staged. He agreed that Lully should again be allowed to write ballets to be inserted into the action, and it was these (in one of which the young King appeared in sun costume), rather than Cavalli's opera, that won approval. Cavalli was disheartened by Lully's intriguing and on his return to Venice devoted himself largely to composing religious music, writing only three more operas in the last fifteen years of his life.

**1663** *Carnival* Première of ***Achille in Sciro*** (Legrenzi/Bentivoglio) – a high point in seventeenth-century Venetian opera – at the Teatro del Conte Bonacossi da Santo Stefano, Ferrara. The subject was also set for Vienna the same year by Draghi – the first of his 172 operas, mostly written for Vienna.

**1666** *20 February* Première of ***Pompeo magno*** (Cavalli/Minato) at San Salvatore, Venice, an extravagant opera that includes dances for horses, madmen and phantoms. The last of Cavalli's operas for which the score has survived, it contains some of his finest music, including Pompey's death scene in the form of a passacaglia.

**1668** *July* Première of ***Il pomo d'oro*** (Cesti/Sbarra) in Vienna, written for the wedding of Leopold I and Infanta Marguerita of Spain, though the performance was delayed for two years until the court theatre had been completed.

**1671** *8 January* Opening of Rome's first public opera house, the Teatro Tordinona, with a performance of Cavalli's ***Scipione affricano*** (1664) with prologue and *intermezzi* by Stradella.

Frontispiece to a set of engravings of Torelli's sets for Caprioli's *Le nozze di Teti e di Peleo*, with a distant view of Paris. The work is dedicated to Cardinal Mazarin.

## Stage spectaculars: the théâtre des machines

Transformation scenes and other sensational stage effects, which had long been one of the chief features of court entertainments, were introduced at the very birth of opera by Bernardo Buontalenti – mechanical genius, supplier of ice to the Medici household, water engineer and architect – who (with Agostino Carracci) designed the *intermedi* in *La pellegrina* at the Medici wedding in 1589, when the new recitative style was first tried out. Among his successors were Giacomo Torelli (1604–1678), known as the 'sorcerer' because of the astonishing scenic transformations he devised, Lodovico Burnacini (1636–1707), who handled huge crowds of people and animals in Vienna, and the Mauro family in Italy and Germany.

Torelli worked in the theatres of Venice, but was brought to Paris for *La finta pazza* in 1645 and returned in 1654 for *Le nozze di Teti e di Peleo*, an opera with music by Caprioli to a libretto by Francesco Buti, librettist of Rossi's *L'Orfeo* (see 1647) and superintendent of Italian artists at the French court. The opening scene of *Teti e Peleo* gives an idea of the spectacle: in the grotto of the centaur Chiron a group of magicians conjures up the chariot of Peleus in a storm of thunder and lightning, through which the chariot rises into the air surrounded by flames and smoke to disappear above the scene. As the flames and smoke subside a new scene is revealed – a view over the sea, above which Jupiter appears mounted on an eagle amid the clouds, while on the right of the stage characters emerge from the open jaws of hell and on the left Juno is carried across the waves in a chariot drawn by peacocks.

*La monarchia latina trionfante*, performed at the Viennese court in 1678, had music by Antonio Draghi, but it was notable principally for the production by Lodovico Burnacini, the last that he designed. It was an allegorical work with fantastic tableaux, which included elephants and camels, performed to celebrate the birth of Prince Josef. The scene here shows Peace, Religion, Abundance and Earth in an underground grotto, which opens up to show the Olympian gods in the heavens.

Architect's drawing for the stage and proscenium arch of the new Théâtre de la Salle des Machines in the Tuileries Palace.

*3 March* Première of ***Pomone*** (Cambert/Perrin) at the Jeu de Paume de la Bouteille, Paris. A *pastorale*, this was recorded as the first French opera to be performed at the Académie Royale de Musique.

**1672** *November* Première of ***Les Fêtes de l'amour et de Bacchus*** (Lully/Quinault with the collaboration of Molière and de Benserade) at the Jeu de Paume de la Bouteille, Paris. This was Lully's first pastoral opera, mostly using music taken from earlier works.

**1673** *27 April* Première of ***Cadmus et Hermione*** (Lully/Quinault) at the Jeu de Paume de la Bouteille, Paris. This was the first *tragédie-lyrique*, in which Lully adapted the Italian recitative style to the rhythms of French speech as it was declaimed in the theatre. Long melodies in irregular speech patterns were interspersed with formal airs, choruses and dances.

**1674** *19 January* Première of ***Alceste, ou Le Triomphe d'Alcide*** (Lully/Quinault) at the Opéra, Paris, the first opera performed at the company's new home in the theatre at the Palais-Royal.
*10 April* Première of ***Ariane, ou Le Mariage de Bacchus*** (Cambert/Perrin) at Drury Lane Theatre, London, the opening opera of the Royall Academy of Musick, founded by Cambert after Lully had taken over the Académie Royale in Paris. An English libretto was provided – 'a meer Translation and nothing else...thought absolutely necessary for the satisfaction of those, who being unacquainted with the French tongue, and who being Spectators, would find themselves necessitated to see the most pressing of their Senses go away from the Theatre ungratified, by their not understanding the Subject that brought them thither.'

**1675** *12 January* Première of ***Thésée*** (Lully/Quinault) at Saint-Germain-en-Laye. It remained in the repertory until 1779, longer than any other of Lully's operas.
*9 March* Première of ***Psyche*** (Locke/Shadwell, based on the *tragédie-ballet* by Molière, P. Corneille and Quinault produced in Paris in 1671) at Dorset Gardens, London. This has a better claim than *The Siege of Rhodes* – still more masque than opera – to being the first English opera.

**1676** *10 January* Première of ***Atys*** (Lully/Quinault) at Saint-Germain-en-Laye – Louis XIV's favourite opera, known as 'the King's opera'.
*Carnival* Première of ***Il Trespolo tutore balordo*** (Stradella/Villifranchi after Ricciardi) at the Teatro in Borgo, Rome. The opera was commissioned by Prince Colonna and gives a satirical portrayal of a ridiculous tutor, one of the first operatic roles to be written for a *buffo* bass.

**1678**
**1702**

# France, Germany, England

*As the form of* opera seria *became increasingly standardized in Italy and the south German courts, musical theatre was becoming more established in northern Europe; the last quarter of the century saw the flowering of the Académie Royale de Musique (or Opéra) in Paris, the opening of the first German opera house in Hamburg, and the production of a series of dazzling semi-operas by Purcell in London.*

### DATES

**1683**
Defeat of the Turks following their siege of Vienna

**1685**
Louis XIV's revocation of the Edict of Nantes compels Protestants to emigrate from France

**1688**
English Revolution in which James II is succeeded by William III and Mary II

**1689**
Cardinal Pietro Ottoboni becomes Pope Alexander VIII (to 1691)

**1700**
Death of Charles II of Spain leads to outbreak the following year of the War of Spanish Succession (to 1713), at the end of which Philip V, grandson of Louis XIV, is confirmed as the first Bourbon king of Spain

**1702**
Anne becomes Queen of England

Design by Jean Bérain for the costume of Pluto, god of the underworld, in Lully's *Proserpine*, first performed for Louis XIV at Saint-Germain-en-Laye in 1680.

**1678** *2 January* Première of ***Adam und Eva, oder der erschaffene, gefallene und wiederaufgerichtete Mensch*** (Theile/Richter) to inaugurate the Theater am Gänsemarkt, Hamburg, the first German opera house. In its 72 years of existence more than 280 operas were produced there.
*8 October* Première of ***La monarchia latina trionfante*** (Draghi/Minato) at the Viennese court.
*10 November* Première of ***La forza dell'amor paterno*** (Stradella/Marchese Rodolfo Brignole Sola) at the Teatro Falcone, Genoa. This opera, commissioned by the librettist, has many innovative features, including a mixture of serious and comic episodes and extremely melodic, almost *arioso*-like recitatives.

**1679** *6 January* Opening of Rome's second public opera house, the Teatro Capranica, with the première of ***Dov'è amore, è pietà*** (Pasquini/after Moniglia's *L'Hipermestra*).
*February* Première of the pastoral opera ***Gli equivoci nel sembiante*** (A. Scarlatti/Contini) at the Teatro Capranica, Rome, the thirty-year-old composer's first extant opera; a private performance was arranged for Queen Christina of Sweden, and the following year Scarlatti entered her service.

**1680** *3 February* Première of ***Proserpine*** (Lully/Quinault) at Saint-Germain-en-Laye, the opera in which Lully used accompanied recitative for the first time.
*3 February* Première of ***L'honestà negli amori*** (A. Scarlatti/'Felice Parnasso') in Rome at the palace of Queen Christina, to whom the opera was dedicated.
*8 November* Première of ***Berenice vendicativa*** (Freschi/Rapparini) in the private theatre of the Venetian procurator Marco Contarini at Piazzola, near Padua. It was a work of incredible extravagance, with lavish scenery, massive choruses, stables of horses, and elephants.

**1683** *6 January* Première of ***Phaéton*** (Lully/Quinault) at the Théâtre de la Cour, Versailles. Because of its sensational special effects the work became known as 'l'opéra du peuple', and several parodies were given at the Comédie-Italienne during the first half of the eighteenth century.

**1684** *18 January* Première of ***Amadis de Gaule*** (Lully/Quinault) at the Académie Royale, Paris. The subject of the opera, based on the medieval chivalric romance, was proposed by Louis XIV.
*31 January* Performance of ***Pompeo*** (A. Scarlatti/Minato) at San Bartolomeo, Naples, written for Rome the previous year; of the ten male roles four were sung by *castrati* (the role of Mitridate by Siface making his Naples début), three by natural male voices and three by women. In mid-February Scarlatti was appointed *maestro di cappella* to the court of Naples and took over the direction of the theatre company, which consisted of nine singers, five instrumentalists and a copyist. Of his some 115 operas (fewer than 40 of which survive) around 70 were written for Naples, and these provided the foundation for the city's great operatic tradition, both in comic opera, of which Scarlatti was a pioneer, and in *opera seria.*
*17 April* Second performance of ***Venus and Adonis*** (Blow/unknown) at Josias Priest's Boarding School, Chelsea (the date and place of the première are unknown). In this 'Masque for the Entertainment of the King' Venus was sung by Mary Davies, who had become Charles II's mistress in 1667, and Cupid by their daughter, Lady Mary Tudor, born in 1673.

Portrait of Henry Purcell (1658–1695).

## Purcell's semi-operas

In England there were only isolated attempts to write operas in the Italian style with recitative. Musical theatre generally took the form of the semi-opera, in which the main roles were spoken but there were musical interludes or 'masques'. Purcell was a master of this medium, and the succession of semi-operas he wrote for London theatres in the 1690s, especially *The Fairy Queen* (1692), are works of outstanding quality which did much to prepare English audiences for the arrival of Italian opera after the turn of the century. Purcell's one opera, *Dido and Aeneas* (1689), was written for amateur performance (at a Chelsea girls' school run by the choreographer of the Theatre Royal in Dorset Gardens). Since its rediscovery two hundred years later, it has become one of the most loved of all seventeenth-century operas.

Scene design by J. O. Harms for the German production of Steffani's *Enrico Leone* in Hamburg in 1696 – as *Heinrich der Löwe*. Agostino Steffani, a priest and diplomat, rose to become prime minister of the Palatinate. He also composed some fifteen operas, which did much to bring Italian opera to Germany, where he spent his whole career.

Scene by Jean Bérain of the destruction of Armida's palace by the devils she has herself summoned at the end of Lully's *Armide* (1686). Earlier, Armide, in a monologue that was the most famous scene in the opera, had conjured up demons to kill the sleeping Renaud (Rinaldo), but they were transformed into little Zephirs who brought garlands to wreathe the sleeping hero. His dream, in which this action took place, was – as with so many dream scenes in baroque opera – represented by a ballet.

**1685** *8 January* Première of ***Roland*** (Lully/Quinault after Ariosto) at the Théâtre de la Cour, Versailles, one of the composer's most successful operas.

**1686** *15 February* Première of ***Armide*** (Lully/Quinault after Tasso) at the Académie Royale, Paris, with designs by Bérain. The last and finest of Lully's *tragédies-lyriques*. In 1690 it was performed in Rome, the first French opera to be given in Italy.
*6 September* Première of ***Acis et Galatée*** (Lully/Campistron) at the Château d'Anet. A *pastorale héroïque* – Lully's last work.

**1687** *22 March* Death of Lully in Paris. Quinault died the following year.

**1688** *28 February* Première of ***David et Jonathan*** (Charpentier/ Bretonneau), at the Collège Louis-le-Grand, Paris. Charpentier's first full-length *tragédie en musique*, it was performed at the Jesuit school with each act preceded by a spoken play on the same subject.

**1689** *30 January* Première of ***Enrico Leone*** (Steffani/Mauro) to inaugurate the Italian opera house in Hanover.
*Spring* Première of ***Dido and Aeneas*** (Purcell/Tate) at Josias Priest's Boarding School, Chelsea.

**1690** *June* Première of ***The Prophetess or The History of Dioclesian*** (Purcell/Betterton after Beaumont and Fletcher), a semi-opera, at the Dorset Gardens Theatre, London.
*28 December* Première of ***Il Colombo, ovvero L'India scoperta*** (Ottoboni/Pasquini) at the Teatro Tordinona, Rome. The libretto for this, the first of numerous operas on the subject of Columbus's voyage, was written by Cardinal Pietro Ottoboni.

**1691** *May or June* Première of ***King Arthur, or The British Worthy*** (Purcell/Dryden), a semi-opera, at the Dorset Gardens Theatre, London. Described by Dryden as a 'dramatick opera', it received several revivals in the eighteenth century.

**1692** *2 May* Première of ***The Fairy Queen*** (Purcell/after Shakespeare), a semi-opera, at the Dorset Gardens Theatre, London; it was repeated there the following year.

## Lully and the Académie Royale

The royal opera company had been founded in 1669 by a consortium led by the poet Pierre Perrin with Robert Cambert as his composer. Within five months the first opera house in Paris had been constructed in the rue Vaugirard on the site of an old tennis court. However, three years later, Perrin was in a debtor's prison and the concession for opera had been purchased by Lully, who did his best to ensure that his operas would be protected from any competition. The Académie was granted the exclusive privilege for the performance of all dramas entirely set to music. Upheld into the nineteenth century, this privilege led to the separate development of the Opéra, as the Académie came to be known, and the Opéra-Comique, where works were always performed with spoken dialogue.

From the 1660s Lully had collaborated with Molière on a number of *comédies-ballets*, but after a quarrel in 1671 Lully collaborated principally with Philippe Quinault (while Molière worked with Charpentier, whom Lully ruthlessly excluded from the Académie Royale), producing a succession of *tragédies-lyriques*. These established a style of great grandeur, with sumptous sets and costumes, rich orchestration and elaborate ballets, which became the hallmark of French *grand opéra*. Many remained in the repertory of the Opéra well into the eighteenth century, and as late as 1777 traditionalists were shocked when Gluck made a new setting of Quinault's libretto for *Armide*.

Stage set in a new theatre designed by Francesco Bibiena, 1703. The Galli da Bibiena family – Ferdinando, his brother Francesco and his sons Giuseppe and Antonio – were the most important theatre architects of the eighteenth century, including in their work set designs with *quadratura*, illusionistic architectural painting that extends the real architecture into imaginary space. In their theatre sets they pioneered diagonally planned scenes, creating a more complex space than the simple perspective designs of the seventeenth century.

Illustration of André Campra's *Le Carnaval de Venise*, 1699. Like *L'Europe galante* (1697), the work was an *opéra-ballet*, a form perfected by Campra, in which each of the acts is a separate entity connected only by a 'collective idea' rather than a dramatic plot.

**1693** *4 December* Première of ***Médée*** (Charpentier/T. Corneille) at the Académie Royale, Paris. It was Charpentier's only work for the Académie, where even after Lully's death he was not accepted; his *tragédie-lyrique* received only a few performances, although it is the most powerfully dramatic opera of the period, with daring harmonic and orchestral writing.

**1694** *28 January* Première of ***Pirro e Demetrio*** (A. Scarlatti/Morselli) at San Bartolomeo, Naples. One of the earliest of Scarlatti's operas to show his personal style, it uses unusual harmonic progressions to underline particularly emotional moments in the text. It was extremely successful and was the first Italian opera to make a mark in London.

**1695** *Autumn* Première of ***The Indian Queen*** (Purcell/Dryden and Howard), a semi-opera, at Drury Lane Theatre, London; a work so popular that it was published immediately (without the composer's knowledge).

**1696** *27 December* Première of ***Il trionfo di Camilla, regina de' Volsci*** (Bononcini/Stampiglia) at San Bartolomeo, Naples. Its flowing melodic style made it enormously successful, with productions throughout Italy and in Vienna, London and Dublin.

**1697** *7 October* Première of ***Issé*** (Destouches/Houdar de la Motte) at Fontainebleau. The Marquis de Dangeau wrote in his journal: 'they played a little opera with music written by a musketeer: the king and courtiers agreed that it is as good as Lully and that it hasn't been stolen.' The opera was revised and amplified in 1708.
*24 October* Première of ***L'Europe galante*** (Campra/Houdar de la Motte), an *opéra-ballet*, at the Académie Royale, Paris. Three of the airs were written by Destouches.
*15 December* Première of ***La caduta de' decemviri*** (A. Scarlatti/Stampiglia) at San Bartolomeo, Naples, with the young *castrato* Nicolini (Nicolò Grimaldi) in a leading role. The opera introduced two novelties: the three-part (fast-slow-fast) 'Italian' overture, rather than the typical Venetian fast overture with a slow introduction, and the inclusion of two comic servants, who have a scene to themselves in each of the acts, anticipating the practice of inserting a comic *intermezzo* between the acts of a serious opera.

**1699** *20 January* Première of ***Le Carnaval de Venise*** (Campra/Regnard) at the Académie Royale, Paris. The work contains an Italian opera (on the Orpheus theme) within an opera.

**1700** Publication in Rome of G. M. Crescimbeni's Arcadian treatise *La bellezza della volgar poesia*, dedicated to Cardinal Pietro Ottoboni.
*21 December* Première of ***Hésione*** (Campra/Danchet) at the Académie Royale, Paris, with designs by Bérain, Campra's first *tragédie-lyrique.*

**1701** *10 November* Première of ***Omphale*** (Destouches/Houdar de la Motte) at the Académie Royale, Paris. This *tragédie-lyrique* was frequently revived.

**1702** *Summer* Première of ***Polifemo*** (Bononcini/Ariosti) at the Lietzenburg (now Charlottenburg) Palace, Berlin, the first opera performed in Berlin. Queen Charlotte played the harpsichord at the first performance.
*7 November* Première of ***Tancrède*** (Campra/Danchet after Tasso) at the Académie Royale, Paris, with the heroine Clorinde sung by Mademoiselle Maupin, celebrated for the beauty of her voice in the low register.

# 1703 / 1716 The Second Century of Opera

*Although operatic music had made little headway in England in the previous century, the appearances of the* castrato *Nicolini in London from 1708 and the arrival of other Italian singers suddenly made opera all the rage. George Frideric Handel, the outstanding master of* opera seria, *made London his home, and it became for him the scene of a succession of operatic triumphs and disasters.*

**DATES**

**1703**
Foundation of St Petersburg by Peter the Great

**1707**
The Austrian army brings an end to Spanish rule in Naples after 200 years

**1713**
At the end of the War of Spanish Succession Milan, Naples and the Netherlands pass from Spain to Austria

**1714**
Death of Queen Anne; succeeded by the Elector of Hanover as George I

**1715**
Death of Louis XIV, succeeded by his five-year-old grandson as Louis XV

First Jacobite Rebellion in Scotland

Set design by James Thornhill for Thomas Clayton's *Arsinoe*, performed at Drury Lane in January 1705.

**1703** Reinhard Keiser was appointed director of the Gänsemarkt theatre in Hamburg, where he had worked since 1695, introducing the practice of incorporating Italian airs into German operas.
*September* Première of ***Arminio*** (A. Scarlatti/Salvi after Tacitus) at the Villa Medici, Pratolino. The libretto, already old, was later set by both Handel and Hasse.
*Autumn* In the absence of his father, Domenico Scarlatti made his début as an opera composer in Naples, with two original works, including ***Giustino*** (libretto by Convo after Beregan) and some reworkings of Venetian operas. The company was quite a family affair: Domenico was composer and arranger, his younger brother Giuseppe painted the sets, one uncle, Nicola Barbapiccola, acted as impresario, another played the double bass, while a third, Tommaso Scarlatti, sang the tenor roles.

*'The beauty of her fine proportion'd figure and exquisitely sweet, silvery tone of voice with the peculiarly rapid swiftness of her throat, were perfections not to be imitated by art or nature.'*

Cibber on Mrs Tofts as Camilla

**1704** *6 May* Première of ***Iphigénie en Tauride*** (Desmarets and Campra/Duché and Danchet) at the Opéra, Paris. This was the earliest opera based on the story of Agamemnon's daughter who finally broke the curse on the house of Atreus. Desmarets had been one of the chief composers of operas for the Académie Royale during the 1690s but had had to flee France in 1699 after having seduced one of his pupils; he had left the score of ***Iphigénie en Tauride***, one of his most original operas, unfinished, and it was completed by Campra.

**1705** *8 January* Première of ***Almira*** (Handel/Feustking after Pancieri) at the Gänsemarkt theatre, Hamburg; Handel's first opera, it contained 41 German and 15 Italian airs. He was to write two more operas for Hamburg, ***Nero*** (which is lost), performed seven weeks after ***Almira*** with Mattheson in the title role, and ***Florinda e Dafne***, performed in two parts in January 1708 on consecutive nights. Keiser produced his own versions of both ***Almira*** and ***Nero*** not long after Handel's had been performed.

Scene from Keiser's *Crösus*, 1711. Like Scarlatti's *Il Ciro*, the opera tells of the Persian king Cyrus (left). The philosopher Solon (centre) had warned the Lydian king Croesus, legendary for his riches, against trusting in worldly happiness, and Croesus has been captured by Cyrus who is about to have him burned at the stake. Solon gives the same warning to Cyrus, who then pardons Croesus. The libretto was based on an Italian opera performed thirty years earlier in Vienna, but the German version expanded the comic scenes for the soldiers and servants.

## Handel's apprenticeship

Handel's first-hand experience of opera began at the Gänsemarkt theatre in Hamburg, where he joined Reinhard Keiser's orchestra as a second violinist in 1703, being promoted to the position of harpsichordist the following year. He wrote three operas for the company, but was not the easiest colleague – he fought a duel with his friend Mattheson after refusing to give up his seat at the harpsichord during a performance of one of Mattheson's operas and may also have excited Keiser's jealousy – and he readily accepted an invitation to go to Italy in 1706. Handel remained indebted to Keiser, not only for the experience of working in an opera house, but also to his music, from which he was to borrow freely.

The invitation had come from the Medici, one of whom had been his patron in Hamburg, and Handel remained in Italy until 1710, spending each autumn in Florence and paying visits to Venice and Naples, but living for the majority of the time in Rome. He was probably introduced to Roman musical circles by Corelli and Alessandro Scarlatti and was invited to meetings of the Arcadian Academy, of which Cardinal Ottoboni, one of his new patrons, was a leading member. The public performance of opera was going through one of its temporary periods of proscription in Rome, but this may have helped Handel in the development of his operatic technique, since in the cantatas and *serenate* which were performed instead – unstaged – the drama had to be contained within the music itself. Each work was made up of a sequence of *scene*, soliloquies consisting of recitative with instrumental accompaniment and an extended aria. The theatrical strength of Handel's later works lies in the inherent dramatic power of his operatic *scene* and their reflection of contrasting emotional states.

*27 January* Première of ***Arsinoe, Queen of Cyprus*** (Clayton/Motteux after Stanzani) at the Drury Lane Theatre, London, the first complete English opera, with Katharine Tofts in the title role. A contemporary critic wrote that 'there is nothing in it but a few Sketches of antiquated Italian Airs, so mangled and sophisticated, that instead of *Arsinoe*, it ought to be called the Hospital of old Decrepid *Italian* Operas.' Of Clayton's second opera, ***Rosamond***, written in 1707 to a libretto by Addison, the composer 'could have collected a Reward for the worst Musick in all the world'.
*20 April* The Haymarket Theatre, London, known as the Queen's – later the King's – Theatre, was inaugurated with the première of Jakob Greber's ***Gli amori di Ergasto*** (libretto after Amalteo), probably the first opera to be performed in Italian in England. The theatre, which soon obtained a monopoly on operatic performances, was to be the principal home of opera in London until the mid-nineteenth century.

**1706** *18 February* Première of ***Alcione*** (Marais/Houdar de la Motte) at the Opéra, Paris. One of Marais's four operas, it contains a notable orchestral storm scene – an early example of operatic 'realism'.
*10 April* Production of Bononcini's ***Camilla*** (see 1696) at the Drury Lane Theatre, London, with music adapted by Haym. Originally it was given in English, then, from 17 December 1707 in English with Italian airs inserted. The opera was performed 110 times in London between 1706 and 1728 and it was this work – a sentimental story with comic servants – that established opera in England. Mrs Tofts, who sang the title role, was ever afterwards known as 'Camilla'.

**1707** *5 January* Première of ***Il Mitridate Eupatore*** (A. Scarlatti/Frigimelica Roberti) at San Giovanni Grisostomo, Venice; Scarlatti's first (and only) opera written for Venice. The composer made a great effort to appeal to Venetian taste and wrote one of his finest scores, with rich orchestration, but Venice was unwilling to acknowledge the work of a Neapolitan.
*October–November* Première of ***Rodrigo (Vincer se stesso è la maggior vittoria)*** (Handel/after Silvani) at the Teatro Cocomero, Florence, the first of Handel's two operas written in Italy.

**1708** *25 December* London début of Nicolini in A. Scarlatti's ***Pirro e Demetrio*** at the Queen's Theatre, sung partly in Italian, partly in English. The *castrato* was an immediate success, even with some of the severest critics of Italian opera, and continued to be acclaimed in London, particular for his role in Mancini's ***Idaspe fedele***, in which he strangled a lion.

Frontispiece to the libretto of Le Sage's *Le Roy de la Chine (Arlequin invisible)*, an operatic parody performed in Paris in 1713 at the Théâtre de la Foire. Music for these works, which were to lead to the development of *opéra-comique*, was generally selected from familiar operas or more popular sources.

## Parodies and comic operas

The public performances of serious operas provided troupes of travelling comedians with a whole range of new material that they could incorporate into their repertory. Although records are far more scarce than for productions in theatres, we know of many operatic parodies, especially in Paris. The stock figures of the *commedia dell'arte* would assume the operatic roles, generally with Harlequin – or occasionally Pierrot – as hero. Lully's operas, in particular, were widely parodied throughout the first half of the eighteenth century, especially *Atys*, 'l'opéra du roi', and *Roland*. A troup of rope-dancers performed a work entitled *Les Fêtes parisiennes* (after Campra's *Les Festes vénitiennes*) in 1711, and the same opera was parodied by Charles Favart in 1740 as *Les Fêtes villageoises*, which was staged at the Opéra-Comique in 1740. Most of Favart's early libretti were parodies, so that *grand opéra* and *opéra-comique* were to this extent founded on a common tradition.

**1709** *26 December* Première of ***Agrippina*** (Handel/Grimani) at San Giovanni Grisostomo, Venice, with Margarita Durastanti in the title role; the composer's first dramatic masterpiece and a great success, with a run of 27 performances.

**1710** *16 June* Handel was appointed Kapellmeister to the Elector of Hanover but was almost immediately given leave to go to London, where he arrived in November.
*17 June* Première of ***Les Festes vénitiennes*** (Campra/Danchet) at the Opéra, Paris.

**1711** *Carnival* Première of ***Crösus*** (Keiser/Minato, trans. Lucas von Bostel) at the Gänsemarkt theatre, Hamburg. The composer's ***Cato*** (libretto by Feind) was performed there later the same year.
*7 March* Première of ***Rinaldo*** (Handel/Gaetano Rossi after Tasso) at the Queen's Theatre, London; the opera was written in the space of fourteen days during Handel's first visit to London and included much music taken from his earlier operas. Nicolini sang the title role, and the audience was particularly impressed with Handel's harpsichord improvisations. The composer subsequently returned to Hanover, but went back to London the following autumn on indefinite leave of absence.

**1712** *12 January* Première of ***Idomenée*** (Campra/Danchet) at the Opéra, Paris. Varesco based his libretto for Mozart's ***Idomeneo*** on Danchet's text for this *tragédie-lyrique*.
*9 March* Gasparini's ***Ambleto*** (libretto by Zeno and Pariati) was performed successfully at the Queen's Theatre, London. It had been premièred in Venice in 1705.
*3 December* Première of ***Il pastor fido*** (Handel/Rossi after Guarini's pastoral poem) at the Queen's Theatre, London. The work's modest scale was a disappointment to the public, and the composer quickly set about composing a new large opera.
*27 December* Première of ***Il Ciro*** (A. Scarlatti/Pariati) at the Teatro Ottoboni, Rome. It is noteworthy for a number of short dance movements, one followed by a hymn sung by one of the characters and repeated by the chorus.

**1713** *21 January* Première of ***Teseo*** (Handel/Haym after Quinault) at the Queen's Theatre, London. This magical opera, dedicated to Lord Burlington, who became Handel's patron, immediately restored the composer's popularity.

**1714** *19 August* Première of ***Les Festes de Thalie*** (Mouret/de Lafont) at the Opéra, Paris. One of two *opéras-ballets* by Mouret produced in 1714 (the other was ***Ragonde***) into which a comic element was introduced, making them ancestors of the *opéra-bouffe*. Both had a number of revivals in various forms over the following sixty years.

**1715** *16 February* Première of ***Tigrane, overo L'egual impegno d'amore e di fede*** (A. Scarlatti/Lalli) at San Bartolomeo, Naples; one of Scarlatti's most successful operas.
*Carnival* Première of ***Ambleto*** (D. Scarlatti/Zeno and Pariati) at the Teatro Capranica, Rome; only one aria survives. The planned *intermezzo*, ***La Dirindina, ossia Il maestro di cappella*** (libretto by Gigli), was cancelled at the last minute when the singers, led by the *castrato* Cecchino (Francesco de Castris), took exception to its satirical treatment of their art and made sure that it was banned by the censor.
*5 June* Première of ***Amadigi di Gaula*** (Handel/Heidegger) at the King's Theatre, London, in which Nicolini again appeared; Handel's first opera for the English court and another magical subject with impressive stage effects.

Set design by Filippo Juvarra for Alessandro Scarlatti's *Il Ciro*, staged at the small Teatro Ottoboni in the Palazzo della Cancelleria, Rome, in 1712. Juvarra, a good friend of his fellow-Sicilian Scarlatti, was one of the most inventive baroque architects and designed opera productions for several Roman theatres. The unusual format of the engraving reflects the tall and extremely narrow stage at the Teatro Ottoboni.

Title-page of Handel's *Rinaldo*, the first opera he wrote for London. It was played for fifteen days in succession in March 1711 in a sumptuous production, which included live sparrows and chaffinches on stage. The scenario was by Aaron Hill, manager of the Queen's Theatre, whose assistant manager was John Jacob Heidegger, later to be Handel's partner in the Royal Academy of Music. *Rinaldo* was revived in 1713 and 1714 and produced again in a revised version in 1717.

Alcina, who had made the first of her many operatic appearances in 1619, is a leading character in Fux's *Die über die Alcina obsiegende Angelica* (1716), where the wicked enchantress has bewitched the inhabitants of two islands, naturalistically represented on either side of the lake at the imperial villa in Vienna. These huge outdoor spectaculars were Fux's most celebrated operas, and the sets for *Angelica* established Giuseppe Galli da Bibiena's reputation as a stage designer.

**1716** *14 September* Première of ***Die über die Alcina obsiegende Angelica (Angelica, vincitrice di Alcina)*** (Fux/Pariati), in an outdoor performance at the imperial villa La Favorita, Vienna.
*December* The opening of the Italian opera season in London at the King's Theatre (which included revivals of Handel's ***Rinaldo*** and ***Amadigi***) was overshadowed by three English-language operas put on at the Lincoln's Inn Fields Theatre (whose music director was Pepusch), including a revised version of Bononcini's ***Camilla*** (see 1696). A second season of English operas followed at Lincoln's Inn Fields in 1717–18, but Italian opera did not return to the King's Theatre until 1720.

**1717**
**1731**

# Prima Donnas and Castrati

*The nature of* opera seria, *with its strict hierarchy among the singers and ornamented formal structures, led to the idolization of star performers, great rivalry between them and, often, scandalous behaviour. For the first – but not the last – time in the history of opera, singers appeared to have the upper hand, and music was often tailored to suit their voices, talents and demands.*

**DATES**

1727
Death of George I, succeeded by his son as George II

1731
Publication of Abbé Prévost's *Manon Lescaut*

**1717** *23 January* Première of ***L'incoronazione di Dario*** (Vivaldi/Morselli) at Sant'Angelo, Venice. The composer's first opera, ***Ottone in villa***, had been written for Vicenza in 1713.

**1718** *26 November* Première of the full-length *commedia in musica* ***Il trionfo dell'onore*** (A. Scarlatti/Tullio) at the Teatro dei Fiorentini, Naples. The work is a masterpiece of comic opera and one of the very earliest of the long line of Neapolitan comic operas for which this theatre was to be celebrated.

**1719** *13 September* Première of ***Teofane*** (Lotti/Pallavicino) at the Hoftheater, Dresden, for the wedding of Friedrich August of Saxony and Maria Josefa, Archduchess of Austria. The cast included the *castrati* Senesino and Berselli, Margarita Durastanti and Giuseppe Boschi, all of whom were to join Handel's company in London.

**1720** *13 April* Opening of the first season of the Royal Academy of Music at the King's Theatre, London, with the première of ***Numitore*** (Porta/Rolli) directed by Handel. Handel's own opera was saved for a performance that the King would be able to attend.
*8 May* Première of ***Radamisto*** (Handel/Haym after Lalli) at the King's Theatre, London, with Durastanti in the title role, since there was as yet no *castrato* in the company; when the work was revived (with substantial revisions) in December the role was taken over by Senesino, and Durastanti sang Zenobia. Handel's first opera for the Royal Academy was richly orchestrated with the parts for each character composed with great care.
*10 June* ***Narciso*** (D. Scarlatti/Zeno revised Rolli) was the third opera performed in the Royal Academy's first season. Its first performance had been in Rome in 1714, the last of seven operas Scarlatti composed for the private theatre of Queen Maria Casimira of Poland.
*30 November* The Royal Academy's second London season opened at the King's Theatre with a performance of ***Astarto*** (Bononcini/Rolli after Zeno and Pariati), in which Senesino made a sensational début. The opera's great success ensured that Bononcini's operas were performed more often in the early years of the Academy than Handel's. In his next operas Handel simplified the rich orchestration he had been using as Bononcini's popular style was more easily melodic.
*28 August* Début of Farinelli in ***Angelica e Medoro*** (Porpora/Metastasio) in Naples, a *serenata* that was also Metastasio's first libretto (his first full *opera seria* libretto was ***Didone abbandonata***, first set by Sarro for Naples in 1724 with Nicolini as Aeneas and Marianna Bulgarelli as Dido). Farinelli was a pupil of Porpora, who was also the teacher of his great rival Caffarelli.

**1721** *January* Première of ***La Griselda*** (A. Scarlatti/Zeno) at the Teatro Capranica, Rome, Scarlatti's last surviving opera. The *castrato* Giovanni Carestini made his début in the opera as Costanza later the same year,

Caricature portrait of Antonio Vivaldi in 1723 by P. L. Ghezzi. The composer was active as an impresario and opera composer from 1713, although his operas – 19 of some 95 scores survive – have been overshadowed by his instrumental music. Nevertheless, he has been better served by recordings than any of his Venetian contemporaries, and his operas give an idea of the sumptuous Venetian style, which was carried abroad by composers such as Caldara and Lotti who travelled to northern European courts.

Audience, orchestra and stage at the original production of Lotti's *Teofane* at the Dresden court opera in 1719. A pupil of Legrenzi, Lotti had been working in Venice and wrote three operas for Dresden during his stay there from 1717 to 1719 as leader of an Italian opera company.

when Scarlatti added new arias and adapted existing ones for him.
*20 December* Première of ***Floridante*** (Handel/Rolli after Silvani) at the King's Theatre, London, Handel's only new opera in the Royal Academy's third season.

**1722** *5 March* Première of ***La Griselda*** (Bononcini/Zeno after Boccaccio, revised Rolli) at the King's Theatre, London, in which Carestini made his début in the city. The opera had been first performed in Turin in 1718.

**1723** *23 January* Première of ***Ottone, re di Germania*** (Handel/Haym) at the King's Theatre, London, using virtually the same libretto as Lotti's ***Teofane*** (see 1719). The opera was put on for Francesca Cuzzoni's début in London, and it was during rehearsals for this that Handel famously threatened to drop her out of a window unless she sang the part as he had written it.

Faustina and Senesino caricatured by Marco Ricci in 1728, during the final season of the original Royal Academy of Music.

## The castrato

The practice of castrating boys before puberty to preserve their unbroken voices to sing in church choirs went back to at least the sixteenth century, but *opera seria* offered far greater scope for the strong tone and astonishing agility of which these artificially preserved voices were capable. In Rome, since women were forbidden to appear on the public stage, *castrati* took all the leading female roles (tenors would often sing the roles of older women, especially comic characters), but they also had the voice preferred for heroic male roles. Although many of the boys who had undergone this cruel operation – often arranged by their parents – failed to achieve operatic fame, those who did won extraordinary adulation, and often behaved with corresponding wilfulness. One common practice was to insist on the insertion of their favourite arias in whatever opera they were singing (known as their 'suitcase arias'); other demands, including of course their fees, were often outrageous. Several *castrati* achieved fame in the late seventeenth century, notably Matteuccio, Cortona and Siface (almost all the *castrati* were known by nicknames), while Nicolini, whose career spanned the turn of the century, started the English love-affair with Italian opera. Their heyday was from around 1720 to the mid-century, when Senesino, Bernacchi, Carestini, Caffarelli and the great Farinelli were all at the peak of their careers.

Their art survived into the 1820s, and continued to have many admirers. Goethe, who saw *castrati* playing female roles in Rome in Cimarosa's *L'impresario in angustie* in July 1787 wrote that 'in these representations, the concept of imitation and of art was invariably more strongly felt, and through their able performance a sort of conscious illusion was produced. Thus a double pleasure is given, in that these persons are not women, but only represent women. The young men have studied the properties of the female sex in its being and behaviour; they know them thoroughly and reproduce them like an artist; they represent, not themselves, but a nature absolutely foreign to them.'

*25 May* Première of ***Flavio, re di Langobardi*** (Handel/Haym after Noris) at the King's Theatre, London, composed to end the Royal Academy's fourth season. In this work, based on an older Venetian libretto, the customary operatic heroism is replaced with comedy, sentiment and political satire.
*28 August* Première of ***Costanza e Fortezza*** (Fux/Pariati), an open-air performance at the Hradčany Palace, Prague, for the coronation festivities of Emperor Charles VI. It was an allegorical work of spectacular magnificence, in which Carestini sang a principal role.

**1724** *2 March* Première of ***Giulio Cesare in Egitto*** (Handel/Haym after Bussani) at the King's Theatre, London, with Senesino in the title role, Cuzzoni as Cleopatra, Berenstadt (another *castrato*) as Tolomeo, Durastanti as Sesto and Boschi as Achillas. In this superbly sensuous work Handel returned to the richer instrumental colouring he had abandoned in the wake of Bononcini's success, including the use of a stage orchestra.
*11 November* Première of ***Tamerlano*** (Handel/Haym after Piovene) at the King's Theatre, London, for the opening of the Royal Academy's sixth season. Although the cast included Senesino and Cuzzoni, the role of the hero, Bajazet, was written for the tenor Francesco Borosini (who had sung the same role in Gasparini's ***Bajazet***, 1719); his magnificent death scene is the tragic climax of the opera.

**1725** *24 February* Première of ***Rodelinda*** (Handel/Haym after Salvi) at the King's Theatre, London, with the same cast as ***Tamerlano***, but with the focus on the title role sung by Cuzzoni.
*27 September* Première of ***Pimpinone, oder Die ungleiche Heirat*** (Telemann/Praetorius after Pariati), at the Gänsemarkt theatre, Hamburg; an *intermezzo* played between the acts of a performance of Handel's ***Tamerlano***. With ***Der geduldige Socrates***, 1721, the first opera he wrote for Hamburg, ***Pimpione*** is one of the few of Telemann's operatic scores to survive.

**1726** *23 March* Première of ***Scipione*** (Handel/Zeno revised Rolli) at the King's Theatre, London.
*16 May* Première of ***Alessandro*** (Handel/Rolli) at the King's Theatre, London. The Royal Academy decided – most unwisely – to engage Cuzzoni's chief rival, Faustina Bordoni, to join the company. Handel

The soprano *castrato* Farinelli (Carlo Broschi) in a female role, caricatured by P. L. Ghezzi in Rome in 1724.

George Frideric Handel during his years as music director of the Royal Academy of Music.

## The Royal Academy of Music

At the end of 1718, when London had been without Italian opera for two seasons, a group of noblemen, including Lord Burlington, Lord Chandos and other members of the 'King's party', set up a new company, the 'Royal Academy of Music' (a name chosen to imitate the French Académie Royale), with Handel as chief composer and 'master of the orchestra', Paolo Rolli, whom Burlington had brought to London in 1715, as librettist and Heidegger as manager. The enterprise was to be funded by public subscription. In May 1719 Handel travelled to Germany to engage singers for the first season – the *castrato* Senesino was considered essential, and while Handel was in Dresden he also engaged Durastanti, Berselli and Boschi, although only Durastanti, Handel's first Agrippina, was able to sing in the first season. In the years that followed most of the finest singers in Europe were heard in operas by Handel (making up roughly half the total of performances), Bononcini, Ariosti and others. The Royal Academy lasted until 1728, when after fierce internal quarrels the company failed.

In 1729 Handel revived the Academy, but poor relations between the composer and some of the singers, particularly Senesino, led to the foundation of a rival company, the 'Opera of the Nobility', which also engaged Farinelli for the 1733–4 season. London was unable to support two Italian opera companies paying colossal fees to their singers and after the 1734–5 season both collapsed.

The fashions for Italian opera and Palladian architecture – both led by the Earl of Burlington – were satirized together by Hogarth in his *Masquerades and Operas: Burlington Gate*, published in 1724. On the left the impresario Heidegger leans out of the window, while on the banner Cuzzoni (seen with the *castrati* Senesino and Berenstadt) is shown refusing a fee of £8,000.

balanced the parts in his opera, in which Senesino also appeared, with the greatest care, including a duet for the two ladies, but relations between them soon deteriorated.

*Carnival* Début of the *castrato* Caffarelli (Gaetano Majorano) in a female role in Sarro's ***Il Valdemaro*** at the Teatro delle Dame, Rome.

**1727** *2 June* Friendly contest between the *castrati* Bernacchi and Farinelli in ***La fedeltà coronata*** (Orlandini) in Bologna. Bernacchi, who was celebrated for his brilliant technique and elaborate ornamentation, was judged superior on this occasion, although Farinelli was later to be famous for the pathos as well as the technical perfection of his performances.

*6 February* Première of ***Don Chisciotte in corte della duchessa*** (Caldara/Pasquini after Cervantes), at the court theatre, Vienna. The work was described as an *opera serioridicola.* Composer and librettist produced a sequel, ***Sancio Pansa, governatore dell'isola Barattaria,*** in 1733.

*11 February* Première of ***Admeto, re di Tessaglia*** (Handel/composer) at the King's Theatre, London. Senesino, Faustina and Cuzzoni again sang together, but the rivalry of the prima donnas was becoming increasingly bitter, culminating in a brawl on stage during a performance of Bononcini's ***Astianatte*** on 17 June 1727, while their supporters fought in the audience.

Scene from the ballad opera *The Devil to Pay*, 1731. It was performed throughout the English-speaking world, with performances in Dublin (1732), Edinburgh (1734), Charleston, S.C. (1736), New York (1751), Annapolis (1752), Philadelphia (1766), Kingston, Jamaica (1779) and Cape Town (1802).

**Carlo Goldoni on the disposition of parts in *opera seria***

*'The three principal personages of the drama ought to sing five airs each; two in the first act, two in the second, and one in the third. The second actress and the second soprano can have only three, and the inferior characters must be satisfied with a single air each, or two at the most. The author of the words must furnish the musician with the different shades which form the chiaroscuro of music, and take care that two pathetic airs do not succeed one another. He must distribute with the same precaution the bravura airs, the airs of action, the inferior airs, and the minuets and rondeaus. He must, above all things, avoid giving impassioned airs, bravura airs, or rondeaus, to inferior characters.'*

*22 November* Première of ***Riccardo primo, re d'Inghilterra*** (Handel/Rolli after Briani) at the King's Theatre, London. The first of three operas Handel wrote for the final season of the Royal Academy.

**1728** *9 February* Première of ***The Beggar's Opera*** (Pepusch et al./Gay) at Lincoln's Inn Fields, London.
*28 February* Première of ***Siroe, re di Persia*** (Handel/Haym after Metastasio) at the King's Theatre, London, followed by ***Tolomeo, re di Egitto*** (libretto by Haym) premièred on 11 May. The final performance of the Royal Academy, on 12 June, was of ***Admeto*** (see 1727).

**1729** *13 December* Première of ***Lotario*** (Handel/after Salvi) at the King's Theatre, London. After a season without Italian opera, Handel and Heidegger revived the Royal Academy, but the singers Handel had been able to engage the previous summer – including the *castrato* Bernacchi, the tenor Fabri and the prima donna Anna Maria Strada – were a disappointment after the stars of the old Academy.

**1730** *4 February* Première of ***Artaserse*** (Vinci/Metastasio) at the Teatro delle Dame, Rome, Vinci's last and most celebrated opera, and the first of 107 settings of Metastasio's libretto. It was a tremendous success, particularly for the *castrato* Gizziello who was making his début. Dr Burney said of Vinci that 'he was the friend, though not the slave to poetry, by simplifying and polishing melody, and calling the attention of the audience chiefly to the voice part, by distinguishing it from fugue, complication and laboured contrivance.'
*February* Première of ***Artaserse*** (Hasse/Lalli after Metastasio) at San Giovanni Grisostomo, Venice, as the last opera of the Carnival season. Hasse, who had studied with Alessandro Scarlatti, had been resident in Venice since 1727 and married Faustina Bordoni there in 1730, after which singer and composer pursued their careers together.
*7 March* Première of ***Partenope*** (Handel/adapted from Stampiglia) at the King's Theatre, London. Although the work is a mock-heroic comedy with extremely attractive music, London audiences would not accept Bernacchi as a replacement for their idol Senesino.

**1731** *13 February* Première of ***Poro, re dell'Indie*** (Handel/after Metastasio) in London. It was the only new opera Handel wrote for the second season of the new company, for which he had now – at enormous expense – rehired Senesino.
*16 August* Première of ***The Devil to Pay, or The Wives Metamorphos'd*** (Seedo et al./Coffey) at Drury Lane, London.This ballad opera with 16 songs was a huge success and was much imitated in France and Italy, while performances in German translation are credited with giving rise to the *singspiel* movement.
*13 September* Première of ***Cleofide (Alessandro nell'Indie)*** (Hasse/Boccardi after Metastasio) at the Hoftheater, Dresden, with Faustina as prima donna (J. S. Bach was in the audience). Hasse and Faustina returned to Dresden in 1734, where Hasse was to be court composer for the next thirty years.
*December* Première of ***La Salustia*** (Pergolesi/Morelli) at San Bartolomeo, Naples; Pergolesi's first opera and no great success. Nicolini, now aged 58, was to have taken part, but quarrelled with the impresario and withdrew; he died the following January.

Ticket (designed by Hogarth) for a performance of *The Beggar's Opera* at Covent Garden as a benefit for Thomas Walker, the first Macheath. He stands in the centre with, on the left, the Peachums and, on the right, the Lockits.

## The Beggar's Opera

John Gay's *Beggar's Opera* was the greatest success on the London stage in the eighteenth century and was the origin of a new genre – the ballad opera – which was to have a strong influence on the development of opera itself. A series of 69 musical numbers, set to familiar popular tunes, some ballads, some from masques or operas, are joined by spoken dialogue with the Beggar acting as master of ceremonies. The story revolves around the rival loves of Polly and Lucy for the Highwayman Macheath, and the corrupt intrigues of their fathers, the informer Peachum and the gaoler Lockit. There are specific targets for the satire of the piece, political – the corruption of Sir Robert Walpole's government – and aesthetic – the introduction of foreign fashions in music and the other arts, especially the Italian opera – but its popularity was due most of all to its presentation of the operatic world in reverse: the heroic kingdoms of mythical antiquity are replaced with the thieves' kitchens and prisons of London, but the sentiments of love, jealousy (the rivalry between Polly and Lucy alludes to Faustina and Cuzzoni) and intrigue play the same roles, and the Beggar even allows a happy ending 'to comply with the Taste of the Town'.

# 1732 / 1739 The Seeds of Change

*While London, with rival Italian opera companies, briefly attracted all the finest singers in Europe, in Naples the comic* intermezzi *and operas of Pergolesi were investing* opera buffa *with qualities which would allow it to rival and eventually invade the territory occupied by* opera seria, *while in France the new dramatic style of Rameau made its first inroads into the long-standing supremacy of Lully's music.*

Title-page of Rameau's *Hippolyte et Aricie*, 1733. France had resisted *opera seria*, which had captivated the rest of Europe, and the posthumous influence of Lully had preserved a form in which spectacle, chorus and dance played a more important role, although the conventions of French *tragédie-lyrique* were as rigid as their Italian equivalent. Rameau's taut, dramatic music gave new life to this old form, from this, his first stage work, written at the age of fifty.

**1732** *January* Première of ***Il Demetrio*** (Hasse/Metastasio) at San Giovanni Grisostomo, Venice, with the *castrato* Appianino (Giuseppe Appiano), making his début. Mozart attended a performance of the opera in Mantua on 10 January 1770.
*26 January* Première of ***Ezio*** (Handel/adapted from Metastasio) at the King's Theatre, London. The Royal Academy had recruited the virtuoso bass singer Antonio Montagnana, whose abilities are reflected in the music Handel wrote for him.
*26 February* Première of ***Sosarme, re di Media*** (Handel/after Salvi) at the King's Theatre, London.
*28 February* Première of ***Jephthé*** (Montéclair/Pellegrin) at the Opéra, Paris; the first religious opera to be performed at the Opéra and a great success, although it was temporarily banned by the Archbishop of Paris. The biblical story of Jephthah, who vows that if he is victorious he will sacrifice the first person he meets – inevitably his daughter – was enlivened with ballets and the introduction of characters from Greek mythology. Montéclair had played double-bass in the famous storm scene in Marin Marais' ***Alcione*** (1706), while Rameau is said to have been inspired to write for the stage having heard ***Jephthé***.
*28 May* Unauthorized performance of ***Acis and Galatea*** (Handel/Gay) – 'An English Pastoral Opera' – adapted for the stage from a masque Handel wrote in 1719. A partial performance had been given at Lincoln's Inn Fields in April 1731, but this new revival was part of a season organized by English Opera, a newly formed company. Handel responded by directing a performance of the work himself at the King's Theatre on 21 June, but continued to compose Italian rather than English opera.
*27 September* Première of ***Lo frate 'nnamurato*** (Pergolesi/Federico) at the Teatro dei Fiorentini, Naples; Pergolesi's second opera (written in Neapolitan dialect). It was well received.

**1733** *7 February* Première of ***Orlando*** (Handel/adapted from Capece after Ariosto) at the King's Theatre, London. It was Handel's only new opera that season, with a magic plot featuring the benign enchanter Zoroaster (a role written for Montagnana) and bearing the message that one must conquer oneself as well as one's enemies. The opera, a break with the traditional political *opera seria*, has some of Handel's most imaginative pictorial effects, especially in the sleep aria for Orlando (Senesino's role) and in the disrupted rhythm of his vision of Angelica in Hades.
*18 March* Première of ***Rosamond*** (Arne/Addison) at Lincoln's Inn Fields, London, the composer's first opera. Using a text originally set in 1707 by Thomas Clayton, it was part of the English Opera's season.
*28 March* Première of ***L'Olimpiade*** (Caldara/Metastasio) at La Favorita, Vienna. Since his arrival in Vienna in 1730, Metastasio worked closely with Caldara, who made the original settings of eight of the poet's opera libretti.

## La serva padrona

Pergolesi's *intermezzo* in two parts about a servant who tyrannizes her master and tricks him into promising to marry her is always seen as a milestone in the history of comic opera. Yet each of its parts is barely twenty minutes long, and it is written for only two singers (and a third, silent, actor). What distinguished *La serva padrona* from other early comic operatic music was its combination of simplicity with tuneful arias and witty recitative and the way its composer portrayed the mixed feelings of the two characters with such subtlety. Despite writing only nine stage works in his short life, Pergolesi established a vocabulary for *buffo* music that still formed the basis for Rossini's comic writing nearly a century later. *La serva padrona* was frequently revived in Italy (where at least sixty theatres staged it) and abroad and – with only a brief gap in the early nineteenth century – has continuously maintained its place in the operatic repertory.

Caricature portrait of Giovanni Battista Pergolesi by P. L. Ghezzi. The sharply drawn characters and tuneful melodies in both his serious and comic operas distinguished his stage music from that of his contemporaries, while the sentimental character of his comedies anticipated developments in the second half of the century.

*5 September* Première of ***La serva padrona*** (Pergolesi/Federico) at San Bartolomeo, Naples. The two parts, sung by Gioacchino Corrado and Laura Monti, were performed as *intermezzi* between the acts of Pergolesi's *opera seria* ***Il prigionier superbo***.
*1 October* Première of ***Hippolyte et Aricie*** (Rameau/Pellegrin) at the Opéra, Paris (following a private performance at the house of the *fermier général*, M. de la Popelinière); Rameau's first opera to be performed, and a considerable success.
*10 November* Opening of the Royal Academy's new season at the King's Theatre, London, with ***La Semiramide***, a *pasticcio* (to a Metastasio libretto) assembled by Handel from music mostly by Vinci, with Strada, Durastanti (re-engaged though past her prime) and two new *castrati*, Carlo Scalzi and Carestini. It was attended by the whole court, including the Prince of Wales, who was also supporting the rival Opera of the Nobility.

**1734** *9 January* Opening of the Opera of the Nobility season with the première of ***Arianna in Nasso*** (Porpora/Pariati revised Rolli) at Lincoln's Inn Fields Theatre, London, with Senesino, Gismondi and Montagnana; the first of five operas Porpora composed as music director of the company.
*6 February* Première of ***Arianna in Creta*** (Handel/after Pariati) at the King's Theatre, London, the composer's only new opera for the 1733–4 season.
*17 February* Première of ***L'Olimpiade*** (Vivaldi/after Metastasio) at Sant' Angelo, Venice.
*25 October* Première of ***Livietta e Tracollo*** (Pergolesi/Mariani) as a two-part *intermezzo* between the acts of ***Adriano in Siria*** (Pergolesi/Metastasio) at San Bartolomeo, Naples.
*9 November* Première of the *pasticcio* ***Artaserse*** (Broschi, Hasse et al./Metastasio) at the King's Theatre, London, in which Farinelli and Senesino appeared together for the first time. Sir John Hawkins wrote: 'The world had never seen two such singers upon the same stage as Senesino and Farinelli; the former was a just and graceful actor, and in the opinion of very good judges had the superiority of Farinelli in respect of the tone of his voice; but the latter had so much advantage in other respects, that few hesitated to pronounce him the greatest singer in the world.'

## The 'Opera of the Nobility'

By 1733 Handel's popularity in London had been undermined by a series of situations: the English Opera company's success, the composer's identification with the German king (and therefore with his unpopular minister Walpole), and his singers' resentment of his dictatorial behaviour. Senesino approached a group of noblemen (including Lord Burlington and other backers of the original Royal Academy) after the 1732–3 Academy season to form a new opera company, and virtually all of Handel's company (with the exception of Strada) defected. Porpora was appointed music director, and the first season opened in January 1734 with his *Arianna in Nasso*, followed by Bononcini's *Astarto*. However, the real impact of the 'Opera of the Nobility' was felt after the arrival of Farinelli, who first appeared in *Artaserse* in November. For two and a half years there was in London, as a fashionable lady said, 'one God, one Farinelli'.

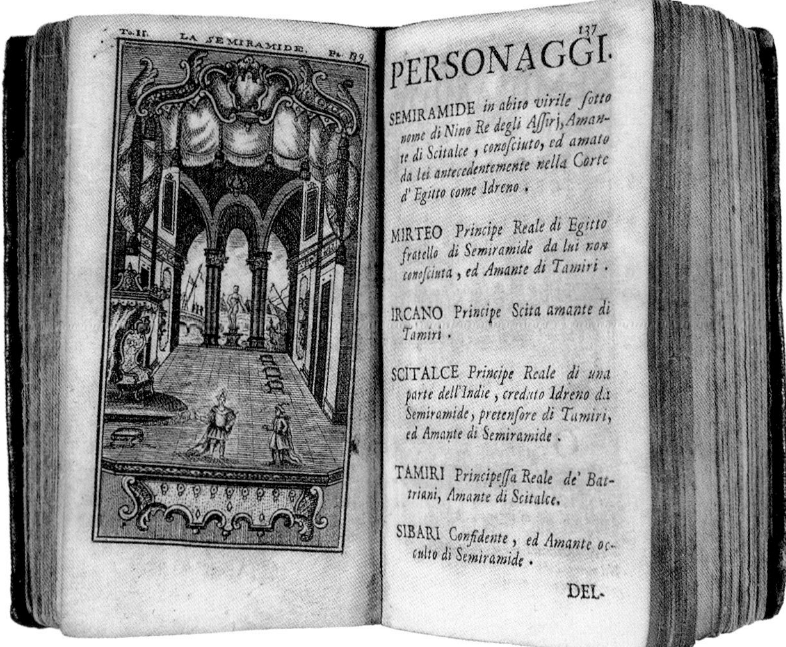

137

PERSONAGGI.

SEMIRAMIDE *in abito virile sotto nome di Nino Re degli Assirj, Amante di Scitalce, conosciuto, ed amato da lei antecedentemente nella Corte d'Egitto come Idreno.*

MIRTEO *Principe Reale di Egitto fratello di Semiramide da lui non conosciuta, ed Amante di Tamiri.*

IRCANO *Principe Scita amante di Tamiri.*

SCITALCE *Principe Reale di una parte dell'Indie, creduto Idreno da Semiramide, pretensore di Tamiri, ed Amante di Semiramide.*

TAMIRI *Principessa Reale de' Battriani, Amante di Scitalce.*

SIBARI *Confidente, ed Amante occulto di Semiramide.*

DEL-

An early edition of Metastasio's *La Semiramide*. The list of characters is typical of the poet's libretti: both Semiramide (who is disguised as a man) and Tamiri love Scitalce; both Mirteo (Semiramide's brother, though she fails to recognize him) and Ircano love Tamiri, to whom Scitalce is betrothed; while both Scitalce and Sibari love Semiramide.

**1735** *2 January* Première of ***L'Olimpiade*** (Pergolesi/Metastasio) at the Teatro Tordinona, Rome. At a performance attended by the poet Thomas Gray the composer was hit on the head by an orange thrown by a dissatisfied member of the audience. A revival in Venice the same year was a huge success thanks to Faustina Bordoni in the prima donna's role.
*19 January* Première of ***Ariodante*** (Handel/adapted from Salvi, after Ariosto) at Covent Garden, London, with Carestini in the title role. The Academy's lease of the King's Theatre had expired at the end of the previous season and been taken over by the Opera of the Nobility, forcing the Academy to move to the Theatre Royal, Covent Garden, which had opened in December 1732. Handel did his best to counter the rival attraction of Farinelli by writing ballets for Maria Sallé's dance troupe into both ***Ariodante*** and ***Alcina***.
*20 January* Première of ***Demofoonte*** (Leo/Metastasio) at San Bartolomeo, Naples; the most successful opera by Leonardo Leo, one of the leading composers of the Neapolitan school.
*18 May* Première of ***La Griselda*** (Vivaldi/Zeno revised Goldoni) at San Samuele, Venice. The title role was written for Anna Girò, whose relationship with the composer led to his being banned from Ferrara by Cardinal Ruffo. The heroine's part is written in a simple dramatic style, which contrasts with the florid ornamentations of the music for the villain, Ottone, sung by a *castrato*.
*24 February* Première of ***Achille et Déidamie*** (Campra/Danchet) at the Opéra, Paris; Campra's last opera, with a prologue which pays homage to Lully and Quinault.
*27 April* Première of ***Alcina*** (Handel/after Ariosto) at Covent Garden, London, with Strada in the title role and Carestini as Ruggiero. The third of Handel's operas based on Ariosto's *Orlando furioso*, it is one of his most effective stage works.

## Metastasio

No poet had more operas composed to his libretti than Metastasio (Pietro Trapassi). He wrote fewer than thirty full-length operatic texts, but they were set to music again and again, as long as *opera seria* remained viable. Trapassi was a godson of Cardinal Ottoboni and sang so beautifully as a child that a rich patron, G. V. Gravina, one of the founders of the Roman Arcadian academy, undertook his education and introduced him to the Arcadia (where he took the name by which he became known). After his first libretto – for Porpora's cantata *Gli orti Esperidi* – was performed in Naples in 1721, the singer of Venus, the soprano Marianna Bulgarelli, encouraged the young man to devote himself entirely to poetry and invited him to live in her house. The heroines' roles in all his earliest works (many of which were first set by Vinci) were written for Bulgarelli, often with Nicolini as her leading man, but in 1729 Apostolo Zeno recommended that Metastasio should succeed him as imperial court poet, and the following year he left his muse and moved to Vienna, where he spent the rest of his life.

Gravina had himself published imitations of Greek tragedies, and he encouraged his protégé to imitate the severe style of the ancient poets. Metastasio went much further than Zeno in his reform of *opera seria*: he restricted the characters to six (occasionally seven) with two female roles, simplified the plots and organized the scenes so that the tone of the work was set at the very beginning and the events followed in a natural sequence. The stories almost always have a political dimension, but there is also rivalry in love (sometimes with multiple triangles), and often one character is disguised, so that – as in ancient drama – there can be a poignant recognition scene. A happy ending is generally brought about by the generosity or clemency of the hero, although a few of the operas end tragically – notably *Catone in Utica* and *Attilio Regolo*. Almost invariably there is a concluding chorus, but very rarely does the chorus – as in *L'Olimpiade* – take a part in the action. Metastasio's verse flows exceptionally freely, and he varied the metres in his arias to reflect different passions, so that the composer's task was made much easier; his libretti show all the possibilities of *opera seria* but also the fatal limitations of a form so circumscribed by convention.

*23 August* Première of ***Les Indes galantes*** (Rameau/Fuzelier) at the Opéra, Paris. The countertenor Pierre de Jélyotte, who had made his début at the Opéra in 1733, scored his first great success in this *opéra-ballet*.
*24 September* Première of ***Tito Vespasiano, ossia La clemenza di Tito*** (Hasse/Metastasio) to inaugurate the Teatro Pubblico, Pesaro. It was revived in Dresden in 1738, where Hasse had been appointed court composer in 1734.
*Autumn* Première of ***Flaminio*** (Pergolesi/Federico) at the Teatro Nuovo, Naples, a full-length comic opera that relies for its effect on sentiment rather than farce, with the rivalries in love, disguises and mistaken identities familiar from *opera seria*.
A performance of ***Flora, or Hob in the Well*** (libretto by Cibber) in Charleston, S.C., is the first recorded production of a ballad opera in America.

**1736** *13 February* Première of ***Achille in Sciro*** (Caldara/Metastasio) at the court theatre, Vienna, for the wedding of Archduchess Maria Theresia and Francis of Lorraine. The work includes a chorus of bacchantes but contains only one solo female role (although Achilles is disguised as a woman for much of the opera). The last of the composer's 87 stage works, ***Temistocle***, was premièred a few weeks before his death in December.
*16 March* Death of Pergolesi at the age of twenty-six.
*23 May* Première of ***Atalanta*** (Handel/adapted from Valeriano) at Covent Garden, London, to celebrate the wedding of Frederick, Prince of Wales, and Princess Augusta of Saxe-Meiningen. The spectacular production with rousing choruses and a firework display ensured that the rival work put on by the Opera of the Nobility was eclipsed. Carestini had left the Academy after the first run of ***Ariodante*** and was replaced by Gizziello both in ***Atalanta*** and in a revival of ***Ariodante*** staged a few days earlier.

**1737** *23 January* Première of ***Arminio*** (Handel/after Salvi) at Covent Garden, London, with Annibali, a *castrato* new to London, in the title role. Only six performances were given.
*27 February* Première of ***Giustino*** (Handel/after Beregan) at Covent Garden, London. Nine performances were given, and the opera was parodied in John Lampe's burlesque opera ***The Dragon of Wortley***, performed – also at Covent Garden – in November of the same year.
*29 May* Première of ***Berenice*** (Handel/after Salvi) at Covent Garden, London, with Strada and Gizziello. This was Handel's third new opera in

Cross-section of the Hoftheater at Mannheim. Built in 1742 to designs by Alessandro Galli da Bibiena, it was the centre of musical life at the court of Elector Carl Theodor, patron of the Mannheim school of composers.

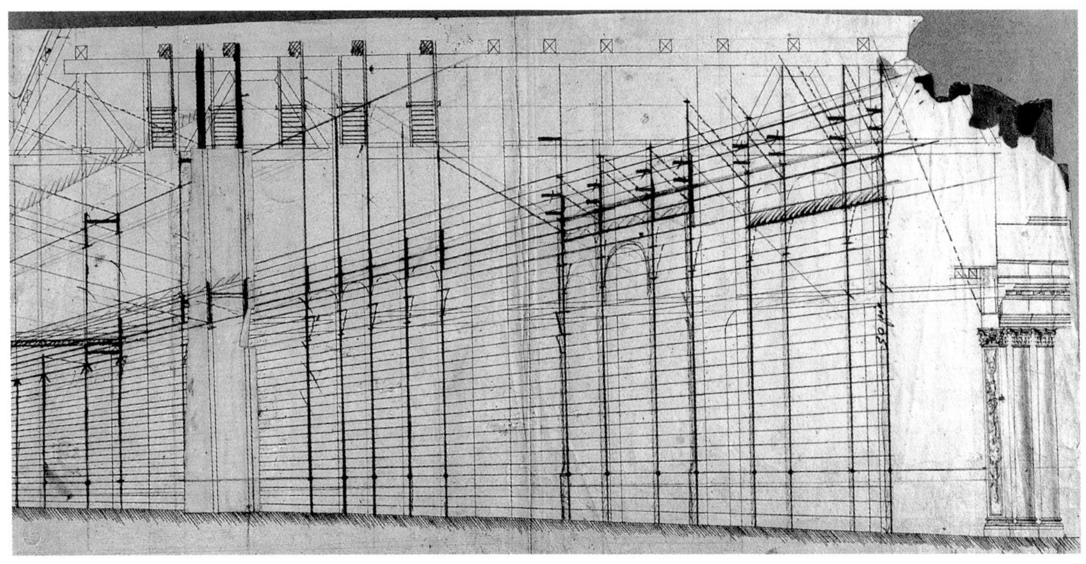

Plan for the enlargement of the stage area of the Salle des Machines in the Tuileries Palace carried out in 1738 by the architect Servandoni, who was also chief decorator at the Opéra from 1726 to 1746.

Faustina Bordoni in *Attilio Regolo* at Dresden in 1750, the setting by her husband Johann Adolf Hasse of Metastasio's libretto written in 1740 but put aside because of the death of Emperor Charles VI.

Performance of Francesco Feo's *Arsace* in the Teatro Regio, Turin, 1740. A contemporary of Porpora, Feo was one of the school of Neapolitan composers writing *opera seria* for Italian theatres.

Costume design by Boquet for the Inca princess in the second *entrée* of Rameau's *Les Indes galantes*, an *opéra-ballet* made up of several separate *entrées* on related themes. The original version (August 1735), consisted of a prologue and three *entrées*, with a new one being added for the revival in March 1736.

the 1736–7 season, in addition to other new productions and revivals. On 24 April he suffered a stroke. Although he recovered, the Academy disbanded – as did the Opera of the Nobility. Handel did set up a new company for the 1737–8 season, for which he wrote ***Faramondo*** (premièred on 14 January 1738) and ***Serse***, but he turned increasingly to oratorio, where the music could suggest the drama without the need for elaborately staged scenic effects.

*24 October* Première of ***Castor et Pollux*** (Rameau/Bernard) at the Opéra, Paris.

*4 November* Inauguration of the Teatro San Carlo, Naples, with a performance of Sarro's ***Achille in Sciro*** (libretto by Metastasio). San Bartolomeo was demolished soon afterwards.

**1738** *16 February* Performance of Hasse's ***Il Demetrio*** (see 1732) at the Teatro de los Caños del Peral, Madrid, where Italian opera became increasingly popular following the arrival of Farinelli in the city the previous year.

*26 April* Première of ***Serse*** (Handel/after Minato) at the King's Theatre, London, with Caffarelli in the title role. The Venetian libretto (originally set by Cavalli) is a satirical comedy, and despite the hero's opening aria 'Ombra mai fu' (later known as 'Handel's Largo') it was not well received.

**1739** *19 November* Première of ***Dardanus*** (Rameau/Le Clerc de la Bruère) at the Opéra, Paris; this powerful *tragédie-lyrique* was revised more than once, and the definitive version was premièred in 1760. The original production was the focus for a dispute between the supporters of Lully's traditional style and Rameau's adherents, who backed his modernizing reforms. Earlier in the year (21 May) his pastoral *opéra-ballet* ***Les Fêtes d'Hébé, ou Les Talents lyriques*** had been premièred at the Opéra.

# 1740 / 1761 The Death of Handel

*By 1759, when Handel died, while* opera seria *was not wholly eclipsed, the ideas of the French Enlightenment were leading to a preference for more natural subjects and less artifical musical forms – a tendency Handel had himself anticipated in his last English opera-oratorios. Comic opera was no longer confined to parody, farce and satire, but reflected the new bourgeois culture that was overtaking the patronage of the court.*

**DATES**

**1740**
Frederick the Great succeeds to Prussian throne (to 1786)

Maria Theresia succeeds to Austrian throne (to 1780)

Publication of Samuel Richardson's *Pamela*

**1743**
War of Austrian Succession (to 1748) with England and Hanover supporting Austria against France, Prussia and Bavaria

**1745**
Rebellion of Bonnie Prince Charlie in Scotland (to 1746)

**1749**
Publication of Fielding's *History of Tom Jones*

**1755**
30,000 people are killed in the Lisbon earthquake

**1756**
Seven Years War (to 1763) with England now supporting Prussia against Austria, France, Russia and Saxony

**1760**
Death of George II, succeeded by his grandson as George III (to 1820)

Revival of Lully's *Acis et Galatée* at Versailles in 1749 with Madame de Pompadour among the cast.

1740 *2 December* Première of ***Imeneo*** (Handel/adapted from Stampiglia) at Lincoln's Inn Fields, London. This and ***Deidamia*** (libretto by Rolli), his last opera, were performed in Handel's final season of Italian opera (mixed with oratorio performances), and both works were anti-heroic. Despite their tuneful, witty scores ***Imeneo*** (written two years earlier) ran for only two nights and ***Deidamia***, premièred on 21 January 1741, for only three.

1741 *13 December* Première of ***Rodelinda*** (Graun/Bottarelli after Salvi) in Potsdam. The composer had been appointed court composer to Frederick the Great the previous year and having been given the task of reviving opera in Berlin had travelled to Italy to recruit singers. ***Rodelinda*** was the first Italian opera given in Berlin, and for the next fifteen years *opera seria* flourished at Frederick's court, although, characteristically, Frederick himself took personal control, selecting (and drafting) libretti, supervising set and costume design, and making sure the singers added no ornamentation that the composer had not written in the score.
*26 December* Première of ***Semiramide riconosciuta*** (Jommelli/Metastasio) at the Teatro Regio, Turin. Jommelli saw the necessity for a reform of *opera seria* to create more genuine drama; the solution he found was to strengthen the role of the orchestra, a change he introduced in ***Semiramide.***

1742 *18 January* Première of ***Lucio Papirio*** (Hasse/Zeno) at the Hoftheater, Dresden. Following the collapse of Italian opera in London, many of the finest singers moved to Dresden, where the court theatre directed by Hasse vigorously upheld the *opera seria* tradition.
*20 January* Première of ***Artaserse*** (Gluck/Metastasio) at the Teatro Regio

## Rameau

Jean-Philippe Rameau was fifty before he wrote his first *tragédie-lyrique* (*Hippolyte et Aricie*, 1733), a composer with a high reputation for his instrumental music and for his writings on musical theory, whose only theatrical experience had been some settings and arrangements for the Théâtres des Foires. Italian opera had made no inroads in France, and the old style of Lully and his successors was still in fashion – indeed Lully's own operas continued to be revived. Rameau's more modern harmonic idiom and his attempts to provide a tauter, more dramatic, musical framework for serious opera met with considerable resistance, although he worked within the traditional French forms of *opéra-ballet* (where each episode has its own plot) and *comédie-lyrique* as well as *tragédie-lyrique*, and maintained the tradition of declamatory recitative. Many of Rameau's earlier stage works were heavily rewritten (both libretto and music) when they were revived, with the constant aim of strengthening their theatrical qualities, and eventually his work was appreciated for its renewal – rather than betrayal – of the French tradition. Indeed, later composers like Traetta, Jommelli and Gluck, who felt constrained by the rigid conventions of *opera seria*, found inspiration in the more open forms of Rameau's operas, for their own movement of reform.

Rameau with Voltaire, many of whose classical tragedies were used as the basis for opera libretti. The print commemorates a meeting in 1765 between the great men, who had collaborated thirty years earlier on *Samson* (an opera which had been banned by the censor) and in 1745 on the *opéras-ballets La Princesse de Navarre* and *Le Temple de la gloire*.

Comedy performed in Paris at the Foire Saint-Germain in the mid-eighteenth century. The parodies of *tragédies-lyriques*, performed with music by both French and Italian companies of comedians at the theatres at Paris's two annual fairs, led to the development of *opéra-comique*. From 1723 the Comédie-Italienne was housed at the Foire Saint-Laurent theatre, while from the following year the Opéra-Comique was accommodated at the Foire Saint-Germain.

Ducale, Milan: Gluck's first opera, written when he was a member of the household of Prince Melzi in Milan, a city (governed by Austria since 1713) not yet distinguished for opera but which welcomed a number of opera composers from the north, including J. C. Bach and the young Mozart.
*7 December* Première of ***Cleopatra e Cesare*** (Graun/Bottarelli after P. Corneille) to inaugurate the Königliches Opernhaus in Berlin.

**1743** *6 January* Première of ***Demofoonte*** (Gluck/Metastasio) at the Teatro Regio Ducale, Milan, the first of Gluck's operas to have some success.
*13 June* Première of ***Demofoonte*** (Jommelli/Metastasio) at the Teatro Obizzi, Padua, in which instrumental obbligato accompaniments are used to set the emotional tone of some of the arias.
*10 October* Première of ***Antigono*** (Hasse/Metastasio) at Schloss Hubertusburg, near Dresden. This was the first libretto Metastasio wrote for Hasse, although the composer had set several of his earlier poems. They were to collaborate on five further operas, and Metastasio particularly liked Hasse's settings, which remained closer than those of most composers to his original texts.

**1745** *16 January* Première of the 'musical drama' ***Hercules*** (Handel/Broughton) at the King's Theatre, London; really a staged oratorio, although it has been claimed as 'the greatest of all English operas.' Neither ***Hercules*** nor the secular oratorio ***Semele***, which had been played at Covent Garden in February 1744, was staged before the twentieth century, and although they closely follow operatic form, there is less vocal virtuosity, the form of many arias is simplified and the chorus assumes a far more important role.
*23 February* Première of ***La Princesse de Navarre*** (Rameau/Voltaire) at the Théâtre de la Grande Ecurie, Versailles, for the wedding of the Dauphin. The intention of the collaboration was to unite comedy, tragedy and opera.
*31 March* Première of ***Platée*** (Rameau/Le Valois d'Orville after Autreau) at the Théâtre de la Grande Ecurie, Versailles, with the counter-tenor Pierre de Jélyotte in the title role of the ugly marsh nymph. This *comédie-lyrique*, also performed during the Dauphin's wedding festivities, is a witty comedy that parodies many of the conventions of serious opera.

Marie Duronceray in the title role of her husband's *Ninette à la cour*, 1755, with music arranged by Egidio Duni.

**1746** *18 January* Reopening of the King's Theatre, London, which had been closed for the duration of the '45 rebellion, with a performance of ***La caduta de' giganti*** (libretto by Vanneschi), a heroic opera by Gluck, newly arrived in London. Gluck was extremely apprehensive that opening a theatre 'in which none but foreigners and Papists were employed' might provoke a riot. The composer wrote a second opera, ***Artamene***, for London before moving on to Copenhagen; the music for both works is largely taken from his earlier Italian operas.

**1748** *9 February* Première of ***Demofoonte*** (Hasse/Metastasio) at the Hoftheater, Dresden, one of the composer's greatest successes.
*14 May* Première of ***Semiramide riconosciuta*** (Gluck/Metastasio) at the Burgtheater, Vienna, for the birthday of Empress Maria Theresia. With this, his twelfth opera, Gluck achieved maturity as a stage composer.
*27 December* Première of ***Bertoldo, Bertoldino e Cacasenno*** (Ciampi/Goldoni) at San Moisè, Venice. The work was highly successful and was produced in Paris in 1753.

**1749** *5 December* Première of ***Zoroastre*** (Rameau/Cahusac) at the Opéra, Paris. The composer's fine *tragédie en musique* with its masonic ceremonials, followed two lighter works, the popular *acte de ballet* ***Pigmalion*** (August 1748) and the *pastorale héroïque* ***Naïs*** (April 1749). It was revived in a revised, much more coherent, form in 1756.

**1750** *12 January* Première of ***Attilio Regolo*** (Hasse/Metastasio) at the Hoftheater, Dresden; the most sensitive setting of this text by Metastasio. His libretto had been written for an opera to celebrate the nameday of Emperor Charles VI in 1740, but this was cancelled when the Emperor died. Unusually, the opera ends with Regulus' tragic farewell to Rome as he departs to certain death.
*14 November* Première of ***Il mondo alla roversa, o sia Le donne che comandano*** (Galuppi/Goldoni) at San Cassiano, Venice. It was one of a

Marie Duronceray (Mme Favart) in Paul Gilbert's opera *Les trois sultanes* to her husband's libretto,1761. Marie Duronceray starred in many of her husband's most successful productions, including a French version of *La serva padrona*, which ran for over a hundred performances in 1754.

Group portrait of Metastasio and friends, the singers Teresa Castellini and Farinelli; painting by Amigoni (who also appears in the group), *c.*1751. Farinelli had been invited to Madrid in 1737 to cure the melancholy of King Philip V, and he remained in Spain for the rest of his career, gaining such influence over the king and his successor, Ferdinand VI, that he became effectively a powerful minister. He persuaded Ferdinand and Queen Barbara (who had been a pupil of Domenico Scarlatti) to open an opera house in 1750, which he directed until 1758, when he retired to Italy.

series of comic operas that this team produced during the 1750s, in which they developed the concerted finale – a loosely constructed musical number made up of several sections, generally at increasingly fast tempi.

**1751** *4 November* Première of ***Il Farnace*** (Traetta/after Zeno) at San Carlo, Naples, the composer's first *opera seria.*

**1752** *1 August* Production of Pergolesi's ***La serva padrona*** (see 1733) by an Italian company at the Opéra, Paris, on a double bill with Lully's ***Acis et Galatée.*** This sparked the pamphlet war known as the 'Querelle des Bouffons' between the defenders of *comédie-lyrique* and the supporters of *opera buffa.*
*6 October* Première of ***Der Teufel ist los, oder Die verwandelten Weiber*** (Standfuss/Weisse after Coffey) in Leipzig. The *singspiel* was translated from ***The Devil to Pay*** (see 1731), earlier versions of which with the original music, one translated by Borcke, Prussian ambassador to London and the translator of Shakespeare's *Julius Caesar*, had been performed in Berlin (1743) and Hamburg (1747).
*18 October* Première of ***Le Devin du village*** (Rousseau/composer) in Fontainebleau, revived with great success at the Opéra on 1 March 1753 and three days later at Bellevue in the private theatre of Madame de Pompadour, who herself took the role of Colin (originally played by Jélyotte). The original version had recitatives written by Jélyotte and Francœur, but Rousseau wrote his own recitatives for the Paris production. The opera was constantly revived and more than 400 performances had been given by 1829.

**1753** *29 May* Performance (possibly première) of ***Der krumme Teufel*** (Haydn/Kurz-Bernardon) at the Kärntnertortheater, Vienna. Haydn may have composed settings for several *singspiele* by the great popular comedian Joseph Felix Kurz, known as Bernardon, though none of the music survives.
*12 October* Inauguration of the Residenztheater, Munich, with the première of ***Catone in Utica*** (Ferrandini/Metastasio). The theatre, designed by the rococo architect Cuvilliès, is still in use.

## The Querelle des Bouffons

The production of Pergolesi's *La serva padrona* in Paris in 1752 sparked off a pamphlet war over the merits of French and Italian opera. The philosopher Jean-Jacques Rousseau, also an accomplished composer and the author of the article on Music in the *Encyclopédie*, argued in his *Letter on French Music* (1753) that Italian *opera buffa* with its sung recitatives was more natural that the more formal French *opéra-comique* with its set pieces and spoken dialogue, and he had already composed *Le Devin du village* to exemplify his ideas. His opponents countered with praise of Rameau, and a revival in 1754 of his comic opera *Platée* proved to be a huge success at the Opéra, eclipsing the performances of the Italian company that had been performing there. There were foolish arguments on both sides, neither of which won a conclusive victory, but a fresh impetus was given to French *opéra-comique* – though spoken dialogue had to be retained since the statutes of the Opéra (Académie Royale de Musique) gave that institution the exclusive right to stage works entirely set to music. The expansion of *opéra-comique* was led by Charles-Simon Favart, a brilliant librettist, actor and impresario, who helped to create a new genre of comic opera, with sentimental plots in modern pastoral settings, known as *comédies larmoyantes* – literally, tearful comedies – which were just the kind of modern works the *philosophes* felt were needed. In 1762 the Opéra-Comique and Comédie-Italienne amalgamated in a company directed by Favart – which might be seen as a resolution of the *Querelle des Bouffons* – and by this time many composers were devoting their attention to the genre; the *Mercure de France* wrote in 1761 that 'music...has now become the interesting part of an *opéra-comique*'.

Charles-Simon Favart in the role of a peasant bagpiper. Favart's early career was spent with the Théâtres des Foires, of which he was appointed director in 1743. Many of his early texts were parodies of grand operas, especially of Lully and Rameau, but by the mid-1750s the popular taste was for sentiment rather than farce, and it was to appeal to this that he produced many original *opéras-comiques*.

**1754** *12 March* New production of ***Admeto*** at the King's Theatre, London, the last of Handel's operas to be revived in his lifetime and the last to be performed before the twentieth century.
*26 October* Première of ***Il filosofo di campagna*** (Galuppi/Goldoni) at San Samuele, Venice. This was Galuppi's most popular opera and one of his most successful collaborations with the great Venetian comic dramatist.

**1755** *6 January* Première of ***Montezuma*** (Graun/Frederick the Great after Voltaire) at the Königliches Opernhaus, Berlin. The following year, after war broke out with Austria, France and Saxony, the opera company was disbanded.
*11 February* Première of ***Pelope*** (Jommelli/Verazi) at the Herzogliches Theater, Stuttgart, the first of the composer's Stuttgart operas to survive. Both composer and librettist used French models to simplify the operatic form, in accordance with the taste of Duke Karl Eugen of Württemberg.
*12 February* Première of ***La Caprice amoureuse, ou Ninette à la cour*** (libretto by Favart after Goldoni's ***Bertoldo***) at the Comédie-Italienne, Paris. The work was a parody of Ciampi's ***Bertoldo*** (see 1748), which had been given in Paris in 1753, but it was Favart's version rather than the original that was widely imitated throughout Europe.

**1756** *23 September* Première of ***La Nitteti*** (Conforto/Metastasio) at the Buen Retiro Palace, Madrid, directed by Farinelli. The libretto, which was to be set several times, was written for Madrid, where Metastasio's friend Farinelli managed the court theatres, for the birthday of King Ferdinand VI.
*18 December* Première of ***Zenobia*** (Piccinni/Metastasio) at San Carlo, Naples, one of the first operas by a composer who twenty years later would become Gluck's rival in Paris.

**1759** *25 April* Death of Handel in London.

**1760** *6 February* Première of ***Cecchina, o La buona figliuola*** (Piccinni/Goldoni, after Samuel Richardson's novel *Pamela*) at the Teatro delle Dame, Rome. The work demonstrates Piccinni's strengths as a comic rather than serious composer and was successful throughout Europe; Piccinni responded brilliantly to the challenge of Goldoni's texts (previously set by Duni) for the concerted finales. It is reported that the opera was performed by Jesuits at the Chinese court during the 1770s. An English adaptation of *Pamela*, ***The Maid of the Mill*** (Arnold/Bickerstaffe), was produced at Covent Garden on 31 January 1765.
*April* Première of ***L'Ivrogne corrigé, ou Le Mariage du diable*** (Gluck/after La Fontaine) at the Burgtheater, Vienna, the most successful of the many *opéras-comiques* Gluck wrote for Vienna.
*15 November* Première of ***L'amante di tutte*** (Galuppi/Antonio Galuppi) at San Moisè, Venice: a burlesque of the Don Juan story.
*28 November* Première of ***Thomas and Sally, or The Sailor's Return*** (Arne/Bickerstaffe) at Covent Garden. This sentimental comedy was written as an 'afterpiece' to follow the performance of a play.

**1761** *3 January* Première of ***Armida*** (Traetta/Durazzo and Migliavacca after Quinault) at the Burgtheater, Vienna. Since his first *opera seria* (see 1751), the composer had fallen under the spell of Rameau and had adapted and set two of his libretti, seeing the French example as a way to give new life to Italian opera. ***Armida*** made Traetta's reputation and brought him into contact with Gluck, who began to modify his own style in the direction of reform.
*11 February* Première of ***L'Olimpiade*** (Jommelli/Metastasio) at the Herzogliches Theater, Stuttgart. The popular libretto set at the Olympic Games was well suited to the added ballet scenes choreographed by Noverre.
*1 May* Haydn entered the service of Prince Paul Anton Esterházy as Vice-Kapellmeister. In March 1762 the prince died and was succeeded by his brother Nicolaus, who was a passionate musician and was to be Haydn's patron for the next twenty-nine years.
*26 December* Première of ***Artaserse*** (J. C. Bach/Metastasio) at the Teatro Regio, Turin, Bach's first opera. It was followed later in the year by a setting of another Metastasio text, ***Catone in Utica***, the first of the two operas the composer wrote for Naples.

Design after Piranesi for the prison scene in Rameau's *Dardanus* in the 1760 production at the Paris Opéra, for which the composer introduced further changes to his radically revised 1744 version of the opera, originally produced in 1739.

Riot during a performance of Thomas Arne's *Artaxerxes*, an English *opera seria*, in 1763, caused by the Covent Garden management withdrawing the concession that allowed spectators to watch the final acts of the opera at half price.

# 2

# 1762–1850

# CLASSICAL AND ROMANTIC OPERA

*The ideals of classicism – a return to purer forms in harmony with nature – and romanticism, which saw music as a way to approach more closely the springs of human emotion and the life of the soul, were allied in their opposition to baroque artifice. Gluck and Mozart, the masters of classical opera, were heroes to the romantics, not only to E. T. A. Hoffmann, the romantics' most imaginative critic, but also to those great masters of romantic music Berlioz, Liszt and Wagner. However, in the years of peace following 1815, though Weber made valiant efforts to establish a new national style of German opera, it was the melodic tradition of Italian opera that carried the day with audiences throughout Europe – in the works of Rossini, Bellini, Donizetti and Verdi sung by stars such as Pasta, Malibran, Grisi, Rubini and Lablache.*

Set for Gluck's *Alceste* (1767) designed by the architect and theatre designer Friedrich von Schinkel for a production at the Berlin Opernhaus in October 1817.

# Classical and Romantic Opera

The Italian Opera House, New York, the first theatre in the USA built specifically for opera. It opened in 1833 with performances by the company of Giacomo Montresor, and one of its promoters was Lorenzo da Ponte, now eighty-four years old. This venture was not a success, but opera became increasingly popular in America during these years.

OPERA SERIA with its *castrato* heroes belonged to the age of absolute monarchy: the formal entrances and exits mirrored the patterns of court etiquette, and the themes – though warning of the dangers of ambition, love, jealousy and other passions – almost always reflected the benevolent powers of a magnanimous monarch. Comic *intermezzi* had provided entertainment with the licensed buffoonery of stock characters, but seldom touched deeper feelings. By the mid-eighteenth century the world had changed; the 'age of reason' saw humanity in a different light, and the sentiments of real people assumed greater importance than the abstract passions of artificial characters. It was in the simpler forms and more natural expression of comic opera that composers and librettists discovered a way to breathe new life into the tradition of serious opera. The reformers – notably Traetta, Jommelli and Gluck – had all been composers of conventional *opera seria*, and it was Gluck who made the most radical changes, borrowing the direct, simple melodic line of French *opéra-comique*, and underpinning it with a subtly coloured orchestral accompaniment that carried the drama forward beneath a new form of dramatic recitative, as well as through the arias, choruses and dances.

Operatic reform had a strong philosophical basis, and the myth of Orpheus, which had been chosen by the first operatic composers to exemplify the power of music, was now treated as a fable about humanity and mortality, while the dismantling of formal structures and the shunning of ornament was based on the 'classical fallacy' that the art of antiquity was the art that was closest to nature. Gluck's reforms had their most profound effect in Paris, which was the intellectual – and operatic – capital of the world. Any new development there would be sure to start a new *querelle*, and while the anti-Gluck party found a champion in the more moderate reformer Piccinni, this campaign was won decisively by the German composer. It was not, however, the end of the war. Although throughout the revolutionary and Napoleonic periods operas with the lofty themes of heroism and endurance, set to music indebted to Gluck's treatment of voices and orchestra, were preferred, Italian melody with brilliantly ornamented parts for virtuoso singers soon came back into favour. By the 1820s Rossini was the fashionable king of Parisian opera – shortly to be followed to the French capital by Bellini and Donizetti. However, they were not unopposed; Berlioz spoke for many serious music-lovers when he condemned Rossini's 'melodious cynicism and contempt for the traditions of dramatic expression' and his supporters' 'blasphemies against Gluck, Spontini and the entire school of feeling and commonsense'. One lasting effect of the operatic style of the revolutionary period was the taste for huge tableaux created by grand musical ensembles and sensational scenic effects. By combining these with Rossinian melody, Meyerbeer created the archetypal French *grand opéra*.

Outside Paris, comic operas – sentimental rather than burlesque – had been growing in popularity, and in England and Germany national styles had begun to emerge around the middle of the eighteenth century. Josef II inaugurated a German Nationalsingspiel in Vienna, which lasted for ten years, and in Leipzig Adam Hiller produced German versions of the most popular French *opéras-comiques*, although the reputation of German music lay in instrumental and symphonic music rather than opera. However, Beethoven's *Fidelio* showed German composers that their supremacy in instrumental music could also form the basis for a national style of opera, and Weber, both in his own compositions and in the works he staged as an opera director, made colossal efforts to realize this ideal, while composers such as Spohr and Marschner gradually added to the repertory, preparing the way for Richard Wagner.

From the mid-eighteenth century operas also began to be produced in America – in English in Philadelphia, New York, Charleston and other cities, and in French in New Orleans – while the courts of northern Europe imported Italian or German composers to direct their opera houses. The most important centre was St Petersburg, where a succession of notable Italian composers worked at the court of Catherine the Great, laying the foundations of the great Russian operatic school of the nineteenth century.

Italy remained the natural home of opera, with performances in dozens of towns as well as in the court theatres and the great cities. Stendhal described a typical Italian company in the early nineteenth century: 'an impresario (very often the richest nobleman in a little town)...forms a little company, always made up of the *prima donna*, the *tenore*, the *basso cantante*, the *basso buffo*, a second female and a third *buffo*. He hires a *maestro* (composer), who writes him a new opera, taking care to suit his arias to the voices of the characters who will sing them. The impresario buys a poem (*libretto*), which costs him 60 or 80 francs. The author is some poor priest, a parasite in some wealthy local house...The impresario, who is the head of one of these houses, hands over the financial affairs of his theatre to a producer, usually a rascally lawyer, who acts as manager; while he, the impresario, becomes the lover of the *prima donna*...After a month of idiotic intrigues, which are the talk of the town, the troupe gives its first performance, and this *prima recita* is the largest public event in the neighbourhood – there is nothing in Paris to compare to it – and for three weeks eight to ten thousand people dispute the merits and faults of the opera...' The emergence of impresarios like Barbaia and Merelli, of music-publishing houses like Ricordi who built their fortunes on opera, and of composers like Rossini, Bellini and Donizetti must be seen in the context of popular opera, where melody, wit and drama were prized above sophistication.

The works of the greatest operatic composer transcend these general developments. The music of Mozart's finest Italian operas is composed with a symphonic sophistication that sets them apart from the genre of *opera buffa*, while his two *singspiele* mix serious elements with the popular songs and pantomime plots: in the first the heroine seems almost to have come from *opera seria*, while his *Die Zauberflöte* is invested with a solemnity unprecedented in works of this kind. However, their success as music theatre is due principally to Mozart's great gift for the delineation of character by musical means. E. T. A. Hoffmann wrote of the instrumental music of the great masters of the Viennese school, all of whom were also great opera composers: 'Haydn interprets the human part of human life in a romantic way...Mozart lays claim to the metaphysical, the wondrous, which dwells in the inner spirit...Beethoven's music moves the lever of fear, of dread, of horror, of pain, and wakens the infinite longing that is the essence of the romantic.'

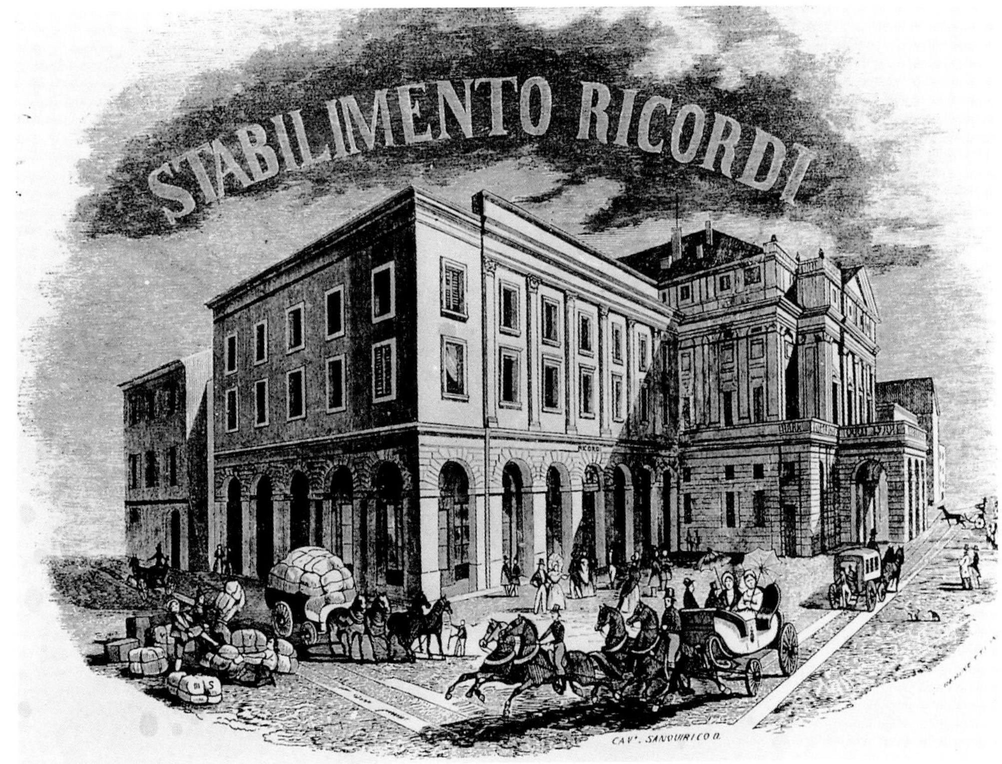


The office of the publishers Ricordi, in part of the building of La Scala in Milan. The publishing house was founded in 1808 by Giovanni Ricordi, who published the works of Rossini, Bellini and Donizetti, and continued by his son Tito and grandson Giulio, who were Verdi's publishers, exercising control over performance as well as publishing rights. From mid-century to the outbreak of the First World War they maintained an almost monopolistic control over opera in Italy.

# 1762–1775 Opera is Reborn

*As the traditional forms of* opera seria *were challenged by new enlightened ideas, comic operas also began to lose their artificiality and take as subject matter the moral and sentimental themes that were becoming popular in English novels and French tales, while their composers searched for a more direct musical style to match this simplicity.*

Gluck and Rameau (who in fact never met), depicted in a print published around the time of the première of *Orphée et Euridice* (1774), the French version of Gluck's opera, at the Paris Opéra, celebrating the German composer as the Frenchman's true successor.

**1762** *2 February* Première of ***Artaxerxes*** (Arne/composer after Metastasio), at Covent Garden, London.
*2 March* Opening of the new Comédie-Italienne (now amalgamated with the Opéra-Comique) at the Hôtel de Bourgogne, Paris – where *opéra-comique* continued to be performed until 1782.
*5 October* Première of ***Orfeo ed Euridice*** (Gluck/Calzabigi) commissioned by Durazzo for the Burgtheater, Vienna, to celebrate the birthday of the Emperor. The title role was sung by the *castrato* Gaetano Guadagni, choreography was by Angiolini and designs by Quaglio. The opera was not well received, and only seven performances were given.
*4 November* Première of ***Sofonisba*** (Traetta/Verazi after Zeno) at the Hoftheater, Mannheim; one of the composer's most successful and innovative operas.
*22 November* Première of ***Le Roi et le fermier*** (Monsigny/Sedaine) at the Comédie-Italienne. In this and later operas on which they collaborated, composer and librettist aimed to provide a strong element of musical continuity in a form that normally consisted simply of a succession of individual numbers.
*8 December* Première of the ballad opera ***Love in a Village*** (Arne/Bickerstaffe), at Covent Garden, London. The music was partly composed by Arne and partly selected from works by other composers. The first American performance was in Philadelphia at the turn of 1766–7, and the work continued to be popular into the 1840s.

**1763** Premières of Haydn's first two Italian operas at Eisenstadt: ***Acide e Galatea*** (11 January, for the wedding of Count Anton, to a libretto by Migliavacca), and the comedy ***La Marchesa Nespola*** (unknown librettist).
*19 February* Première of ***Orione, ovvero Diana vendicata*** (J. C. Bach/Bottarelli) at the King's Theatre, London, in the presence of the King and Queen. The composer's first opera written for the theatre, to which he had been appointed composer in residence the previous year, it enjoyed continuing success.
*4 October* Performance of ***Ifigenia in Tauride*** (Traetta/Coltellini) at Schönbrunn. It was one of the earliest 'reform' operas and may date from as early as 1761. Gluck conducted a performance of the work in Florence in February 1767 and used the subject for an opera of his own in 1779.

**1764** *7 January* Première of ***La Rencontre imprévue*** (Gluck/Dancourt) at the Burgtheater, Vienna. It was the last – and most effective – of the *opéras-comiques* Gluck was commissioned to write for Vienna by Durazzo; in German translation, as ***Die Pilgrime von Mekka***, it became one of the founding works of the German *singspiel.*
*24 April* Première of ***Egeria*** (Hasse/Metastasio), a traditional *opera seria*, at the Burgtheater, Vienna, on the occasion of the coronation of Josef II.
*12 September* Death of Rameau in Paris.

Portrait of Gluck and his wife around 1770.

**1765** *27 February* Première of ***Tom Jones*** (Philidor/Poinsinet after Fielding) at the Comédie-Italienne, Paris, an opera which became an international success. The English novel stimulated the composer to some of his finest music, including a number of concerted numbers in which, as in *opera seria,* the different feelings of the characters are expressed. An English opera based on Fielding's novel was composed in 1769 by Samuel Arnold.

**1766** *15 April* Première of the *ballet-héroïque,* ***Aline, reine de Golconde*** (Monsigny/Sedaine) at the Opéra, Paris. Sedaine's libretto was used by a number of later composers, including Donizetti.
*27 July* Première of ***La canterina*** (Haydn/unknown librettist) at Eisenstadt, an *intermezzo*-like *opera buffa* parodying *opera seria,* later performed at Eszterháza and Pressburg (Bratislava). Comic Italian operas were to become Prince Nicolaus's favourite music.

**1767** *20 January* Première of ***Il Bellerofonte*** (Mysliveček/Bonechi) at San Carlo, Naples, one of the earliest – and best – of the Bohemian composer's serious operas.

## Gluck's reforms

The six operas Gluck wrote for the Paris Opéra from 1774 to 1779 – which included revised versions of two works first performed in Vienna without much success – are seen as a milestone in operatic history, replacing the old form of Italian *opera seria* with a new French style that restored ancient gravity and simplicity in the spirit of the Florentine camerata. The fact that the role of Orfeo, originally written for *castrato*, was now sung by a tenor even seems to symbolize the change to a new order. However, the impetus for the changes came from several different quarters: the writer Francesco Algarotti, who wanted music and poetry, singers, chorus, ballet and spectacle, all to serve the dramatic action; Giacomo Durazzo, appointed director of the court opera in Vienna in 1754, who wanted to introduce French elements into Italian opera to serve the same ends; the librettists Coltellini and Verazi and, above all, Raniero da Calzabigi, who was Gluck's most important collaborator; the dancer-choreographer Gasparo Angiolini, who worked with Gluck on two 'action ballets', *Don Juan* (1761) and *Semiramis* (1765); and composers such as Jommelli, music director in Stuttgart, and Traetta, whose appointment at the Bourbon court of Parma had introduced him to the operas of Rameau and the French school and who provided a model for many of Gluck's reforms. The overall aim was to create a natural style, so that the old pattern of *secco* recitative and static arias might be replaced by a looser and more unified form, in which the orchestra played the leading role, accompanying recitatives, arias, choruses and dances.

Orpheus leading Euridice out of Hades; title page of the libretto of Gluck's opera.

*24 April* Première of ***Lottchen am Hofe*** (Hiller/Weisse after Goldoni and Favart) at the Stadttheater, Leipzig. Composer and librettist did much to further the cause of German *singspiel* with their adaptations of French *opéras-comiques.*

*26 April* Première of ***L'amore artigiano*** (Gassmann/Goldoni) at the Burgtheater, Vienna, a work that enjoyed great success throughout Europe.

*13 May* Première of ***Apollo et Hyacinthus*** (Mozart/Widl) at the University, Salzburg. At the end of each school year it was a tradition that the Salzburg students would put on a performance. This *intermezzo* by the eleven-year-old composer was played between the acts of a Latin tragedy written by his librettist.

*24 November* Première of ***Ernelinde, princesse de Norvège*** (Philidor/Poinsinet) at the Opéra, Paris. It was the composer's principal grand opera and he modified the conventional French form by introducing long Italianate arias.

*26 December* Première of ***Alceste*** (Gluck/Calzabigi) at the Burgtheater, Vienna. This was Gluck's second 'reform' opera. Mozart attended a performance in September 1768. The work was not well received, and Gluck later made several changes to the score.

**1768** *27 January* Première of ***Les Moissonneurs*** (Duni/Favart) at the Comédie-Italienne, Paris - the archetypal *comédie larmoyante.*
*20 August* Première of ***L'Ingénu, ou Le Huron*** (Grétry/Marmontel after Voltaire) at the Comédie-Italienne, Paris. The composer's first success, the opera tells the moral tale of an American Indian (half-French), a noble savage, whose desire to marry a French girl – against the wishes of her father – is finally achieved. The Italianate style of the music and sentimental story were typical of the operas Grétry wrote with Marmontel, who later led the opposition to Gluck in Paris.
*28 September* Première of ***Lo speziale*** [***The Apothecary***] (Haydn/Goldoni), to inaugurate the opera house at Eszterháza.
*3 October* Première of ***The Padlock*** (Dibdin/Bickerstaffe after Cervantes) at Drury Lane, London. It received performances soon afterwards across the English-speaking world: in New York and Philadelphia in 1769, in Dublin in 1770, Montego Bay in 1777, Calcutta in 1789, and was also revived in England and America in the early nineteenth century. The Afro-American actor Ira Aldridge was a famous Mungo, the part originally played by the composer.
*October* Première of ***Bastien et Bastienne*** (Mozart/Weiskern and Schachtner) in the garden of Dr Anton Mesmer in Vienna, a version of Favart's parody of Jean-Jacques Rousseau's ***Le Devin du village.***

**1769** *6 March* Première of ***Le Déserteur*** (Monsigny/Sedaine) at the Comédie-Italienne, Paris, in which the authors carried their plan of musical continuity so far that the finale of the work is virtually through-composed. The opera was performed in Paris throughout the nineteenth century and all over Europe. A version by Dibdin, premièred at Drury Lane in 1773, was performed in 1787 in New York and Philadelphia.
*1 May* Première of ***La finta semplice*** (Mozart/Coltellini after Goldoni) in the Archbishop's Palace, Salzburg. It had been written for Vienna in 1768, but the Burgtheater management decided to revive Piccinni's ***La buona figliuola*** (see 1760) instead.

**1770** *30 May* Première of ***Armida abbandonata*** (Jommelli/de Rogatis after Tasso) at San Carlo, Naples. Mozart and his father attended a performance, and Mozart told his sister: 'the opera is nice, but too clever and too old-fashioned for the theatre'.

*'I have striven to restrict music to its true office of serving poetry by means of expression and by following the situation of the story, without interrupting the action or stifling it with a useless superfluity of ornaments; and I believe that it should do this in the same way as telling colours affect a correct and well-ordered drawing, by a well-assorted contrast of light and shade, which serves to animate the figures without altering their contours.'*

Gluck's introduction to *Alceste* (probably written by Calzabigi)

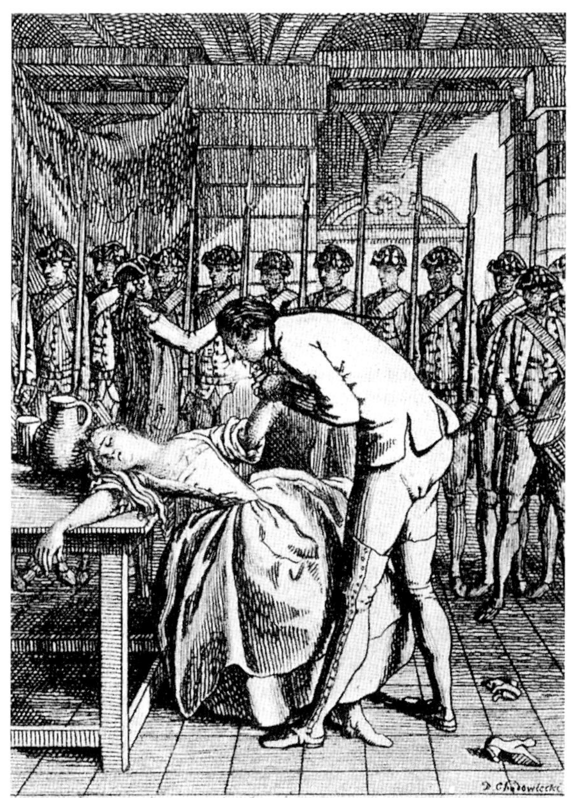

Scene from a production of Monsigny's *Le Déserteur* in Berlin, where the opera was first performed in 1772, three years after its Paris première. The heroine, Louise, faints, when she hears the news that her lover, who has deserted from the army, has been pardoned.

Charles Dibdin as Mungo in his opera *The Padlock* (1768).

Scene from Haydn's *L'incontro improvviso*, performed in the opera house at Eszterháza in 1775. The set was designed by Pietro Travaglia.

*3 November* Première of ***Paride ed Elena*** (Gluck/Calzabigi) at the Burgtheater, Vienna. The dances were directed by Jean-Georges Noverre, but the opera was a failure and, apart from an eighteenth-century performance in Naples, was not revived until the twentieth century.
*26 December* Première of ***Mitridate, re di Ponto*** (Mozart/Cigna-Santi after Racine) at the Teatro Regio Ducale, Milan. There were twenty-two successive performances, but the opera was not revived.

**1771** *2 June* Première of ***Armida*** (Salieri/Coltellini after Tasso) at the Burgtheater, Vienna. It was repeated there in 1776. Salieri, who in 1766 had been brought by Gassmann to Vienna, where he enjoyed the support of Gluck and Metastasio, was a prolific composer of operas, serious and comic.
*17 October* Première of ***Ascanio in Alba*** (Mozart/Parini), a *serenata* for the wedding of Archduke Ferdinand to Princess Maria Ricciarda Beatrice d'Este, at the Teatro Regio Ducale, Milan, with a *castrato* role sung by Giovanni Manzuoli. The previous night had seen the première of ***Ruggiero*** (Hasse/Metastasio), Hasse's last opera. Leopold Mozart told his wife: 'I'm afraid Wolfgang's Serenata eclipsed Hasse's opera so much I can't describe it.' The Archduke was so pleased with Mozart's work that it had to be repeated two nights later.
*9 November* Première of ***Zémire et Azor*** (Grétry/Marmontel) in Fontainebleau. The *comédie-ballet* had a great international success, with performances before 1800 in thirty cities, including Moscow, Warsaw, St Petersburg, New York, Philadelphia, Charleston and Boston.

**1772** *1 May* Première of ***Il sogno di Scipione*** (Mozart/Metastasio) for the installation of the new archbishop, Hieronymus Colloredo, in Salzburg. The libretto had originally been written to celebrate Empress Elisabeth's birthday in 1735 and needed to be adapted to suit the occasion.

## Haydn at Eszterháza

From 1761 to 1790 Haydn was in the service of the Esterházy family, and for much of that time one of his chief duties was running the opera in their new palace at Eszterháza. The household moved there in 1766, the year Haydn was appointed Kapellmeister, and the opera house opened in 1768. Apart from composing operas himself, his main task was the preparation and production of a large repertory of works by leading composers, including Gluck, Piccinni, Paisiello, Anfossi, Sarti, Salieri, Traetta, Cimarosa, Zingarelli and many others. After the opera house had been rebuilt in 1781 following a disastrous fire, it became one of the most active opera houses in Europe – during the 1780s there were around 90 performances in most years, and as many as 125 in 1786 – for which Haydn had total musical responsibility, while from 1782 Pietro Travaglia oversaw the design, lighting and machinery of the productions. Haydn's own operas, mainly comic or 'semi-serious', are among the finest of the period, although they never achieved international success in their time and still remain outside the standard operatic repertory.

*11 November* Première of ***Antigona*** (Traetta/Coltellini) at the court theatre, St Petersburg, the last and most 'modern' of Traetta's operas, with dramatic recitatives and important parts for both chorus and orchestra.
*26 December* Première of ***Lucio Silla*** (Mozart/Gamerra altered by Metastasio) at the Teatro Regio Ducale, Milan. The work is a traditional *opera seria*, but Mozart already showed signs of his greatest talent as an opera composer, giving strong individual character to the different roles. He started by composing the recitatives and choruses, leaving the arias until the final few weeks, when the singers were actually on the spot; the tenor who was to sing the title role did not arrive until the 17th, and there were still four arias to be written for him – two of which Mozart completed within a day.

**1773** *18 January* Première of ***Thetis och Pelée*** (Uttini/Wellander after a play by Gustav III) at the Bollhuset, Stockholm. The first Swedish grand opera, based on a play by the king who appears as the principal character in the original version of Verdi's ***Un ballo in maschera***.
*26 July* Première of ***L'infedeltà delusa*** (Haydn/Coltellini) at Eszterháza. The opera, almost certainly using an old libretto by Coltellini adapted for Haydn, lampoons the aristocracy. It was Haydn's most effective opera to date and has been successful in modern revivals.

Anna Morichelli as Violanta, the heroine of Paisiello's *La frascatana* (1774), which she sang in a 1780 revival of the opera at the Vienna Burgtheater, where it was first performed in 1775.

**1774** *19 April* Première of ***Iphigénie en Aulide*** (Gluck/Lebland du Roullet, after Racine) at the Opéra, Paris, with Madeleine-Sophie Arnould in the title role. Gluck's former pupil, Queen Marie Antoinette, persuaded the Opéra to stage the work, with the stipulation that Gluck agreed to write six operas for them. Their reception justified the gamble on a German composer.
*2 August* Première of ***Orphée et Euridice***, the French version of Gluck's ***Orfeo ed Euridice*** (see 1762) at the Opéra, Paris. The *castrato* title role was now sung by a tenor, and the work took Paris by storm.
*November* Première of ***La frascatana*** (Paisiello/Livigni) at San Samuele, Venice. The composer's operas had been well received in Naples since the mid-1760s, but this was his first runaway success outside that city.

*'M. Grétry is from Liège; he is young, he looks deathly pale, in pain, tormented, with all the symptoms of a man of genius.'*
Baron Friedrich-Melchior Grimm

**1775** *13 January* Première of ***La finta giardiniera*** (Mozart/Petrosellini?) at the Residenztheater, Munich. The opera had been planned to open on 29 December, but was so well liked in rehearsal that the performance was put off to allow for more rehearsal time. The plot is a typical *comédie larmoyante* and the libretto is poorly constructed, consisting mainly of arias with overlong finales. Mozart himself prepared a German version, which was widely performed in Germany from 1779 by Johann Böhm's troupe of travelling actors.
*23 April* Première of ***Il re pastore*** (Mozart/Metastasio) at the Archbishop's Palace, Salzburg, for the visit of Archduke Maximilian.
*29 August* Gala première of ***L'incontro improvviso*** (Haydn/Friberth) composed for a visit by Archduke Ferdinand to Eszterháza. It was the longest and most lavishly orchestrated of Haydn's operas to date, if not his best. The two principal roles were taken by the librettist and his wife. The text is an Italian version of Dancourt's ***La Rencontre imprévue***, which had been set by Gluck (see 1764).
*October* Première of ***Socrate immaginario*** (Paisiello/Galiani and Lorenzi) at the Teatro Nuovo, Naples. A highly original setting of a brilliant libretto, which satirized the fashionable classical craze, it was banned by King Ferdinand as being 'too impertinent'.
*21 November* Première of ***The Duenna*** (Linley/Sheridan) at Covent Garden, London. The Linleys, father and son, composed and compiled the music, and the opera enjoyed a great success.

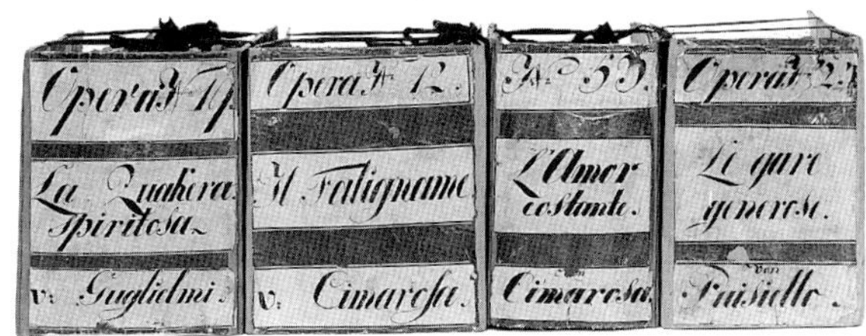

Files of orchestral parts for operas by Guglielmi, Cimarosa and Paisiello performed under Haydn during the 1780s at Eszterháza.

**1776**
**1780**

# Melodrama and Singspiel

*The 1770s saw the growth of a new sense of German culture: the imitations of French and English – rather than Italian – operatic forms began to bear fruit in distinctive German forms: the* singspiel, *with spoken dialogue between musical numbers, and the* melodrama, *in which words were spoken against an orchestral accompaniment throughout.*

Charlotte Brandes, an actress celebrated for her natural expressive gifts, as the heroine of her husband's play *Ariadne auf Naxos*, set by Georg Benda as a melodrama and performed at Gotha in 1775.

Set design by Pierre-Adrien Paris for the prison where Orestes and Pylades are confined in Gluck's *Iphigénie en Tauride*, first performed at the Paris Opéra in 1779, with Levasseur in the title role.

DATES

**1776**
*4 July* American Declaration of Independence (the Revolutionary War continues to 1781)
Publication of Charles Burney's *General History of Music* (to 1789)
**1778**
Deaths of Voltaire and Rousseau
**1780**
Death of Empress Maria Theresia, succeeded by her son as Josef II

**1776** *23 April* Première of the revised version of Gluck's ***Alceste*** (see 1767) at the Opéra, Paris, with Rosalie Levasseur in the title role. It was very coolly received; Gluck's new operas provoked fierce opposition from traditionalists and from those who saw the Italian style as the future for French opera, led by the writer Marmontel, who had provided libretti for a number of Grétry's operas and now arranged for Piccinni to be invited to Paris.
*25 September* Première of the *singspiel* ***Romeo und Julie*** (Benda/Gotter) at Gotha; one of the earliest operas based on Shakespeare's play. The previous year Benda had written two *melodramas*, ***Ariadne auf Naxos*** and ***Medea***, in which the immediacy of the spoken word offered the greatest possible contrast to the artificiality of *opera seria*.

**1777** *Summer* Première of ***Il mondo della luna*** (Haydn/Goldoni) at Eszterháza for the wedding of Count Nicolaus Esterházy. The opera gave the composer the opportunity for parody beyond the stock *buffo* plot, and also for musical scene-painting of the moon landscape.
*23 September* Première of ***Armide*** (Gluck/Quinault) at the Opéra, Paris, with Levasseur in the title role. The composer used the libretto (and original sets) of Lully's ***Armide*** (see 1686), and this new interpretation of Quinault's hallowed text was a provocation that increased the intensity of the arguments with the supporters of Piccinni.

**1778** *27 January* Première of ***Roland*** (Piccinni/Quinault revised by Marmontel) at the Opéra, Paris, also using a libretto that had been set by

Lully (see 1685). The title role was written for Ubalde Arrivée (Gluck's Agamemnon and Orestes in his two ***Iphigénie*** operas); the Gluck party did their best to ensure that the work would fail.
*17 February* Opening of the Nationalsingspiel at the Burgtheater, Vienna, with the première of ***Die Bergknappen*** (Umlauf/Weidmann). Josef II's initiative to promote a national German opera lasted for ten years.
*4 April* Première of ***La clemenza di Scipione*** (J. C. Bach/unknown librettist) at the King's Theatre, London; Bach's last Italian opera, a fine work in which modernizing influences (in arias, chorus, ballet and orchestra) are most pronounced.
*3 August* Opening of La Scala theatre, Milan, with the première of ***Europa riconosciuta*** (Salieri/Verazi), a fairly traditional political *opera seria.*

Madame Stierle as Delda in Ignaz Umlauf's *Die Bergknappen*, which opened the German Nationalsingspiel in Vienna in February 1778.

**1779** *25 April* Première of ***La vera costanza*** (Haydn/Puttini and Travaglia) at Eszterháza, originally set by Anfossi for Rome in January 1776 (a version performed in Vienna a year later). Haydn's version is notable particularly for its sharply characterized arias and fine ensembles.
*18 May* Première of ***Iphigénie en Tauride*** (Gluck/Guillard after Euripides) at the Opéra, Paris, the outstanding example of the composer's mature style. Piccinni's opera on the same subject was premièred on 23 January 1781 but did not stand comparison with Gluck's masterpiece.
*24 September* Première of ***Echo et Narcisse*** (Gluck/Tchudi) at the Opéra, Paris; Gluck's last opera, it failed completely. Gluck returned to Vienna, where he prepared a German version of ***Iphigénie en Tauride***, first performed on 23 October 1781.
*28 December* Première of ***L'italiana in Londra*** (Cimarosa/Petrosellini) at the Teatro Valle, Rome; the composer's first great success, although the twelfth opera he had written.

**1779–80** Composition of ***Zaïde*** (Mozart/Schachtner). Mozart intended the work for Vienna, where it was to be performed by Johann Böhm's troupe, but the death of Empress Maria Theresia in November 1780 frustrated this plan, and the work was abandoned without the overture or final chorus being composed. Two numbers were set as *melodrama*, a form that had impressed Mozart when he heard Benda's ***Medea*** at Mannheim in 1778.

**1780** *23 September* Première of ***Adelheit von Veltheim*** (Neefe/Grossmann) at the Theater in der Junghof, Frankfurt. The most successful opera – with a Turkish subject that anticipates Mozart's ***Entführung*** – by a composer who provides a link between the founder of *singspiel,* Hiller, with whom Neefe collaborated in Leipzig, and Beethoven, who was his pupil in Bonn.

## Opera in St Petersburg

Italian opera had been performed at the Russian court since the 1730s, but it was during the reign of Catherine the Great that St Petersburg saw a succession of the most advanced composers of Italian opera as court composers: Galuppi (1765–8), Traetta (1768–76), Paisiello (1776–83), Sarti (1784–6, 1792–6), Cimarosa (1787–91) and Martín y Soler (1788–94). Catherine (born a German princess) was an enthusiastic follower of the Enlightenment and her musical appointments reflected her rejection of the absolutist principles enshrined in *opera seria*.

With the exception of Traetta – one of the most notable 'reform' composers, who was joined four years after his arrival by the librettist Coltellini – her *maestri di cappella* were masters of sophisticated comedy. One of the outstanding comic operas of the period, Paisiello's *Il barbiere di Siviglia* (1782), received its first performance in St Petersburg. Catherine also promoted the work of Russian composers, including Fomin and Pashkeevich, both of whom wrote operas to libretti written by the Empress herself.

# 1781/1786 Mozart in Vienna

*Mozart was desperate to escape from the restrictions imposed by his employer, the Archbishop of Salzburg, and* Idomeneo *was written with the hope of obtaining a court appointment in Munich. When this failed, he moved to Vienna, quit the Archbishop's service and made his own way in the Austrian capital.*

Aloysia Weber as the heroine of Grétry's *Zémire et Azor* (1771) in a revival of the opera at the Vienna Burgtheater in 1784.

**1781** *29 January* Première of ***Idomeneo, re di Creta*** (Mozart/Varesco) at the Residenztheater, Munich, with Anton Raaff in the title role. The libretto was based on one by Danchet that had been set by Campra in 1712.
*25 February* Première of ***La fedeltà premiata*** (Haydn/after Lorenzi) for the inauguration of the new theatre at Eszterháza (the old one was destroyed in a fire in November 1779, in which many instruments and scores also perished). The libretto (which had been set in 1779 by Cimarosa) was based on a pastoral tale by Guarini, and the opera is one of Haydn's most richly orchestrated vocal works.
*13 August* Première of ***Montezuma*** (Zingarelli/Cigna-Santi) at San Carlo, Naples, the composer's second opera and a notable success. It was performed under Haydn at Eszterháza in spring 1785. The Mexican king had already made several operatic appearances: in a setting by Graun (1755) of a libretto by Frederick the Great of Prussia and in two earlier settings of Cigna-Santi's libretto, by Majo (1765) and Mysliveček (1771).
*10 September* Première of ***La serva padrona*** (Paisiello/Federico) at Tsarskoe Selo to celebrate the nameday of Grand Duke Alexander. The composer reused the libretto set by Pergolesi in 1733.
*28 November* Première of ***The Banditi, or Love's Labyrinth*** (Arnold/O'Keeffe) at Covent Garden, London. The score was partly composed and partly compiled by Arnold, and the opera became extremely popular in Britain and America under the title ***The Castle of Andalusia.***

**1782** *16 July* Première of ***Die Entführung aus dem Serail*** (Mozart/Stephanie) at the Burgtheater, Vienna. The libretto was adapted from one that Bretzner – who objected to Mozart's setting – had written for Johann André. It seems ultimately to have been derived from Bickerstaffe's ***The Captive***, which had been performed as a *pasticcio* in London in 1769.
*August* Première of ***Orlando Paladino*** (Haydn/Badini and Porta) at Eszterháza. This was Haydn's most successful opera, later frequently performed throughout Germany in translation as ***Ritter Roland.***
*14 September* Première of ***Fra i due litiganti il terzo gode*** (Sarti/Goldoni) at La Scala, Milan. The opera was an immediate success throughout Europe, enjoying special popularity in Vienna, where it was first performed at the Burgtheater on 28 May 1783. It was so well known that Mozart introduced a favourite number into the finale of his ***Don Giovanni.***
*26 September* Première of ***Il barbiere di Siviglia*** (Paisiello/Petrosellini) at the Hermitage Theatre, St Petersburg. The opera, based on Beaumarchais's play (which had originally been designed as an opera libretto and was rewritten by the author after it had been rejected by the Opéra-Comique), was hugely successful, with performances in Vienna and Naples the following year and soon afterwards throughout Europe, until it was finally eclipsed by Rossini's setting of the story.

Title page of the printed libretto of Mozart's *Idomeneo* (1781), written for Elector Carl Theodor's Residenztheater in Munich.

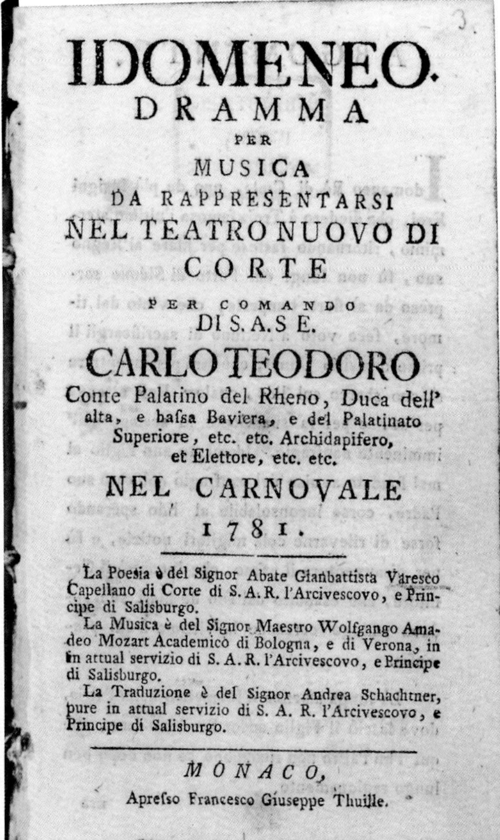

IDOMENEO.
DRAMMA
PER
MUSICA
DA RAPPRESENTARSI
NEL TEATRO NUOVO DI
CORTE
PER COMANDO
DI S.A.S E.
CARLO TEODORO
Conte Palatino del Rheno, Duca dell' alta, e baſsa Baviera, e del Palatinato Superiore, etc. etc. Archidapifero, et Elettore, etc. etc.
NEL CARNOVALE
1781.

La Poesia è del Signor Abate Gianbattista Varesco Capellano di Corte di S. A. R. l'Arcivescovo, e Principe di Salisburgo.
La Musica è del Signor Maestro Wolfgango Amadeo Mozart Academico di Bologna, e di Verona, in in attual servizio di S. A. R. l'Arcivescovo, e Principe di Salisburgo.
La Traduzione è del Signor Andrea Schachtner, pure in attual servizio di S. A. R. l'Arcivescovo, e Principe di Salisburgo.

*MONACO,*
Apreſso Francesco Giuseppe Thuille.

## Idomeneo and Die Entführung aus dem Serail

By the time he came to write his first two mature operas, Mozart had gained considerable experience of operatic composition. He had written several Italian operas during his teens, and in 1778 he composed a number of arias for members of the Mannheim company, including the tenor Anton Raaff and the soprano Aloysia Weber, with whom he was in love (and whose sister Constanze he was to marry). That same year, Elector Carl Theodor, the patron of the Mannheim orchestra and singers, moved his household to Munich, and it was for his new court that Mozart wrote *Idomeneo*. Although he was quite familiar with Gluck's innovations (one of his arias for Aloysia was for insertion in Gluck's *Alceste*), his new opera was in the modern *opera seria* vein of Traetta and Piccinni – whose *Roland* Mozart had heard in Paris in 1778 – rather than the French style of Gluck, despite the French origin of his libretto. There are many splendidly characterized arias, but the orchestrated recitatives lend continuity to the dramatic action, and the choral and ensemble numbers are particularly fine. Mozart's first full-length *singspiel*, *Die Entführung aus dem Serail*, also took full advantage of the currency of a variety of styles at the time: some of the arias sung by the servants, Pedrillo, Blondchen and Osmin, are like the popular melodies of contemporary French and English comic operas; the hero, Belmonte, is a modern operatic hero; the role of the heroine, Constanze – written for Salieri's mistress Caterina Cavalieri and sung by Aloysia Weber in 1784–5 – is in full *opera seria* style; while the ensembles combine comedy and pathos in a uniquely Mozartian way. It was surely its transcendence of the *singspiel* genre that provoked Emperor Josef II's alleged comment, 'Too many notes my dear Mozart.' The composer is said to have replied, 'Just as many as are necessary, sire.'

Bassa Selim with his harem, in a scene from Mozart's *Die Entführung aus dem Serail* (1782).

*30 November* Opening of the new Royal Opera House in Stockholm with the première of ***Cora och Alonzo*** (Naumann/Adlerbeth). The plot is based on Marmontel's novel *Les Incas* and was also the subject of an opera composed in 1785 by Méhul (premièred at the Paris Opéra in February 1791).
*31 December* Première of ***Rosina*** (Shield/Mrs Brooke) at Covent Garden, London. Based on Favart's ***Les Moissonneurs*** (see 1768), this ballad opera made an immediate mark, with performances in Dublin, Edinburgh, Montego Bay, New York and Philadelphia within five years.

**1783** *July–October* Mozart worked on two new operas, neither of which he completed: the first, to a feeble libretto by Abbé Varesco, was ***L'oca di Cairo***; the second, to a libretto that may be by Petrosellini, ***Lo sposo deluso, ossia La rivaltà di tre donne per un solo amante.***
*30 October* Première of ***La Caravane de Caire***, (Grétry/Morel de Chédeville) in Fontainebleau. Louis XVI himself is supposed to have assisted with the libretto of this *opéra-ballet*. The work was an enormous success, with over 500 performances at the Opéra in the course of forty-five years.
*14 December* First performance of da Ponte's Italian version of Gluck's ***Iphigénie en Tauride*** at the Burgtheater, Vienna.

**1784** *26 February* Première of ***Armida*** (Haydn/Durandi after Tasso) at Eszterháza. It was Haydn's last opera for Eszterháza and Prince Nicolaus Esterházy's favourite, receiving fifty-four performances at the opera house.
*26 April* Première of ***Les Danaïdes*** (Salieri/Lebland du Roullet and Tchudi) at the Opéra, Paris. The work was originally announced as by Gluck and Salieri, but after several successful performances Gluck announced that it was by his pupil alone.
*17 September* Première of ***Agatka, czyli Przjazd pana*** [***Agatha, or The Arrival of the Master***] (Holland/Radziwill) in Nieświcz. One of the earliest Polish operas, produced for a visit by King Stanislaw Poniatowski to Prince Radziwill's estate.
*21 October* Première of ***Richard Cœur-de-Lion*** (Grétry/Sedaine) at the Comédie-Italienne, Paris (now established in the Salle Favart). The plot anticipates the heroic rescue operas of the revolutionary period. In 1786 there were rival London productions at Covent Garden and Drury Lane, and by the end of the century it had been heard in Boston (23 January 1797), Philadelphia (23 March 1798) and New York (21 May 1800).

**1785** *12 October* Première of ***La grotta di Trofonio*** (Salieri/Casti) at the Burgtheater, Vienna, a comic pastoral opera which became one of Salieri's greatest successes.

**1786** *4 January* Première of ***Oedipe à Colone*** (Sacchini/Guillard) at Versailles, the composer's chief work, written at the end of his life.
*19 January* Première of ***Gustaf Wasa*** (Naumann/Kellgren) at the Royal Opera House, Stockholm, composed to a scenario written by Gustav III. The opera, on a national theme, was frequently revived throughout the next hundred years.
*7 February* Premières of ***Der Schauspieldirektor*** (Mozart/Stephanie) and ***Prima la musica e poi le parole*** (Salieri/Casti) at a garden party given by Josef II at Schönbrunn. Both works, commissioned by the Emperor, were satires on the intrigues of singers, patrons, librettists and composers in grand opera.
*Carnival* Première of ***La vendetta di Nino*** (Prati/Giovannini) at the Teatro della Pergola, Florence. Based on Voltaire's version of the Semiramis legend (also recounted in a libretto by Metastasio which had been set dozens of times), Prati's opera is one of the first to be written

Scene from Naumann's *Cora och Alonzo* (1782), which tells of the forbidden love of the Inca princess Cora, a virgin priestess of the temple of the sun, for Alonzo, a Spaniard who is an opponent of the conquistadors and befriends the Incas. They are discovered together after the temple is destroyed in an earthquake, and Cora is condemned to be buried alive, but Alonzo eventually persuades the Incas to spare her life, and the lovers are permitted to marry.

with a tragic end. After 1790, in the wake of the French revolution, tragic endings became increasingly common in serious opera.

*1 May* Première of ***Le nozze di Figaro*** (Mozart/da Ponte after Beaumarchais) at the Burgtheater, Vienna. Although the play was banned in Vienna, da Ponte appears to have persuaded the Emperor that the subversive elements had been removed from the opera. The work was not especially well received by the Viennese, who preferred more conventional compositions, but it was a triumph in Prague, where it received its first performance in December of the same year.

*11 July* Première of ***Doktor und Apotheker*** (Dittersdorf/Stephanie) at the Burgtheater, Vienna. This was the greatest success of one of the leading *singspiel* composers of the period.

*17 October* Première of ***Azémia, ou Le nouveau Robinson*** (Dalayrac/ Lachabeaussière) at Fontainebleau. Five months earlier another of the composer's most successful works, ***Nina, ou La Folle par amour*** (libretto by Marsollier), had received its first performance at the Comédie-Italienne in Paris.

*17 November* Première of ***Una cosa rara, o sia Bellezza ed onestà*** (Martín y Soler/da Ponte) at the Burgtheater, Vienna, one of the most popular operas of the whole period, a number from which is quoted in the last act of Mozart's ***Don Giovanni.***

*27 December* Première of ***Gli equivoci*** (Storace/da Ponte) at the Burgtheater, Vienna. One of the best of the early adaptations of Shakespeare's plays (it is based on the *Comedy of Errors*), by the Anglo-Italian brother of Mozart's first Susanna. The following year Storace returned to London, where he composed a succession of English operas, the most successful of which was ***The Pirates*** (1792), which reuses a substantial part of the music written for ***Gli equivoci.***

Wolfgang Amadeus Mozart portrayed in silhouette in 1786.

Francesco Benucci and Nancy (Anna Selina) Storace, who sang Figaro and Susanna in the first production of *Le nozze di Figaro* in Vienna. Benucci was also the first Guglielmo in *Così fan tutte*, and sang Leporello in the first Viennese production of *Don Giovanni*, as well as creating the title role in Salieri's *Axur*. Storace had been Salieri's mistress for a time, before she returned to London – with her husband – in the spring of 1787.

# 1787 / 1791 Mozart's Last Operas

*Le nozze di Figaro and the four operas Mozart wrote in the final years of his life provide a touchstone for the judgment of every other opera ever written. No composer since Monteverdi had managed to allow music to express so clearly, so subtly and so completely the shades of human passions and aspirations, and the intricate interplay of their relationships.*

**DATES**

**1789**
Start of French Revolution

George Washington inaugurated as first president of the USA

Death of Josef II, who is succeeded by his brother as Leopold II

**1787** *5 February* Première of ***Don Giovanni Tenorio, o sia Il convitato di pietra*** (Gazzaniga/Bertati) at San Moisè, Venice. There had been earlier Don Juan operas, but it was Bertati's libretto that da Ponte used as the basis of his text for Mozart (see 29 October 1787).
*8 June* Première of ***Tarare*** (Salieri/Beaumarchais) at the Opéra, Paris. Although his plays about Figaro and Count Almaviva were adapted for two of the most famous operas in the repertory, Beaumarchais wrote only one opera libretto himself – for Salieri's most successful opera.
*22 July* Première of ***Electra*** (Häffner/Ristell) at Drottningholm Palace. The Swedish libretto was based on the play by Guillard after Sophocles (which had been set by Lemoyne in 1782); this was one of the earliest Swedish operas of real character.
*4 August* Première of ***Inkle and Yarico*** (Arnold/Colman) at the Little Haymarket Theatre, London. This Barbadian story of rescue and betrayal – Inkle, who has been saved by the Amerindian maiden Yarico, sells her into slavery (though the opera is given a happy ending) – was one of the most popular operas of the period, with performances in Kingston (Jamaica), New York, Philadelphia and Calcutta within a few years of its première.

A contemporary relief depicts the scene in which Don Giovanni, in Mozart's opera, invites the stone statue of the man he has killed to dinner.

Lorenzo da Ponte, poet for the Italian opera in Vienna from 1782 to 1790 and librettist for Mozart's three greatest operas.

## Mozart and da Ponte

Lorenzo da Ponte had arrived in Vienna in 1782, after various picaresque adventures, with a recommendation from his friend Caterino Mazzolà (poet at the Dresden court and in 1791 librettist for Mozart's *La clemenza di Tito*) to the court composer Salieri. Emperor Josef II was about to sponsor a new Italian opera in Vienna and the recent arrival was lucky enough to receive a court appointment as librettist to the company. In the prevailing atmosphere of jealousy and intrigue da Ponte appears to have kept the Emperor's goodwill, and he suggested to Mozart (whom Josef considered an instrumental rather than an opera composer) that they collaborate on an opera. The choice of *Le nozze di Figaro* was an audacious one, since performances of Beaumarchais's play had recently been banned by the Emperor, but da Ponte omitted the most subversive passages and the work was passed by the censor.

Da Ponte continued to write libretti for other composers – notably Martín y Soler and Salieri – but collaborated with Mozart on two other operas, *Don Giovanni* and *Così fan tutte*, until, on Josef's death, he was forced to leave Vienna. (Mozart turned down a proposal that they should go to London together and write an opera there.) Their three operas are unequalled. The beauty of Mozart's music was matched by the brilliance and subtlety of his musical craftsmanship in orchestration, vocal writing and in the overall structures created by patterns of keys and tempi. But the success of their collaboration lies in the lifelike depictions of each character and their interplay in the duets, trios and ensembles, particularly in the concerted finales of acts. The complexity of the music at first baffled the Viennese, who were used to the simpler melodious style of Paisiello, Martín and Salieri, but the characters were drawn with such precision and so much humanity that every strand in the tangle of emotions explored in each opera stands out with absolute clarity. These works, on their own, are enough to justify opera as an artistic medium.

After its last recorded performance in New York in 1844 it was not revived until 15 March 1997, when it was produced in Barbados in a version by Roxanna Panufnik and Eddy Grant.

*29 October* Première of ***Il dissoluto punito, ossia Il Don Giovanni*** (Mozart/da Ponte) at the National Theatre, Prague. The original cast was drawn from the Italian opera company of Pasquale Bondini, who had commissioned the opera following the great success of ***Le nozze di Figaro*** in Prague the previous year. After a shaky start, the success was repeated, though not at first in Vienna, where it was first performed – ending with Don Giovanni dragged off to hell – at the Burgtheater on 7 May 1788. Mozart described it as a 'dramma giocosa', and, as in earlier operas, he adopted a variety of styles: while the music for Leporello, Don Giovanni's servant, is of typical *buffo* character, that for the noble Donna Anna and Don Ottavio is in *opera seria* style.

*15 November* Death of Gluck in Vienna.

**1788** *8 January* Première of ***Axur, re d'Ormus*** (Salieri/da Ponte), an Italian version of ***Tarare***, performed at the Burgtheater, Vienna, to celebrate the wedding of Archduke Franz. Da Ponte also provided a libretto for a comic opera by the composer, ***Il talismano***, produced at the Burgtheater later the same year (10 September).

*12 January* Première of ***Ifigenia in Aulide*** (Cherubini/Moretti) at the Teatro Regio, Turin. The last opera Cherubini wrote before leaving Italy, ***Ifigenia in Aulide*** was a great success. The same year Cherubini moved to Paris, where he composed his first French opera, ***Démophoön***. Audiences

Neues Singspiel.

Im kaiserl. königl. Naztional = Hoftheater
wird heute Dienstag den 26ten Jäner 1790 aufgeführt:
(zum erstenmal)

COSI FAN TUTTE,
O SIA:
LA SCOLA DEGLI AMANTI.
So machen sie's, oder: die Schule der Liebhaber.

Ein komisches Singspiel in zwey Aufzügen.

Die Poesie ist vom Hrn. Abbate da Ponte, Dichter des italiänischen Singspiels beym k. k. Hoftheater.

Die Musik ist vom Herrn Wolfgang Mozart, Kapellmeister in wirklichen Diensten Sr. Majestät des Kaisers.

Die Bücher sind bloß italiänisch beym Logenmeister für 24 kr. zu haben.

Es ist am verflossenen Sonntage in den k. k. Redoutensaälen eine goldene Frauenzimmerdose verlohren worden, wer selbe gefunden, wird höflichst gebeten, sie gegen gute Rekompens an die theatralische Kasse zu überbringen.

Der Anfang ist um 7 Uhr.

The Théâtre de la Porte Saint-Martin had been established in 1781 by Queen Marie Antoinette (the sister of Josef II) for the performance of opera in Paris. As a symbol of the old régime, it was stormed by revolutionaries in 1789, two days before the fall of the Bastille.

Playbill for the première of Mozart's *Così fan tutte*. Fiordiligi was sung by Adriana Ferrarese, who had recently become da Ponte's mistress, a circumstance that was indirectly responsible for his fall from grace at the Imperial court.

in the French capital were not satisfied with an easy melodic Italian style, and in Cherubini's later operas – he remained in France to reach a position of great eminence in the musical world there – the music is more closely tied to the dramatic situations of the plot.
*Autumn* Première of ***L'amor contrastato (La molinara)*** (Paisiello/Palomba) at the Teatro dei Fiorentini, Naples. It was performed in Madrid and Paris in 1789, in Eszterháza, Turin, Vienna and Dresden in 1790, in Warsaw in 1792–3, Berlin and Lisbon in 1793, London (Haymarket) in 1794–5 and Prague in 1796–7. In Vienna it remained the most frequently performed opera at the Burgtheater for twenty years, and Beethoven wrote variations on one of the most celebrated arias.

Pierre-Augustin Caron de Beaumarchais, playwright, politician, spy and adventurer, whose plays about Count Almaviva and his servant Figaro were the basis both for *Il barbiere di Siviglia* by Paisiello (and later for Rossini's opera) and for Mozart's *Le nozze di Figaro*. While the first was a traditional story of a young woman escaping the attentions of her guardian to marry a young student who turns out to be a nobleman, the second, where the Count's attempted infidelities are thwarted by his servants, contained highly subversive social criticism. Beaumarchais's own libretto for Salieri's *Tarare* varies the same theme in its depiction of a valiant soldier who eventually triumphs over a corrupt and cruel monarch.

**1789** *26 January* Opening of the Théâtre de Monsieur (later Théâtre Feydeau) in Paris with a performance of ***Le avventure amorose*** (Tritto/'Timido P. A.'), first performed in Rome in 1787.
*9 February* Première of ***Gorebogatyr*** [***The Errant Knight***] (Martín y Soler/Catherine the Great and Khrapovitsky) at the Hermitage Theatre, St Petersburg, in the presence of the French and Austrian ambassadors. The opera was a satire directed against Gustav III of Sweden (also an opera librettist), who had recently declared war on Russia.
*12 June* Première of ***Nina, o sia La pazza per amore*** (Paisiello/Carpani after Marsollier) at the Palace of Caserta, Naples. Marsollier's sentimental text, with one of the earliest operatic representations of madness, had been used three years earlier by Dalayrac, and Paisiello's version, which remained in the repertory for many years, set a standard for Italian *opera semiseria* as an equivalent to French *comédie larmoyante.*
*29 July* Première of ***Claudine von Villa Bella*** (Reichardt/Goethe) at the Schlosstheater, Charlottenburg; a first public performance followed five days later at the Berlin Opernhaus. Goethe had written the text in 1774 – the first of three *singspiele* that he wrote, in addition to a sequel to ***Die Zauberflöte*** – and it had already been set by Kayser (and was to be set again by Schubert in 1815). Reichardt's version was the first German opera to be staged successfully at the Prussian court.

**1790** *26 January* Première of ***Così fan tutte, ossia La scuola degli amanti*** (Mozart/da Ponte) at the Burgtheater, Vienna. It is possible that the mysogynistic theme of the opera – in which two sisters are seduced for a wager by their lovers in disguise and each 'marries' the other's girlfriend in a fake wedding ceremony – was suggested to da Ponte by the Emperor himself, although amorous confusion of identity had been an operatic mainstay from Cavalli's ***La Calisto*** to Haydn's ***La fedeltà premiata***; in Mozart's opera, however, the situation becomes painfully believable. The work was almost universally condemned as immoral in the nineteenth century, and its place in the repertory is a comparatively recent one.
*14 June* A French version of Pergolesi's ***La serva padrona*** (1733) was performed in Baltimore (and repeated in New York on 9 December).
*23 August* Première of ***Les Rigueurs du cloître*** (Berton/Fiévée) at the Comédie-Italienne, Paris. One of the earliest 'rescue operas', it anticipates both Cherubini's ***Les deux journées*** and Beethoven's ***Fidelio***.
*4 September* Première of ***Euphrosine, ou Le Tyran corrigé*** (Méhul/F. B. Hoffmann) at the Comédie-Italienne, Paris. This was the first of the nine operas Méhul had already written to receive a performance. Subsequently he had an unbroken run of success, producing thirty-two more *opéras-comiques* over the next twenty-seven years. The quality of his music is uneven, but he excelled at descriptive music for romantic scenes – moonlit nights, storms at sea – and in depicting villainy. ***Euphrosine*** is notable for a musical motif associated with the pervading strain of jealousy. Méhul

used both dialogue and melodrama (speech over music) to achieve the most striking dramatic effects.

*9 September* Première of ***Das Sonnenfest der Braminen*** (Müller/Hensler) at the Leopoldstadt Theater, Vienna. Wenzel Müller was to become the most prolific composer of *singspiele* and incidental music for comedies in Vienna across the turn of the century. This was his first major success, with subsequent productions in Prague, Graz, Hamburg, Weimar (staged by Goethe), Brno, Berlin, Temesvar, Bern and even Paris. The opera was admired by both Mozart and Haydn.

Irena Tomeoni as the mad bride Nina, in a Vienna production of Paisiello's popular *Nina, o sia La pazza per amore*.

**1791** *9 April* Première of ***Guillaume Tell*** (Grétry/Sedaine) at the Opéra-Comique, Paris, the first opera by France's leading composer with a clearly revolutionary subject to be staged in Paris after the Revolution – though Grétry's treatment is disappointingly conventional.

*18 July* Première of ***Lodoïska*** (Cherubini/Filette-Loraux) at the Théâtre Feydeau, Paris. Described as a *comédie héroïque*, it uses the Neapolitan *opera buffa* form – with emphasis on orchestra, ensembles and finales – to deal with a heroic drama. The heroine does not appear until Act II (her voice is heard offstage at the end of Act I, which is otherwise written entirely for male voices). Both the baritone villain Dourlinski and the use of a trumpet call to announce the rescue are elements taken over by Beethoven in ***Fidelio.*** Cherubini's new style proved somewhat too 'learned' for French audiences, and his operas had a greater success in Germany; a better reception was given in Paris to Rodolphe Kreutzer's opera (written for the Comédie-Italienne the same year) using this libretto, which was also set five years later by Simon Mayr.

*6 September* Première of ***La clemenza di Tito*** (Mozart/Mazzolà) at the National Theatre, Prague, at the coronation festivities of Leopold II. It was based on a libretto by Metastasio, and although considerably modernized with many arias omitted, ensembles added and a concerted finale written to conclude the first act, it still retained the static quality of *opera seria*, despite the strongly drawn characters. It was characterized by the new empress as 'porcheria tedesca' – 'German trash' – but remained one of

The set for the Vienna production of Paisiello's *La molinara*, a comic opera with marriage proposals, mistaken identities and real and feigned madness, that was the great favourite of Viennese audiences.

## Die Zauberflöte

*'Sarastro's arias are the only music fit for God to sing.'*
G. B. Shaw

Mozart's last two operas were quite different from the three he had written with da Ponte. *La clemenza di Tito*, written for a ceremonial occasion, was in the old-fashioned *opera seria* tradition; the other breathed life into popular German *singspiel*. In his earlier German opera, *Die Entführung aus dem Serail*, Mozart worked with a typical comic opera plot, but the text written by the actor-manager Emanuel Schikaneder for *Die Zauberflöte* [*The Magic Flute*] was in the true tradition of Viennese popular pantomime, with a Harlequin character (the bird-catcher Papageno), transformation scenes and archetypal heroes and villains. At the same time, there is a deeply serious theme, in which the conflict of good and evil is played out on a symbolic plane, defined by the ideals and rituals of freemasonry.

The powers of light and darkness fight for the souls of the noble human couple Tamino and Pamina, and their trials are shared and parodied by Papageno and his mate, whose aspirations never rise above food, drink and sex. Mozart's music, while ranging from tuneful popular songs for Papageno through acrobatic vengeance arias for the Queen of the Night to hymnlike music for Sarastro and his priests – even a chorale with fugal accompaniment in the style of Bach – miraculously welds all the disparate elements into a harmonious unity. Even in *singspiel*, with its separate numbers connected by spoken dialogue, the composer, having established the character of each role in an aria, shades the development of the interplay between them in ensemble numbers, in which representatives of the three worlds come together. Just as Mozart's Italian operas were an inspiration to Rossini and Verdi, there is a direct line that leads from *Die Zauberflöte* to Beethoven, Weber and, ultimately, Wagner.

Schikaneder as Papageno in the original production of Mozart's *Die Zauberflöte* at the Theater auf der Wieden, Vienna.

Mozart's most popular operas well into the nineteenth century, although today it is performed less frequently than any of his other mature operas.
*30 September* Première of ***Die Zauberflöte*** (Mozart/Schikaneder) at the Theater auf der Wieden, Vienna. The work was an immediate success, and performances were given throughout the operatic world within a very few years.
Composition of ***L'anima del filosofo, ossia Orfeo ed Euridice*** (Haydn/Badini), a 'reformed' *opera seria* with an important role for the chorus. Haydn had accepted an invitation to London after the death of his patron Prince Nicolaus Esterházy, and was commissioned to write the opera for Sir John Gallini's company at the new King's Theatre, but royal permission to perform opera in the theatre was withheld, and no performance took place. The opera ends tragically, without the consoling conclusion of previous settings, from Peri and Monteverdi to Gluck.
*5 December* Death of Mozart in Vienna.

# 1792/1804 Opera after the French Revolution

*Paris after the Revolution continued to attract the leading composers of opera, but artificiality and erotic sentiment were now replaced with violent tragedy and heroic plots, where men and – even more frequently – women are seen to triumph over tyranny and misfortune. As war and disorder spread through Europe similar ideological themes were taken up by opera composers in Italy and Germany.*

Ferdinando Paer, music director of the Kärntnertortheater in Vienna at the turn of the century and the author of *Leonora*, which was produced in Dresden in 1804, though it was unknown to Beethoven.

The Paris Opéra-Comique during the revolutionary period. The work being performed is a revival of Monsigny's *Le Déserteur*, a classic tale of struggle against authority.

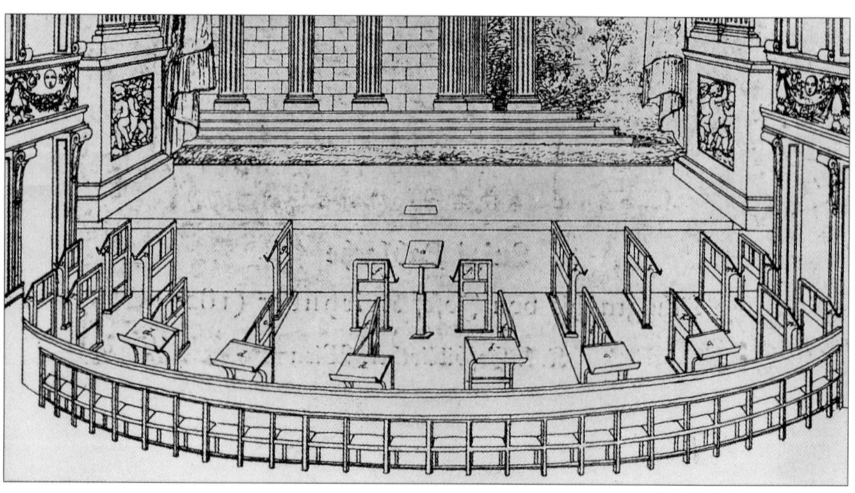

Orchestra pit of the Kärntnertortheater, Vienna, the principal public opera house in the city during the early nineteenth century.

**1792** *7 February* Première of ***Il matrimonio segreto*** (Cimarosa/Bertati after Colman and Garrick) at the Burgtheater, Vienna, with many of the singers who had taken part in Mozart premières: Dorotea and Francesco Bussani, Benucci and Mandini. Emperor Leopold II liked it so much that he invited the composer and performers to dinner after the première and then insisted that they return to the theatre and repeat the performance.

**1793** *11 February* The Comédie-Italienne, performing in the Salle Favart, is renamed Théâtre de l'Opéra-Comique National.
*16 February* Première of ***La Caverne*** (Lesueur/Dercy) at the Théâtre Feydeau, Paris. Based on Le Sage's *Gil Blas* and Schiller's *Die Räuber*, the story of Séraphine abducted to a brigands' cave captures the spirit of the Reign of Terror, matched by the expressive chromaticism of Lesueur's score. The subject was also set by Méhul.
*9 October* Première of ***Roméo et Juliette*** (Steibelt/de Ségur) at the Théâtre Feydeau, Paris. The subject was also set by Dalayrac, but Steibelt's was the best of the early operatic versions of Shakespeare's play.

**1794** *18 February* Première of ***Saffo*** (Mayr/Sografi) at La Fenice, Venice. The composer, whose musical education was entirely Italian, was a successful oratorio composer whom Piccinni had encouraged to try his hand at opera: the work was well received.
*24 June* Possible first American performance of Gluck's ***Orphée et Euridice*** at Charleston, S.C. Mozart's ***Le nozze di Figaro*** may have been performed in New York five years later.

**1796** *30 January* Première of ***Giulietta e Romeo*** (Zingarelli/Foppa after Shakespeare) at La Scala, Milan, the composer's best known work. Napoleon liked this version of the opera, in which Romeo dies but Juliet survives. Romeo was sung by one of the last great *castrati*, Girolamo Crescentini, who was even credited with the composition of the opera's most famous aria, 'Ombra adorata aspetta'.
*26 December* Première of ***Gli Orazi ed i Curiazi*** (Cimarosa/Sografi) at La Fenice, Venice, starring Crescentini as Curiazio. The libretto is relentlessly tragic, ending with the heroine being stabbed by her brother; Sografi had already introduced stage deaths in operas about Semiramis and Cleopatra (both 1791), and in 1803 was to write the libretto for Zingarelli's ***La distruzione di Gerusalemme.***

**1797** *13 March* Première of ***Médée*** (Cherubini/F. B. Hoffmann) at the Théâtre Feydeau, Paris. The work had little success in Paris (although two parodies appeared within a few days of the première), but was often revived in Germany – a frequent occurrence with Cherubini's operas. The title role, a 'grand fiendish part' was created by Julie Scio, and her over-exertion is said to have led to her early death. The greatest Medeas since that time have been Therese Tietjens in the 1860s and Maria Callas in the 1950s, both of whom used recitatives composed in 1855 by Franz Lachner; the original version, as an *opéra-comique*, was performed with spoken dialogue, which allowed for much tighter dramatic action.

**1798** *January* Première of ***Griselda, ossia La virtù al cimento*** (Paer/Anelli after Boccaccio) at the Teatro Ducale, Parma. The composer's first opera, ***Circe***, had been performed in Venice in 1792, but this was his earliest real success, composed a year after he had been appointed music director of the Kärntnertortheater, Vienna. Anelli's text had been set by Piccinni in 1793, and libretti he had written were later used for two of the greatest comic operas: Rossini's ***L'italiana in Algeri*** and Donizetti's ***Don Pasquale*** – although neither of these was the original setting.

Domenico Cimarosa, leading composer of the Neapolitan school, who wrote *Il matrimonio segreto* and *Gli Orazi ed i Curiazi*.

Caricature of Cherubini by Jean-Baptiste Isabey.

Jean-François Lesueur, who was appointed court composer to Napoleon in 1804.

**1799** *1 January* Première of ***Elisca, ou L'Amour maternel*** (Grétry/Favières) at the Opéra-Comique, Paris, an opera based on the tales of two travellers who explored Madagascar.
*3 January* Première of ***Falstaff, ossia Le tre burle*** (Salieri/Defranceschi after Shakespeare), at the Kärntnertortheater, Vienna. The following year composer and librettist adapted another Elizabethan play for the theatre, Ben Jonson's *The Epicoene.*
*23 February* Première of ***Camilla, ossia Il sotterraneo*** (Paer/Carpani after Marsollier) at the Kärntnertortheater, Vienna, the composer's finest opera. The original French libretto had been set by Dalayrac.

**1800** *16 January* Première of ***Les deux journées*** [***The Water Carrier***] (Cherubini/Bouilly) at the Théâtre Feydeau, Paris. An archetypal rescue opera, it is based (like Bouilly's ***Léonore***, set by Gaveaux in 1798, and the origin of Beethoven's ***Fidelio***) on a real incident during the reign of terror, although it is set in seventeenth-century Paris. It had 200 consecutive performances in Paris and was also a success outside France, particularly in Germany.
*16 September* Première of ***Le Calife de Bagdad*** (Boieldieu/Godard d'Aucour de Saint-Just) at the Opéra-Comique, Paris. Boieldieu had written the first of his many comic operas, ***La Fille coupable*** (to a libretto by his father), at the age of eighteen and it had been performed in his native town of Rouen in 1793.

**1801** *21 January* Première of ***I baccanali di Roma*** (Nicolini/Romanelli) at La Scala, Milan. The composer's most important opera, also notable as the first great success for the tempestuous prima donna Angelica Catalani, who had made her début in Venice a year earlier in Mayr's ***Lodoïska*** (an opera first performed in 1796).
*17 February* Première of ***L'Irato, ou L'Emporté*** (Méhul/Marsollier) at the Opéra-Comique, Paris. This brilliant one-act comedy, a pastiche of Paisiello, enjoyed international success. Its score bears a dedication to Napoleon Bonaparte, first consul of the French Republic.
*21 April* Première of ***Ginevra di Scozia*** (Mayr/Rossi after Ariosto) for the inauguration of the Teatro Nuovo, Trieste.

**1802** *23 March* Performance of Cherubini's ***Lodoïska*** staged by Schikaneder at the Theater an der Wien, the first French revolutionary opera to reach Vienna. In August ***Les deux journées*** was produced on successive nights at the Burgtheater and the Theater an der Wien, and

## Napoleon's court composers

After the execution of the King and Queen in 1793 the Opéra, which was associated with the court, was shunned, but *opéra-comique* continued in Paris, both at the Salle Favart and the Théâtre Feydeau, even though their resources were rather strained when singers trained in declamation rather than operatic singing had to cope with the orchestration of Méhul or Cherubini. Many of the leading French composers had composed patriotic hymns and marches in the years immediately following the Revolution, but after 1800 operatic activity gathered momentum, and Napoleon applied his organizing spirit to this as to every other aspect of life. He amalgamated the two homes of comic opera in 1801 and in the same year appointed Paisiello, who had supported the French when they invaded Naples in 1799, as his court composer. In 1804, the year in which Napoleon assumed the title of Emperor, the Opéra resumed its importance in the musical life of the capital, and the influence of his own musical tastes was clearly felt: Lesueur, who was appointed to succeed Paisiello, finally saw a few of his grandest operas produced; Spontini, named the Empress's director of music in 1806, took over the Théâtre-Italien in 1810; Cherubini, who did not share Napoleon's musical ideas, left for Vienna, but was summoned back as soon as the French armies reached the Austrian capital; Méhul's *Joseph* was named 'opera of the year' by the Emperor in 1807. All these composers produced grand operas on lofty themes which anticipate the works of Meyerbeer, Verdi and Wagner.

Set design in neoclassical style by Anton de Pian for the production of Cherubini's *Médée* at the Kärntnertortheater, Vienna, in 1802.

Set by Percier, Fontaine and Thibault for Grétry's *Elisca* (1799). The designs were made after careful research into the native vegetation of Madagascar and the method of construction of the raised bamboo houses.

Costume designs by Berthélémy for Lesueur's *Ossian, ou Les Bardes*, based on the Celtic epic poem which (although it turned out to be a fake) provided a new noble mythology for the early romantic period.

performances followed soon after of ***Médée*** (November 1802), ***Elisa*** (December 1802), Lesueur's ***La Caverne*** (June 1803 in two theatres), and Méhul's ***Ariodant*** (February 1804).
*5 April* Première of ***Une Folie*** (Méhul/Bouilly) at the Opéra-Comique, Paris; the most successful of Méhul's comic operas, performed worldwide. In England and America it was given – as ***Love Laughs at Locksmiths*** (first performed in 1803) – in a version by Colman recomposed by Michael Kelly, who explained that 'the original music was very good but not calculated for an English audience'. In Denmark a version, ***Ungdom og Galskab*** (1806), with music by Edouard Dupuy, the 'Don Juan of the north', was the most popular opera of the period in that country.

**1803** *March* Première of ***Peter Schmoll und seine Nachbarn*** (Weber/Türke after Cramer) in Augsburg. Weber's second completed opera, it was written in Salzburg in 1801–2, but the performance was not well received. The same year Weber was appointed conductor of the theatre at Breslau (Wroclaw), through the influence of his teacher, the Abbé Vogler. He remained there until 1806, initiating an ambitious programme of operatic reform, with intensive rehearsals, a new seating arrangement for the orchestra and a new repertory of operatic works.

**1804** *27 November* Première of ***Milton*** (Spontini/Etienne de Jouy and Dieulafoy) at the Opéra-Comique, Paris. The composer, who had made his name as an operatic composer in Naples, had moved to Paris early in the year, and his ***La finta filosofa*** (1799) had been given at the Opéra-Comique in February. ***Milton*** was the second of two new works he put on there, and it established him in the musical world of Paris.
*10 July* Première of ***Ossian, ou Les Bardes*** (Lesueur/Dercy and Deschamps), the first opera performed at the new Académie Impériale de Musique (Opéra) in Paris. The subject had been suggested by Napoleon, who attended the second performance on 13 July. Since his success with ***La Caverne*** Lesueur's opera projects had been too demanding in expensive production effects to mount, and even with the support of the Emperor few of his later operas were performed; the last to be staged was ***Le Mort d'Adam*** (1809, written 1799), based on Klopstock, Milton and the Bible.
*3 October* Première of ***Leonora, ossia L'amore conjugale*** (Paer/Schmidt) at the Hoftheater, Dresden, where Paer had been appointed Kapellmeister the previous year. In contrast to Beethoven's version of the story (produced the following year), the music is conventional in its Italian melodiousness.

**1805**
**1816**

# Opera during the Empire

*The years of Napoleon's reign in Europe had been marked at first by grand historical operas that reflected his imperial style, but later they witnessed the emergence of the irresistible Rossini. As if to establish the start and end of an era,* Fidelio, *Beethoven's great hymn to political freedom, was first performed in its original version the year after Napoleon became Emperor and in its definitive version the year before his final defeat.*

**DATES**

**1805**
Napoleon is crowned King of Italy in Milan Cathedral

French victory at Austerlitz over the Austrians and Russians

**1806**
Joseph Bonaparte named King of Naples and Louis Bonaparte King of Holland

Napoleon enters Berlin after defeating the Prussians at Jena

**1808**
Joseph Bonaparte named King of Spain; Joachim Murat replaces him as King of Naples

Goethe's *Faust* part 1 published

**1809**
Napoleon annexes the Papal States, taking the Pope prisoner

**1810**
Sir Walter Scott's *The Lady of the Lake* published

**1812**
Grande armée destroyed in retreat from Moscow

Louisiana becomes a state of the USA

USA at war with Britain

**1813**
French defeated in Battle of the Nations at Leipzig

**1814**
Napoleon banished to Elba

Congress of Vienna opens

**1815**
Napoleon returns for 100 days but is defeated at Waterloo and banished to St Helena

Angelica Catalani, one of the most brilliant and successful prima donnas of the age, making her London début as the heroine in Portugal's *La morte di Semiramide* at the King's Theatre, London, in December 1806. She continued to perform in London until 1814, and during these years, the climax of her singing career, she amassed a huge fortune. From 1814 to 1817 she directed the Théâtre-Italien in Paris, but this proved a financial disaster, and she resumed her singing career until 1828.

*'When she throws out all her voice to the utmost, it has a volume and strength that are quite surprising, while its agility in divisions, running up and down the scale in semitones, and its compass in jumping over two octaves at once, are equally astonishing ... but her taste is vicious, her excessive love of ornament spoiling every simple air...'*

Lord Mount Edgcumbe on Angelica Catalani

**1805** *20 November* Première of first (three-act) version of ***Leonore*** (Beethoven/Sonnleithner after Bouilly) at the Theater an der Wien, Vienna, a week after the Napoleonic army had occupied the city. The title role was sung by the nineteen-year-old Anna Milder.

**1806** *25 February* Première of ***Faniska*** (Cherubini/Sonnleithner) at the Kärntnertortheater, Vienna. The opera had been commissioned for Vienna, and while the composer was supervising the production he was forced to accept the post of Director of Music to Napoleon at Schönbrunn.
*13 December* Angelica Catalani's London début at the King's Theatre in the title role of ***La morte di Semiramide*** (Portugal/Caravita), originally produced at São Carlos, Lisbon, in 1801. She was to sing the role of Susanna in the first London production of ***Le nozze di Figaro*** at the King's Theatre in June 1812.

**1807** *17 February* Première of ***Joseph en Egypte*** (Méhul/Duval) at the Opéra-Comique, Paris. Despite its biblical subject, the work was not performed at the Opéra because of its spoken dialogue. It was a considerable international success and – with his Ossianic ***Uthal*** of 1806 – marked the high point of Méhul's career.
*15 December* Première of ***La Vestale*** (Spontini/Etienne de Jouy) at the Opéra, Paris. Spontini reflected the richness of Etienne de Jouy's dramatic tableaux with powerful music and colourful orchestration, pacing the build-up of musical effects to produce striking climaxes.

**1808** *16 April* Première of ***Les Voitures versées*** (Boieldieu/Dupaty) at the Hermitage Theatre, St Petersburg. In 1803 the composer had taken up an appointment at the Russian court, where he remained until 1810.

**1809** *7 October* Appointment of Domenico Barbaia as director of the San Carlo and Teatro Nuovo opera houses in Naples. He later also assumed responsibility for the Teatro del Fondo and Teatro dei Fiorentini.
*28 November* Première of ***Fernand Cortez, ou La Conquête du Mexique*** (Spontini/Esménard and Etienne de Jouy) at the Opéra, Paris. This sumptuous opera, commissioned by Napoleon to commemorate his military victories, was premièred just as the Emperor began his Spanish campaign, and despite – or because of – the public's enthusiasm for the opera's celebration of Spanish heroism, it was almost immediately withdrawn. It was put on again in 1817 and continued to be revived throughout the nineteenth century.

**1810** *18 January* A private performance of Cimarosa's ***Gli Orazi ed i Curiazi***, starring the *castrato* Crescentini, was given in Paris for Napoleon. The following year, on 1 October, Mozart's ***Così fan tutte*** was performed for the Emperor and his court at Compiègne.
*16 September* Première of ***Silvana*** (Weber/Hiemer) in Frankfurt; the first of Weber's operas to achieve some success. The story is steeped in medieval chivalry and is one of the earliest romantic operas to draw on this source. The title role was sung by Carolina Brandt, whom Weber married in 1817.
*3 November* Première of ***La cambiale di matrimonio*** (Rossini/Rossi after Federici) at San Moisè, Venice, Rossini's first opera to be staged.

**1811** *4 June* Première of ***Abu Hassan*** (Weber/Hiemer, after *1001 Nights*) at the Residenztheater, Munich; a typical *singspiel* with exotic 'Turkish' material (and a hero plagued, like the composer, with debts), that has continued to maintain an occasional place in the repertory.

Marietta Marcolini, who sang the role of the heroine Isabella in the first production of Rossini's *L'italiana in Algeri* in Venice in May 1813. She had also played leading roles in several of Rossini's earliest operas and was for a time the composer's mistress. She was a celebrated Tancredi and continued to sing Rossini roles until her retirement in 1820.

Wilhelmine Schröder-Devrient as Leonora in an early revival of *Fidelio*.

## Fidelio

Beethoven's apprenticeship in opera came as a member of the Bonn court orchestra, in which he played works by Cimarosa, Paisiello, Salieri, Martín y Soler, Grétry, Monsigny, Dittersdorf, Benda and Mozart. He was also familiar with Gluck's operas and is reputed to have played *Iphigénie en Tauride* through to a group of French officers in Vienna in 1805. The form of *Fidelio* (originally titled *Leonore*) – with its spoken dialogue and melodrama, its mixture of simple airs and duets with more complex ensembles and finales, its domestic setting and the happy end brought about by an act of superhuman courage – derives from French revolutionary opera (*Lodoïska* is an obvious precedent), but Beethoven's music transcends all comparisons. The opera was commissioned by Schikaneder – who originally gave the composer a hopelessly inadequate grand opera libretto of his own, *Vestas Feuer*, to set – and Beethoven had started work on it by the end of 1803. The story (which the Viennese censor insisted had to be set in sixteenth-century Spain, although it referred to a recent incident) had already been set by Gaveaux (1798) and Paer (premièred in Dresden six weeks before Beethoven's work), and the title was changed before the première to avoid confusion with Paer's opera. A revised version of the opera, reduced from three to two acts was premièred at same theatre on 29 March 1806 and the definitive version, now entitled *Fidelio*, was first performed at the Kärntnertortheater, Vienna, on 23 May 1814, with Anna Milder again taking the role she had created in the original production.

Scene from Rossini's *Tancredi*. The hero, who has been unjustly banished, surveys his homeland across the river. This was the occasion for the opera's most famous number, cherished for its patriotic sentiment as well as its irresistible music, 'Tu che accendi…Di tanti palpiti.'

Isabella Colbran, star of the Teatro San Carlo in Naples and wife of Rossini. She is portrayed in 1817 in the title role of Mayr's *Saffo* (1794).

Scene from Rossini's *L'inganno felice*, 1812.

One of Schinkel's set designs for the revival of Mozart's *Die Zauberflöte* at the Berlin Schauspielhaus in 1815.

*12 November* Première of ***Berenice, regina d'Armenia*** (Zingarelli/Ferretti after Zeno) at the Teatro Valle, Rome. This was the last opera by Zingarelli, whose traditional style was unable to survive the sudden popularity of Rossini.

**1812** *8 January* Première of ***L'inganno felice*** (Rossini/Foppa after Palomba) at San Moisè, Venice, the opera with which Rossini scored his first big success. Two more followed in quick succession, the sacred opera ***Ciro in Babilonia*** at Ferrara during Lent and ***La scala di seta***, again at San Moisè on 9 May.
*4 April* Première of ***Jean de Paris*** (Boieldieu/Godard d'Aucour de Saint-Just) at the Opéra-Comique, Paris. The work was a great success, particularly in the German version, which Weber conducted in Prague on 8 January 1814, later using the work to contrast the *esprit* of French opera with the emotion and sentiment of German and Italian works.
*18 May* Première of ***Demetrio e Polibio*** (Rossini/Viganò-Mombelli after Metastasio) at the Teatro Valle, Rome. Rossini wrote the opera at the age of sixteen in 1807 as a commission from the tenor Domenico Mombelli.
*26 September* Première of ***La pietra del paragone*** (Rossini/Romanelli) at La Scala, Milan, Rossini's first opera for La Scala and a triumph.
*24 November* Première of ***L'occasione fa il ladro*** (Rossini/Prividali after Scribe) at San Moisè, Venice, followed two months later by ***Il signor Bruschino, ossia Il figlio per azzardo***.

**1813** *6 February* Première of ***Tancredi*** (Rossini/Rossi after Voltaire and Tasso) at La Fenice, Venice. The first serious opera Rossini had written, the work became a runaway success and established the composer's reputation as the rising star of Italian opera.

The tenor Giovanni David, jun. as Lindoro in Rossini's *L'italiana in Algeri*.

*21 February* Première of ***La rosa bianca e la rosa rossa*** (Mayr/Romani) at the Teatro San Agostino, Genoa. This story of the English Wars of the Roses, based on a French libretto, was the first operatic text by Felice Romani, who was to become the finest librettist of Italian romantic opera, writing some ninety texts which were used for over 200 operas.
*22 May* Première of ***L'italiana in Algeri*** (Rossini/Anelli) at San Benedetto, Venice. Rossini's first comic success, this was the first of his operas to be heard in Spain (1815), Germany (1816) and France (1817). When it was put on in Naples in October 1815, Isabella's aria 'Pensa alla patria' had to be omitted for fear it would incite a revolution.
*9 September* Weber made his conducting début as the new director of the German Opera in Prague with a performance of Spontini's ***Fernand Cortez*** (1809), which was given an anti-Bonapartist slant to suit a city that had become a haven for opponents of the Emperor. Weber also performed Beethoven's ***Fidelio*** there (after fourteen rehearsals) on 21 November 1814, and built up a repertory of sixty-two operas that included ***Don Giovanni, Le nozze di Figaro, La clemenza di Tito, Les deux journées, La Vestale, Joseph*** and Spohr's ***Faust.***

## Domenico Barbaia and his four tenors

Domenico Barbaia (1778–1841) was that great rarity, an opera impresario who was never short of money. His fortune did not come from the operas he put on, but from organized gambling. Italian opera houses, since they were a focus of social life, frequently had gambling tables in the foyer, and while he was still in his twenties Barbaia took over the gambling concession at La Scala, taking advantage of the wealth of the profiteers who were supplying the French armies in the city. In 1809, he was appointed impresario of the royal theatres in Naples with, again, the concession to run the gambling. Barbaia assembled a team of brilliant singers in Naples, especially noted for their florid ornamentation, including the soprano Isabella Colbran (the mistress of both Barbaia and the King of Naples) and four great tenors, Manuel Garcia, sen., Andrea Nozzari, Giovanni Battista Rubini and Giovanni David, jun. In 1815 Barbaia invited Rossini to become musical and artistic director of his Naples theatres, supervising all productions and training the singers in their parts. Since the singers would have protested if a composer were paid the same fees that they received, Barbaia supplemented Rossini's salary with a share of the profits from the gaming tables: this was the foundation of Rossini's fortune.

Rossini was able to write great dramatic parts for Colbran (whom he married in 1822), then nearing the end of her career, and roles of great virtuosity for his tenors. In *Elisabetta* the hero (Leicester) was sung by Nozzari, the villain (Norfolk) by Garcia; Garcia travelled with Rossini to Rome to sing Almaviva in *Il barbiere di Siviglia*; and in *Otello* the title role, written for Garcia, was eventually taken by Nozzari, while David sang Rodrigo. Rubini joined the company in 1815, but his association with Rossini was more fruitful when he was one of the Italian singers working for the composer in Paris in 1825. All these tenors sang the florid music written in the higher part of their register with a 'head voice' or falsetto, although tenors who could sound a ringing high C with a chest voice were soon to be heard – to Rossini's dismay.

Barbaia's activities did not come to an end when Rossini left with Colbran in 1822. He had already taken on the additional post of manager of the Kärntnertor-theater in Vienna in 1821, where he arranged a hugely successful Rossini season with the composer and his Neapolitan team and commissioned Weber to write *Euryanthe*. The following year he hired Donizetti to take charge of productions at the Teatro del Fondo in Naples, and, from the mid-1820s, took on yet another theatre – La Scala in Milan, where he commissioned Bellini's *La straniera*. By his nurturing of composers and singers Barbaia did more to sustain and develop Italian opera than anyone during these years.

**1814** *23 May* Première of the definitive version of Beethoven's ***Fidelio*** at the Kärntertortheater, Vienna, with Anna Milder as Leonora and Michael Vogl, the great interpreter of Schubert's songs, as Pizarro. Allied troops had entered Vienna on 11 April, and on 26 September a gala performance of the opera was given for the delegates assembled for the Vienna Congress, which was to establish a new post-Napoleonic order in Europe.
*14 August* Première of ***Il turco in Italia*** (Rossini/Romani) at La Scala, Milan, with Filippo Galli as the Turk. Although one of Rossini's most engaging comic operas – with a poet on stage writing the opera as the action takes place – it had a very hostile reception from the Milanese, who accused the composer, with no justification, of reusing the music of ***L'italiana in Algeri***, rather than writing them a new work.

**1815** Schubert wrote five works for the stage, none of which was produced at the time.
*4 October* Première of ***Elisabetta, regina d'Inghilterra*** (Rossini/Schmidt after Federici) at San Carlo, Naples, with Isabella Colbran as Queen Elizabeth, Garcia as Leicester and Nozzari as Norfolk. As this was Rossini's first opera in his new post as music director of the Naples opera houses, he could safely recycle much music from earlier operas. During his years there (1815–22) Rossini wrote ten operas for Naples and a further ten for Rome, Milan, Venice and Lisbon.

**1816** Début of nineteen-year-old Giuditta Negri (later Pasta) at the Théâtre-Italien, Paris. It was not an auspicious beginning, and she was relaunched at the same theatre in 1821, when she began to take leading roles in Rossini's serious operas.
*20 February* Première of ***Il barbiere di Siviglia*** (Rossini/Sterbini after Beaumarchais) with the title ***Almaviva, ossia L'inutile precauzione*** at the Teatro Argentina, Rome.
*3 August* Première of ***Undine*** (Hoffmann/La Motte Fouqué) at the Schauspielhaus, Berlin, E. T. A. Hoffmann's high point as a composer. The production had magnificent sets by Schinkel, the most extravagant being the Water Palace of Kühleborn. Schinkel designed sets for thirty-two operatic and dramatic productions at the theatre from 1813 to 1832, including Mozart's ***Die Zauberflöte*** (1815), Gluck's ***Alceste*** (1817) and operas by Méhul and Spontini.
*1 September* Première of ***Faust*** (Spohr/Bernard) at the Estates Theatre, Prague, conducted by Weber. The opera had been written for the Theater an der Wien, Vienna, where Spohr was music director from 1813 to 1816, but it was not performed there for another two years. Like ***Der Freischütz*** its plot revolves around a pact with the devil, though it has nothing to do with Goethe's *Faust*. It is one of the earliest German operas to be through-composed (without dialogue) and has been seen to anticipate Wagner's use of leitmotifs.
*4 December* Première of ***Otello, ossia Il moro di Venezia*** (Rossini/Berio di Salsa after Shakespeare) at the Teatro del Fondo, Naples; the role of Desdemona was written for Colbran. Rossini was starting to break down the conventional framework of opera, allowing the numbers to flow into each other more freely, and in the final act he allowed Desdemona's simple willow song to break off incomplete.

Geltrude Righetti-Giorgi, a childhood friend of Rossini's, who played Rosina to Manuel Garcia's Almaviva in the Rome première of *Il barbiere di Siviglia* in 1816.

## Il barbiere di Siviglia

It was still a commonplace for successful libretti to be set again and again by different composers, but it was a bold step for Rossini to choose the subject of one of the most popular operas of the period, Paisiello's *Il barbiere di Siviglia*, even though its elderly composer had fallen into disfavour with the defeat of Napoleon. It was, indeed, a last-minute decision, since the composer had agreed to compose an opera for Rome and *Il barbiere* could not create problems with the censor. It was written in less than three weeks and put on in great haste, and a series of ludicrous accidents which played into the hands of Paisiello's supporters made the première, conducted by Rossini, a disaster. However, when the work was repeated in Bologna in August (two months after Paisiello's death) it was immediately acclaimed. It has remained one of the most popular operas ever written.

# 1817 / 1821 Weber and German Romanticism

*Carl Maria von Weber, both as a composer and as director of the Dresden opera, was the champion of the movement to develop a German operatic style, to match their great achievements in instrumental music and to oppose the triumphant progress of Rossini across Europe.*

**DATES**

**1820**
Revolutions in Spain and Portugal
Publication of Pushkin's *Ruslan and Ludmila*

**1821**
Start of national rising in Greece (to 1827)
Death of Napoleon on St Helena

**1817** *25 January* Première of ***La Cenerentola, ossia La bontà in trionfo*** (Rossini/Ferretti) at the Teatro Valle, Rome, with Geltrude Righetti-Giorgi in the title role. The opera has more than a tinge of sentiment in its *buffo* version of the Cinderella story.
*30 January* Weber's début as music director of the new German Opera in Dresden conducting a performance of Méhul's ***Joseph***, seventeen days after his arrival in the city. In August his appointment was confirmed for life, although his plans for promoting German opera were opposed by factions at court led by the Italian court composer Morlacchi.
*31 May* Première of ***La gazza ladra*** (Rossini/Gherardini after Baudouin d'Aubigny and Caigniez) at La Scala, Milan. Stendhal said that the first night of this *semiseria* work was the most successful he had ever attended.

Lucia Elizabeth Vestris as Don Giovanni in the parody of Mozart's opera put on in London in 1817.

Opening night, 16 April 1821, in the new theatre for the Opéra on the rue Peletier with a performance of Catel's *Les Bayadères*.

*'The novelty is now* Der Freischütz *of Weber – performing at the Lyceum and the music is wild but often beautiful – when the magic bullets are cast they fill the stage with all sorts of horrors – owls flapping their wings – toads jumping about – fiery serpents darting – ghastly hunters in the clouds, while every now and then [in] a stream of wild harmony comes a crashing discord – all forms I assure you of a very fine scene, while every part of the house except the stage is envelloped in darkness.'*

Mary Shelley to Leigh Hunt, 22 August 1824

Set for the production of *Der Freischütz* in Weimar, a year after its Berlin première, depicting the Wolf's Glen, where the magic bullets are cast.

Scenery workshops for the new Paris Opéra in 1821.

## A German national opera

The German-speaking world, which had been fragmented for centuries, found a spiritual unity after it was freed from the occupation of Napoleon, and the search for a cultural identity, begun in the late eighteenth century, was pursued with new vigour. German instrumental music had already established a native tradition, but opera was still dominated by the Italians: they held most of the main operatic posts, even in Paris, although *singspiel*, based initially on the models of English ballad opera and French *opéra-comique*, had begun to establish a new direction. Weber had a vision of serious German opera as 'a work of art complete in itself, with all its parts well finished and fused together in beautiful unity', and aimed to achieve this both in his activities as an opera director and in his compositions. As director of the 'German Opera', first in Prague then in Dresden, Weber's preference for French opera over Italian indicated where he believed the origins of German opera must lie, but it was only through his own work that he could establish a new pattern. Spohr's *Faust* and Hoffmann's *Undine* had drawn on the German romantic folklore that had previously been used only for popular *singspiel*, but Weber's *Der Freischütz* with its sinister supernatural plot, expertly developed by his librettist Friedrich Kind, offered a far more powerful interpretation of national myth. The music too, with its hunting chorus, lyrical evocations of nature and references to folk music has a marked local character, and its development from overture to finale – despite the interruptions of spoken dialogue – has a unity, reinforced by the use of reminiscence motifs, that follows the tradition of German instrumental music. The opera was completed on 13 May 1820 after three years of work; an immediate success, its historical importance has been matched by its enduring popularity.

Agathe in *Der Freischütz* played by Henriette Sontag, a celebrated early interpreter of the role, who made her adult début in Prague in 1821 after playing a succession of juvenile roles.

Giuditta Pasta (born Giuditta Negri) who, after a failed début at the Théâtre-Italien in 1816, returned to the same stage in 1821, at the start of a brilliant career, in which she was celebrated especially for her Rossini roles. She appears here as Medea in Mayr's *Medea in Corinto*.

At the London première of the opera (10 March 1821) the leading role was sung by Lucia Elizabeth Vestris, who had made her name in 1817 playing Don Giovanni in a parody of Mozart's opera.
*19 July* Première of ***Romilda e Costanza*** (Meyerbeer/Rossi) in Padua, the first of the composer's six Italian operas, all but the last closely imitating the style of Rossini, just as his earlier German opera ***Akimelek*** (1813) had been modelled on Weber.
*27 July* Destruction of the Berlin Schauspielhaus by fire during a performance of Hoffmann's ***Undine***. The new opera house, designed by Schinkel, opened in 1821.
*11 November* Première of ***Armida*** (Rossini/Schmidt after Tasso's *Gerusalemme Liberata*) at the Teatro San Carlo, Naples, with Colbran in the title role. Stendhal said that one of the love duets, 'Amor, possente nome' was found so sensual that 'the ladies were embarrassed to praise it'.
*27 December* Première of ***Adelaide di Borgogna*** (Rossini/Schmidt) at the Teatro Argentina, Rome.
*30 December* Première of ***Adelaide e Comingio*** (Pacini/Rossi) at the Teatro Re, Milan; Pacini's fifteenth opera, and his first real success.

**1818** *5 March* Première of ***Mosè in Egitto*** (Rossini/Tottola after Ringhieri) at San Carlo, Naples, with Colbran singing the role of Anaide. The work was in fact a staged oratorio – *azione tragico-seria* – for Lent. The famous prayer, 'Dal tuo stellato soglio', was added for a revival at the theatre a year later.
*14 November* Première of ***Enrico di Borgogna*** (Donizetti/Merelli) at San Luca, Venice, the composer's first opera. Twelve years later he reused one of the arias; as 'Al dolce guidami' it was the highpoint in ***Anna Bolena***, the first opera to win him an international reputation.
*3 December* Première of ***Ricciardo e Zoraide*** (Rossini/Berio di Salsa) at San Carlo, Naples.

**1819** *27 March* Première of ***Ermione*** (Rossini/Tottola after Racine) at San Carlo, Naples.
*24 April* Première of ***Eduardo e Cristina*** (Rossini/Schmidt after Pavesi) at San Benedetto, Venice.
*26 June* Première of ***Emma di Resburgo*** (Meyerbeer/Rossi) at San Benedetto, Venice. This opera, on a Nordic theme, was successful in Italy.
*19 August* Première of ***L'apoteose d'Ercole*** (Mercadante/Schmidt) at San Carlo, Naples; Mercadante's first opera, commissioned by Rossini.
*24 September* Première of ***La donna del lago*** (Rossini/Tottola after Scott) at San Carlo, Naples. The part of Roderick Dhu was originally written for a tenor but was altered by Rossini for the 1824 Paris production so that it could be sung by the baritone Antonio Tamburini.
*26 December* Première of ***Bianca e Falliero, ossia Il consiglio dei tre*** (Rossini/Romani) at La Scala, Milan.
*26 December* Première of ***Il falegname di Livonia, o Pietro il grande, czar delle Russie*** (Donizetti/Bevilacqua-Aldovrandini) at San Samuele, Venice, a work which met with little success.

**1820** *13 February* Murder of the Duc de Berry, heir to the French throne, at the Opéra on the rue Richelieu. The theatre was demolished by order of the Archbishop of Paris, and a new opera house opened the following year.
*14 June* Première of ***Die Zwillingsbrüder*** (Schubert/von Hofmann) at the Kärntnertortheater, Vienna. It was the composer's friend Michael Vogl who initiated Schubert's operatic projects, and the tenor played a double role in this first work. The same team produced a second opera, ***Die Zauberharfe***, at the Theater an der Wien two months later (19 August),

but neither work was well received. They were the only two of Schubert's operas to be performed in his lifetime. The overture to ***Die Zauberharfe*** is his best known piece of operatic music, as he reused it as an overture to Helmine von Chezy's play *Rosamunde*, which was performed with his incidental music in 1823.

*14 November* Première of ***Margherita d'Anjou*** (Meyerbeer/Romani after Pixérécourt) at La Scala, Milan; the composer's first opera for La Scala.

*3 December* Première of ***Maometto II*** (Rossini/della Valle) at San Carlo, Naples. The title role was written for Filippo Galli, originally a tenor, who became one of the greatest bass singers of the period; his first appearance as a bass was in the première of Rossini's ***L'inganno felice*** (see 1812) and the leading role in ***La gazza ladra*** (see 1817) was also written for him.

*Carnival* Première of ***Le nozze in villa*** (Donizetti/Merelli) at the Teatro Vecchio, Mantua; the composer's first *opera buffa.*

**1821** *24 February* Première of ***Matilda di Shabran, ossia Bellezza e cuor di ferro*** (Rossini/Ferretti) at the Teatro Apollo, Rome, conducted by Paganini. The libretto was based on F. B. Hoffmann's ***Euphrosine***, set by Méhul in 1790.

*12 March* Première of ***L'esule di Granata*** (Meyerbeer/Romani) at La Scala, Milan.

*29 March* Première of ***Le Maître de chapelle, ou Le Souper imprévu*** (Paer/Gay) at the Opéra-Comique, Paris; it was eventually to prove a more lasting success than Paer's serious operas, with revivals in many countries throughout the nineteenth century and into the twentieth.

*16 April* Opening of the new 'temporary' house for the Opéra on the rue Peletier with a performance of ***Les Bayadères*** (Catel/Etienne de Jouy), which had been premièred in the old Salle Montansier on 8 August 1810. The rue Peletier remained the home of the Paris Opéra until 1875.

*14 May* Spontini inaugurated his tenure as music director of the Berlin Opernhaus by conducting a performance of his own opera ***Olimpie*** (libretto by Dieulafoy and Brifaut after Voltaire) in a translation by E. T. A. Hoffmann. It had been premièred at the Paris Opéra on 22 December 1819. Feeling against France and Italy was still strong (use of Italian in the opera house had been outlawed since the Battle of Jena in October 1806), and after a few performances the house was half-empty.

*18 June* Inauguration of the new Schauspielhaus in Berlin with the première of ***Der Freischütz*** (Weber/Kind after Apel and Laun) on the sixth anniversary of the Battle of Waterloo, with Karoline Seidler singing the role of Agathe. Censorship caused absurd cuts for the opera's première in Vienna (3 November 1821), where Schröder-Devrient sang her first Agathe on 7 March 1822 with Weber conducting: Rossini attended a performance on 27 March. The success of ***Der Freischütz*** in Germany was soon rivalled in Paris and London.

***Die beiden Padagogen*** (Mendelssohn/Casper after Scribe) was performed in a private house in Berlin. This slight Mozartian *singspiel* written when the composer was twelve years old was one of Mendelssohn's few ventures into opera. With the exception of his oratorios, Mendelssohn's music was almost entirely instrumental: even his 'Songs without Words'.

*Autumn* Composition of ***Alfonso und Estrella*** (Schubert/Schober); its first documented performance was given under Liszt at Weimar in 1854.

*30 October* Première of ***Elisa e Claudio*** (Mercadante/Romanelli) at La Scala, Milan. It was the young composer's first major success, and performances were given over the next three years in London, Paris, Barcelona and Vienna.

FOR THE BENEFIT OF
Mr. HEWLET.

Mr. BROWN has spared neither time or expense in rendering this Entertainment agreeable to the Ladies and Gentlemen of Colour, being the third attempt of this kind in this City, by persons of Colour.

AN OPERA
Will take place corner of Mercer and Bleecker-st.
On MONDAY EVENING, Oct. 1st.

SONGS.

| | |
|---|---|
| "Behold in his soft expressive face," | Mr. Hewlet. |
| The Light House, | Hutchington. |
| "Scots wha' hae' wi Wallace bled," | Hewlet. |
| Corporal Casey, | Thompson. |
| "Is there a heart that never loved," | Hewlet. |
| "I knew by the smoke that so gracefully curl'd," | Hutchington. |
| "My Deary," | Hewlet. |
| Maid of the Mill, | Hewlet. |
| Robin Adair, | Hewlet. |
| The Hunter's Horn, | Hewlet. |

After which will be performed, for the last time this Season, the TRAGEDY of

Richard the Third.

| | |
|---|---|
| KING HENRY, | Mr. Hutchington. |
| PRINCE OF WALES, | Miss S. Welsh. |
| RICHARD, | Mr. Hewlett. |
| BUCKINGHAM, | Hutchington. |
| LORD STANLEY, | J. Hutchington. |
| RICHMOND, | Mathews. |
| LADY ANN, | Miss Welsh. |
| QUEEN ELIZABETH, | J. Welsh. |

PANTOMIME ASAMA.

| | |
|---|---|
| ASAMA, | Mr. Hewlet. |
| ASANA, | S. Welsh. |

The BALLET got up under the direction of Mr. Hewlet, being received on Monday evening, Sept. 24, with unbounded applause, will be repeated again on Monday Evening, October 1st, 1821.

| | | | |
|---|---|---|---|
| Columbine, | Miss S. Welsh. | Old Man, | Thompson. |
| Daphne, | Mr Hewlet. | Servant, | Master Geib. |

ADMITTANCE 50 CENTS.

Playbill for an 'operatic' concert on 1 October 1821 at the African Grove, New York, one of the first African-American musical venues.

**1822**
**1828**

# Romantic Opera

*While Rossini went from triumph to triumph, several younger composers, including Gaetano Donizetti and Vincenzo Bellini, began to come to prominence. Meanwhile, the taste for romantic literature inspired a new range of sources for opera plots: the historical novels of Sir Walter Scott and his imitators began to be mined by librettists, while Shakespeare's plays were given a new romantic interpretation.*

Set for the production of Rossini's *Semiramide* at La Scala, Milan, which was staged soon after the première of the opera in Venice in February 1823. The designs were by the principal scenic artist at La Scala, Alessandro Sanquirico.

**1822** *28 January* Première of ***Zoraida di Granata*** (Donizetti/Merelli) at the Teatro Argentina, Rome. The commission had probably been passed on by Mayr, and it was Donizetti's first real success, bringing him to the notice of Barbaia, who commissioned works for La Scala and for Naples, where he gave the composer a post on his musical staff. Merelli, who had written three earlier libretti for Donizetti, was later impresario of the Teatro Carlo Felice in Genoa and then Barbaia's successor as impresario of La Scala.
*6 February* Première of ***Aladin, ou La Lampe merveilleuse*** (Isouard and Benincori/Etienne) at the Opéra, Paris, with decoration by Pierre Cicéri, chief painter at the Opéra 1816–48, and Louis Daguerre. The designers, who used gas lighting and introduced panoramas and dioramas to theatre decoration, produced such a brilliant spectacle that the opera was played one hundred times within three years.

*16 February* Première of ***Zelmira*** (Rossini/Tottola after Dormont de Belloy) at San Carlo, Naples. Rossini himself conducted performances of the opera in Vienna (13 April 1822), London (24 January 1824) and Paris (14 March 1826). The Vienna performance, which starred Colbran with other members of the San Carlo opera company was the beginning of a Rossini season, organized by Barbaia at the Kärntnertortheater, that lasted until 8 July; the London performance also started a season in which eight of the twelve operas performed were by Rossini. The production at the Paris Opéra, which starred Pasta, Rubini and Nicolas Levasseur and was designed by Cicéri, was extraordinarily lavish, although the administration refused to authorize expenditure of over 12,000 francs on new costumes for some 120 soldiers and priests.
*12 May* Première of ***La zingara*** (Donizetti/Tottola) at the Teatro Nuovo, Naples. The composer's first Neapolitan work for Barbaia was an *opera semiseria* with spoken dialogue which met with local success. The same year (26 October) Donizetti worked with Felice Romani for the first time, producing ***Chiara e Serafina, o I pirati*** (also for Barbaia) at La Scala, but the Milanese audience was not impressed.

**1823** *25 January* Première of ***Leicester, ou Le Château de Kenilworth*** (Auber/Scribe and Mélesville) at the Opéra-Comique, Paris. The opera, based on Scott's novel, was the first collaboration of one of the most successful operatic teams of the period.
*3 February* Première of ***Semiramide*** (Rossini/Rossi after Voltaire) at La Fenice, Venice, the last opera Rossini composed in Italy. He wrote the title role for Colbran, by now his wife. At the London première in 1824 the role was sung by Pasta (with Vestris as Arsace), and by Joséphine Fodor at the Paris première at the Théâtre-Italien in December 1825.
*April* Schubert completed ***Die Verschworenen*** (first performed in 1861) and, in the summer, ***Fierrabras*** (first performed in 1897). The libretto of the first (a variant of Aristophanes' *Lysistrata*, in which women refuse their men sex to prevent them from fighting wars) was written by Castelli, a friend of both Beethoven and Weber, and published in 1823 as an example of a good libretto for German composers to set. It elicited some of Schubert's finest operatic music.
*29 April* Wilhelmine Schröder-Devrient's first appearance as Leonore in ***Fidelio***, at the Königliches Oper, Dresden, under the direction of Weber.
*28 July* Première of ***Jessonda*** (Spohr/Gehe after Lemierre) at the Hoftheater, Kassel, the composer's principal opera, in which he abandoned the alternation of recitative and aria for a through-composed score. It was a success throughout Germany and northern Europe.

Costume designs by Hippolyte Lecomte for the original production of Auber's *La Muette de Portici* at the Opéra in February 1828.

Set design by Cicéri for *Pharamond*, an opera premièred at the Opéra on 10 June 1825 with music by four of the most fashionable French composers, Boieldieu, Berton, Kreutzer and Daussoigne (Méhul's adopted son). The druidic subject, typical of romantic sensibility, anticipated Bellini's *Norma* by six years.

## Romance and tragedy

Idealized visions of the Middle Ages – the crusading chivalry, the selfless patriotism, the tragic romances – caught the popular imagination and were most vividly recounted in the novels of Sir Walter Scott. The earliest Italian opera with a libretto based on Scott was Rossini's *La donna del lago* (1819), based on the poem 'The Lady of the Lake' (1810). During the 1820s and later, Scott's Scottish novels and medieval English romances were used by librettists who included Scribe and Hans Christian Andersen and composers from Rossini, Carafa and Pacini to Auber, Boieldieu, Marschner, Nicolai, Bellini and Donizetti. Two operas based on *Ivanhoe* (one in Paris in 1826, one in London three years later) were even cobbled together from items taken from *Semiramide* and other Rossini operas.

The Tudor period had provided the setting for a rash of historical operas, but Shakespeare's plays, which had been a popular source for libretti in the late eighteenth century, were now seen in a new light and became the basis for another group of romantic tragedies. Rossini's *Otello* was the first of these, while *Macbeth* and *Romeo and Juliet* were also set during the 1820s. Felice Romani, who wrote an *Amleto* which was set by Mercadante in 1822, viewed *Hamlet* as a modern *Oresteia* (the sequence of Greek tragedies that had been the origin of Gluck's *Iphigénie* operas and many other works). Berlioz, after seeing the English actress Harriet Smithson as Ophelia and Juliet in Paris in 1827, wrote: 'Shakespeare, coming upon me unawares, struck me like a thunderbolt. The lightning flash of that discovery revealed to me at a stroke the whole heaven of art, illuminating it to its remotest corners. I recognized the meaning of grandeur, beauty, dramatic truth…'

The subject of Heinrich Marschner's *Der Vampyr* (1828) is taken from a poem thought at the time to be by Byron. Lord Ruthven, the vampire, is allowed to return to life on the condition that he procures three young girls for the devil, but is thwarted by the determined innocence of the third. The original captions for the illustrations read: 'Aubrey falls down. The moon shines brightly on Ruthven's pale face,' and 'George: Alas! She lies there lifeless covered in blood!' In 1829, the opera had a run of sixty performances at the Lyceum Theatre, London, in an English version by Planché.

The illustration of the apparition of the woman in white is taken from *Guy Mannering*, one of the two novels by Sir Walter Scott that served as the basis for Boieldieu's *La Dame blanche* (1825). The plot, set in Scotland in 1759, involves the discovery of the true heir to an ancestral castle.

*25 October* Première of ***Euryanthe*** (Weber/Helmine von Chezy) at the Kärntnertortheater, Vienna, with seventeen-year-old Henriette Sontag in the title role. The opera was commissioned by the ubiquitous Barbaia, following his triumphant Rossini season, as an opera 'in the manner of *Der Freischütz*', although the composer intended it to be a more serious work, a grand heroic romantic opera, through-composed, whose traditional numbers were replaced by integrated scenes. The libretto is very weak, and the first performance was badly received, although the opera became a success in Dresden and elsewhere in Germany.

**1824** *4 February* Première of ***L'ajo nell'imbarazzo*** (Donizetti/Ferretti) at the Teatro Valle, Rome, a successful romantic comedy, in which Tamburini played the comic father. The opera was revived in London in 1846 as ***Don Gregorio.***

*7 March* Première of ***Il crociato in Egitto*** (Meyerbeer/Rossi) at La Fenice, Venice; the last and most successful of Meyerbeer's Italian operas, with a leading role written especially for Giovanni Battista Velluti – the final great *castrato* part in opera. The supporting cast included Malibran and

Maria Caradori. Rossini's staging at the Théâtre-Italien, Paris, on 25 September 1825 led to the start of Meyerbeer's international recognition.
*August* Rossini was appointed co-director (with Paer) of the Théâtre-Italien in Paris. He agreed to produce the operas he had written in the past, to compose new operas and to stage other Italian works. The following year, Pacini, at the height of his success, was appointed music director at the Teatro San Carlo, Naples, a post he held until 1830.
*7 December* Première of ***Robin des bois*** (the French version of ***Der Freischütz***, adapted by Castil-Blaze) at the Théâtre de l'Odéon, Paris. Although he described it as 'a great travesty, hacked and mutilated', Berlioz attended every performance until he had committed the work to memory.

**1825** Most Italian theatres were closed, since the Pope had declared 1825 a 'Holy Year'.
*February* Première of ***Adelson e Salvini*** (Bellini/Tottola) at the Teatro del Conservatorio di San Sebastiano, Naples. Bellini's graduation opera from the Conservatory was performed by an all-male cast.
*19 June* Première of ***Il viaggio a Reims, ossia L'albergo del giglio d'oro*** (Rossini/Balocchi), to celebrate the coronation of Charles X, at the Théâtre-Italien, Paris. Much of the score was reused for ***Le Comte Ory*** (1828).
*17 October* Première of ***Don Sanche, ou Le Château d'amour*** (Liszt/Théaulon de Lambert and de Rancé after Florian) at the Opéra, Paris. The composer, who was thirteen at the time, was a sensation in Paris as a piano prodigy and had studied opera composition with Paer; this was to be his only opera. The title role was sung by Adolphe Nourrit, who had made his début at the Opéra in Gluck's ***Iphigénie en Tauride*** in 1821 and became the company's leading tenor until 1837.
*31 October* Première of ***Giulietta e Romeo*** (Vaccai/Romani after Shakespeare) at the Teatro della Canobbiana, Milan. In a revival of the opera in Florence in 1829 Giulietta was sung by Giulia Grisi and Romeo by Giuditta Pasta, roles that both were to sing in Bellini's setting of the libretto (see 1830), though never together.
*29 November* The first opera to be sung in Italian in New York was Rossini's ***Il barbiere di Siviglia*** performed at the Park Theatre by the Garcia company, with Manuel del Popolo Vicente Garcia in the role of Almaviva (which he had created), his daughter Maria as Rosina and his son Manuel Patricio Garcia as Figaro.
*10 December* Première of ***La Dame blanche*** (Boieldieu/Scribe) at the Opéra-Comique, Paris, based on Scott's *Guy Mannering* and *The Monastery*. It was the composer's last opera, written after his return from Russia, and was one of the most successful of all French *opéras-comiques* (its 1000th performance at the Opéra-Comique was given on 16 December 1862). Its richly melodic score, with unornamented vocal lines, colourful orchestration and expressive use of chromaticism was admired by Wagner.

**1826** *12 April* Première of ***Oberon, or The Elf King's Oath*** (Weber/Planché after Wieland) at Covent Garden, London, conducted by the composer. The work was typical of the London musical theatre, with a mixture of musical and dramatic forms and an extremely lavish production. It was a great success there, but not on the continent. Weber was as driven as ever with rehearsals and overseeing the details of the production, and his efforts no doubt hastened the progress of his tuberculosis. He died in London on the night of 4–5 June.
*30 May* Première of ***Bianca e Gernando*** (Bellini/Gilardoni) at San Carlo, Naples, a rescue opera commissioned as a result of the success of the

## The Garcia family

The Italian opera season initiated by the Garcias at New York's Park Theatre in November 1825 was a milestone in the history of opera in America, but also a symptom of the growing popularity of Italian opera – and especially Rossini – worldwide. The core of Manuel Garcia's company was his family: he himself was the leading tenor, his son Manuel, jun., was the baritone, and the female roles were sung by his daughter Maria, later Maria Malibran, and his wife (their younger daughter Pauline, later another great singer, was still only a child). Other Rossini operas put on during the season included *Tancredi* (31 December 1825), *Otello* (7 February 1826) and *La Cenerentola* (27 June). Garcia also put on operas he had composed himself and Zingarelli's *Giulietta e Romeo*, but these were not much liked. He was more successful with Mozart's *Don Giovanni* (23 May 1826), although it had proved impossible to get satisfactory singers and the first performance was a near-disaster; the opera ran for ten performances. After *Otello* the great English actor Edmund Kean came backstage to congratulate Manuel Garcia on his performance, but it was Maria who was the star of the company and on her return to Europe she rivalled Pasta as the supreme prima donna of the age.

Manuel Garcia, sen., in an oriental role. A tenor known for his elegant ornamentation and strength of tone, Garcia trained in his native Spain and made his Paris début in 1808 in Paer's *Griselda*, later becoming a member of Barbaia's company in Naples. He was also a composer of operas and one of the leading singer teachers of his generation, whose pupils included not only his three children but also Henriette Méric-Lalande and Adolphe Nourrit.

composer's student opera. The cast included Méric-Lalande, Rubini and Lablache.

*9 October* Première of ***Le Siège de Corinthe*** (Rossini/Soumet and Balocchi) at the Opéra, Paris, a revised version of ***Maometto II*** (see 1820). The score was simplified to suit the French singing style of Nourrit and Cinti – who were acclaimed at the première – while Cicéri, the designer, created a spectacular effect for when the city burns down in the final act.

**1827** *26 March* Première of ***Moïse et Pharaon, ou Le Passage de la mer rouge*** (Rossini/Balocchi and Etienne de Jouy) at the Opéra, Paris, a revised version of ***Mosè in Egitto*** (see 1818), with Cinti, Nourrit and Levasseur in the cast.

*Autumn* Rossini arranged for William Balfe's operatic début as Figaro in ***Il barbiere di Siviglia*** at the Théâtre-Italien, Paris.

*27 October* Première of ***Il pirata*** (Bellini/Romani) at La Scala, Milan, with Méric-Lalande (who had made her Milan début the previous year), Rubini and Tamburini. Bellini's third opera was a great success, with performances worldwide in the 1830s.

*21 November* Première of ***Le convenienze ed inconvenienze teatrali*** (Donizetti/composer after Sografi) at the Teatro Nuovo, Naples. It was the best of Donizetti's farces, a satire on old-fashioned *opera seria*, with a

The Salle Favart in Paris, which housed the Théâtre-Italien from autumn 1825 to January 1838, when it burned down; after it was rebuilt it became the home of the Opéra-Comique. In Rossini's time there, it was known for its brilliant ensemble of singers, while the Opéra specialized in spectacularly designed productions.

character (the mother of the seconda donna) sung by a baritone *en travesti*. Berlioz thought well of it.

**1828** *29 February* Première of ***La Muette de Portici*** (Auber/Scribe and Delavigne), at the Opéra, Paris, starring Cinti, Nourrit and Dabadie. It was Scribe's first outstanding success as a librettist and initiated a new style of *grand opéra* in which sentiment was combined with spectacular production effects (designed by Cicéri, who had travelled to Milan to consult La Scala's resident designer Sanquirico). The eruption of Vesuvius forms the climax of the opera.
*29 March* Première of ***Der Vampyr*** (Marschner/Wohlbrück after Nodier) at the Stadttheater, Leipzig. Marschner had assumed Weber's mantle as the leading composer of new German romantic opera.
*7 April* Revival of Bellini's ***Bianca e Fernando*** (see 1826) with altered title and libretto revised by Romani, commissioned by Merelli to inaugurate the new Teatro Carlo Felice in Genoa.
*5 June* Première of ***Pan Tvardovsky*** (Verstovsky/Aksakov and Zagoskin) at the Bolshoi Theatre, Moscow. The composer had already written several vaudevilles, but this was his first opera, written in the Weberian romantic style. Weber's ***Der Freischütz*** had been performed in St Petersburg in 1824 and in Moscow in 1825.
An Italian touring company led by Luigi Zamboni (the original Figaro in Rossini's ***Barbiere***) visited St Petersburg with the intention of forming a permanent Italian opera there. Glinka was apprenticed to the company's coach and became immersed in the Rossinian style, but the company failed after its third season.
*20 August* Première of ***Le Comte Ory*** (Rossini/Scribe and Delestre-Poirson) at the Opéra, Paris, a farcical opera given the fashionable romantic setting of the crusades. Some of the score was taken from ***Il viaggio a Reims*** (1825). The title role was written for the distinctively French timbre of Adolphe Nourrit, whose co-stars in the première included Cinti and Levasseur.

Maria Malibran, the elder daughter of Manuel Garcia, as Leonore in the prison scene of Beethoven's *Fidelio*. The emotional power of Malibran's performances, which could at times overwhelm their musical quality, made her the most idolized opera singer of her day, and her death at the age of twenty-eight was universally mourned.

Bellini's *Il pirata* is set in thirteenth-century Sicily, and the typically romantic plot involves Gualtiero, a nobleman forced to become a pirate, and his victorious enemy, the Duke of Caldora, who has forced Gualtiero's lover Imogene to marry him. Gualtiero kills the Duke in a duel, is then executed by the Duke's subjects, and the opera, which had begun with a storm and shipwreck, ends with the heroine going mad with grief. The writing of the tenor role of Gualtiero was strongly influenced by Bellini's friendship with Giovanni Battista Rubini, who supposedly lodged with the composer while he was working on the opera. The print shows Rubini as Gualtiero and his wife, Adele Comelli, as Imogene.

# 1829 1835 Bel Canto

*As increasing prosperity in the great cities of Europe led opera to regain the social prestige it had enjoyed in the eighteenth century, attention began to be focused again on the star singers, for whom the fashionable composers wrote great showpieces. Their spectacular techniques and their rivalries absorbed rather more attention than the music itself, to the disgust of composers and critics, led by Berlioz, who believed that opera should have a more noble and serious intent.*

Henriette Méric-Lalande as Alaide in Bellini's *La straniera*, a role she created at La Scala in 1829. A member of Barbaia's company in Naples, where she had studied under Manuel Garcia, sen., she was the heroine in several premières of Bellini's operas and also created the role of Lucrezia Borgia for Donizetti.

**1829** *14 February* Première of ***La straniera*** (Bellini/Romani after Darlincourt), at La Scala, Milan, with Méric-Lalande, Tamburini and Caroline Unger (later a celebrated Lucrezia Borgia). Commissioned by Barbaia, the work was a close collaboration between composer and librettist: in the case of the final aria 'Or sei pago, o ciel tremendo' the music was composed first, and the librettist supplied words as soon as he heard the melody.

*16 May* Première of ***Zaira*** (Bellini/Romani after Voltaire), commissioned by Merelli to inaugurate the Teatro Regio Ducale, Parma, after Rossini had turned the project down. Apart from Méric-Lalande and Lablache, the cast were unequal to the composer's demands and the opera was unsuccessful, much of the music being reused in ***I Capuleti e i Montecchi*** (see 1830).

*12 June* Première of ***Agnes von Hohenstaufen*** (Spontini/Raupach and Lichtenstein) at the Opernhaus, Berlin, with sets by Schinkel. The German subject of the composer's last opera was an attempt to make his grand spectacular productions appeal to the Berlin public, but the new German romantic style initiated by Weber proved far more popular.

The sleepwalking scene from Bellini's *La sonnambula* from the original production at the Teatro Carcano, Milan, in 1831 with sets designed by Sanquirico.

## Bellini

The Sicilian Vincenzo Bellini achieved his pre-eminence in Italian romantic opera with only ten works, in contrast to the great productivity of Donizetti, or of Rossini in his early years. His style, too, was distinguished from that of his contemporaries by the remarkable extension and purity of the vocal line, within which any decoration was contained rather than being superimposed as added ornamentation. This melodic gift allowed him to write arias of intense beauty such as Norma's 'Casta diva', but also to build up a dramatic situation by repeating the same long phrase with varied accompaniment in set pieces such as the Act I finale of *La sonnambula*, which depicts a scene of confusion and jealousy after the heroine has been discovered in another man's room. Bellini's music was appreciated not only by singers, for whom it provided a marvellous vehicle for expressive performance, and by the public, but also by fellow musicians: Wagner praised *Norma* for its melodic inspiration, its profound reality and its deep passion. Bellini was also lucky to have worked with Felice Romani on most of his operas, a close collaboration rather than the usual perfunctory relationship between composer and librettist; while the plots are typical of romantic opera, the poetry written for the composer's long melodies is of outstanding quality, perfectly matching the tone and expression of the music.

Group portrait of the leading members of the company at the Teatro Carcano in 1830–1, at a time when a group of wealthy Milanese were hoping to outdo La Scala. Giuditta Pasta is in the centre with (top) N. Molinari and L. Henry, (centre) Filippo Galli and G. B. Rubini, and (bottom) Donizetti, Frezzolini, Romani and Bellini.

*6 July* Première of ***Elisabetta, o Il castello di Kenilworth*** (Donizetti/Tottola after Scott) at San Carlo, Naples. This was the composer's first opera on a Tudor subject and the first in which he had two leading female roles. The Neapolitan censor was delighted with the happy end, where the two lovers are pardoned by a beneficent monarch.

*3 August* Première of ***Guillaume Tell*** (Rossini/Etienne de Jouy and others after Schiller) at the Opéra, Paris, Rossini's last opera and, apart from ***Il barbiere di Siviglia***, his greatest success. The cast included Cinti-Damoreau (Mathilde), Nourrit (Arnold), Levasseur (Walter) and Dabadie (Tell), but the work is dominated by ensembles rather than solo arias, and the chorus takes a central role both musically and dramatically. At the first Italian production, at Lucca on 17 September 1831, Arnold was sung by Gilbert-Louis Duprez.

**1830** *28 January* Première of ***Fra Diavolo, ou L'Hôtellerie de Terracine*** (Auber/Scribe and Delavigne) at the Opéra-Comique, Paris. This hugely popular – if musically rather superficial – bandit opera was the greatest triumph of all the collaborations between Scribe and Auber. The title role was written for the eminent tenor-baritone Jean-Baptiste Chollet.

*25 February* Première of Victor Hugo's *Hernani* at the Théâtre-Français, Paris, a revolutionary drama that helped provoke the overthrow of Charles X in July. Bellini and Romani planned an opera based on the play, but they were forced to abandon the project after the composer had already

## Rossini in Paris

Rossini held his official appointment at the Théâtre-Italien from 1824 to 1829, but after the revolution of July 1830, when he returned to Paris from Bologna, he moved into an apartment in the theatre and continued to be closely involved in the productions, including new works by Bellini and Donizetti. Pasta, Malibran and Grisi were members of the company there as well as Rubini, Donzelli, Tamburini and Lablache, and throughout this period Rossini fostered a fluent Italian style of singing to counteract what he described as 'urlo francese' (French shouting). His works for the Opéra, especially *Guillaume Tell*, balanced the demands for lavish productions with showpieces for the star singers, particularly Cinti, Nourrit and Levasseur. These singers were in demand in foreign opera houses, but the ensembles Rossini welded together in Paris helped the city retain its position as the world's opera capital well into the second half of the nineteenth century.

Scene illustrating the story of *Guillaume Tell* from a series of drawings made by Charles Chasselat in 1816. Tell, who has been taken prisoner, is brought across the lake, but when a storm arises he is released from his chains since he is the only one who can control the boat; as it reaches land he jumps ashore and pushes the boat with his enemies back into the waves. The incident occurs in the final scene of Rossini's opera.

written music for five scenes (much of which he later recycled) because of the problems of censorship.

*11 March* Première of ***I Capuleti e i Montecchi*** (Bellini/Romani) at La Fenice, Venice, with Giuditta Grisi (Romeo), Maria Caradori (Giulietta) and Lorenzo Bonfigli (Tebaldo). The opera, a setting of the libretto first set by Vaccai (see 1825), had originally been commissioned from Pacini. Bellini (who happened to be in Venice, as did Romani) was called in as a last-minute replacement, reusing part of the score of ***Zaira*** (see 1829) in order to complete the work in time. In many later performances Vaccai's last act was substituted for Bellini's.

Set design for the final scene of Auber's *Fra Diavolo* in the original production at the Opéra-Comique in January 1830.

Caricatures by Dantan of two of the leaders of French romanticism, Hector Berlioz (right) and Victor Hugo. Hugo's play *Hernani* was premièred in February 1830, while December of the same year saw the first performance of Berlioz's dramatic *Symphonie fantastique*.

*25 August* A performance of Auber's ***La Muette de Portici*** (see 1828) in Brussels sparked off the Belgian revolution, which led to the country's independence (its first performance there had been on 12 February 1829). The same opera had been performed at the opening of the Opéra three weeks earlier, following the revolution in Paris, and Nourrit had sung the Marseillaise at the end.
*5 December* A concert of Berlioz's music conducted by Habeneck at the Paris Conservatoire included the first performance of his orchestral *Symphonie fantastique.* The same evening the actress Harriet Smithson, the model for the artist's beloved in the symphony, appeared as the mute girl Fenella in a performance of ***La Muette de Portici*** at the Opéra.
*26 December* Première of ***Anna Bolena*** (Donizetti/Romani) at the Teatro Carcano, Milan, with Pasta, Elisa Orlandi, Rubini and Galli and sets by Sanquirico. The success of the composer's thirtieth opera (his first setting of a libretto by Romani) raised him to the first rank. Much of the composition was carried out while he was staying in Pasta's villa on Lake Como.

**1831** *6 March* Première of ***La sonnambula*** (Bellini/Romani) at the Teatro Carcano, Milan, with Pasta (the first of three great parts the composer wrote for her), Rubini and Luciano Mariani. The libretto was based on a ballet (1827) by Hérold and Scribe, and Pasta may have suggested the subject to the composer. By 1850 the opera had been sung in fifty-five cities in twelve countries. Glinka, travelling in Italy, was moved to tears at the première and later wrote a *Divertimento brillante* based on themes from ***La sonnambula*** (published by Ricordi) as well as a *Serenata* on themes from ***Anna Bolena.***

*'However barbarous Spontini's music is now acknowledged to be, it is like Cimarosa beside the music of this lunatic who fancies himself a Beethoven because he combines in himself in exaggerated form all the defects of that celebrated composer and none of his qualities.'*

Adolphe Adam, in *Lettres sur la musique française,* on Berlioz

## Berlioz's operas of the imagination

Hector Berlioz was surely the finest French dramatic composer of the nineteenth century. However, if the social and musical conditions in Paris were ideal for Rossini, they were hostile to Berlioz's deeply serious attitude to musical drama; it was nearly impossible for him to arrange performances of the operas he wanted to write. He admired Gluck, Weber and Spontini – whose work was far removed from the 'cheap sensationalism' of the Opéra – and in trying to follow their example he took refuge in non-operatic forms. The *Symphonie fantastique* ('Episodes in the life of an artist') is highly dramatic: the March to the Scaffold (in which the hero dreams he has killed his beloved, is condemned, led to the guillotine and witnesses his own execution), was taken without alteration from an earlier opera, *Les francs juges* (1825), of which only fragments survive. As Berlioz himself said, the written programme of the symphony functions like the spoken dialogue in an opera in that 'it provides the motivation and explains and justifies the mood of the successive movements'. *Roméo et Juliette* (1839) is written for voices and chorus, but, except for the character of Friar Lawrence, they are used only tonarrate the action, and the depiction of the lovers is entirely orchestral.
*La Damnation de Faust* (1846) is written in dramatic form, complete with stage directions, but was intended for concert performance. All three works can be seen as operas of the imagination, attempts to fuse opera with the symphonic tradition, and they were to prove as influential as the three operas Berlioz did complete, *Benvenuto Cellini* (1838), *Béatrice et Bénédict* (1862) and *Les Troyens* (1858), the last of which never received a complete performance in the composer's lifetime.

The final scene of Hérold's *Zampa*, where the wicked pirate Zampa is seized by the ghost of the girl he has seduced and abandoned, to be dragged into the abyss. The print shows the 1832 Vienna production, staged a year after the Paris première.

*3 May* Première of ***Zampa, ou La Fiancée de marbre*** (Hérold/Mélesville) at the Opéra-Comique, Paris, starring Chollet. This ghoulish French variation on Weber's romanticism was, with ***Le Pré aux clercs***, Hérold's most lasting success.
*20 June* Première of ***Le Philtre*** (Auber/Scribe) at the Opéra, Paris. The libretto, a parody of the legend of Tristan and Iseult, was later adapted by Romani for Donizetti's ***L'elisir d'amore*** (see 1832).
*1 September* Donizetti's ***Anna Bolena*** was performed at the Théâtre-Italien with Pasta in the title role: the first Donizetti opera to be given in Paris.
*21 November* Première of ***Robert le diable*** (Meyerbeer/Scribe and Delavigne) at the Opéra, Paris. Meyerbeer's first French opera, it took the city by storm, although it had taken five months of rehearsals at the composer's expense to perfect both the score and the performance. The original cast included Dorus-Gras, Cinti-Damoreau, Nourrit, Levasseur and, in the mimed role of the Abbess, the great ballerina Marie Taglioni; the sets were by Cicéri. The opera was also an immediate success abroad, and rival productions opened in London within three months in different versions and with different titles – at Covent Garden on 20 February 1832 and at Drury Lane the following night.
*26 December* Première of ***Norma*** (Bellini/Romani after Soumet) at La

Painting of the last act trio, 'Que faut-il faire?' from Meyerbeer's *Robert le diable* (1831) with Nicolas Levasseur as Bertram, Adolphe Nourrit as Robert and Cornélie Falcon as Alice. The two men had created these roles, while Falcon had made her début at the Opéra in 1832 in the part created by Dorus-Gras. In the opera Robert is torn between his love for Princess Isabella and the temptation to commit evil deeds, encouraged by Bertram, who turns out to be both his father and the devil. A conventful of unchaste nuns are in fact ghostly spectres, and having defied his conscience to steal a magic branch which confers wealth, power and immortality, Robert attempts to rape Isabella but is dissuaded by her anguished pleas. In the final act his virtuous half-sister Alice persuades him to reject Bertram's offer of a pact with the devil, and as he prays to heaven for assistance the scene changes to a magnificent cathedral, in which he is finally united with Isabella in marriage. This painting by Lepaulle was a tombola prize at the 1834 Opéra ball where it was won – or bought later – by Nourrit.

Giuditta Pasta as Donizetti's *Anna Bolena*, a role she created in 1830. Delacroix, who considered her controlled expressiveness ideal, wrote that in 1831 'at Milan, she created Norma with extraordinary brilliancy; people no longer talked of la Pasta, but la Norma', though he went on to say that after Malibran had appeared in the same part, it was she who became la Norma.

Scala, Milan, with Pasta in the title role, Giulia Grisi (later a famous Norma) as Adalgisa, Donzelli, and Negrini; the sets were by Sanquirico. After an uncertain first night, which drove the composer to tears, the opera became a great international success, particularly in London, where it was premièred at the Haymarket Theatre on 20 June 1833 with Pasta, Méric-Lalande, Donzelli and Galli.

**1832** *12 May* Première of ***L'elisir d'amore*** (Donizetti/Romani after Scribe) at the Teatro della Canobbiana, Milan, with Dabadie as Nemorino and Giuseppe Frezzolini as Dulcamara. It followed two serious operas Donizetti had already written that year – for Naples and La Scala.
*15 December* Première of ***Le Pré aux clercs*** (Hérold/Planard after Mérimée) at the Opéra-Comique, Paris, the opera regarded as the composer's finest work.

**1833** *2 January* Première of ***Il furioso all'Isola di San Domingo*** (Donizetti/Ferretti after Cervantes) at the Teatro Valle, Rome, the first of four new full-length serious operas by the composer staged in 1833. As with several of his operas at this time, the hero's role is written for a baritone rather than a tenor.
*14 February* Première of ***Caterina di Guisa*** (Coccia/Romani) at La Scala, Milan. The best of thirty-seven operas, many on historical subjects, written by one of the more innovative Italian composers in the age between Paisiello – whose pupil Coccia had been – and Verdi.

Giulia Grisi and Luigi Lablache in the first act of Bellini's *I puritani*. Grisi had made her début in Bologna at the age of seventeen; three years later, in 1823, she was taken on at La Scala (where she sang Adalgisa in the original production of *Norma*). She broke her contract in 1832 to join the company at the Théâtre-Italien in Paris, where she sang until 1849, also appearing regularly in London from 1834 to 1861 and making her last appearance there (as Lucrezia Borgia) in 1866. She was a great beauty and had a superb voice – pure *bel canto* as opposed to the expressive qualities of Pasta and Malibran. Lablache spent his early career in Naples and made his début at La Scala in 1817 in Rossini's *La Cenerentola*. He was a regular performer in London and Paris from 1830 to 1856.

*27 February* Première of ***Gustave III, ou Le Bal masqué*** (Auber/Scribe) at the Opéra, Paris. The work (to a libretto rejected by Rossini) was a great international success everywhere – except in Sweden – and achieved its 100th performance at the Opéra by 4 January 1837.
*16 March* Première of ***Beatrice di Tenda*** (Bellini/Romani) at La Fenice, Venice. Romani was slow in producing the libretto and Bellini brought police proceedings against him, which created a lasting breach between them. It was also the last role the composer created for Pasta; having always had problems with intonation, her voice was now failing, although, unwisely, she continued to perform for a number of years.
*17 March* Première of ***Parisina d'Este*** (Donizetti/Romani after Byron) at the Teatro della Pergola, Florence, the composer's favourite of all his operas. In the finest scene the jealous Azzo hears his wife utter her lover's name in her dreams and furiously awakens her.
*24 May* Première of ***Hans Heiling*** (Marschner/Devrient) at the Opernhaus, Berlin, the most successful opera of German national character before Wagner.
*9 September* Première of ***Torquato Tasso*** (Donizetti/Ferretti) at the Teatro Valle, Rome. In this *opera semiseria* (with rather inappropriate comic elements) the hero's role was again written for a baritone, after the tenor Rubini had turned it down.
*18 November* Inaugural performance of Rossini's ***La gazza ladra*** at the Italian Opera House in New York, the first theatre in the city built specifically for opera. The first season, jointly promoted by Lorenzo da Ponte and Chevalier Riva-Finoli, was poorly supported and only one more season was put on there.
*26 December* Première of ***Lucrezia Borgia*** (Donizetti/Romani after Hugo) at La Scala, Milan, with Méric-Lalande, Luciano Mariani and Marietta Brambilla. The opera, one of Donizetti's most lasting successes, ran into difficulties with the censors because of its political implications – it revolves around a conspiracy against an unpopular ruler – and was performed under a number of different titles. After its first Paris performance at the Théâtre-Italien on 27 October 1840 Victor Hugo sued successfully for infringment of his rights, and the scene of the opera, now entitled ***La rinnegata***, was changed to Turkey. Performances were never permitted in Naples during the composer's lifetime.

**1834** *13 January* Première of ***Das Nachtlager in Granada*** (Kreutzer/Braun von Braunthal after Kind) at the Josefstadt Theater, Vienna. This romantic *singspiel* is the most lasting work by Conradin Kreutzer (not to be confused with the Frenchman Rodolphe Kreutzer), who was music director of several Viennese theatres during the 1820s and 1830s.
*15 May* Malibran's La Scala début: as Norma.

## Opera in New Orleans

John Davis and James Caldwell, two rival impresarios, were responsible for the revival of opera in New Orleans, an important centre for French opera until the war of 1812–14; they made the city America's operatic capital for over twenty years. Davis had built the Orleans Theatre in 1819 and continued to concentrate on the French repertoire, while Caldwell brought his Virginia company to the city in 1820, at first sharing Davis's theatre but moving to the Camp Street Theatre in 1824. From that year Davis began to take his company on the road, and until 1833 they provided the northern cities of New York, Philadelphia, Boston and Baltimore with their main experience of European opera. Meanwhile, Caldwell continued to promote the cause of opera in English, including versions of Mozart's *Le nozze di Figaro*, Rossini's *La Cenerentola*, Weber's *Der Freischütz* and Auber's *Fra Diavolo*. After the competing versions of Meyerbeer's *Robert le diable* in 1835, Caldwell stepped up his enterprise by bringing over Italian companies, who made a tremendous impression with several of Bellini's operas and Donizetti's *Lucia di Lammermoor*, while the climax of Davis's activity was a production of *Les Huguenots*, which opened on 30 April 1839.

*25 September* Première of ***Le Châlet*** (Adam/Scribe and Mélesville) at the Opéra-Comique, Paris, Adam's first and greatest hit (its 1000th performance at the Opéra-Comique took place on 5 February 1873). Donizetti's ***Betly, ossia La capanna svizzera*** (1836) was also based on Scribe's libretto.

**1835** *24 January* Première of ***I puritani di Scozia*** (Bellini/Pepoli after a play by Ancelot and Saintine taken originally from Scott) at the Théâtre-Italien, Paris, with Grisi, Rubini, Tamburini and Lablache. In Bellini's last opera, set in Plymouth (which the librettist located in Scotland), the absence of Romani's hand in the libretto is clearly noticeable, but the composer adopted a more monumental style to suit a work commissioned for Paris, and the score contains some wonderful music, especially the celebrated quartet 'A te, o cara'. The four singers in the original cast became known as the 'Puritani Quartet' and held opera managers to ransom by refusing to appear unless all four of them (Rubini was later replaced by Grisi's husband, Mario) were engaged.
*23 February* Première of ***La Juive*** (Halévy/Scribe) at the Opéra, Paris, with Dorus-Gras, Falcon, Nourrit and Levasseur. The work (to another libretto Rossini had turned down) was the composer's only lasting success. Nourrit was responsible for the role of the father being given to a tenor and is supposed to have written the words for Eléazar's aria 'Rachel! Quand du seigneur'. Halévy's most successful comic opera, ***L'Eclair***, was premièred the same year at the Opéra-Comique.
*12 March* Première of ***Marino Faliero*** (Donizetti/Bidera after Delavigne and Byron) at the Théâtre-Italien, Paris. The first opera commissioned from Donizetti for the French capital, it was eclipsed by the success of Bellini's last compositions – and was not one of Donizetti's best works.
*30 March* First performance of ***Robert le diable*** in New Orleans by James Caldwell's American company (in a double bill with 'Jump Jim Crow'). A rival French production by John Davis followed on 12 May.
*July* Giuseppe Verdi conducted a run of Rossini's ***La Cenerentola*** in Milan, after his first conducting engagement – as a last-minute stand-in at a performance of Haydn's *Creation* in April 1834 – had brought him to the attention of the Milanese musical world.
*23 September* Death of Bellini at Puteaux near Paris.
*26 September* Première of ***Lucia di Lammermoor*** (Donizetti/Cammarano after Scott) at San Carlo, Naples, written on the composer's return from Paris specifically for Fanny Persiani as Lucia and Gilbert-Louis Duprez as Edgardo. The story had been utilized in 1829 for an opera by Carafa and in 1832 by H. C. Andersen in a libretto for Bredal, but Donizetti's opera become one of the masterpieces of Italian romantic opera: the mad scene for the heroine with flute obbligato is one of the great *bel canto* set pieces.
*28 September* Première of ***Askol'dova mogila*** [***Askold's Grave***] (Verstovsky/Zagoskin) at the Bolshoi Theatre, Moscow. Verstovsky, who was heavily indebted to Weber, tried to integrate Russian themes into a mainstream romantic opera, which proved an enormous success in Russia.
*29 October* Première of ***The Siege of Rochelle*** (Balfe/Fitzball after de Genlis) at Drury Lane, London. Balfe had been engaged as a singer at the Théâtre-Italien in Paris and had produced his first opera, ***I rivali di se stessi***, in Palermo, where he was the principal baritone in the 1829–30 season. Following the success of ***The Siege of Rochelle*** he tried to establish an English opera in London, but thwarted by quarrels and intrigues he returned to Paris.
*30 December* Première of ***Maria Stuarda*** (Donizetti/Bardari after Schiller) at La Scala, Milan, with Malibran in the title role. An earlier version, altered to take account of censorship in Naples and titled ***Buondelmonte*** had been performed at San Carlo on 18 October 1834.

Fanny Persiani as Lucia in Donizetti's *Lucia di Lammermoor*, the role she created in 1835. She specialized in parts that demanded the light, agile *coloratura* of which she had such brilliant command, and the part of Lucia was tailored by the composer to the character and flexibility of her voice.

'I saw *La Juive* at the Grand Opera... and I say that I saw it because as for popular music it has none. Illusion is carried to the extreme...You would swear that everything is real. Real silver and cardinals who are almost real. The king's armoury real, the costumes of the armed men, doublets, lances etc. real; and those which were false – the doublets of the extras – were copied from real ones and cost 1,500 francs each. Too much truth...the final scene too horrible because of so much illusion. At Constance a Jewess, because of her relations with a Christian, is thrown with her father into a cauldron of boiling oil. Before it comes to that, we go through a thousand surprises, but everything is rich and everything is magnificent – if one closes one eye.'

Donizetti writing to a friend

# 1836
# 1841

# Successors to Rossini

*The mantle of Rossini, who wrote no more operas after* Guillaume Tell, *was assumed jointly by Bellini (until his death in 1835), Meyerbeer and Donizetti. However, the late 1830s saw the emergence of two young composers, Richard Wagner and Giuseppe Verdi, who would revolutionize and divide the operatic world.*

One of the sets for Louise Bertin's *Esméralda* (1836), each of which depicted the cathedral of Notre-Dame from a different angle. Although the press was universal in its praise for Charles Cambon's designs, they failed to satisfy Victor Hugo, the author of the libretto and of the novel on which it was based. Bertin was the daughter of the proprietor of the influential *Journal des débats*, for which Berlioz wrote music criticism.

**DATES**

**1836**
Independence of Texas from Mexico
**1837**
Victoria comes to the British throne
Death of Alexander Pushkin in a duel
**1838**
Louis Daguerre takes his first photographs

**1836** *29 February* Première of ***Les Huguenots*** (Meyerbeer/Scribe and Deschamps) at the Opéra, Paris, with Falcon, Dorus-Gras, Nourrit and Levasseur. It was the composer's most successful work, although censorship created problems in many cities: in Vienna (where the opera was not performed until 1839) all religious references were removed and it was entitled ***Die Gibellinen in Pisa.***
*29 March* Première of ***Das Liebesverbot, oder Die Novize von Palermo*** (Wagner/composer after Shakespeare's *Measure for Measure*) at the Stadttheater, Magdeburg. The opera was taken off after one performance.
*23 September* Death of Maria Malibran. Delacroix, comparing her passion and spontaneity to the calculated dignity of Pasta, wrote that 'she achieved moments full of energy and seemingly full of truth, but it also happened that she would seem exaggerated and faulty in her timing, and as a consequence unbearable. I do not recall ever having seen her *noble*.'
*13 October* Première of ***Le Postillon de Longjumeau*** (Adam/Brunswick and de Leuven) at the Opéra-Comique, Paris, with a cast headed by Jean-Baptiste Chollet.
*14 November* Première of ***Esméralda*** (Bertin/Hugo) at the Opéra, Paris. Hugo based the libretto on his own novel *Notre-Dame de Paris* (1831). Berlioz had wanted to turn this into an opera, but deferred to Louise Bertin and even supervised the rehearsals of her work, although this met with little success. The subject was later used in at least seven more operas.

Pauline Viardot and Marietta Alboni in a London production of Meyerbeer's *Les Huguenots* during the 1840s. Pauline, the younger of Manuel Garcia's daughters, played several of the roles with which her sister, Maria Malibran, had been identified, including Desdemona in Rossini's *Otello* (her début role in 1837 in Brussels) and *Norma*. She married the director of the Théâtre-Italien, Louis Viardot, in 1841 and was later important both as a highly intelligent singer and a patron of young composers. Alboni was one of the great operatic stars of the mid-century, though her size led Rossini to compare her to 'an elephant which has swallowed a nightingale'.

Music cover showing Jenny Lind in the title role of Donizetti's *La Fille du régiment*, one of her most famous roles.

## Meyerbeer

Giacomo Meyerbeer (born Jakob Beer) was the phenomenon of French grand opera. After trying out both German and Italian opera, like Gluck in the previous century, he found his true self in his French works, which formed a synthesis of the styles then current in Paris: the melodic ease derives from Rossini, the monumentality is in the tradition that led from Gluck through the revolutionary composers to Spontini, while the historic subjects in Scribe's libretti and the lavish settings and scenic effects designed by Cicéri and his successors followed in the wake of the spectacular operas of Boieldieu, Hérold and Auber. There was a sensationalism that appealed to the opera-going public and a musical technique that won praise from such stern critics as Berlioz and Wagner. Schumann, however, attacked both the pretensions and commercialism of Meyerbeer's operas, and, viewed from a modern perspective, it is clear that they depended too much on their calculated climactic tableaux without providing either the singers' showpieces or the musical qualities of his great Italian contemporaries. Delacroix wrote perceptively of *Les Huguenots* after the magic had begun to wear off: 'It occurs to me that he is too much taken up with local colour...the increasing heaviness of his work, and the bizarre quality in the singing derive in large part from this exaggeration in his interest.'

Design for the hero's costume in the carnival scene of Berlioz's *Benvenuto Cellini*. The role was sung at the première – unwillingly – by Gilbert-Louis Duprez.

*'Initiated into all the secrets of Italian song and German harmony, the composer has delved deep into those of Russian melody. Richly talented, he has proved with his brilliant enterprise that Russian melody, whose nature seems at one moment sad, at another cheerful, at another quite uninhibited, can be elevated to a tragic style. With Glinka's opera...a new period is initiated in the history of art: the period of Russian music.'*

Prince Vladimir Odoyevsky on Glinka's *A Life for the Tsar*

Gilbert-Louis Duprez as Polyeucte, the role he created in Donizetti's *Les Martyrs* at the Opéra in 1840. Duprez had taken Nourrit's place as leading tenor at the Opéra in 1837 after spending more than ten years singing in Italy. He was celebrated for his ringing high C produced with full chest voice (which was not to Rossini's liking when he sang Arnold in *Guillaume Tell*, his first role at the Opéra), but his career as a singer was quite short and he later turned to teaching and composition.

*19 November* Première of ***L'assedio di Calais*** (Donizetti/Cammarano) at San Carlo, Naples, his third new opera that year. The work was written in the French style with a full-length ballet in an attempt to attract a commission from the Opéra.
*9 December* Première of ***Zhizn za tsarya*** [***A Life for the Tsar***] (Glinka/Rozen) as the inaugural performance in a rebuilt Bolshoi Theatre, St Petersburg. The music reflects the cosmopolitan nature of Russian society at the time, combining Russian folksong and Viennese dance music with the Italian melodic style of Rossini and Bellini. Nevertheless, its national character was considered too strong by the westernizing clique at the Russian court.

**1837** *11 March* Première of ***Il giuramento*** (Mercadante/Rossi after Hugo) at La Scala, Milan; one of several successes the composer had at this period and generally considered to be his finest opera.
*23 August* Première of ***La double échelle*** (Thomas/Planard) at the Opéra-Comique, Paris. It was the composer's first opera and a marked success, although it was followed by a succession of less successful *opéras-comiques*.
*29 October* Première of ***Roberto Devereux, Conte d'Essex*** (Donizetti/Cammarano after Ancelot) at San Carlo, Naples, the last opera the composer wrote for the city. A number of circumstances – the death of his wife, the censor's ban on ***Poliuto*** because of its religious subject matter and a contract to write two operas for the Paris Opéra – contributed to Donizetti's decision to move to Paris.
*22 December* Première of ***Zar und Zimmermann, oder Die zwei Peter*** (Lortzing/composer after Mélesville, Merle and Cantiran de Boirie, 1818) at the Stadttheater, Leipzig. This comic, satirical treatment of the story of Peter the Great working in the shipyards became one of the most frequently performed of all operas.

**1838** *7 March* Début of Jenny Lind as Agathe in ***Der Freischütz*** in Stockholm. The 'Swedish nightingale' went on to become one of the most celebrated singers of the Victorian age.
*10 September* Première of ***Benvenuto Cellini*** (Berlioz/Wailly and A. Barbier) at the Opéra, Paris, with Duprez, Dorus-Gras and Stoltz. A hostile reception at the opera's première led to Duprez's departure after only three performances, and the composer faced opposition from the management, and the musicians, who sabotaged several performances; twenty-nine rehearsals were followed by only seven performances. The opera was revived by Liszt in Weimar in 1852.

**1839** *6 August* Production of a French version of Donizetti's ***Lucia di Lammermoor*** adapted by the composer (who had arrived in Paris the previous October) for the Théâtre de la Renaissance. He also wrote ***L'Ange de Nisida*** for the same theatre, but this closed and, as the management of the Opéra had rejected his partly composed ***Le Duc d'Albe***, he rewrote the new work for the Opéra to a partly new libretto as ***La Favorite***.
*17 November* Première of ***Oberto, conte di San Bonifacio*** (Verdi/Piazza, revised by Merelli and Solera) at La Scala, Milan. This was Verdi's first opera, though it may have been based on an earlier operatic composition, ***Rocester***, started in 1836. Its favourable reception led Merelli to offer Verdi a three-opera contract for La Scala. Ricordi published the score, thus enabling the composer to settle in Milan.
*24 November* First of three performances at the Paris Conservatoire of Berlioz's 'dramatic symphony' ***Roméo et Juliette***, conducted by the composer.

## Donizetti

Donizetti, a native of Bergamo, where he studied with Simon Mayr, was the first young composer to make a mark at a time when Rossini dominated the operatic scene in Italy; the music of his early operas is cast very much in Rossini's mould. In 1822 he came to the notice of Barbaia, who brought him to Naples, where he composed a succession of operas in all the current genres. Although he wrote several very witty *buffo* operas, his style was best suited to works with highly dramatic situations, violent conflicts, pathetic mad scenes and tragic deaths, but he was hampered in Naples by the strict censorship imposed by a shaky régime, and it was only with the production in Milan of his thirtieth opera, *Anna Bolena*, in 1830 (which gave him his first opportunity to work with Felice Romani), that his tragic gifts were given free rein. Thereafter he wrote a succession of works for Naples, Milan, Venice, Paris and Vienna, mostly in the genre of romantic *melodramma* but including two brilliant comedies, *L'elisir d'amore* and *Don Pasquale*. He came to be regarded – together with Bellini – as the successor to Rossini, whose last opera had been written in 1829. Donizetti was astonishingly prolific, writing over seventy operas in his twenty-five-year career.

Self-caricature of Donizetti in 1841, when he was living in Paris.

Eugène Scribe, the most prolific of all French librettists. Composers with whom he collaborated included Boieldieu, Cherubini, Rossini, Donizetti, Hérold, Halévy, Balfe, Adam, Thomas and Verdi. His most long-standing association was with Auber and the one that added most lustre to his name that with Meyerbeer. He worked with Berlioz on *La Nonne sanglante*, commissioned by the Opéra, from 1841 to 1846, but it was never realized. Neither Verdi nor Halévy were prepared to set the libretto, which was eventually composed by Gounod.

**1840** *11 February* Première of ***La Fille du régiment*** (Donizetti/Saint-Georges and Bayard) at the Opéra-Comique, Paris. The composer adapted his style so successfully in this, his first French opera, that the work has come to be seen as the quintessential *opéra-comique*, especially Marie's air in Act II, 'Salut à la France'. In the autumn, Donizetti travelled to Milan to arrange the Italian version of the work, premièred at La Scala on 3 October. Its London première (in Italian) was at Her Majesty's Theatre on 27 May 1847, starring Jenny Lind.
*10 April* Première of ***Les Martyrs*** (Donizetti/Scribe) at the Opéra, Paris, with Dorus-Gras and Duprez. The original version, ***Poliuto*** (libretto by Cammarano after Corneille), had been composed in 1838 with the leading role written for Nourrit – who had moved to Naples in 1837 after Duprez had joined the Opéra – but it was banned by the censor, probably because of Nourrit's reputation as a radical as much as for its sacred subject.
*23 June* Première of ***Hans Sachs*** (Lortzing/after Deinhardstein) at the Stadttheater, Leipzig. The operetta anticipates Wagner's ***Die Meistersinger*** in both subject matter and in its characterization of the hero.
*5 September* Première of ***Un giorno di regno, ossia Il finto Stanislao*** (Verdi/Romani) at La Scala, Milan. The *buffo* libretto had previously been set by Gyrowetz (in 1818) and this was the first of the operas in Verdi's contract with Merelli. Tragically, his wife and child died during the composition of the work, and its – undeserved – failure determined Verdi to abandon opera composition.
*29 November* Première of ***Saffo*** (Pacini/Cammarano) at San Carlo, Naples, the composer's most important work. Marietta Alboni, one of the great contraltos of the century, made her début in the title role in a revival of the opera in Bologna in 1842.
*2 December* Première of ***La Favorite*** (Donizetti/Royer and Vaëz, revised by Scribe, after Baculard d'Arnaud) at the Opéra, Paris. The leading roles were sung by Rosine Stoltz, current star of the Opéra (and mistress of its director), Duprez and Levasseur, while the ballet starred Carlotta Grisi, the singer's cousin. It was the work originally written as ***L'Ange de Nisida*** for the Théâtre de la Renaissance.

**1841** *26 December* Première of ***Maria Padilla*** (Donizetti/Rossi after Ancelot) at La Scala, Milan, for the opening of the carnival season.

# 1842 1850 Verdi and Wagner

*The two composers whose work would dominate the operatic world in the second half of the nineteenth century were both born in 1813 – Wagner was four and a half months older – and both came to prominence in the decade before 1850. While Wagner embodied the ideals of the movement for German national opera, Verdi gave a new dimension to the Italian tradition with the deep psychological insight of his music.*

**DATES**

**1844**
Dumas père's *Le Comte de Monte Cristo* published

**1847**
Start of the first California gold rush

**1848**
Insurrection in Paris forces abdication of Louis-Philippe

Austrians expelled from Milan in the 'cinque giornate' of March

Uprisings in Vienna, Berlin and Venice

Murger's *Scènes de la vie de Bohème* published

**1849**
Rome proclaimed a republic

Uprisings in Dresden and Baden

**1842** *9 March* Première of ***Nabucco (Nabucodonosor)*** (Verdi/Solera) at La Scala, Milan. Merelli used a ruse to get Verdi to return to operatic composition, and the work became a colossal success. Features that were to be typical of Verdi's later compositions were the dramatic use of the chorus (especially in the celebrated 'Va pensiero, sull'ali dorate') and the father-daughter/ baritone-soprano relationship.
*19 May* Première of ***Linda di Chamounix*** (Donizetti/Rossi) at the Kärntnertortheater, Vienna, with Eugenia Tadolini, Marietta Brambilla, Napoleone Moriani and Felice Varesi, all later to be celebrated as Verdi singers. It was the first of two operas the composer wrote for Vienna after he had accepted an offer from Merelli (co-director of the theatre in Vienna as well as of La Scala) to become director of the Italian season (April–June) there. Meyerbeer was appointed Generalmusikdirektor at the Berlin Opernhaus, replacing Spontini, who returned to Paris to intrigue against his successor. The German composer remained in Berlin until 1847 and his productions included Gluck's ***Armide***, Spohr's ***Faust*** and Wagner's ***Der fliegende Holländer*** as well as ***Les Huguenots*** and a new German opera of his own.
*20 October* Première of ***Cola Rienzi, der letzte der Tribunen (Rienzi)*** (Wagner/composer after Bulwer-Lytton) at the Hofoper, Dresden.
*9 December* Première of ***Ruslan i Lyudmila*** (Glinka/Shirkov and others after Pushkin) at the Bolshoi Theatre, St Petersburg. The libretto was originally to have been written by Pushkin himself, but after his death in a duel it was put together by various hands. Both text and music incorporate folk material, and the opera is in a more personal style than Glinka's earlier opera, but its national character again offended the court, so that its initial success was modest.
*31 December* Première of ***Der Wildschütz, oder Die Stimme der Natur*** (Lortzing/composer after Kotzebue) at the Stadttheater, Leipzig, a Weberian romantic opera inspired by the German countryside.

**1843** *2 January* Première of ***Der fliegende Holländer*** (Wagner/composer after Heine et al.) at the Hofoper, Dresden, with Schröder-Devrient as Senta, Karl Risse as Daland and Johann Michael Wächter as the Dutchman.

Giuseppina Strepponi, with the score of Verdi's *Nabucco*. She had helped to arrange a performance of Verdi's first opera, *Oberto*, at La Scala in 1839. She sang the role of Abigaille in *Nabucco*, the opera which established his reputation, in March 1842 (although the composer was opposed to her taking the part). She was later to become Verdi's companion, living with him from 1848 and marrying him in 1859.

# Der fliegende Holländer, Tannhäuser, Lohengrin

Wagner's early musical career as a conductor gave him an intimate familiarity with the operatic repertory, and his first works show influences as varied as Weber, Bellini and Meyerbeer. However, in the three operas that followed Wagner was determined to use truly German subjects and to find a style suited to his developing conception of the future of German opera. *Der fliegende Holländer* is set in a mood of romantic gloom reminiscent of Spohr's *Faust* or Marschner's *Der Vampyr*, but the story of the captain of the phantom ship condemned to sail the seas until redeemed by a woman's love is made more powerful by the strength and vividness of the orchestration – the overture immediately suggests the overwhelming force of the ocean – and also by the composer's tendency to break down the traditional elements of opera (recitative, aria, chorus, ensemble) to make a more coherent dramatic flow.

Both *Tannhäuser* and *Lohengrin* are set in the middle ages, but their mood is quite different from the misty Gothic legends that had been the stuff of so many Italian romantic operas. In the Nordic medieval myths Wagner had found the world in which his dramas of power, love, renunciation and death could be played out. With each opera the music became more seamless, and he began to introduce leitmotifs: fragments of melody associated with individual characters or with the overriding themes of the drama. In *Lohengrin* the most pervasive leitmotif is that of the Unanswered Question.

Scene from the 1843 revival of Wagner's *Rienzi* in Dresden, whose cast included Josef Tichatschek and Henriette Kriete (replacing Wilhelmine Schröder-Devrient, who had sung in the première). The work, a grand opera in the manner of Meyerbeer, was intended for Paris, but, despite Meyerbeer's support, was rejected by the Opéra administration. It was well received in Dresden, where it was generally performed over two evenings, but had only modest success elsewhere.

Design for one of the original sets for Wagner's *Der fliegende Holländer*, 1843.

Gilbert-Louis Duprez and Rosine Stoltz in Act II of the first production of Donizetti's last opera *Don Sébastien*, 1843.

*3 January* Première of ***Don Pasquale*** (Donizetti/composer and Ruffini after Anelli) at the Théâtre-Italien, Paris, with Grisi, Mario, Tamburini and Lablache. The first performance in Italy followed at La Scala on 17 April 1843.
*11 February* Première of ***I lombardi alla prima crociata*** (Verdi/Solera after Grossi) at La Scala, Milan, with Erminia Frezzolini as Giselda. Verdi supplied several new numbers, including a ballet, for the première in Paris (26 November 1847), where it was known as ***Jérusalem.***
*5 March* Revival of Gluck's ***Armide*** at the Hofoper, Dresden, conducted by Wagner. In February 1847 he also put on his own version of ***Iphigénie en Aulide***, reorchestrated and with new recitatives.
*5 June* Première of ***Maria di Rohan*** (Donizetti/Cammarano) at the Kärntnertortheater, Vienna. The title role in an exceptionally melodramatic plot was written for Tadolini.
*13 November* Première of ***Don Sébastien, roi de Portugal*** (Donizetti/Scribe) at the Opéra, Paris, the last opera that Donizetti wrote. ***Caterina Cornaro***, completed a few months earlier, had its première at San Carlo, Naples, two months later.
*27 November* Première of ***The Bohemian Girl*** (Balfe/Bunn after Saint-Georges) at Drury Lane, London, the most successful English opera of the first half of the nineteenth century and the only one to gain international renown. Its American première at New York's Park Theatre on 25 November 1844 was a groundbreaking event for opera in America, as the work achieved a popularity that won a whole new audience for the medium.

**1844** *27 January* Première of ***Hunyadi László*** (Erkel/Egressy after Tóth) in Budapest, a work which became Hungary's national opera.
*12 February* Rossini's ***La Cenerentola***, played in Sydney in an English translation, was the first opera to be performed in Australia.
*9 March* Première of ***Ernani*** (Verdi/Piave after Hugo) at La Fenice, Venice, the first of nine works Verdi wrote in collaboration with Francesco Maria Piave. The scale of the opera was governed by the smaller theatre for which it was written, enabling the composer to put more emphasis on the individual characters than on building up grand dramatic effects with chorus and orchestra. The opera made Verdi's name and from November 1844 to July 1847 he composed six more: a period he referred to as his 'years in the galleys'.
*3 November* Première of ***I due Foscari*** (Verdi/Piave after Byron) at the Teatro Argentina, Rome. The opera is notable for Verdi's device of using a specific theme for each character, played each time they appear.
*7 December* Reopening of the Berlin Opernhaus, closed by fire the previous year, with ***Ein Feldlager in Schlesien*** (Meyerbeer/Rellstab), the composer's last German opera. Retitled ***Vielka***, its title role offered Jenny Lind an opportunity for one of her first great successes when she sang it at the Theater an der Wien, Vienna (18 February 1847).

Schröder-Devrient and Tichatschek as Venus and Tannhäuser in the first production of Wagner's opera at the Dresden Hofoper in 1845. The roles of Elisabeth and Wolfram were sung by Johanna Wagner and Anton Mitterwurzer.

**1845** *15 February* Première of ***Giovanna d'Arco*** (Verdi/Solera after Schiller) at La Scala, Milan, in which the composer returned to the epic scale, writing the title-role for the soprano Erminia Frezzolini, one of the outstanding interpreters of his music. ***Alzira***, premièred at San Carlo, Naples, in August, was one of the composer's least successful works.
*4 June* Première of ***Leonora*** (Fry/J. R. Fry after Bulwer-Lytton) at the Chestnut Street Theatre, Philadelphia; the first publicly performed grand opera by a native-born American.
*19 October* Première of ***Tannhäuser und der Sängerkrieg auf Wartburg*** (Wagner/composer) at the Hofoper, Dresden.

**1846** *17 March* Première of ***Attila*** (Verdi/Solera and Piave) at La Fenice,

Set for Act II of Verdi's *Giovanna d'Arco* (1845) at La Scala with Giuseppe Bertoja's fanciful re-creation of Rheims cathedral.

## Verdi's early operas

The uncompromising nature of Verdi's personality shines through the story of the composer's early life and career. He was, to start with, a reluctant opera composer, and after his first success with *Ernani* he resented the constant demands for new compositions; nevertheless, each new work enlarged the boundaries of operatic form. The overriding principle of his method of composition was truth to the dramatic situation, while his greatest gift was for the musical delineation of character with an insight that only Mozart among his predecessors had ever achieved. In *Ernani*, where the heroine Elvira is loved by tenor, baritone and bass, the tragic dénouement is brought about by Ernani's promise to kill himself if he hears Silva sound his horn. Verdi was pressed by the soprano Sofie Löwe to end the opera with the customary solo *scena* for the heroine, but he insisted on concluding with a final trio after the horn call to preserve the dramatic integrity of the work. *Macbeth* gives an even clearer insight into his way of working: he knew precisely what he wanted from his libretto, and his copious correspondence with Piave shows his determination that everything should be exactly right. For the role of Lady Macbeth he rejected a soprano who sang 'too perfectly', because he wanted a 'rough, hollow, stifled' voice and he insisted that her two big scenes 'must not be sung at all: they must be acted and declaimed in a voice that is hollow and veiled'. Rehearsals for the opera were endless; it took three months to perfect the sleepwalking scene, which is the masterpiece of the opera.

Costume design in Egyptian style for Auber's biblical opera *L'Enfant prodigue*, which enjoyed international success in the years following its première at the Paris Opéra in 1850.

Scene from William Wallace's *Maritana* (libretto by Fitzball) premièred at the Drury Lane Theatre, London, on 15 November 1845. The opera was a great success on English stages throughout the world, though it made little impact elsewhere.

'She can read any piece at sight. Her voice is a little harsh in the high register, and a little weak in the low, but by dint of study she has managed to make it so flexible in the high register that she can overcome the most incredible difficulties. Her trills are matchless, she has unequalled agility, and she generally shows off her technical skill with *fioriture*, *gruppetti* and trills: things which went well in the last century, but not in 1847... Her face is ugly, serious and somewhat Nordic, which I find unpleasant, and she has a very large nose, very large hands and feet...'

Muzio on Jenny Lind

'Who could describe those long notes, drawn out until they quite melt away; that shake which becomes softer and softer; those very piano- and flute-like notes, and those round, fresh tones that are so youthful?'

Queen Victoria on Lind's *Amina* at Her Majesty's in the last of her three operatic seasons in London (1849)

Venice. After supervising the première of the opera Verdi suffered a nervous collapse.
*12 May* Première of ***Liden Kirsten*** [***Little Cristina***] (J. P. E. Hartmann/H. C. Andersen) in Copenhagen. The opera, based on one of Andersen's own stories, was a lasting success in Denmark.
*30 May* Première of ***Der Waffenschmied*** (Lortzing/after von Ziegler) at the Theater an der Wien, Vienna, where the composer was appointed Kapellmeister the same year.
*6 December* Concert première of ***La Damnation de Faust*** (Berlioz/composer and Gandonnière after Nerval and Goethe) at the Opéra-Comique, Paris. Despite Gustave Roger in the role of Faust, the two performances of the work went virtually unnoticed. Berlioz's 'dramatic legend' incorporates (in highly revised form) much of the composer's *Eight Scenes from Faust* written in 1828–9, and he considered preparing an operatic version (for the intended 1848–9 season of Jullien's Drury Lane company), but the work remains an 'opera of the imagination'. The first stage production of the work was by Raoul Gunsbourg at Monte Carlo in 1893.

**1847** *14 March* Première of ***Macbeth*** (Verdi/Piave and Maffei after Shakespeare) at the Teatro della Pergola, Florence. The title role was sung by Felice Varesi and the role of Lady Macbeth by Marianna Barbieri-Nini.
*Spring* The Royal Italian Opera was established at Covent Garden. Operas performed in the first season included ***Ernani, I due Foscari*** (10 April), ***Maria di Rohan*** (8 May), ***Semiramide*** and ***L'elisir d'amore***, and the singers included Giulia Grisi, Fanny Persiani, Marietta Alboni, Lorenzo Salvi and Agostino Rovere. As a competitive enterprise the promoter Louis-Antoine Jullien tried to establish a Grand English Opera Company at Drury Lane, bringing Berlioz to London as its conductor. They performed ***Lucia di Lammermoor*** and Balfe's ***The Maid of Honour***, but audiences were too sparse and the initiative ended with Jullien's bankruptcy.
*15 April* ***Ernani***, performed by the Havana opera company at the Park Theatre, New York, was the first Verdi opera played in the USA. It was followed in June by ***I due Foscari*** and works by Donizetti. Another visit with works by the same two composers was made in 1850.
*22 July* Première of ***I masnadieri*** (Verdi/Maffei after Schiller) at Her Majesty's Theatre, London, the only opera Verdi wrote for London, and the only one in which Jenny Lind created a role. Lind performed for two further seasons in London and in 1850 made a concert tour of the USA (with no operatic performances) organized by P. T. Barnum, which created a wave of 'Lindomania' in America.
*22 November* Opening of Astor Place Opera House (whose principal lessee was Salvatore Patti, the father of Adelina) with a performance of ***Ernani***.
*25 November* Première of ***Martha, oder Der Markt zu Richmond*** (Flotow/Friedrich) at the Kärntnertortheater, Vienna. The opera owed its enormous popularity to the composer's incorporation of popular airs, including 'The Last Rose of Summer'.

**1848** *8 April* Death of Donizetti in Bergamo.
Liszt took up his appointment as Kapellmeister at Weimar. During his ten years at the Hoftheater he arranged revivals of the operas of Gluck, Mozart, Beethoven and Schubert, and promoted new works by Schumann, Berlioz and Wagner. His 'new German school' was strongly opposed by the conservatives of Dresden and Leipzig.
*25 October* Première of ***Il corsaro*** (Verdi/Piave after Byron) at the Teatro Grande, Trieste.

**1849** *27 January* Première of ***La battaglia di Legnano*** (Verdi/

Cammarano) at the Teatro Argentina, Rome. Since Rome was on the verge of declaring itself a republic, the success of this patriotic opera was guaranteed.
*9 March* Première of ***Die lustigen Weiber von Windsor*** (Nicolai/Mosenthal after Shakespeare) at the Opernhaus, Berlin. This was Nicolai's last and most successful opera, whose flowing, melodic style shows the influence of the years he had spent in Italy.
*16 April* Première of ***Le Prophète*** (Meyerbeer/Scribe) at the Opéra, Paris, with Pauline Viardot (as Fides) and Gustave Roger (as the anabaptist preacher John of Leyden), as well as Castellan and Levasseur. The obligatory ballet was a Dutch skating scene performed on roller-skates (whose music, as *Les Patineurs*, has remained Meyerbeer's best known work). Chopin dragged himself to the première and was horrified – as was Delacroix, who called it 'the annihilation of art'.
*8 December* Première of ***Luisa Miller*** (Verdi/Cammarano after Schiller) at San Carlo, Naples, with Marietta Gazzaniga in the title role.

**1850** *20 April* Première of ***Le Songe d'une nuit d'été*** (Thomas/Rosier and de Leuven) at the Opéra-Comique, Paris. Shakespeare's life is interwoven with themes from *A Midsummer Night's Dream*, and Falstaff and Queen Elizabeth as well as the playwright himself appear among the cast.
*25 June* Première of ***Genoveva*** (Schumann/composer after Tieck and Hebbel) at the Stadttheater, Leipzig. Schumann had considered both *Till Eulenspiegel* and the Nibelung legend as operatic subjects, but finally settled on another medieval story, saddling himself, as Wagner told him, with a very poor libretto. Despite postponements and a first night ruined by an accident, the opera was quite well received; it was revived by Liszt in Weimar in 1855 and maintained its place in repertory in Germany into the 1880s.
*29 July* Bellini's ***La sonnambula*** was the first opera to be performed in Chicago. On its second night Price's Theater caught fire and burned down after Act I.
*28 August* Première of ***Lohengrin*** (Wagner/composer) at the Hoftheater, Weimar, conducted by Liszt. The opera had been written for Dresden, but Wagner was now a political exile in Switzerland, and the cast assembled for the first performance was a very poor one.
*16 November* Première of ***Stiffelio*** (Verdi/Piave after Souvestre and Bourgeois) at the Teatro Grande, Trieste. The modern setting was not liked by the audience and the opera was later rewritten as ***Aroldo*** (see 1857), set in the middle ages.

LOHENGRIN.

Romantische Oper in drei Acten,
(letzter Act in zwei Abtheilungen)
von
RICHARD WAGNER.
Als Manuscript gedruckt.

Title page of the published libretto of Wagner's *Lohengrin*, showing the arrival of the hero in his boat drawn by a swan.

The spinning scene in Act II of Flotow's *Martha* in the original production in 1847 in Vienna, where the opera enjoyed its greatest success.

3

# 1851–1914

# INTERNATIONAL OPERA

*At a time when opera singers, like instrumental virtuosi, were travelling throughout Europe and to America, creating the beginnings of a standard repertory common to the world's leading opera houses, nationalist movements, particularly in Eastern Europe, were encouraging the composition of operas that would reflect local traditions – the rhythms of their dances, their speech patterns, their history and folklore. Verdi and Wagner, now in their maturity, continued to work, in very different ways, towards a more unified operatic form, in which the alternation of recitative and aria would yield to a continuous musical narrative. Wagner's approach was the more radical; for his 'music of the future' he created colossal symphonic structures bound together with fragments of melodic material, leitmotifs, each of which was invested with symbolic significance, so that at a profound level the development of the plot is narrated by the music itself.*

Final scene of Wagner's *Tristan und Isolde*.

# International Opera

Most of the current standard repertory of opera houses around the world is made up of works composed during this period – the best known works of Verdi, Wagner, Puccini and Richard Strauss, as well as *Faust, Carmen* and *Pagliacci* among other familiar operas – yet as one surveys the sequence of compositions and performances it hardly seems like a golden age. For some time Paris remained the centre of the operatic world, but the social performance was becoming increasingly dominant. A ballet had to be included in the second act of any opera staged at the Opéra, so that the members of the Jockey Club need attend only enough of the performance to see the girls of the *corps de ballet* on stage and then meet them in the passage de l'Opéra on rue Peletier at a suitable time to take them off to a *souper intime*; Wagner was not forgiven for placing the ballet he wrote for the Paris production of *Tannhäuser* in Act I. It was a rule of the Opéra that composers could not conduct their own operas, and Berlioz as well as Wagner suffered from the indifference of unsympathetic musicians. However, they were not entirely without friends: Pauline Viardot, the younger daughter of Manuel Garcia, is one of the heroines of the age, a serious and intelligent singer and teacher who gave encouragement and practical support to Gounod and Saint-Saëns as well as to Berlioz and Wagner. Another important figure was Léon Carvalho, who maintained adventurous repertories at the Théâtre-Lyrique and Opéra-Comique. Such efforts sustained the French operatic tradition, embodied by Gounod, Bizet and Massenet, even after the catastrophic end of the Second Empire in 1870.

Wagner's own attitude to opera was, by contrast, a deeply serious one. He not only wanted to compose 'music of the future' but also to create a *Gesamtkunstwerk* – a total work of art – in which every aspect of an opera performance, including the theatre and the audience, would be an expression of the composer's will. Between *Lohengrin* in 1850 and *Tristan und Isolde* in 1865 there was no new Wagner opera, and throughout this period (much of it spent in exile in Switzerland) the composer was writing and composing the great works that were to follow. Once the Bayreuth Festivals began in 1876 Wagner was at last triumphant: almost the whole musical world – Verdi was among the few exceptions – was enthralled.

The sense of national identity proclaimed so forcibly by Wagner, both in his music and his writings, was symptomatic of a dissatisfaction throughout Europe with the old system of European empires that seemed to have been reimposed after

Verdi continued to be a vocal supporter of the movement for the liberation and unification of his country, which now hoped to place Vittorio Emanuele on the Italian throne. Performances of Verdi's operas were sometimes the occasion for public demonstrations, where cries of 'Viva Verdi' stood also for 'Viva Vittorio Emanuele, Re d'Italia'. Here, during the unrest of 1859, the same slogan is written up on the walls of Milan.

the defeat of Napoleon. Verdi's name became a symbol for the movement to free the lands of northern Italy from Austrian rule and unite it with the south. Elsewhere operas with more obviously patriotic themes acted as a focus for national feelings: Erkel's earliest Hungarian operas date from the 1840s, and he was followed by Moniuszko in Poland and Smetana in Czechoslovakia; in every case the music drew extensively on local sources. Russia had enjoyed a long tradition of operatic performances, but the court favoured a policy of cultural assimilation with Western Europe, and the group of nationalist composers – few of whom were professional musicians – wanted to create genuinely Russian operas. Rimsky-Korsakov was the most prolific opera composer, but a more radical work and an undoubted masterpiece was Mussorgsky's *Boris Godunov*.

In Italy, the home of opera, dissatisfaction with tradition led a group who called themselves the *Scapigliati* (unkempt ones) to form a new movement for reform, although, ironically, it was Verdi, one of their principal targets, whose late works matched many of their ideals most closely. Indeed, two of their leaders, Franco Faccio and Arrigo Boito, later became two of Verdi's most trusted collaborators. However, younger composers were caught up with the revolutionary spirit and saw the future not with historical operas but with dramas of the present day. Literary and dramatic realism – as found in the novels of Zola, the plays of Sardou and, later, Belasco, and the stories of the Sicilian Giovanni Verga – were the stimulus for operatic *verismo* (although 'realism' has to be understood in a comparative sense), of which the great master was Puccini.

Operatic performance and operatic audiences before 1850 had been fairly local in scale, but the opening of the US market and the firm establishment of opera as a destination for bourgeois patronage caused changes that altered patterns of performance and, ultimately, changed the nature of opera itself. In 1850 P. T. Barnum promoted a tour for the 'Swedish nightingale', Jenny Lind, throughout the USA. She sang no operas but opened up a new sensibility to operatic music all over America. Other musicians followed, some of whom also included Mexico and South American cities on their itineraries, and many decided to settle. New York, in particular, became an important stop on the tours of the great singing stars, and amid all the anecdotes of spoilt prima donnas and wily impresarios it is easy to lose sight of the overwhelming artistic impact of fine performances of great operas. Walt Whitman, who loved opera, wrote that without it he could never have composed *Leaves of Grass*.

In all the principal opera houses, in Paris, London, Vienna or New York, the core of the repertory was the same. As the producers and consumers of opera became increasingly separated, this repertory changed less and less (Bellini, Donizetti, Meyerbeer and Verdi made up the most significant part of it), although a new work that was assured of box office success – Verdi's latest or a *Faust* or a *Carmen* – might be rushed into production by rival impresarios in London or New York, each trying to outdo the other with a roster of top singers. During the opening season of the Metropolitan Opera in 1883 nineteen operas were played: nine of them were by the four composers named above, and only six (four French and two Italian) were less than thirty years old. Long before the first recordings – which have often been blamed for this – opera was diverging into a contemporary art form and a museum art.

The relative importance of famous singers and a young composer is clearly shown in this caricature which appeared after the première of Massenet's first work written for the Paris Opéra, *Le Roi de Lahore*. The most celebrated of the four singers is the baritone Jean Lassalle (second from left) who went on to become one of the stars of New York's Metropolitan Opera in the 1890s.

The challenge for opera directors was to integrate these two strands, by having the finest musicians interpret new works, despite the increasing technical demands they made on performers, and by presenting old works with the same freshness as operas being heard for the first time. This was done with outstanding success by Gustav Mahler, not an opera composer himself. Mahler's ten-year reign at the Vienna Hofoper set new musical standards, as the wishes of the composer – alive or dead – were once again given priority over those of the singers; he used sets, costumes and light not only to provide a spectacle for the audience but also to create a total work of art.

# 1851–1857 Verdi's Middle Period

*While Verdi's remarkable productivity continued into the 1850s, with his three most popular operas appearing in a space of twenty months, Wagner, in exile, worked on his plans to produce the 'music of the future'. In Paris the Opéra persuaded Verdi to write new works, but its repertory was otherwise rooted in the past, and the new companies established in New York and London were no more adventurous, relying for their success on international singing stars.*

**DATES**

**1852**
Following a coup d'état in December 1851, Louis Napoleon assumes title of emperor of France as Napoleon III

**1853–6**
Crimean War between Russia and Turkey; England and France are engaged as allies of Turkey

**1853**
Haussmann begins the reconstruction of Paris

**1855**
First version of Walt Whitman's *Leaves of Grass* published

**1857**
Publication of Baudelaire's *Les Fleurs du mal*

**1851** *24 January* Bellini's ***La sonnambula*** (1831) was the first opera performed in San Francisco in a season that also included Verdi's ***Ernani.***
*11 March* Première of ***Rigoletto*** (Verdi/Piave after Hugo) at La Fenice, Venice. There were many censorship problems with the Austrian authorities because of the 'immorality' of the plot, but Verdi eventually managed to get the libretto approved with a minimum of changes.
*16 April* Première of ***Sapho*** (Gounod/Augier) at the Opéra, Paris, with Pauline Viardot in the title role. In this, the composer's first opera, he hoped to rival the simplicity of Gluck and Spontini rather than following the grand tradition of Rossini and Meyerbeer. It was Viardot who encouraged Gounod to write the opera and who arranged for its performance at the Opéra.
*22 November* Première of ***La Perle du Brésil*** (David/Gabriel and Saint-Etienne) at the Opéra National, Paris. Félicien David had followed his musical studies with a period as a missionary in the Ottoman Empire, and his music, which is tinged with orientalism, exerted a strong influence on the next generation of French operatic composers: Gounod, Thomas, Saint-Saëns and Massenet. The new Opéra National (the old one had closed after the 1848 Revolution) had opened in September; its name was changed to Théâtre-Lyrique the following April.

**1852** *4 September* Première of ***Si j'étais roi*** (Adam/d'Ennery and Brésil) at the Théâtre-Lyrique, Paris. It was the most lasting success of the three successful operas (the others were ***La Poupée de Nuremberg***, February, and ***Le Farfadet***, March) by Adam staged in Paris in 1852.
*October* Opening of an Italian opera season at the Astor Place Opera House, New York, in which Alboni and Alessandro Bettini starred.

Sheet of costumed characters from *Rigoletto*, 1851, published by Ricordi. With its intimate connection with La Scala, the Ricordi dynasty exerted an almost monopolistic power over much of Italian opera during the nineteenth century, while Verdi's works provided a significant proportion of the firm's income.

Set for the gypsy camp in Act II of *Il trovatore* in the production at La Fenice, Venice, which opened less than a year after the original Rome production. The sets were by La Fenice's resident designers Giuseppe and Pietro Bertoja.

**1853** *19 January* Première of ***Il trovatore*** (Verdi/Cammarano completed by Bardare after García Gutiérrez) at the Teatro Apollo, Rome. In the Paris première (23 December 1854) the leading roles were sung by Erminia Frezzolini and Mario, while in London (10 May 1855) the role of Azucena was taken by Viardot. The New York première was at the Academy of Music under Max Maretzek on 2 May 1855.
*4 February* Première of ***Les Noces de Jeannette*** (Massé/Barbier and Carré) at the Opéra-Comique, Paris. The composer's finest opera, it was a huge success, with the 1,000th performance at the Opéra-Comique being given on 10 May 1895.
*6 March* Première of ***La traviata*** (Verdi/Piave after Dumas) at La Fenice, Venice. The opera was at first unsuccessful, but its revival fourteen months later at the Teatro San Benedetto sealed its popularity. It reached Paris in 1856 with Mario as Alfredo and Marietta Piccolomini as Violetta. During this period Verdi worked on an opera based on King Lear (an old project of his), commissioning a libretto from Somma, but the work was again abandoned in 1857.

## Rigoletto, Il trovatore and La traviata

Although the atmosphere of each of these operas is very different, they are unified by the tragedies which befall innocent and guilty alike, and they display related aspects of Verdi's operatic genius. *Il trovatore* is the most conventional, not only in its medieval Spanish setting and convoluted plot with gypsies and changelings, but also in its form: the libretto follows the traditional structure of individual numbers, chiefly arias, but the musical characterization is strong, particularly that of Azucena, the vengeful gypsy. In both *La traviata* and *Rigoletto*, the dramatic tension is increased by the part given to the baritone: not a conventional rival with the tenor for the heroine's love, but in one case the hero's father, who persuades the heroine to abandon his son, and in the other the father of the heroine – a relationship that clearly had a deep personal significance for Verdi. Musically, *Rigoletto* is the most innovative, in that the musical plot of the opera is frequently carried by the orchestra while the characters converse above it (Rigoletto himself has no formal arias), so that the use of reminiscences (Monteroni's curse or the Duke's song) form a natural part of the score.

**1854** *16 February* Première of ***L'Etoile du nord*** (Meyerbeer/Scribe) at the Opéra-Comique, Paris (reusing numbers from ***Ein Feldlager in Schlesien***: see 1844). The opera is about Peter the Great and his tsaritsa Catherine.
*18 February* Première of ***Halka*** (Moniuszko/Wolski after Wójcicki) in Vilnius; a concert performance of a two-act version had been given by amateurs in the same city on 1 January 1848, and the work was revived (with revisions) in Warsaw ten years to the day after this, becoming a cornerstone of Polish national culture – several performances in the original language have been given in the USA. Following the Warsaw production Moniuszko was appointed conductor at the opera and professor at the Conservatoire.
*17 June* Death of Henriette Sontag while on tour in Mexico. She had returned to the stage in 1849 after a retirement of nearly twenty years and resumed several of her old roles, including Lucrezia Borgia, her last part.
*24 June* Première of ***Alfonso und Estrella*** (Schubert/Schober) at the Hoftheater, Weimar, under Liszt. The work had been written in 1821–2.
*2 October* ***Norma*** with Grisi and Mario opened the first season of the New York Academy of Music, an opera company directed by Max Maretzek. It was the principal home of opera in New York until the opening of the Metropolitan Opera House in 1883.
*18 October* Première of ***La Nonne sanglante*** (Gounod/Scribe and Delavigne) at the Opéra, Paris, a setting of the libretto originally provided for Berlioz.

Liszt as conductor at Weimar, where for a decade (1848–58) with his small company he staged the most imaginative repertory of operatic works anywhere in the world.

**1855** *14 May* Première of ***Jaguarita l'indienne*** (Halévy/Saint-Georges and de Leuven) at the Théâtre-Lyrique, Paris. Wallace based his last opera, ***The Desert Flower*** (Covent Garden, 12 October 1863) on the same libretto.
*13 June* Première of ***Les Vêpres siciliennes*** (Verdi/Scribe and Duveyrier) at the Opéra, Paris. The libretto had originally been written for Donizetti as ***Le Duc d'Albe***. The first of Verdi's two French operas, it was not a success despite Verdi having included all the requisite elements for a French *grand opéra*, including an Act III ballet. The composer disliked these requirements of the opera house that he called the '*grande boutique*'.

**1856** *4 March* Covent Garden Theatre destroyed by fire during a costume ball. Frederick Gye the younger had been manager of the theatre since 1849 and ran the opera house until his death in 1878. While the theatre was being rebuilt, Italian opera performances were put on at the Lyceum.

Wagner was banished from Germany for his activities during the revolutions of 1848–9 and lived mainly in Switzerland until 1859. He was active as a conductor there, including works by Mozart and Gluck in his repertoire, which he adapted to match his own musical aesthetic. This playbill is for his production of *Don Giovanni* at the Stadttheater, Zurich, in March 1851.

## Liszt at Weimar

Liszt was appointed Kapellmeister to the Grand-Duke of Sachsen-Weimar in 1844, and his opera productions at the Hoftheater from 1848 helped to counterbalance the conventional taste of Paris and the regional German opera houses. His first major première was that of *Lohengrin* (28 August 1850, following a production of *Tannhäuser* in February 1849), and he was a great supporter of Berlioz, staging *Benvenuto Cellini* twice (20 March 1852; 1856), but he also revived the operas of Gluck, Mozart, Beethoven, Schubert (putting on the first performance of *Alfonso und Estrella*) and Weber. The repertory did embrace works from the standard Italian repertory (including Verdi's *I due Foscari* in 1856), but Liszt was conspicuous in his support for the 'new German' school, and Weimar productions included Raff's *König Alfred* (9 March 1851), Dorn's *Die Nibelungen* (22 April 1854, a few weeks after the Berlin première), Schumann's *Genoveva* (9 April 1855), Lassen's *Landgraf Ludwigs Brautfahrt* (10 May 1857) and Sobolewski's *Komala* (30 October 1858). In December 1858 it was the production of *Der Barbier von Bagdad* by his secretary Peter Cornelius that polarized his supporters and opponents and led to his resignation.

The German contralto Sofia Cruvelli (Sophie Crüwell) as Hélène in the original production of *Les Vêpres siciliennes* at the Paris Opéra in 1855. Cruvelli, who had sung Abigaille in the 1846 London première of *Nabucco* (performed as *Nino* because of English objections to biblical subjects portrayed on stage) and was the current star of the Opéra, disappeared with her lover while the opera was in rehearsal, though she returned in time to make a triumphant appearance in the première.

'Seems to me now when I look back, the Italian contralto Marietta Alboni (she is living yet, in Paris, 1891, in good condition, good voice yet, considering) with the then prominent histrions Booth, Edwin Forrest, and Fanny Kemble and the Italian singer Bettini, have had the deepest and most lasting effect upon me. I should like well if Madame Alboni and the old composer Verdi, (and Bettini the tenor, if he is living) could know how much noble pleasure and happiness they gave me, and how deeply I always remember them and thank them to this day.'

Walt Whitman, *Old actors, singers, shows, &c., in New York*

Elsewhere he wrote: 'I wonder if the lady [Alboni] will ever know that her singing, her method, gave the foundation, the start, thirty years ago, to all my poetic efforts since...But for the opera, I could never have written *Leaves of Grass*.'

*16 May* Première of ***Rusalka*** (Dargomizhsky/composer after Pushkin) at the Teatr-tsirk, St Petersburg. Working with a libretto based on a Russian folktale, the composer gave the music a strongly Russian character by moulding its rhythms and inflections to the patterns of Russian speech, creating a new recitative style in which little space is found for formal arias. The work, widely considered the composer's masterpiece, exerted a powerful influence on the group of young nationalist composers in St Petersburg known as the *moguchaya kuchka* ('Mighty Handful'); Dargomizhsky's posthumous Don Juan opera ***The Stone Guest*** (1872) was completed by two of their number.
*30 August* Première of ***I promessi sposi*** (Ponchielli/after Manzoni) at the Teatro della Concordia, Cremona. This first production was quite well received, but the opera's revival at the Teatro dal Verme, Milan, in 1872 established its composer's reputation.
*22 October* Play-through of the first version of ***Die Walküre*** at the Hotel Baur au Lac, Zurich, with Liszt at the piano and Wagner singing the roles of Siegmund and Hunding. The poem of ***Der Ring des Nibelungen*** had been completed at the end of 1852 and Wagner had given a reading of it at the same hotel over four evenings in February 1853.

Nestroy as 'Landgraf Purzel' in his wonderful parody of Wagner's *Tannhäuser* (performed in 1857 shortly after the Vienna première of the opera), in which the Venusberg was transformed in to an 'underground Delikatessenkeller'. It was extremely popular, running for seventy-five performances until 1862.

**1857** *12 March* Première of the original version of ***Simon Boccanegra*** (Verdi/Piave after García Gutiérrez) at La Fenice, Venice. It only achieved success when revived with many revisions in 1881.
*16 August* Première of the revised version of Verdi's ***Aroldo*** (previously ***Stiffelio***; see 1850) to inaugurate the Teatro Nuovo, Rimini, conducted by Angelo Mariani, who became a close friend of the composer. To overcome the resistance to an opera with a contemporary setting, the scenario was transferred to medieval Scotland and England.
*28 August* Vienna première of Wagner's ***Tannhäuser*** at the Thalia Theater, the first Wagner opera produced in the city. It was followed on 31 October by a parody by the great comic actor-dramatist Nestroy.
*29 October* Première of ***The Rose of Castile*** (Balfe/Harris and Falconer) at the Lyceum Theatre, London. The opera, which was performed a hundred times in under a year, was based on a libretto set in 1854 by Adam as ***Le Muletier de Tolède***.

# 1858–1867 The Second Empire

*Although Paris remained the centre of the operatic world, Verdi's new operas (and the disastrous production of* Tannhäuser*) were almost the only new works of interest staged at the Opéra, which was caricatured in a series of brilliant operettas by Offenbach. However, Léon Carvalho's programme at the Théâtre-Lyrique was extremely innovative, with imaginative revivals and the introduction of several works which have remained in the repertory, most notably Gounod's* Faust *and Berlioz's* Les Troyens à Carthage.

**DATES**

**1858**
*14 January*
Assassination attempt on Napoleon III and Empress Eugénie outside the Opéra (where they were to attend a benefit for the tenor Massol) by the Italian patriot Felice Orsini leaves many wounded and several dead

**1859**
Austrian army defeated by the French and Sardinian forces and Lombardy gains its freedom from Austria

**1858–65**
Destruction of old fortifications of Vienna and building of the Ringstrasse

**1860**
Following the liberation of Sicily and Naples, Victor Emmanuel, King of Sardinia, is proclaimed 'King of Italy'

**1861–5**
American Civil War

**1864**
Ludwig II comes to the Bavarian throne

**1864–9**
Publication of Tolstoy's *War and Peace*

**1867**
Exposition Universelle in Paris kindles interest in Japanese culture

Model of Philippe Chaperon's set for Act II of Wagner's *Tannhäuser*, which the composer had extensively revised in the hope of making a breakthrough in Paris. In the event, the performances of the opera in March 1861 were disrupted by members of the Jockey Club, infuriated that there was no Act II ballet, and by the disgruntled claque which the composer refused to pay. Wagner withdrew the work after the third performance.

**1858** *15 January* Première of ***Le Médecin malgré lui*** (Gounod/composer, Barbier and Carré) at the Théâtre-Lyrique, Paris. This effective adaptation of Molière was the composer's first *opéra-comique*, successfully evoking the atmosphere of seventeenth-century France.
*13 April* London début of Therese Tietjens as Valentine in Meyerbeer's ***Les Huguenots*** at Her Majesty's Theatre, with Queen Victoria in the audience.
*15 May* Opening of the rebuilt Covent Garden theatre with a new production of ***Les Huguenots***, conducted by Costa with a cast including Grisi and Mario. Building work went on until the very last minute, while at the performance it took so long to shift the scenery and work the new machinery that the curtain did not fall at the end of the third act until after midnight, and the opera was left incomplete.
*21 October* Première of ***Orphée aux enfers*** (Offenbach/Crémieux and L. Halévy) at the Bouffes-Parisiens, Paris (a revised version was premièred at the Gaîté Parisienne in 1874). The first full-length *opérette*, the work followed the old tradition of operatic parodies with its classical setting

Dido's palace at Carthage, set by Chaperon for the production of Berlioz's *Les Troyens à Carthage* at the Théâtre-Lyrique in November 1863. The epic character of the opera made no concessions to the fashionable taste for sentimentality and vocal virtuosity but paid tribute to the two operatic composers Berlioz most admired: Gluck, whose simple, direct style is reflected in the arias, and Spontini, whose grand tableaux influenced the monumental set pieces.

Pauline Viardot as Orphée in Gluck's opera, produced in Berlioz's version at the Théâtre-Lyrique in 1859. Viardot, though less of a phenomenon as a singer than her elder sister Maria Malibran, was a great influence for good in the operatic world, supporting Saint-Saëns, Berlioz and Wagner among many others. Like her brother, Manuel Garcia, jun., she was also an influential singing teacher.

and quotations from Gluck, but it also provided a racy spectacle that delighted Second Empire Paris.
*15 December* Première of ***Der Barbier von Bagdad*** (Cornelius/composer) at the Hoftheater, Weimar. It was the first opera by Cornelius, Liszt's secretary at Weimar and champion of Wagner and the 'New German School'. The single performance of the opera was disrupted by opponents of Liszt, and the uproar led Liszt to quit his post at Weimar, and Cornelius to move to Vienna, although his second opera, ***Der Cid***, was premièred in Weimar in 1865. ***Der Barbier von Bagdad*** only became successful after its revival in 1884, newly orchestrated by Felix Mottl.

**1859** *17 February* Première of ***Un ballo in maschera*** (Verdi/Somma after Scribe) at the Teatro Apollo, Rome.
*19 March* Première of ***Faust*** (Gounod/Barbier and Carré after Goethe) at the Théâtre-Lyrique, Paris, with Marie Miolan-Carvalho as Marguerite. In its original version ***Faust*** was an *opéra-comique* with spoken dialogue; recitatives were written for a production in Strasbourg in April 1860. The intimate scale and clear delineation of character show Gounod's rejection of the grand style of Meyerbeer, a course he continued with ***Mireille*** and ***Roméo et Juliette.***
*4 April* Première of ***Le Pardon de Ploërmel (Dinorah)*** (Meyerbeer/Barbier and Carré) at the Opéra-Comique, Paris, conducted by the composer in the presence of Napoleon III and Empress Eugénie, with a cast that included Jean-Baptiste Faure as Hoël.
*4 April* A production of ***Tannhäuser*** at the Stadt Theater, New York, was the first performance of a Wagner opera in the Americas.
*11 October* Première of ***Mohega, die Blume des Waldes*** (Sobolewski/composer) in Milwaukee. The plot, based on an incident in the Revolutionary War, was set by the composer the year he arrived in America and is among the early performances of opera in German in the USA. (Milwaukee, a city which had expanded after an influx of German refugees after 1848, was to stage ***La traviata*** in German two years later.)

The assassination of Riccardo (Gustav III in the original libretto) in the first production of Verdi's *Un ballo in maschera* in Rome, 1859. The original setting (used in Auber's 1833 version of the libretto and again in 1843 by Mercadante) had to be changed because the censors in Naples, where the opera had been due to have its première, forbade its performance after Orsini's attempt on the life of Napoleon III. A version of Verdi's opera with the original Swedish characters was first performed in Copenhagen on 25 September 1935.

*18 November* Revival of Gluck's ***Orphée et Euridice*** in a version by Berlioz, based on both the Italian and French scores, at the Théâtre-Lyrique, Paris, with Pauline Viardot as Orphée. Berlioz's version of ***Alceste*** was premièred two years later (21 October 1861) at the Opéra, again with Viardot in the title role.
*24 November* New York début of sixteen-year-old Adelina Patti (as 'the little Florinda') at the Academy of Music as Lucia. Her Edgardo was Pasquale Brignoli, the leading Italian tenor in New York during the 1850s.

**1860** *25 January; 1, 8 February* Wagner concerts were given at the Théâtre-Italien, Paris, in which the composer conducted excerpts of ***Der fliegende Holländer***, ***Lohengrin***, ***Tannhäuser*** and ***Tristan und Isolde***. In May, in the presence of Berlioz, Wagner played through Act II of ***Tristan und Isolde*** at the house of Pauline Viardot, who sang the role of Isolde; and in August he published his essay on '*Zukunftsmusik*' (music of the future).
*7 February* Première of ***Hrabina*** [***The Countess***] (Moniuszko/Wolski) at the Wielki Teatr, Warsaw. The opera includes arias based on the Polish national dances, the polonaise and mazurka.

**1861** *13 March* First performance of ***Tannhäuser*** (revised version) at the Opéra, Paris, after 164 rehearsals, with Albert Niemann in the title role and Marie-Constance Sasse (a former café singer of *chansonettes*) as Elisabeth. The opera was withdrawn after the third performance and in order to make use of the expensive sets and costumes Adam and Melésville produced an opera also set in the Wartburg – ***La Voix humaine***, premièred on 30 December 1861 – which, however, ran for only thirteen performances.

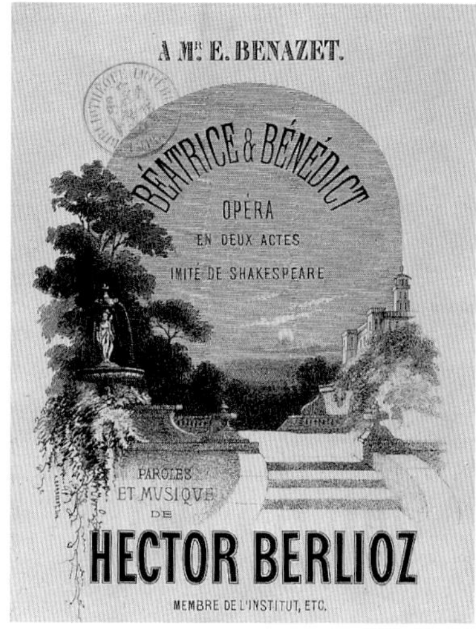


Vocal score of Berlioz's *Béatrice et Bénédict*, 'a caprice written with the point of a needle' for the the new theatre at Baden-Baden opened by the manager of the casino there, Edouard Bénazet, for whom Berlioz had conducted a series of concerts for several years and to whom he dedicated the opera. The composer wrote that 'this work is difficult of performance, especially in the men's parts, but I think it one of the most spirited and original I ever wrote. Unlike *Les Troyens*, its production entails no expense.'

Scene from Gounod's *Faust* at Covent Garden in 1864 with Jean-Baptiste Faure (Méphisto) Adelina Patti (Marguerite) and Mario (Faust), three of the greatest opera stars of the period.

*11 April* Première of ***La Statue*** (Reyer/Barbier and Carré) at the Théâtre-Lyrique, Paris. Based on a story from *The Thousand and One Nights*, it was the composer's second opera for this theatre and won the approval of Berlioz.
*14 May* Covent Garden début of Adelina Patti (now eighteen) as Amina in Bellini's ***La sonnambula.*** She sang Zerlina in ***Don Giovanni*** later in the same season, when Grisi was singing one of her last Donna Annas. Patti made her Paris début the following year.
*15 June* First performance of Verdi's ***Un ballo in maschera*** in London at Mapleson's Lyceum Theatre with Luigi Arditi as Riccardo and Tietjens as Amelia. While this production was already in rehearsal, Gye tried to race Mapleson with a cast including Mario and Miolan-Carvalho, but his production at Covent Garden opened a week later.
*29 August* Stage première of ***Die Verschworenen, oder Der häusliche Krieg*** (Schubert/Castelli, after Aristophanes' *Lysistrata*) in Frankfurt, following a concert performance given in Vienna on 1 March 1861 (see 1823).

**1862** *10 February* Première of ***The Lily of Killarney*** (Benedict/Oxenford and Boucicault) at Covent Garden, London. This was the most successful of the eleven operas written by the Anglo-German composer and operatic conductor, maintaining a place in the repertory of English-language opera houses into the twentieth century.
*28 February* Première of ***La Reine de Saba*** (Gounod/Barbier and Carré after Nerval) at the Opéra, Paris. The work, the composer's first for the Opéra since ***La Nonne sanglante*** (1854), failed on account of its supposed Wagnerism.
*9 April* Première of ***Estrella de Soria*** (Berwald/Prechtler trans. Wallmark) at the Royal Opera House, Stockholm. The opera had been written in 1841 during the composer's stay in Vienna, but, like the rest of his visionary œuvre, was neglected by his fellow-countrymen until the last years of his life; his only other surviving opera, ***Drottningen av Golconda*** (1864–5) was not performed until 1968.
*12 May* Première of ***Lalla-Roukh*** (David/Lucas and Carré after Moore) at the Opéra-Comique, Paris, another of the composer's orientalist operas. A different version of the story, set by Anton Rubinstein and titled ***Feramors*** was staged at Dresden the following year.
*9 August* Première of ***Béatrice et Bénédict*** (Berlioz/composer after

## International star singers

The marketing of Jenny Lind by P. T. Barnum in 1850 had created an international market for opera singers – primarily sopranos – which impresarios, managers and singing teachers did their best to exploit. Their core repertory was quite narrow: Bellini's *La sonnambula* and *I puritani* were ideal vehicles for the display of *coloratura*, while *Norma* and Donizetti's *Lucrezia Borgia* and *La Favorite* were favourite dramatic roles; Meyerbeer's operas gave scope for several star performances as well as providing lavish visual spectacle (and plenty of dull moments for the audience to concentrate on conversation and the social performance). Gounod and Thomas created a new kind of heroine, softer and more sentimental, and their latest operas, like those of Verdi, were seized on by impresarios, sometimes racing their rivals to put on a production first.

The supreme prima donna was Adelina Patti, born to an operatic family who moved to New York when she was three. Her repertory was extremely limited and she was not a great actress, but her vocal technique was peerless, and she could command the highest fees in America, London, Paris and Vienna. Among her rivals were: Therese Tietjens, a German dramatic soprano who was a mainstay of the London opera seasons from 1858 to her death in 1877 and also appeared at the New York Academy; Marie Miolan-Carvalho; Pauline Lucca, a temperamental Viennese singer known as the 'demon wild-cat', who broke her life-contact with the Vienna Hofoper to sing at the New York Academy from 1872; the American Clara Louise Kellogg, who sang in London as well as her native country, where she later ran an English-language opera troupe; Minnie Hauk, from New York, who established her career in Vienna and became one of the great singing actresses of the era; the sublime contralto from Maine, Annie Louise Cary, whose voice Anton Rubinstein called the most beautiful in the world; the beautiful Swedish soprano Christine Nilsson, who sang in Paris, Vienna and London, toured the USA and appeared in the first season of the Metropolitan Opera in 1883–4; and the Canadian Emma Albani, who married the son of Frederick Gye, manager of Covent Garden, where she was a great favourite. None of these divas was Italian, and Italy, even La Scala, seldom played an important part in their careers: the division between the indigenous tradition of opera composition and performance and the international opera circus had already begun.

Poster for Verdi's *Don Carlos*, first performed at the Opéra in 1867. It depicts the scene in prison after Rodrigo has been shot and Don Carlos confronts his father Philip II.

Shakespeare) at the Stadttheater, Baden-Baden, conducted by the composer with artists from the Paris Opéra, including Anne-Arsène Charton-Demeur as Béatrice.

*10 November* Première of ***La forza del destino*** (Verdi/Piave after Saavedra), the composer's last collaboration with Piave, at the Bolshoi Theatre, St Petersburg.The Roman tenor Enrico Tamberlik, who sang Alvaro, had been involved in getting Verdi to write the opera for Russia. In less than five years it had also been heard in Rome, Madrid, New York, Vienna, Buenos Aires and London. Verdi prepared a second version, with a full-scale overture and the libretto revised by Ghislanzoni, which was sung for the first time in Milan (La Scala) on 27 February 1869.

**1863** *March–April* Wagner gave a series of concerts in St Petersburg, where he spent time with Anton Rubinstein and Alexander Serov, and in Moscow.

## Tristan und Isolde

During his Swiss exile, Wagner was diverted from his work on the *Ring* by the need to give musical expression to his love affair with Mathilde Wesendonck, and *Tristan und Isolde* was composed in 1857–9. Based on the tragic medieval love story, *Tristan* gave opera a radically new form, which Wagner was to develop in all his subsequent works. The overall musical structure, unbroken by individual 'numbers', was bound together by thematic leitmotifs associated both with the characters and the underlying themes of the work, establishing an entirely new relationship between singers and orchestra. Though technically as taxing as any traditional operatic roles, the vocal parts offered no opportunity for individual virtuosity, and even characterization was submerged beneath the overwhelming, fatalistic, musical drive. More than any other of the composer's operas, *Tristan und Isolde* converted the musical public to Wagnerism, although its difficulties were initially considered insuperable. Wagner, who had been enormously impressed by the Vienna performance of *Lohengrin* in 1861, wanted *Tristan* to be premièred there, but in 1863, after seventy-seven rehearsals, the work had to be abandoned; it was premièred in Munich in 1865, but its overwhelming international triumph only began in the 1880s.

Opening scene of *Tristan und Isolde* on board the ship in which Tristan brings Isolde from Ireland to be the bride of King Marke of Cornwall.

*28 May* Première of ***Judith*** (Serov/composer and Maikov after Giacometti) at the Maryinsky Theatre, St Petersburg. The composer – an internationalist rather than a Russian nationalist – had visited Germany in 1858, becoming an enthusiast for Wagner's music, though both ***Judith***, his first opera, and its even more spectacular successor, ***Rogneda*** (1865), were modelled on Meyerbeer rather than Wagner.

*11 June* The first of two rival productions of Gounod's ***Faust*** was staged in London – at Colonel Mapleson's Lyceum Theatre (in Italian) with Tietjens, Giuglini, Gassier, Trebelli and Santley; Gye's production at Covent Garden (in French) followed on 2 July with the orginal Marguerite (Miolan-Carvalho), Tamberlik as Faust and Faure as Méphisto. Thereafter ***Faust*** was given at Covent Garden every season until 1911. The opera's US première took place in Philadelphia on 18 November 1863 (in German), followed by rival performances in New York on 25 November (in Italian) and 18 December (in German).

*14 June* Première of ***Die Loreley*** (Bruch/Geibel) at the Nationaltheater, Mannheim, a setting of a libretto originally written for Mendelssohn, who composed only a few fragments of the music.

*30 September* Première of ***Les Pêcheurs de perles*** (Bizet/Cormon and Carré) at the Théâtre-Lyrique, Paris. The opera is noteworthy for the composer's adventurous harmonic writing, but it was taken off after eighteen performances and only became successful after Bizet's death. He had already written two comic operas, ***Le Docteur Miracle*** (1856) and ***Don Procopio*** (1858–9), and the grand opera ***Ivan IV*** (1862, not staged until 1946, though some of the music was reused in later operas).

*4 November* Première of ***Les Troyens à Carthage*** (part 2 of ***Les Troyens***) at

the Théâtre-Lyrique, Paris, conducted by the composer with Charton-Demeur as Dido (the whole work was not performed until 1890). Despite its production difficulties, this is one of the greatest operas written between 1850 and 1900.
*11 November* Première of ***I profughi fiamminghi*** (Faccio/Praga) at La Scala, Milan. The work was a conscious attempt to renew the operatic form, and Boito's 'Ode to Italian Art' which it occasioned offended Verdi and alienated him for some time from Faccio, Boito and their associates.
*25 November* Production of Gounod's ***Faust*** (in Italian) at the New York Academy with Clara Louise Kellogg as Marguerite, a character whom the singer described as 'innocent to the verge of idiocy'. For decades ***Faust*** was the most popular of all operas in the USA.

**1864** *19 March* Première of ***Mireille*** (Gounod/Carré after Mistral) at the Théâtre-Lyrique, Paris, with Miolan-Carvalho in the title role. The opera, with its pronounced Provençal flavour, underwent extensive revisions before its success was finally achieved with a revival at the Opéra-Comique twenty-five years later.
*2 May* Death of Meyerbeer in Paris.
*4 May* Wagner's first meeting with the eighteen-year-old King Ludwig II of Bavaria, who provided him with financial support, specifically for the ***Ring***. The king also planned a Wagner Festival Theatre in Munich and commissioned designs from the architect of the Dresden Hofoper, Gottfried Semper.
*27 October* Operatic début of Christine Nilsson as Violetta in ***La traviata*** at the Théâtre-Lyrique, Paris.
*17 December* Première of ***La belle Hélène*** (Offenbach/Meilhac and L. Halévy) at the Théâtre des Variétés, Paris, with Hortense Schneider in the title role. Offenbach again caricatured both the Opéra (Rossini and Wagner are among the targets) and Second Empire society, finding in Schneider, already famous for her lovers, an ideal heroine, 'exciting, modern, ironic, the froth of the champagne'.

**1865** *21 April* Première of the revised version of ***Macbeth*** (Verdi) in French (translated by Nuitter and Beaumont) at the Théâtre-Lyrique, Paris.
*28 April* Posthumous première of ***L'Africaine*** (Meyerbeer/Scribe and Fétis) at the Opéra, Paris. The title role (Sélika) in Meyerbeer's last opera was created by Sasse – the composer had wanted Pauline Lucca, but she did not sing French – and the role of Nélusko by Faure. It received more than one hundred performances within a year.
*30 May* Première of ***Amleto*** (Faccio/Boito) at the Teatro Carlo Felice, Genoa, the second and last of the composer's operas. He and his librettist had been close friends since they were fellow-students at the Milan Conservatorio and were leading members of the *Scapigliati*, who assailed bourgeois artistic ideals. The excellent libretto of ***Amleto*** is the first of Boito's adaptations of Shakespeare, and the experience served him well when he later worked with Verdi.
*10 June* Première of ***Tristan und Isolde*** (Wagner/composer) at the Hofoper, Munich, conducted by Hans von Bülow with Ludwig and Malwine Schnorr von Carolsfeld in the title roles.
*28 September* Première of ***Straszny dwór*** [***The Haunted Manor***] (Moniuszko/Checiński) at the Wielki Teatr, Warsaw. The work contains fine ensemble writing as well as a brilliant virtuoso role for the leading soprano.
*9 December* Première of ***Le Voyage en Chine*** (Bazin/Labiche and Delacour), at the Opéra-Comique, Paris, the composer's most successful work. The elaborate scenery by Philippe Chaperon included the deck of a

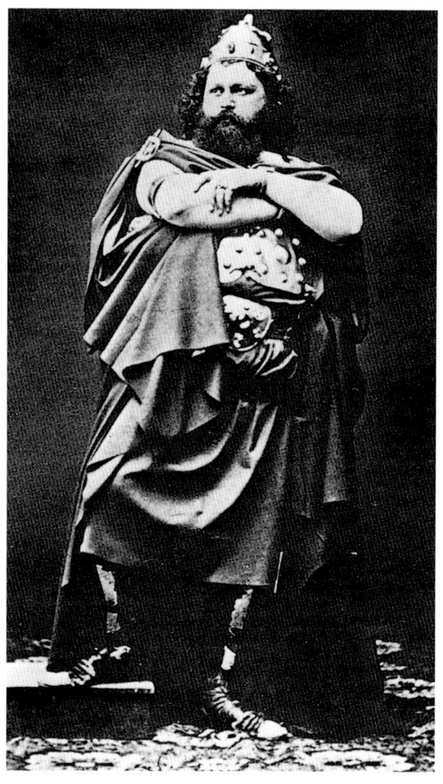

Ludwig Schnorr von Carolsfeld as Tristan, the role he created in 1865, shortly before his death.

Caricature of Offenbach in 1866 (with his faithful librettists Meilhac and Halévy clinging to his coat-tails), suggesting his dominance of the light operatic world; each box represents a theatre in which he is involved, from the Palais-Royal (where *La Vie parisienne* was premièred on 31 July 1866) to the Variétés (where *Barbe-Bleu* opened on 5 February), the Bouffes (his own theatre), the Châtelet etc., with the Opéra and Opéra-Comique (where his *Robinson Crusoé* opened the following year), as well as Vienna, Berlin and Baden-Baden in the background.

steamboat, and in the early performances real smoke billowed out of the funnel and the back curtain painted with the horizon moved to give the illusion of the pitching and rolling of the ship; both effects, however, had to be suppressed as on some nights smoke poured into the auditorium and the illusion of movement made the audience feel dizzy.

Marie Miolan-Carvalho as Juliette in Gounod's opera, a role she created in 1867. She was the wife of Léon Carvalho, who took over as director of the Théâtre-Lyrique in 1856 and ran it until 1860 and then again, after it had reopened in its new home in the place du Châtelet, from 1862 to 1868. His productions there included Gounod's *Faust* (in which his wife created the role of Marguerite); the same composer's *Mireille* (in which she created the title role) as well as works by Mozart and Weber; Berlioz's revivals of Gluck's operas (Marie sang Euridice) and *Les Troyens à Carthage*; Bizet's *Les Pêcheurs de perles*; and Verdi's *Macbeth*.

**1866** *April–May* Rival productions of Mozart's ***Don Giovanni*** in Paris: at the Opéra (from 2 April, with added ballet music from Mozart's works arranged by Auber) and at the Théâtre-Lyrique (from 10 May, in a musical arrangement by J. F. E. Gautier). Berlioz attended eight consecutive performances of the latter production.
*30 May* Première of ***Prodaná nevěsta*** [***The Bartered Bride***] (Smetana/Sabina) at the Provisional Czech Theatre, Prague, which had opened in 1862 with the aim of promoting national opera. The work (revised in 1870) has music that matches the witty Bohemian peasant story and has been a lasting success, although initially less favoured than the composer's serious historical opera (with the same librettist) ***Braniboři v Čechách*** [***The Brandenburgers in Bohemia***], which had been premièred at the beginning of the year.
*13 October* Début of the fourteen-year-old soprano Minnie Hauk as Amina in ***La sonnambula*** at the Brooklyn Academy of Music. She repeated the role two years later at Covent Garden. Later she was to be the first American Juliette (1867), Carmen (1878) and Manon (1885).
*17 November* Première of ***Mignon*** (Thomas/Barbier and Carré after Goethe) at the Opéra-Comique, Paris, Thomas's finest work, whose initial success was ensured by the performance of the mezzo Marie-Célestine Galli-Marié in the title role. Like Gounod, Thomas believed that the quality of French opera would be raised by basing libretti on great literature (Goethe, Shakespeare et al.), although he saw nothing wrong in giving Goethe's tragic tale a happy ending.

**1867** *11 March* Première of ***Don Carlos*** (Verdi/Méry and du Locle after Schiller) at the Opéra, Paris, sung in French, with Sasse as Elisabeth de Valois and Faure as Posa. Empress Eugénie was offended by the heretical opinions expressed in the opera and turned her back on the performance. The first Italian production of the opera was at Covent Garden on 4 June, the first in Italy, with Teresa Stolz as Elisabetta, in Bologna on 27 October.
*27 April* Première of ***Roméo et Juliette*** (Gounod/Barbier and Carré after Shakespeare) at the Théâtre-Lyrique, Paris, with Miolan-Carvalho as the heroine. It is the composer's most original work, centring on the two lovers, who have four duets in the course of the opera (including – in defiance of Shakespeare – one as Romeo is dying).
*18 November* Première of ***Bogatyri*** [***Heroes***] (Borodin/Krylov) at the Bolshoi Theatre, Moscow. V. A. Krylov wanted Borodin to set the whole of his witty libretto with parodies in the grand operatic styles of Rossini and Meyerbeer, but time was so short that over half the numbers were set to existing music by Meyerbeer, Offenbach and other western composers. The principal target of the satire was Serov's pompous mythological opera ***Rogneda*** (see 1863), which flew in the face of everything the nationalist composers were trying to do, and excerpts from this were also used.
*26 December* Première of ***La jolie fille de Perth*** (Bizet/Saint-Georges and Adenis after Scott) at the Théâtre-Lyrique, Paris. The role of Catherine was to have been sung by Nilsson but she broke her contract to sing Ophélie at the Opéra and it was taken instead by the young Jane Devriès. The picturesque score is far better than the libretto (only loosely based on Scott), which features a lascivious duke, mistaken identities and a last-act mad scene.

# 1868 1875 The New Repertory

*Boito's* Mefistofele, *Verdi's* Aida, *Mussorgsky's* Boris Godunov *and Bizet's* Carmen *all had their first productions in these years, helping to modernize the international repertory; at the same time the premières of* Die Meistersinger, Das Rheingold *and* Die Walküre *(following that of* Tristan und Isolde *in 1867) converted many more musicians to Wagner's music, and performances outside Germany became more frequent – a new initiative in Paris, and the first Wagner productions in London and in Italy.*

**DATES**

**1869**
Opening of Suez Canal

**1870**
*19 July* Outbreak of war between France and Prussia. In Paris the Third Republic is proclaimed and the city besieged by the Prussians

Rome becomes the capital of Italy

**1871**
Fall of Paris and rule of the Commune for two months

Chicago destroyed by fire

**1873**
Collapse of financial markets in Vienna (May) and New York (September)

**1874**
First Impressionist exhibition in Paris

**1868** *5 March* Première of ***Mefistofele*** (Boito/composer), conducted by the composer at La Scala, Milan. The performance, eagerly anticipated, lasted 5½ hours and was a disaster, leading Boito, who found the criticisms of his fellow-*scapigliato* Ghislanzoni particularly hurtful, to burn much of the score. He eventually revised what had survived, and the new version was premièred at the Teatro Comunale, Bologna, on 4 October 1875, with Italo Campanini in the role of Faust. Unlike Gounod's ***Faust***, the opera draws on both parts of Goethe's drama and is a much more profound exploration of the conflict of good and evil.

*9 March* Première of ***Hamlet*** (Thomas/Barbier and Carré) at the Opéra, Paris, with Faure as Hamlet and Nilsson as Ophélia. Shakespeare is smothered by the conventions of French *grand opéra* (including a happy end), of which this is a last flowering. Nilsson repeated her performance the following year at Covent Garden (where the opera was sung in Italian) with Sir Charles Santley as her Hamlet.

*16 May* Gala première of ***Dalibor*** (Smetana/Wenzig trans. Špindler) at the New Town Theatre, Prague. This tragic tale of a national hero was staged to commemorate the laying of the foundation stone of the new Czech National Theatre.

Manet's drawing of Jean-Baptiste Faure as Hamlet in Ambroise Thomas's opera of the same name. Faure made his début at the Opéra-Comique in 1852 and was the leading baritone there for nearly twenty-five years, outstanding in both the French and Italian repertoires. He was also an important collector of Impressionist paintings, particularly those of Manet.

Scene from Act II of the original production of Wagner's *Die Meistersinger von Nürnberg* at Munich in 1868.

*21 June* Première of ***Die Meistersinger von Nürnberg*** (Wagner/composer) at the Hofoper, Munich, conducted by Hans von Bülow with Franz Betz (Sachs), Mathilde Mallinger (Eva), Franz Nachbaur (Stolzing), Carl Schlosser (David). The opera represents Wagner's musical ideology through the character of Stolzing, who has learned his music in the school of nature rather than following the pedantic rules of the musicians' guild, but nevertheless wins the singing competition and thus the hand of Eva through the guidance of the benevolent cobbler-poet Hans Sachs.
*13 November* Death of Rossini in Paris.

**1869** *11 February* Première of ***Voevoda*** (Tchaikovsky/composer and Ostrovsky) at the Bolshoi Theatre, Moscow. The composer's first opera was not a success and he destroyed the score; however, much of the music was reused in ***Oprichnik*** (1870–2) and in the ballet *Swan Lake* (1875–6). Another operatic project the same year, ***Undine***, was abandoned.
*26 February* Première of ***William Ratcliff*** (Cui/Pleshcheev and Krylov after Heine) at the Maryinsky Theatre, St Petersburg. Composed over ten years and described by Vladimir Stasov as 'one of the most important compositions of our time', it was the first opera to be completed by any of the Mighty Handful, although its romanticism hardly conformed with their operatic manifesto.

'1. The new school wants dramatic music to have its own value as absolute music independent of the text. One of the characteristics of this school is the avoidance of banality and vulgarity.
2. Vocal music in the theatre should correspond exactly to the text sung.
3. The forms of operatic music do not depend in any way on the traditional moulds established by routine. They should be born freely from the dramatic situation and from the specific requirements of the text.
4. It is necessary to translate into music with the maximum of contrast the character and type of the different persons, not to commit anachronisms in historical works, and to render local colour faithfully.'

Manifesto of the Mighty Handful

Heinrich and Therese Vogl as Siegmund and Sieglinde in the original production of *Die Walküre* in Munich in 1870. The cast also included August Kindermann as Wotan and Sophie Stehle as Brünnhilde.

*27 February* Première of the revised version of Verdi's ***La forza del destino*** at La Scala, Milan, Verdi's first association with the opera house since 1845. The work was conducted by Mariani with his lover Teresa Stolz as Leonora.
*3 March* Opéra première of Gounod's ***Faust*** with added ballet music, sung by a cast including Nilsson and Faure. A parody, ***Le petit Faust*** (Hervé/Crémieux and Jaime), was put on at the Théâtre des Folies-Dramatiques on 23 April, starring the celebrated courtesan Blanche d'Antigny as Marguerite (Hervé was one of her innumerable lovers).
*8 March* Death of Berlioz in Paris.
*30 March* Opening of the new season at Covent Garden, for which Gye and Mapleson went into partnership, so that they could pool their resources of musicians. The first opera under their joint management was ***Norma***, starring Tietjens, while on 4 May Nilsson made her London début as Lucia, and the company also included Patti and Lucca. In ***Don Giovanni*** Patti, Tietjens and Nilsson all appeared, with Faure as the Don and Mario (still singing in London two years later) as Ottavio. However, the partnership of Gye and Mapleson lasted only two seasons.
*6 April* French première of ***Rienzi*** at the Théâtre-Lyrique, Paris, under Jules Pasdeloup, Carvalho's successor, to whom Wagner had granted his French rights and who planned to produce all the composer's operas (until the Franco-Prussian War intervened). ***Rienzi*** was greeted with continuing hostility by many of the Paris audience: Bizet had described it as 'music of decadence rather than of the future'.
*25 May* Opening of new Hofoper on the Ringstrasse, Vienna, with a performance of Mozart's ***Don Giovanni***. Amalie Materna, well known as an operetta singer, made her grand opera début there in Meyerbeer's ***L'Africaine*** later the same season.
*22 September* Première of ***Das Rheingold*** (Wagner/composer) at the Hofoper, Munich under Franz Wüllner, with August Kindermann (Wotan), Sophie Stehle (Fricka), Heinrich Vogl (Loge), Karl Fischer (Alberich) and Carl Schlosser (Mime) among the cast. The composer, dissatisfied with a dress rehearsal at the beginning of the month, had left Munich and protested against the performance.

**1870** *19 March* Première of ***Il Guarany*** (Gomes/Scalvini revised by d'Ormeville) at La Scala, Milan, with Victor Maurel, making his Milan début, in the leading role. The exotic opera by the Brazilian composer (himself part Guarany Indian) was an immediate success.
*26 June* Première of ***Die Walküre*** (Wagner/composer) at the Hofoper, Munich, despite objections from the composer.
*23 July* A performance of ***Der fliegende Holländer*** (in Italian) at Drury Lane, London, with Santley as the Dutchman, was the first production of a Wagner opera in England.

**1871** *18 January* Première of ***Ali Babà*** (Bottesini/Taddei) by the 'Opera Buffa' at the Lyceum Theatre, London. The composer of several operas, though better known as 'the Paganini of the double-bass', Bottesini was also a noted conductor, who directed the first performance of ***Aida*** in Cairo at Verdi's request.
*12 May* Wagner announced plans for the Bayreuth Festival Theatre in which the first complete performance of ***Der Ring des Nibelungen*** was to take place. The following year he moved with his family to Bayreuth.
*1 November* The Italian première of ***Lohengrin*** conducted by Mariani, in the Teatro Comunale, Bologna, was the first production of a Wagner opera in Italy. It had been planned for some time by the Milan publisher Lucca as a way of breaking Ricordi's stranglehold over the Italian operatic

Scene from Act I of Rimsky-Korsakov's *Pskovityanka* in the original production at the Maryinsky Theatre, St Petersburg. The score combined the influences of Dargomizhsky's recitative style, Russian folk music and the music of Mussorgsky (who shared a room with Rimsky-Korsakov in 1871–2 while he was working on the revisions to *Boris Godunov*). The work was well received, but the composer later felt that the harmony, counterpoint and orchestration were inadequate, and he revised it in 1876 and – as *Ivan the Terrible* – in 1894.

world, and the rivalry of Wagner and Verdi was built up by the press. Bologna was the venue for the Italian premières of several other Wagner operas.

*24 December* Première of ***Aida*** (Verdi/Ghislanzoni after du Locle), at the Khedival Theatre, Cairo, conducted by Bottesini. The opera had been commissioned by Ismail Pasha for his new theatre, which had opened with a production of ***Rigoletto*** on 6 November 1869. While the orchestra plays a more important part than in any of his earlier operas, Verdi's outstanding achievement in ***Aida*** was the convincing portrayal of individual passions and tragedies within a framework of magnificent splendour.

**1872** *8 February* Italian première of Verdi's ***Aida*** at La Scala, Milan, conducted by Franco Faccio, with Stolz in the title role. Verdi's increasingly close association with his leading lady – as well as Angelo Mariani's defection to Wagner – had disrupted his friendship with Mariani and also put a serious strain on his own marriage.

*28 February* Posthumous première of ***Kamenny Gost*** [***The Stone Guest***] (Dargomizhsky/Pushkin) at the Maryinsky Theatre, St Petersburg, conducted by Eduard Nápravník, with Fedor Komisarzhevsky as Don Juan and Ivan Mel'nikov, Yuliya Platonova and Osip Petrov. The opera had been orchestrated by Rimsky-Korsakov (at the request of the dying composer) and was furnished with an overture by Cui. It was a complete setting of Pushkin's *Don Juan* poem, composed largely in the recitative style Dargomizhsky had used for ***Rusalka*** (see 1856).

*22 May* Première of ***Djamileh*** (Bizet/Gallet after Musset) at the Opéra-Comique, Paris. The title role was sung by the Baronne de Presles (known as Alice Prelly), formerly Mme de Pomeyrac, described by Henri Gauthier-Villars as 'the voiceless Venus'. The melodramatic plot, unsatisfactory performance and adventurous harmonic writing conspired to make the opera a failure.

*12 June* Première of ***La Princesse jaune*** (Saint-Saëns/Gallet) at the Opéra-Comique, Paris. The composer's first opera started the fashion for Japanese subjects.

*30 November* Première of ***Don César de Bazan*** (Massenet/Chantepie after d'Ennery and Dumanoir) at the Opéra-Comique, Paris, the second of two *opéras-comiques* with which the composer began his operatic career.

Clara Louise Kellogg, the American soprano, as Aida, one of her most celebrated roles.

## Boris Godunov

Modest Mussorgsky in 1873, around the time the revised score of *Boris Godunov* was completed.

Modest Mussorgsky was the outstanding operatic composer of the new Russian school, although only one of his operas was complete at the time of his death. As a teenager he started to set Victor Hugo's *Han d'Islande* – the earliest operatic project by one of the Mighty Handful – and, after studying in 1857 with Dargomizhsky and Balakirev, he embarked on an opera, *Oedipus in Athens,* after Sophocles. However, he set this aside and in 1863 started on a new opera based on Flaubert's *Salammbô*, with music that was orientalist rather than Russian in character; again, after three years, when he had written some 1½ hours of music, he abandoned this, though he reused parts of the score in *Boris Godunov*. Yet another unfinished project was an opera based on Gogol's *The Marriage*, which he had been encouraged to write by Dargomizhsky; he played through the first act in October 1868, and his audience were astonished at the accuracy with which he captured the rhythms and inflections of Russian speech, but doubted if it was 'musicianly and artistic'.

By this time he had already started the first version of *Boris Godunov*. It was finished the following year, and Mussorgsky submitted it to the Imperial Theatres in July 1870. Six months later it was rejected, and Mussorgsky began to rework it, to overcome some of the objections that had been made: quite apart from its provocative subject, the first version had no leading female role (or ballet) and was through-composed – with dialogues, choruses and monologues for the hero, but no arias. In the second version, which he completed by July 1872, the composer included a new third act, in which the Polish princess is introduced, and three scenes were performed at the Maryinsky Theatre on 17 February 1873. The opera was finally accepted for production when the soprano Yuliya Platonova insisted that it should be given for her benefit performance, and twenty-six performances (with one scene censored) were given after the première in February 1874 before it was completely banned by the censor. When it was revived in December 1896, Mussorgsky's harmonic irregularities and harsh orchestration were ironed out in Rimsky-Korsakov's version. Other later versions continued to 'correct' the composer, so that it is only quite recently that the intended character of Mussorgsky's masterpiece has been restored.

P. A. Lody as Andrei Morozov, the tragic hero of Tchaikovsky's *Oprichnik*, a role he created in 1874. This historical opera (the *oprichnik* were Ivan the Terrible's guardsmen) had been written two years earlier very much under the influence of the nationalist movement. It was well received, although the composer was dissatisfied with it.

**1873** *13 January* Première of ***Pskovityanka*** [***The Maid of Pskov***] (Rimsky-Korsakov/composer after Mey) at the Maryinsky Theatre, St Petersburg. The composer's first opera, begun in 1868.
*24 May* Première of ***Le Roi l'a dit*** (Delibes/Gondinet) at the Opéra-Comique, Paris; the first of two substantial operatic works by a composer experienced in both *opérettes* and ballet music.
*25 November* American première of ***Aida*** at the New York Academy, with Ottavia Torriani supported by Cary, Campanini and Maurel (making his New York début). The Academy, directed during the 1870s by Maurice Strakosch, relied on a brilliant group of singers, with the quartet of Nilsson, Cary, Campanini and Giuseppe del Puente appearing in several productions, including ***Les Huguenots***, ***Il trovatore*** and ***Lohengrin***.

**1874** Début of Giovanni de Reschi (Jean de Reszke) in the baritone role of Alfonso in ***La Favorite*** in Venice. He went on to become the greatest tenor of his generation.
*8 February* Première of ***Boris Godunov*** (Mussorgsky/composer after Pushkin and Karamzin) at the Maryinsky Theatre, St Petersburg, conducted by Nápravník and with a cast including Mel'nikov in the title role, Platonova, Petrov and Komisarzhevsky.
*27 March* Première of ***Dvě vdovy*** [***The Two Widows***] (Smetana/Züngel after Mallefille) at the Provisional Czech Theatre, Prague (revised version 1878).
*5 April* Première of ***Die Fledermaus*** (Johann Strauss/Haffner and Genée after Meilhac and L. Halévy) at the Theater an der Wien, Vienna. Strauss's sublime operetta was only accepted into the opera house proper after the failure of his one attempt at a major operatic work, ***Ritter Pázmán*** (1892).
*24 April* Première of ***Oprichnik*** (Tchaikovsky/composer after Lazhechnikov) at the Maryinsky Theatre, St Petersburg, under Nápravník.

*11 October* Première of ***Der Widerspenstigen Zähmung*** [***The Taming of the Shrew***] (Goetz/composer and Widmann after Shakespeare) at the Nationaltheater, Mannheim. Goetz's first opera, a mainstay of the German repertory for many years, exemplified his belief that closed forms (recitatives, arias, ensembles) were an essential requirement for operatic composition.

**1875** *5 January* Opening of the new Paris Opéra (architect: Garnier; decorations by Baudry and others). The first new opera given there (on 5 April) was Mermet's ***Jeanne d'Arc***.

*25 January* Première of ***Demon*** (Rubinstein/Viskovatov after Lermontov) at the Maryinsky Theatre, St Petersburg. The title role in Rubinstein's most successful opera became a brilliant vehicle for dramatic singers, most notably Chaliapin, who first sang it in 1893 in Tblisi.

*3 March* Première of ***Carmen*** (Bizet/Meilhac and L. Halévy after Mérimée) at the Opéra-Comique, Paris, with Galli-Marié in title role and Paul Lhérie as Don José. The first performance of the opera outside Paris, replacing the *mélodrame* as well as some unaccompanied dialogue with recitatives by Ernest Guiraud, was in Vienna on 23 October.

*10 March* Première of ***Die Königin von Saba*** [***The Queen of Sheba***] (Goldmark/Mosenthal) at the Hofoper, Vienna, with Materna as the Queen. No money was available for new scenery, so scenery from a ballet, *Sardanapale*, had to be reused, but the work was well received and went on to international success.

*8 May* First performance of a Wagner opera at Covent Garden: ***Lohengrin***, sung in Italian. Lohengrin was sung by Patti's husband Ernest Nicolini, Wolfram by Maurel and Elsa by Emma Albani. Later the same month Mapleson mounted a rival ***Lohengrin*** with Campanini, Nilsson, Tietjens and Antonio Galassi.

*22 November* The Paris version of ***Tannhäuser*** received its first performance in German at the Hofoper, Vienna, rehearsed by the composer and conducted by Hans Richter, the first of a series of Wagner performances arranged by the new musical director of the Hofoper, Franz Jauner. The cast included Materna, Bertha Ehnn, the Swedish tenor Leonard Labatt and Emil Scaria, all of whom also sang in the Vienna première of ***Die Walküre*** in March 1877. All four operas of the ***Ring*** had been given by February 1879.

Print commemorating the first production of *Carmen* at the Opéra-Comique in March 1875.

## Carmen

Bizet's masterpiece had an inauspicious beginning. The opera had been extensively reworked during rehearsals, which began in October 1874, and after the first night its success was still uncertain. During the thirty-third performance, on 3 June, Bizet died; before the news reached the theatre, Galli-Marié, playing Carmen, almost collapsed on stage during the scene in which the cards foretell death, and later she collapsed in the wings. Tchaikovsky had praised the way the singer 'managed to combine with the display of unbridled passion an element of mystical foreboding'. She was soon rivalled by other singers, who saw the part as an opportunity for a display of sensuality and dramatic power offered by none of their traditional roles. Outstanding Carmens included Minnie Hauk, who insisted on selecting her own cast for productions in 1878 in London and New York (Campanini as Don José, del Puente as Escamillo and Alwina Valleria as Micaela), Pauline Lucca (in Vienna and at Covent Garden), and, most famous of all, Emma Calvé, who sang the first performance in French at the Met with Jean de Reszke, Jean Lassalle and Emma Eames.

Set for the final scene, in the desert, of Goldmark's *Die Königin von Saba* in the first Italian production at Turin in 1879. With its combination of passionate roles for the leading singers with choruses and ensembles of great solemnity, this remains one of the finest German operas of its period.

# 1876 / 1882 Bayreuth

*The completion of the cycle of* Der Ring des Nibelungen *and the opening of the Festival Theatre at Bayreuth realized Wagner's dream of creating opera in a setting totally removed from the social milieu of the fashionable city opera house. From the outset musicians came to Bayreuth as pilgrims to the shrine of the new religion of music.*

The Festspielhaus at Bayreuth soon after its completion.

The orchestra pit at Bayreuth during the first cycle of *Der Ring des Nibelungen*.

**1876** *8 April* Première of ***La gioconda*** (Ponchielli/Boito after Hugo) at La Scala, Milan. The celebrated 'Dance of the Hours' shows the influence of French conventions on Italian operatic form, as the leading composer of the generation after Verdi tried to emerge from the shadow of the great man. ***La gioconda*** was a notable success and has held a place in the repertory. Boito, shamed by the disaster of his ***Mefistofele*** (see 1868) wrote the libretto under an anagrammatic pseudonym.

*11 April* Première of ***Piccolino*** (Guiraud/Sardou and Nuitter) at the Opéra-Comique, Paris. The composer, best known for completing ***Les Contes d'Hoffmann*** (1881) and writing recitatives for ***Carmen*** (1875) and ***Lakmé*** (1883), wrote a number of successful *opéras-comiques*, of which ***Piccolino*** was the best known abroad. Victorien Sardou, author in 1887 of the play ***Tosca***, on which Puccini was to base his opera (see 1900), had been writing libretti for the Opéra-Comique since 1862.

*13, 14, 16, 17 August* Première of ***Der Ring des Nibelungen*** (Wagner/composer) at the Festspielhaus, Bayreuth, conducted by Hans Richter. The performances on 16 and 17 August were the premières of ***Siegfried*** and ***Die Götterdämmerung***. Kaiser Wilhelm I and Emperor Don Pedro II of Brazil were in the first-night audience; King Ludwig II had attended the dress rehearsals.

*7 November* Première of ***Hubička*** [***The Kiss***] (Smetana/Krásnohorská, after Světlá) at the Provisional Czech Theatre, Prague. Written at a time when the composer had recently become completely deaf, this slight comic opera, with overtones of folk music, was an immediate success.

Amalie Materna as Brünnhilde, the role she played in the first *Ring* cycle. Other leading roles were sung by Franz Betz (Wotan), Josephine Schefsky (Sieglinde), Albert Niemann (Siegmund), Georg Unger (Siegfried), Eugen Gura (Donner and Gunther) and Karl Hill (Alberich); Lilli Lehmann sang the roles of a Rhinemaiden, a Valkyrie and the Wood Bird.

> *Experience is everything. Moreover, Siegfried alone (man by himself) is not the complete human being: he is merely the half; it is only along with Brünnhilde that he becomes the redeemer. To the isolated being not all things are possible; there is need of more than one, and it is woman, suffering and willing to sacrifice herself, who becomes at last the real, conscious redeemer: for what is love itself but the 'eternal feminine'?*
>
> Wagner on the *Ring*

A commemorative print (1906) showing Siegfried's encounter with the Rhinemaidens in *Die Götterdämmerung.*

## The Ring

Wagner had had plans for using the myth of Siegfried, celebrated both in the Icelandic sagas and in medieval German epics, since 1848, and within five years he had not only enlarged the scheme to embrace a four-part operatic cycle about the destructive ambition of the Norse gods, ending with the immolation of Valhalla, but had written and published the poem that would serve as a libretto for his scheme. However, although fragments of the music were written, the project was put aside until both *Tristan* and *Die Meistersinger* had been completed. The realization of the *Ring* was made possible by his meeting with the eighteen-year-old Ludwig II of Bavaria, who had just ascended the Bavarian throne and developed an all-consuming passion for Wagner and his works. He was willing to finance the production of the *Ring*, and as Wagner resumed work on the composition, Ludwig embarked on plans to build a special theatre in Munich for the performance. Political opposition made this impossible, but the first two parts, *Das Rheingold* and *Die Walküre*, were performed at the Munich Hofoper in 1869 and 1870, while the composer arranged to have a special festival theatre built at Bayreuth. Even with Ludwig's backing, this was a colossal enterprise to finance, but in August 1876 the theatre opened with the first complete cycle of *Der Ring des Nibelungen*.

Wagner had by now fully developed the use of leitmotifs in his music, and these fragments of thematic material are used not simply to identify the characters, but to unify the colossal musical structure and to underline the recurring themes of love, heroism, anger, revenge, greed and renunciation. However, the compelling appeal of Wagner's opera lies ultimately in the individual relationships between the characters – the rivalry between Wotan and Alberich, the love stories of Siegmund and Sieglinde or Siegfried and Brünnhilde, the jealousy of Fricka, Gutrune and Hunding, and perhaps above all the tragic devotion of Wotan to his daughter Brünnhilde.

*6 December* Première of ***Kuznets Vakula*** [***Vakula the Smith***] (Tchaikovsky/Polonsky after Gogol) at the Maryinsky Theatre, St Petersburg, conducted by Nápravník. Gogol's robust story of the smith who cheats the devil is set by Tchaikovsky to music that Cui described as 'melancholy, elegiac, sentimental'; but, if the spirit of Gogol is absent, this is one of the composer's finest operatic scores with many reminiscences of Russian and Ukrainian folk music. It was revived in 1885 as ***The Slippers***.

Title page of the score of Ponchielli's *La gioconda*, 1876, with its Venetian setting.

**1877** *27 April* Première of ***Le Roi de Lahore*** (Massenet/Gallet) at the Opéra, Paris, with Lassalle as Scindia. This was the composer's first work for the Opéra. Its success overshadowed one of the late operas of his predecessor, Gounod, ***Cinq Mars***, which Carvalho – now director of the Opéra-Comique – had premièred there three weeks earlier in the hope of reviving Gounod's career after his exile in England.
*19 May* Therese Tietjens made her final appearance as Lucrezia Borgia at Her Majesty's Theatre, London, shortly before her death.
*7 June* Marcella Sembrich made her first appearance on the operatic stage as Elvira in ***I puritani*** in Athens. She had studied violin and piano, but when she played and sang for Liszt, the composer advised her to choose singing as a career.
Mapleson leased the New York Academy of Music for a touring company of operatic stars, returning for several seasons until the mid-1880s, when the loss of Patti and the overwhelming success of the seasons of German opera at the Metropolitan forced him to quit.
*2 December* Première (in German) of ***Samson et Dalila*** (Saint-Saëns/Lemaire) at the Hoftheater, Weimar. The composer had played through the first act with Viardot in the title role at the singer's summer house in 1875. Act II was given a concert performance the same year at the Théâtre du Châtelet in Paris, but was disliked by the critics, being considered too 'symphonic' and serious for any French theatre. Liszt then offered to stage it in Weimar, but it was not performed in France until 1890 (in Rouen) and not at the Opéra until 23 November 1892; from that time it began to enjoy the great success that has kept it in the repertory ever since.

**1878** *27 January* Première of ***Šelma sedlák*** [***The Cunning Peasant***] (Dvořák/Veselý) at the Provisional Czech Theatre, Prague. A little over a year earlier the composer had written a tragic opera, ***Vanda***, which had failed completely, but he replaced the derivative style of that work – an amalgam of Smetana, Meyerbeer and Wagner – with music of a much more individual, tuneful character in this light comedy, which was a notable success in his homeland and was performed in several German cities in the 1880s.

**1879** *11 January* Première at the Teatro Regio, Turin, of ***Ero e Leandro*** (Bottesini/Boito), the most enduring of Bottesini's operas, setting a libretto which Boito had originally intended for himself.
*29 March* Première of ***Evgeny Onegin*** (Tchaikovsky/composer and Shilovsky after Pushkin) at the Little Theatre of the Imperial College of Music, Moscow. The opera made little impression until its revival in Moscow in October 1884. Tchaikovsky identified strongly with the characters in the opera, not so much with the man of the world Onegin as with the emotional Tatyana, whose reaction to Onegin's love letter is a turning point in the opera. Tchaikovsky had himself received a love letter from a woman he did not know containing threats of suicide if he did not respond, as a result of which – seven weeks after their first meeting – he contracted a disastrous marriage with her.
*9 November* The tenor title role in ***Robert le diable*** was sung for the first

time in Madrid by Jean de Reszke, who never again sang a baritone role.
*30 December* Première of ***The Pirates of Penzance (or The Slave of Duty)*** (Sullivan/Gilbert) at the Royal Bijou Theatre, Paignton. The performance was given to establish copyright the night before the proper première at the Fifth Avenue Theatre, New York. The London première followed in 1880. Like most of the collaborations of Gilbert and Sullivan, the operetta took grand opera as one of the many targets of its satire.

**1880** *21 January* Première of ***Maiskaya noch*** [***May Night***] (Rimsky-Korsakov/composer after Gogol) at the Maryinsky Theatre, St Petersburg, conducted by Nápravník, with Mel'nikov and Fedor Stravinsky in the cast. The opera, based on a Ukrainian folk tale, tells of village lovers whose rivalry is resolved by the queen of the water sprites.
*5 March* Première of ***Kupets Kalashnikov*** [***The Merchant Kalashnikov***] (Rubinstein/Kulikov after Lermontov) at the Maryinsky Theatre, St Petersburg. Its brilliant local colour was considered dangerously nationalistic, and the opera was banned after its second performance.
*26 December* Première of ***Il figliuol prodigo*** (Ponchielli/Zanardini after Scribe) at La Scala, Milan, with Tamagno and E. de Reszke.

**1881** *10 February* Posthumous première of ***Les Contes d'Hoffmann*** (Offenbach/Barbier and Carré) at the Opéra-Comique, Paris, so successful that it was repeated one hundred times in its opening year. The composer had died the previous October and his score was completed and orchestrated by Guiraud; the drinking song and Giulietta's Barcarolle were taken from ***Die Rheinnixen*** (Vienna, 1864). Adèle Isaac sang all four heroines, with Alexandre Talazac as Hoffmann.
*25 February* Première of ***Orleanskaya deva*** [***The Maid of Orleans***] (Tchaikovsky/composer) at the Maryinsky Theatre, St Petersburg, conducted by Nápravník (to whom the opera is dedicated), with Mariya Kamenskaya in the title role and F. Stravinsky as Dunois. The libretto is based on Zhukovsky's version of Schiller's play, and the opera is the composer's only – and rather unsuccessful – attempt to write a grand opera of the Meyerbeer type.
*24 March* Première of the revised version of Verdi's ***Simon Boccanegra*** at La Scala, Milan, with Maurel, Tamagno, E. de Reszke and Anna d'Angeri, conducted by Faccio. Ricordi, who had been trying unsuccessfully to get Verdi to write a new opera, sponsored this revival of an opera nearly twenty-five years old (see 1857) with an exceptionally strong cast and arranged for Boito to collaborate on the revision of the libretto.

Playbill for the opening night of the new Czech National Theatre, Prague, 11 June 1881. Smetana's *Libuše*, written in 1871–2, portrays a great Bohemian heroine and was immediately adopted as the Czech national opera.

Ensemble from Rimsky-Korsakov's *Maiskaya noch*, with the bass Fedor Stravinsky (father of the composer) second left.

The trio of aesthetes from the first production of Gilbert and Sullivan's *Patience*, 1881.

*28 March* Death of Mussorgsky in St Petersburg.
*1 April* Première of ***Le Tribut de Zamora*** (Gounod/d'Ennery and Brésil) at the Opéra, Paris. It was the composer's last opera and failed to match the success of ***Faust*** or ***Roméo et Juliette.***
*23 April* Première of ***Patience, or Bunthorne's Bride*** (Sullivan/Gilbert) at the Opera Comique, London, a satire on the aesthetic movement.
*11 June* Première of ***Libuše*** (Smetana/Wenzig, trans. Špindler) for the opening of the new Czech National Theatre in Prague.
*8 December* During the second performance of ***Les Contes d'Hoffmann*** at the Ringtheater, Vienna, the first production outside Paris, the theatre burned down. On the same night the new Czech National Theatre in Prague also burned down.
*19 December* Première of ***Hérodiade*** (Massenet/Milliet, Hartmann and Zanardini after Flaubert) at the Théâtre de la Monnaie, Brussels, an opera house that pioneered the performance of Wagner's operas in French and was to champion the music of the French Wagnerians.

**1882** *10 February* Première of ***Snegurochka*** [***The Snow Maiden***] (Rimsky-Korsakov/composer after Ostrovsky) at the Maryinsky Theatre, St Petersburg, conducted by Nápravník, with Kamenskaya and F. Stravinsky among the cast. A revised version was premièred in the same theatre in

Toulouse-Lautrec's drawing of Ambroise Thomas rehearsing his opera *Françoise de Rimini*, produced at the Opéra in 1882. The composer of *Mignon* and *Hamlet*, who had been director of the Conservatoire since 1871, was discouraged by the failure of his new work and wrote no more operas.

The Austrian soprano Gabrielle Krauss as Hermosa, the role she created in Gounod's *Le Tribut de Zamora* at the Paris Opéra on 1 April 1881.

Amalie Materna as Kundry and Hermann Winkelmann as Parsifal, the roles they sang in the première of *Parsifal* at Bayreuth, 26 July 1882.

## Bayreuth and Parsifal

The Bayreuth Festspielhaus was as revolutionary as *Der Ring des Nibelungen*, the work for which the theatre was designed. Wagner insisted that the plans should be determined solely by artistic considerations, particularly the building's acoustics. He had greatly expanded the traditional opera orchestra, and his solution to the problem of balance with the singers was to position the players in a covered pit partly beneath the stage. The effect of the box-like shape of the auditorium was to increase the reverberation time, so that, although music and words would be less clearly articulated, a fuller and more thoroughly blended tone might be heard. Wagner also wanted to do away with all notions of a social distinction between different parts of the auditorium, so that the experience could be untainted by non-artistic distractions.

It was specifically for this theatre that he composed his last opera, *Parsifal*. As with the *Ring*, he had long been planning an opera based on the medieval epic of the 'holy fool' and his search for the holy grail, but it was only after the first Bayreuth Festival that Wagner started on the composition, which was not completed until January 1882. *Parsifal* is a religious opera, but its Christianity is strongly tinged with the very personal beliefs of its composer, and its themes are more universal: heroism, sensuality, the triumph of good over evil and transfiguration in death. Wagner lived for only a few months after the opera's first performance, and his widow insisted – ultimately unsuccessfully – that the opera should only ever be performed in the sacred surroundings of Bayreuth.

1898. This allegorical fairy-tale about the change from winter to spring was the first of the composer's operas in which his technique was sufficiently developed to be able to give coherent form to his inspired musical ideas, and it remained his favourite. An earlier revival in Moscow in October 1882 (designed by Viktor Vasnetsov) was the first production by the Private Russian Opera founded by S. I. Mamontov, which introduced many new works by Russian composers to the public in productions designed by leading artists.

*14 April* Première of ***Françoise de Rimini*** (Thomas/Barbier and Carré after Dante) at the Opéra, Paris.

*May–June* Season of Wagner operas given under Hans Richter at Her Majesty's Theatre, London, at the start of a tour organized by Angelo Neumann which continued through Europe and to New York: the season began with a complete ***Ring*** cycle with most of the original cast (though Fricka and Brünnhilde were sung by Hedwig Reicher-Kindermann, daughter of the original Munich Wotan); this was followed by ***Lohengrin***, ***Holländer***, ***Tannhäuser***, ***Meistersinger***, Weber's ***Euryanthe*** and ***Tristan***. Rosa Sucher sang the roles of Elsa, Elisabeth, Eva and Isolde, partnered by Hermann Winkelmann as Lohengrin, Tannhäuser, Walther and Tristan, while Eugen Gura sang Wolfram and Sachs. ***Tristan***, being heard in London for the first time, made the strongest impression, both positive and negative; one critic later described it as 'the ripest fruit from a tree of good and evil, especially evil'.

*26 July* Première of ***Parsifal*** (Wagner/composer) at the Festspielhaus, Bayreuth, conducted by Hermann Levi. The title role was taken by Winkelmann, with Emil Scaria (Gurnemanz), Karl Hill (Klingsor), Theodor Reichmann (Amfortas) and Amalie Materna alternating with Marianne Brandt as Kundry.

*8 October* Première of ***Dimitrij*** (Dvořák/Červinková-Riegrová) at the New Czech Theatre, Prague, the composer's only grand historical opera, which contains some of his most effective dramatic music, suited to the pan-Slavic theme.

*29 October* Première of ***Čertova stěna*** [***The Devil's Wall***] (Smetana/Krásnohorská) at the New Czech Theatre, Prague, the composer's last completed opera.

# 1883–1895 Perfect Wagnerites

*The institution of Bayreuth as a pilgrimage site for musicians helped turn Wagnerism into a massive cult. In France the* Revue wagnérienne, *published from 1885 to 1887, discussed and elaborated the master's aesthetic philosophy, leading not only to the deployment by composers of a new harmonic language but also to a conscious development of 'national' musical characteristics.*

**DATES**

**1889**
Universal Exposition in Paris, of which the Eiffel Tower was the centrepiece

**1890**
First moving-picture shows in New York

**1894**
Alfred Dreyfus arrested for treason and deported

**1883** *13 February* Death of Wagner in Venice.
*5 March* Première of ***Henry VIII*** (Saint-Saëns/Détroyat and Silvestre) at the Opéra, Paris, with Lassalle in the title role. Although the grand historical subject is reminiscent of Meyerbeer, the musical setting is more forward-looking, though hardly attractive enough to hold an operatic audience.
*17 March* Première of ***Dejanice*** (Catalani/Zanardini) at La Scala, Milan. The composer's earliest opera had been ***La falce*** (1875, with libretto by his fellow-*scapigliato* Boito); both ***Dejanice*** and ***La Wally*** (1892) show Wagner's influence more strongly than any operas by Catalani's Italian contemporaries.
*14 April* Première of ***Lakmé*** (Delibes/Gondinet and Gille) at the Opéra-Comique, Paris. The title role of this exotic tragedy was written as a vehicle for the beautiful Brooklyn *coloratura* soprano Marie Van Zandt, who sang in the première with Talazac as Gérald. Recitatives to replace the spoken dialogue were written by Guiraud, so that the work could be performed abroad.
*22 October* The first season at the Metropolitan Opera, New York, opened with a production of Gounod's ***Faust*** (in Italian). The principals, Nilsson as Marguerite, Campanini as Faust and Novara as Méphisto, had previously sung these roles at the Academy of Music for Mapleson, who now offered Patti as a rival attraction at the Academy. ***Faust*** became so popular at the Met that the house became known as the Faustspielhaus; the archetypal cast there in the 1890s included the de Reszke brothers and Nellie Melba.

**1884** *7 January* Première of ***Sigurd*** (Reyer/du Locle and Blau) at the Théâtre de la Monnaie, Brussels. The composer, who had written three operas earlier in his career (see 1861), was best known as Berlioz's successor as music critic for the *Journal des débats.*
*19 January* Première of ***Manon*** (Massenet/Meilhac and Gille after Prévost) at the Opéra-Comique, Paris, with Marie Heilbronn as Manon and Talazac as Des Grieux. The Italian rights in the work were purchased by Ricordi, but he delayed the first performance until after Puccini's opera on the same subject had been performed in 1893.
*15 February* Première of ***Mazepa*** (Tchaikovsky/composer and Burenin after Pushkin) at the Bolshoi Theatre, Moscow. Despite its grand historical setting, the opera focuses on the personal tragedy of the leading characters, with some of the composer's most effective dramatic music.
*4 May* Première of ***Der Trompeter von Säckingen*** (Nessler/Bunge after von Scheffel) at the Stadttheater, Leipzig, a comic opera which was enormously popular in Germany.

*'To be devoted to Wagner merely as a dog is devoted to his master, sharing a few elementary ideas, appetites and emotions with him, and, for the rest, reverencing his superiority without understanding it, is no true Wagnerism.'*

G. B. Shaw in his preface to *The Perfect Wagnerite*, 1898

The Swedish soprano Christine Nilsson portrayed in *Gypsy Girl with Mandolin* by Camille Corot in 1874. She was the principal star of the inaugural season of New York's Metropolitan Opera in 1883–4, although she was then vocally past her best.

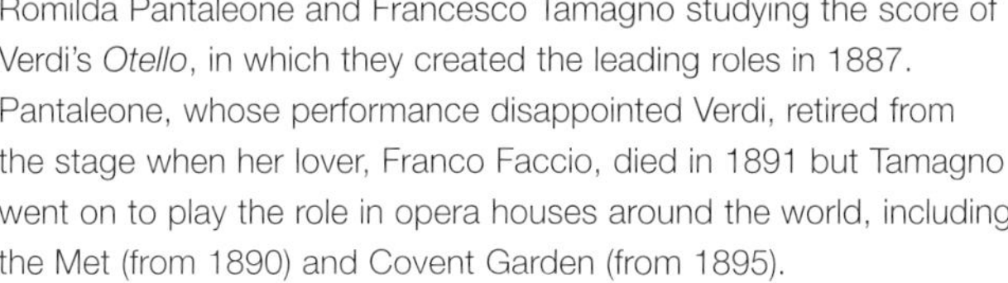

Romilda Pantaleone and Francesco Tamagno studying the score of Verdi's *Otello*, in which they created the leading roles in 1887. Pantaleone, whose performance disappointed Verdi, retired from the stage when her lover, Franco Faccio, died in 1891 but Tamagno went on to play the role in opera houses around the world, including the Met (from 1890) and Covent Garden (from 1895).

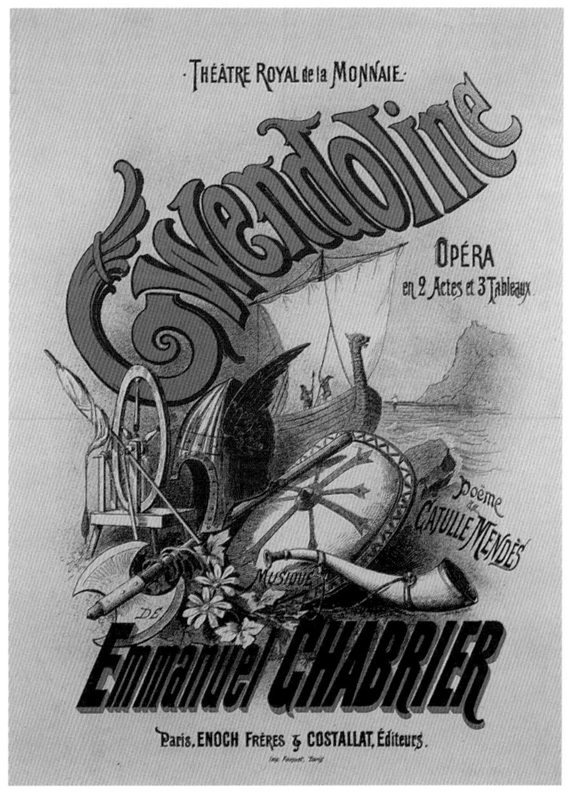


Poster for the première of Chabrier's Viking epic *Gwendoline*, first performed at the Théâtre de la Monnaie, Brussels in 1886. French versions of many Wagner operas had been given there – *Lohengrin* (1870), *Der fliegende Holländer* (1872), *Tannhäuser* (1873), the *Ring* cycle (1883) and *Die Meistersinger* (1885) – and it was the theatre where many French Wagnerian works received their first performances. It was also here that Nellie Melba made her début as Gilda in 1887.

Edouard and Jean de Reszke as Don Diègue and his son Rodrigue, roles they created in Massenet's *Le Cid* at the Opéra in November 1885. Born in Poland, the de Reszke brothers became the star male singers of their generation. Jean was unrivalled as a tenor until the advent, shortly before his retirement in 1902, of Caruso, and his repertoire, which also included Wagner, was broader than the Italian's; Edouard, five years younger than his brother, was a bass equally at home in serious or *buffo* roles.

*31 May* Première of ***Le villi*** (Puccini/Fontana) at the Teatro dal Verme, Milan, whose orchestra included Mascagni as a double-bass player. Ricordi soon put Puccini on a monthly retainer, though he later threatened to terminate this if his third opera, ***Manon Lescaut*** (on which the composer started work in 1890), was not a success.

**1885** *14 March* Première of ***The Mikado, or The Town of Titipu*** (Sullivan/Gilbert) at the Savoy Theatre, London. It was the most successful of Sullivan and Gilbert's operettas and the only one to enter the repertory outside the English-speaking world.
*17 March* Première of ***Marion Delorme*** (Ponchielli/Golisciani after Hugo) at La Scala, Milan, the composer's last opera and one of many works of the period – from ***La traviata*** to ***Thaïs*** and ***Manon Lescaut*** – to be based on the tragedy of a reformed prostitute. The title role was created by Romilda Pantaleone, to whom the work was dedicated, and Didier by Tamagno.
*25 April* Posthumous première of ***Une Nuit de Cléopâtre*** (Massé/Barbier after Gautier) at the Opéra-Comique, Paris, a work of extreme sensuality.
*24 October* Première of ***Der Zigeunerbaron*** (J. Strauss/Schnitzer after Jókai) at the Theater an der Wien, Vienna, a comic opera which reflects the Hungarian gypsy plot in its colourful music.
*30 November* Première of ***Le Cid*** (Massenet/d'Ennery, Blau and Gallet after Corneille) at the Opéra, Paris, a work that typifies the Opéra audience's taste for visual and musical spectacle.
*1 December* US première of ***Tristan und Isolde*** at the Metropolitan Opera, New York, with Niemann and Lehmann in the title roles; it became an immediate success, enormously strengthening the Wagnerian movement in America.

**1886** *21 February* Première of ***Khovanshchina*** (Mussorgsky/composer and Stasov), composed between 1872 and 1880, in an amateur production at Kononov's Hall, St Petersburg (a version completed and orchestrated by Rimsky-Korsakov). The official première was at the Maryinsky Theatre, St Petersburg, on 20 November 1911 with Chaliapin in the leading role.
*10 April* Première of ***Gwendoline*** (Chabrier/Mendès) at the Théâtre de la Monnaie, Brussels. The work was produced at the height of the Wagnerian craze in Paris, and the influence is only too apparent in Chabrier's opera, based on one of the Nordic sagas. The composer had

## First seasons at the Metropolitan Opera

The new house, created and owned by members of the 'Knickerbocker aristocracy', was designed to bring new standards both to the performance of opera in New York and to its social ambience. The nineteen operas given in 1883–4 are a good guide to the current international repertory; the season opened with Gounod's *Faust* and continued with a mixture of French, Italian and German works (though all were sung in Italian): *Robert le diable*, *Les Huguenots* and *Le Prophète* by Meyerbeer; *Mignon* and *Hamlet* by Thomas; Bizet's *Carmen*; Mozart's *Don Giovanni*; Rossini's *Il barbiere di Siviglia*; *I puritani* and *La sonnambula* by Bellini; *Lucia di Lammermoor* by Donizetti; *Il trovatore*, *La traviata* and *Rigoletto* by Verdi; Boito's *Mefistofele*; Ponchielli's *La gioconda*; Flotow's *Martha*; and Wagner's *Lohengrin*. The international roster of singers, most of whom had appeared in recent seasons at the Academy of Music, included sopranos Christine Nilsson, Marcella Sembrich (a sensational newcomer to New York, who made her début as Lucia) and Alwina Valleria; mezzos Sofia Scalchi, Zelia Trebelli (Guillebert) and Emmy Fusch-Madi; tenors Italo Campanini, Victor Capoul and Roberto Stagno; baritones Giuseppe del Puente and Giuseppe Kaschmann; and basses Achile Augier, Giovanni Mirabella, Baldassare Corsini and Franco Novara (Frank Nash). Not surprisingly, the season was a financial disaster, losing $250,000, and it was followed by seven years of German opera. The first of these was organized and conducted by Leopold Damrosch. He and his successor Anton Seidl brought over a company of singers which included the Bayreuth artists Materna, Lehmann, Brandt, Alvary, Niemann, Reichmann and Fischer. Wagner naturally figured large (with a full *Ring* cycle in March 1889), as did Meyerbeer, while other operas performed – in German – included *Fidelio*, *Guillaume Tell*, *Fernand Cortez*, *Norma*, *Un ballo in maschera*, *Die Königin von Saba* and *Carmen*.

The Swiss soprano Lucienne Bréval (Bertha Schilling) as Salammbô in a revival of Ernest Reyer's opera based on Flaubert's exotic novel. She made her début in 1892 and during the 1890s was a prominent Wagnerian singer in Paris, creating the role of Brünnhilde (in *Siegfried* and *Die Götterdämmerung*) in French; after 1900 Bréval sang regularly both at the Met and Covent Garden.

The baritone Jean Lassalle as Benvenuto Cellini in Saint-Saëns's *Ascanio*, premièred at the Opéra in March 1890. Lassalle, who had made his début in Brussels in 1871, was a prominent artist at the Met in 1892–3 and later seasons.

already composed two *opérettes*, ***L'Etoile*** (1877) and ***Une Education manquée*** (1879), both charming works, though at the time they too were accused of excessive Wagnerism.
*30 June* During a performance of ***Aida*** at Rio de Janeiro, audience hissing forced a staff conductor from the podium mid-performance and his place was taken by a nineteen-year-old cellist from the orchestra – Arturo Toscanini.
*31 July* Death of Liszt in Bayreuth.

**1887** *5 February* Première of ***Otello*** (Verdi/Boito after Shakespeare) at La Scala, Milan, conducted by Faccio. Otello and Iago were sung by Tamagno and Maurel (who later sang these roles at the Met and elsewhere) and Desdemona by Pantaleoni.
*18 May* Première of ***Le Roi malgré lui*** (Chabrier/de Najac and Burani after Ancelot) at the Opéra-Comique, Paris. Although this belongs to the genre of *opéra-comique*, its success has always been limited by the complexity of both the plot and the musical treatment, with its Wagnerian colouring and harmonies.
*1 November* Première of ***Charodeika*** [***The Enchantress***] (Tchaikovsky/Shpazhinsky) at the Maryinsky Theatre, St Petersburg, a highly melodramatic opera that takes the redeeming power of love as its theme.

**1888** *7 May* Première of ***Le Roi d'Ys*** (Lalo/Blau) at the Opéra-Comique, Paris, a richly coloured Wagnerian work based on Breton legends, completed in 1880. It was rejected by the Opéra but attained great popularity when eventually staged at the Opéra-Comique with a cast that included Talazac as Mylio.
*24 May* London début of Nellie Melba as Lucia at Covent Garden.
*29 June* Posthumous première of ***Die Feen*** (Wagner/composer after Gozzi) at the Hoftheater, Munich, the composer's first opera, composed (in 1833 in Würzburg) in the Weberian romantic vein.
Début in The Hague of Sibyl Sanderson (protégée of Massenet and former fiancée of Randolph Hearst), as Manon, a role she also created at the Met on 16 January 1895 with Jean de Reszke, Mario Ancona and Plançon.

**1889** *12 February* Première of ***Jakobín*** [***The Jacobin***] (Dvořák/Červinková-Riegrová) at the Czech National Theatre, Prague. Set in a Bohemian village, the plot of the opera concerns the reconciling power of music, a theme which elicited some of the composer's most sensitive writing.
*21 April* Première of ***Edgar*** (Puccini/Fontana after Musset) at La Scala, Milan, with Giovanni Battista de Negri and Pantaleone in the leading roles. The libretto was unsatisfactory, failing to provide convincing motivation for the characters, and in future operas Puccini was always closely involved in the development of the text.
*14 May* Première of ***Esclarmonde*** (Massenet/Gallet and de Gramont) at the Opéra-Comique, Paris. The work was written as a vehicle for Sanderson to perform during the Paris Exposition.
*1 July* Performance of ***Le Prophète*** (Meyerbeer) in Brisbane sung in the international utopian language Volapük.
*9 December* Opening of the Chicago Auditorium, designed by Louis Sullivan and Dankmar Adler, with a gala concert by Patti and other artists. The theatre, which seats 6,000, was not used exclusively as an opera house, although it was the home of opera in Chicago until 1929.

**1890** *10 February* Première of ***Salammbô*** (Reyer/du Locle) at the Théâtre de la Monnaie, Brussels, with Rose Caron, the leading singer of French Wagnerian opera, in the title role. It was Reyer's last opera.
*21 March* Première of ***Ascanio*** (Saint-Saëns/Gallet after Dumas and Meurice) at the Opéra, Paris, based on the life of Benvenuto Cellini.

The cast included Lassalle as Cellini and Eames as Colombe.
*17 May* Première of ***Cavalleria rusticana*** (Mascagni/Menasci and Targioni-Tozzetti after Verga) at the Teatro Costanzi, Rome, with Gemma Bellincioni as Santuzza and Roberto Stagno (whom she later married) as Turiddu.
*4 November* Première of ***Knyaz Igor*** [***Prince Igor***] (Borodin/composer after Stasov) at the Maryinsky Theatre, St Petersburg, with additions by Rimsky-Korsakov and Glazunov. The title role was sung by Mel'nikov. Borodin had started work on the opera in 1869, and Galitzky's celebrated aria had been premièred in a concert in 1879 by Fedor Stravinsky.
*6–7 December* Posthumous première (in a German translation) of both parts of ***Les Troyens*** (Berlioz/composer after Virgil) at the Hoftheater, Karlsruhe, under the direction of Felix Mottl. The first part (Acts I and II) had previously only been given concert performances (originally in 1879 with Charton-Demeur, the first Dido, singing the role of Cassandra). Part II was revived at the Opéra-Comique, Paris, in 1892 with the role of Dido sung by Marie Delna, who also played Cassandra when Part I was finally performed at the Opéra (in a reduced version) in 1899.
*19 December* Première of ***Pikovaya dama*** [***The Queen of Spades***] (Tchaikovsky/composer and M. Tchaikovsky after Pushkin) at the Maryinsky Theatre, St Petersburg, conducted by Nápravník, with Mariya Slavina (as the sinister Countess), Nikolai Figner, his wife Medea Mei and Ivan Mel'nikov. Tchaikovsky identified deeply with Hermann's obsessive search for love, a search that is thwarted by his sense of alienation and by the inexorable progress of fate. The opera – unlike Pushkin's poem – ends with the hero's suicide.

Cover of *L'illustrazione italiana* featuring Victor Maurel as Verdi's *Falstaff*, premièred at La Scala in February 1893. After the English première of the opera, at Covent Garden on 19 May 1894, a reviewer for *The Times* wrote: 'It remains to be seen whether the subscribers and the fashionable world in public will care for an opera which, since it contains no dull moments, allows no opportunities for comfortable conversation during the music.'

**1891** *31 January* Première of ***Ivanhoe*** (Sullivan/Sturgis after Scott) to inaugurate Richard d'Oyly Carte's Royal English Opera House, London, with the Welsh tenor Ben Davies in the title role. Although the work, Sullivan's only grand opera, ran for a record 160 consecutive performances, it was a critical and financial failure and Carte soon had to sell his theatre.
*18 June* Première of ***Le Rêve*** (Bruneau/Gallet after Zola) at the Opéra-Comique, Paris. The composer, a former pupil of Massenet, whose direct musical style mirrored the sincerity and intensity of Zola's realism, was hailed as the hero of a new revolution. He collaborated with Zola on three more operas, but his music has not held a place in the repertory.
*31 October* Première of ***L'amico Fritz*** (Mascagni/Daspuro after Erckmann-Chatrian) at the Teatro Costanzi, Rome, with Calvé, Lhérie and Fernando de Lucia. This simple, romantic opera fulfilled the high expectations that followed the overwhelming success of Mascagni's first opera.

**1892** *20 January* Première of ***La Wally*** (Catalani/Illica after Hillern) at La Scala, Milan, with Hariclea Darclée in the title role. It was Catalani's last and finest opera, set in the Tyrol, and includes the great soprano aria 'Ebben? Ne andró lontano'.

## Boito and Verdi

Verdi's reluctance to compose another opera after *Aida* was the cause of great concern to his publisher Giulio Ricordi, since the firm's income relied so heavily on publishing and performance rights from Verdi's works. Boito had written the text for a hymn Verdi composed for the 1862 Exhibition in London, but shortly after that he and his friend Faccio had offended Verdi (see 1863); nevertheless, he was the one librettist who might be able to get Verdi to compose again, so Ricordi, Faccio (now back on good terms with Verdi) and the composer's wife all encouraged the idea of a collaboration on a new version of Shakespeare's *Othello*. The first approaches were made in 1879, but despite a continuing correspondence, Verdi remained reluctant, and only in 1884 did he start composing. By the end of 1885 the score was nearly complete, and the opera that resulted is arguably the most perfect collaboration between poet and composer. When Boito showed the composer a first sketch for a new Shakespearean opera, *Falstaff*, in the summer of 1889, Verdi took less than a week to decide to renew the collaboration, and their comic masterpiece was first performed in February 1893.

Poster for Puccini's *Manon Lescaut*, premièred in Turin in February 1893. The title role was created, in her native city, by Cesira Ferrani (Zanazzio), whom Puccini described as 'the ideal Manon, in appearance, talent and voice'.

Portrait (by Léon Glaize) of the seventeen-year-old Marie Delna as Dido in the revival of Berlioz's *Les Troyens à Carthage* which opened at the Opéra-Comique on 9 June 1892. The young mezzo received plaudits both for the beauty of her singing and for her natural acting and diction, and she was a natural choice for the role of Cassandra when the first part of Berlioz's masterpiece was staged at the Opéra on 15 November 1899.

A popular print of the tragic dénouement of Mascagni's *Cavalleria rusticana*, first performed in Rome in May 1890. Modern novels and dramas with realist contemporary settings were already familiar, but 'veristic' opera was quite new, and Mascagni's work, written as a competition entry when he was an unknown orchestral musician, not only challenged other composers to emulate his achievement but also to develop a suitably natural musical style.

Scene of the destruction of the temple in the Paris première (31 October 1890) of Saint-Saëns's *Samson et Dalila* at the Nouveau Théâtre-Lyrique (Eden-Théâtre), with Alexandre Talazac as Samson. A production had opened in Rouen on 3 March the same year, but the work was not staged at the Opéra until November 1892.

*16 February* Première (in German translation) of ***Werther*** (Massenet/Blau, Milliet and Hartmann after Goethe) at the Hofoper, Vienna, conducted by Richter, with Ernest Van Dyck as Werther and Marie Renard as Charlotte. Working on an intimate scale, the composer captured the romantic sentimentality, if not the irony, of Goethe's novel.
*21 May* Première of ***Pagliacci*** (Leoncavallo/composer) at the Teatro dal Verme, Milan, conducted by Toscanini with a cast including Fiorello Giraud, Victor Maurel, Adelina Stehle and Mario Ancona. Boito considered it a 'vile spectacle'.
*June–July* Guest season at Covent Garden conducted by Gustav Mahler, in which, as well as ***Fidelio***, ***Tannhäuser*** and ***Tristan***, the complete ***Ring*** was performed – though ***Siegfried*** was given first so that the 'Teuton Adonis', Max Alvary, could make his début as young Siegfried – with singers including Klafsky, Sucher, Reichmann and Ernestine Schumann-Heink.
*6 October* Première of ***Cristoforo Colombo*** (Franchetti/Illica) at the Teatro Carlo Felice, Genoa, composed as part of the celebrations for the anniversary of Columbus's voyage.
*1 November* Première of ***Mlada*** (Rimsky-Korsakov/composer after Krylov) at the Maryinsky Theatre, St Petersburg. The opera-ballet had originally been commissioned from five composers (the others were Borodin, Cui, Mussorgsky and Minkus) but was not completed. Rimsky-Korsakov rewrote all the text and music himself.
*25 November* First appearance of Calvé, the most famous of all Carmens, in that role at the Opéra-Comique, Paris. She performed her first Carmen at the Met the following year.
*18 December* Première of ***Iolanta*** (Tchaikovsky/M. Tchaikovsky after Hertz) at the Maryinsky Theatre, St Petersburg, conducted by Nápravník, with Figner and Mei. Tchaikovsky's last opera, put on in a double-bill with the ballet *The Nutcracker*, was based on a fairy tale in the manner of H. C. Andersen.

**1893** *30 January* Première of ***Madame Chrysanthème*** (Messager/Hartmann and Alexandre after Loti) at the Théâtre-Lyrique de la Renaissance, Paris. The story with its Japanese local colour was one of the sources for Long's *Madam Butterfly* story – which led to Puccini's opera – though Messager's opera has a happy end.
*1 February* Première of ***Manon Lescaut*** (Puccini/Praga, Oliva and Illica after Prévost) at the Teatro Regio, Turin. Seven librettists were involved; the first was Leoncavallo, with whom the composer did not get on, but he found ideal collaborators in Illica, an excellent librettist who had also worked with Franchetti and Catalani, and Giacosa, a lecturer in literature at the Milan Conservatory, who versified the text. Puccini, who had been to Bayreuth in 1889, derived from Wagner not only his use of identifying themes for the characters but also the augmented chords and unresolved dissonances which helped create the characteristic 'Puccini sound'.
*9 February* Première of ***Falstaff*** (Verdi/Boito after Shakespeare) at La Scala, Milan, with Victor Maurel in the title role. The opera is unified by the 'orchestral continuity' Verdi first tried out in ***Rigoletto*** (1851) and had continued to develop, so that in ***Falstaff*** the musical material is given an almost symphonic development.
*18 February* Première of the operatic version of Berlioz's ***La Damnation de Faust*** (see 1846), adapted for the stage by Raoul Gunsbourg, at the Théâtre du Casino, Monte Carlo, with Jean de Reszke as Faust.
*9 May* Première of ***Aleko*** (Rachmaninov/Nemirovich-Danchenko after Pushkin) at the Bolshoi Theatre, Moscow, a prize-winning student work about jealousy and murder in a band of gypsies.
*7 November* The Liceo opera house, Barcelona, was bombed by the

anarchist Santiago Salvador during a performance of ***Guillaume Tell***. Twenty people were killed and many injured.
*23 December* Première of ***Hänsel und Gretel*** (Humperdinck/Wette after brothers Grimm) at the Hoftheater, Weimar. The composer of this most popular of all 'children's operas' was a dedicated disciple of Wagner.

**1894** *4 March* Première of ***Hulda*** (Franck/Grandmougin after Bjørnson) at the Théâtre du Casino, Monte Carlo. The first of Franck's two operas, neither of which was produced in his lifetime.
*16 March* Première of ***Thaïs*** (Massenet/Gallet after France) at the Opéra, Paris. The name part in this sensational story of the temptation of a desert monk was written for Sanderson.
*April* Début of Enrico Caruso in Mario Morelli's ***L'amico Francesco*** at the Teatro Nuovo, Naples, taken off after two nights. However, he was heard by the impresario of the Teatro Cimarosa in Caserta and sang there in both ***Cavalleria rusticana*** and ***Faust*** in April 1895.
*10 May* Première of ***Guntram*** (Strauss/composer) at the Hoftheater, Weimar, the composer's first, Wagnerian, opera, with Pauline de Ahna as Freihild. In August Strauss conducted at Bayreuth for the first time – ***Tannhäuser*** with de Ahna (whom he married in September) as Elisabeth.
*20 June* Première of ***La Navarraise*** (Massenet/Claretie and Cain) at Covent Garden, London, with Calvé as Anita, a role she repeated at the Opéra-Comique and the Met the following year. The composer wrote this melodramatic work as a riposte to the *verismo* of Mascagni's ***Cavalleria rusticana*** (and of Bruneau's ***Le Rêve***).
*16 December* Première of ***Donna Diana*** (Reznicek/composer after Moreto) at the New German Theatre, Prague, conducted by the composer. Rooted in the German romantic tradition, it was the only one of the composer's operas to achieve lasting international fame.
*24 December* 'Night of the seven stars' at the Metropolitan Opera, New York, when ***Les Huguenots*** was performed by Lillian Nordica, Sofia Scalchi, Melba, the de Reszke brothers, Plançon and Maurel.

**1895** *8 February* Première of ***La Montagne noire*** (Holmès/composer) at the Opéra, Paris. The last opera written by the French-Irish composer Augusta Holmès and the only one to be performed. Her admiration for Wagner is reflected all too strongly in the work's overcharged orchestration.
*16 March* Première of ***La Dolores*** (Bretón/composer after Feliú y Codina) at the Teatro de la Zarzuela, Madrid. In addition to many *zarzuelas*, the composer wrote some twenty operas, of which this enjoyed the greatest success.
*4 May* Première of ***Der Evangelimann*** (Kienzl/composer after Meissner) at the Opernhaus, Berlin.The work, which has remained popular, is a Wagnerian *volksoper* on the themes of jealousy, betrayal and forgiveness.
*20 November* Revival of Purcell's ***Dido and Aeneas*** (the first since the seventeenth century) at the Royal College of Music, London, as part of the celebrations for the bicentenary of Purcell's death.
*10 December* Première of ***Noch pered rozhdestvom*** [***Christmas Eve***] (Rimsky-Korsakov/composer after Gogol) at the Maryinsky Theatre, St Petersburg, conducted by Nápravník. The royal figure – clearly intended to be Catherine the Great, though not named – was recognized by a member of the royal family at a preview of the opera, and the part had to be rewritten for a baritone, since representation of members of the royal house on stage was forbidden.

Poster for the October 1895 Opéra-Comique production of Massenet's *La Navarraise*, featuring Emma Calvé as Anita, a role that Massenet had written especially for her. G. B. Shaw described Calvé as 'a living volcano, wild with anxiety…mad with joy, ecstatic with love, desperate with disappointment'.

The composer Augusta Holmès. Her opera *La Montagne noire* (1895) was the first new work staged at the Opéra after Verdi's *Otello*; the sets were largely taken over from productions that had been staged in 1893–4 – Vidal's ballet *La Maledetta* (1893), *Die Walküre* and *Thaïs* – and only thirteen performances were given.

# 1896 / 1902 The Turn of the Century

*The years around 1900 saw a mass of new works, some by established operatic composers such as Mascagni, Leoncavallo, Puccini, Massenet and Rimsky-Korsakov, others by young composers of all nations trying to make their names in the lyric theatre, often with operas based on local themes.*

**DATES**

**1897**
Zionist Congress in Basel

**1898**
Zola publishes his open letter 'J'accuse' about the Dreyfus case

Spanish–American War results in the loss of the Spanish colonies

Empress Elisabeth of Austria murdered by an Italian anarchist

**1899**
Start of Boer War in South Africa

**1900**
Assassination of King Umberto I of Italy, who is succeeded by Victor Emmanuel III

**1901**
Death of Queen Victoria, who is succeeded by Edward VII

US President McKinley assassinated, succeeded by Theodore Roosevelt

Trans-Siberian Railway reaches Port Arthur

Postcards issued by Puccini's publisher Ricordi to commemorate the première of *La Bohème*, 1896.

Poster for the first production of Puccini's *Tosca*, showing the scene of Tosca's murder of Baron Scarpia. These roles were created by Hariclea Darclée and Eugenio Giraldoni.

**1896** *5 January* Première of ***Pepita Jiménez*** (Albéniz/Money-Coutts) at the Liceo, Barcelona; the composer's most successful opera, written to a libretto by his English patron, Francis Burdett Money-Coutts.
*1 February* Première of ***La Bohème*** (Puccini/Giacosa and Illica after Murger) at the Teatro Regio, Turin, conducted by Toscanini, with Cesira Ferrani as Mimì. The opera initially had a cool reception, but a second production in Palermo two months later was a great success, propelling Puccini to international stardom.
*2 March* Première of ***Shamus O'Brien*** (Stanford/Jessop after Le Fanu) at the Opera Comique, London, the Irish composer's most successful opera.
*10 March* Première of ***Chatterton*** (Leoncavallo/composer after de Vigny) at the Teatro Argentina, Rome. This was Leoncavallo's first opera, which had been written almost twenty years earlier.
*21 March* Première of ***Das Heimchen am Herd*** [***The Cricket on the Hearth***] (Goldmark/Willner after Dickens) at the Hofoper, Vienna.
*28 March* Premièrc of ***Andrea Chenier*** (Giordano/Illica) at La Scala, Milan. Set at the time of the French Revolution, the opera was immediately popular and has held its place in the repertory. Illica wrote the libretto for Franchetti, who allowed Giordano to take it over, and his music effectively matches the vein of *verismo* in a romantic costume drama.
*7 June* Première of ***Der Corregidor*** (Wolf/Mayreder after Alarcón) at the Nationaltheater, Mannheim, Hugo Wolf's only work for the stage. It contains wonderful individual numbers but lacks dramatic drive. Mahler's refusal to stage the work in Vienna was a devastating blow to Wolf, provoking delusions that he himself was director of the Hofoper.
*23 September* First performance of ***Der vierjährige Posten*** (Schubert/Körner), a *singspiel* written in 1815, in Dresden. Schubert's ***Fierrabras***

# Puccini: La Bohème and Tosca

Puccini's earlier operas – most recently *Manon Lescaut* – had presented quite traditional operatic themes, but *La Bohème* puzzled its first audiences: although the opera is set in 1830, its characters are quite ordinary people, students in Paris, while the sentiment and comedy of the first two scenes gives way to an increasingly tragic mood in the second half of the work. However, Puccini unified the opera with thematic fragments associated with his characters (they can hardly be called leitmotifs) and heightened the pathos by returning to themes associated in the early part of the opera with happiness or love at its tragic dénouement. After a little hesitation the public accepted this new formula, and the blatant sentiment of the music brought a new audience to the opera house. Murger's *Scènes de la vie de Bohème* had been brought to Puccini's attention as a source for an opera by Leoncavallo, who was planning to use it himself, and the friendship of the composers was strained by Puccini's taking the material and producing his opera before Leoncavallo's was finished.

The source for *Tosca*, Puccini's next opera, was a play by Victorien Sardou, which had also been considered by other composers (including Verdi). Puccini had seen Sarah Bernhardt perform the tragic role on stage in Italy some years earlier, and, once he began to work on the opera, he travelled to Paris to get the playwright's approval of his adaptation of the work. Puccini adds pathos to the melodramatic plot by using the music not only to define little details of the stage action but also to paint descriptive tableaux around the brutal second act, in which attempted rape is countered by murder: the interior of the church when the Te Deum is sung at the end of Act I and the scene of day breaking over Rome at the start of Act III with the sound of sheep's bells and church clocks striking.

Puccini's scores were written with immense care, and, although he was a great admirer of Wagner, they represent a continuation of the Italian operatic tradition rather than essays in the more symphonic German style. The melodic vocal lines are perfectly placed for his singers, whether the character of the music is lyric or dramatic, and the score serves always to support and define the dramatic action; Puccini's works are not operas of the imagination, but operas for the stage.

Poster for Mascagni's *Iris*, which starred Hariclea Darclée, 1898. As the poster suggests, the opera catered to the contemporary taste for Japonaiserie.

(libretto by Kupelwieser), commissioned in 1821 by the Kärntnertortheater, Vienna, but never performed, received its first stage production five months later in Karlsruhe.
*7 November* Première of ***Jungfrun i tornet*** [***The Maiden in the Tower***] (Sibelius/Herzberg), in an amateur production at the City Hall, Helsinki. It was to be Sibelius's only opera.

**1897** *19 February* Première of ***Messidor*** (Bruneau/Zola) at the Opéra, Paris, a work in which the *vérisme* shown in the earlier collaborations of composer and author is modified by a symbolic dimension to the plot.
*12 March* Première of ***Fervaal*** (d'Indy/composer) at the Théâtre de la Monnaie, Brussels. The composer of this symbolist music drama based on Celtic legend was the most passionate Wagnerian among French composers, but he promoted the nationalist ideal of Ars Gallica more successfully with the revivals of early opera he staged as head of the Schola Cantorum than through his own compositions.
*8 April* Mahler accepted the post of music director of the Hofoper, Vienna. His first engagement was as conductor of *Lohengrin* on 11 May. Mahler's ten year 'reign' marked the highest point in the history of the Vienna opera.
*6 May* Première of ***La Bohème*** (Leoncavallo/composer after Murger) at La Fenice, Venice. Despite Puccini's opera, Leoncavallo's was an international, albeit brief, success.
*27 November* Première of ***L'arlesiana*** (Cilea/Marenco after Daudet) at the Teatro Lirico, Milan, with Caruso creating the tenor role – his first great success. The singer's Milan début had been one week earlier at the same theatre, in ***La gioconda***.

The heroic tenor Leo Slezak, who made his stage début in Brno in 1896 as Lohengrin and went on to become one of the great stars of the Vienna Hofoper, the Metropolitan and other international opera houses.

*28 December* Première of ***Šárka*** (Fibich/Schulzová) at the Czech National Theatre, Prague, one of the last and finest works of one of the leading Czech nationalist composers.

**1898** *7 January* Première of ***Sadko*** (Rimsky-Korsakov/composer and Bel'sky) by Mamontov's Private Russian Opera at the Solodovnikov Theatre, Moscow, with Sekar-Rozhansky in the title role, Chaliapin as the Viking merchant and Zabela-Vrubel as the Princess. Rimsky-Korsakov reused much of the music he had written for his orchestral suite on the same subject in 1867, and the opera is a series of tableaux created with his vivid orchestral palette.
Appointment of Giulio Gatti-Casazza as manager of La Scala. He engaged Toscanini as chief conductor, and together they did much to raise standards of performance, although the Teatro Lirico was more enterprising in mounting new operas.
*17 November* Première of ***Fedora*** (Giordano/Colautti) at the Teatro Lirico, Milan, conducted by the composer, with Gemma Bellincioni, Caruso and Delfino Menotti. The opera was based on a melodrama written by Victorien Sardou for Sarah Bernhardt and was another of Caruso's early successes. Giordano's music suited the new generation of singers trained in the *verismo* style perfectly, and his reputation was second only to that of Puccini until the 1920s.
*22 November* Première of ***Iris*** (Mascagni/Illica) at the Teatro Costanzi, Rome, conducted by the composer, with Darclée and de Lucia in the leading roles.
*7 December* Première of ***Mozart i Salieri*** (Rimsky-Korsakov/Pushkin) by Mamontov's Private Russian Opera at the Solodovnikov Theatre, Moscow, with the tenor Vasily Shkafer as Mozart and Chaliapin as Salieri. In this work the composer went back to the earlier form of Russian recitative opera pioneered by Dargomizhsky.

**1899** *22 January* Première of ***Der Bärenhäuter*** (S. Wagner/composer) at the Hofoper, Munich; the first and best received of a series of operas written by Wagner's son Siegfried.
*21 March* Première of ***Messaline*** (de Lara/Silvestre and Morand) at the Théâtre du Casino, Monte Carlo.
*24 May* Première of ***Cendrillon*** (Massenet/Cain after Perrault) at the Opéra-Comique, Paris.
*25 July* Première of ***Yupanky*** (Berutti/Rodríguez Larreta) at the Teatro de la Opera, Buenos Aires. Caruso took the title role in this Inca opera by the Argentine composer, who two years earlier had written the patriotic opera ***Pampa***.
*3 November* Première of ***Tsarskaya nevesta*** [***The Tsar's Bride***] (Rimsky-Korsakov/Tyumenev after Mey) by the Private Russian Opera at the Solodovnikov Theatre, Moscow.
*23 November* Première of ***Čert a Káča*** [***The Devil and Kate***] (Dvořák/Wenig) at the Czech National Theatre, Prague. Based on a folk tale, the opera is constructed with long recitative passages following Czech speech rhythms, a technique later adopted by Janáček.
Revival of Haydn's ***Lo speziale*** (1768) at the Hofoper, Vienna, in a 'free arrangement' under Mahler; the first Haydn opera to be revived since the eighteenth century.

**1900** *14 January* Première of ***Tosca*** (Puccini/Giacosa and Illica after Sardou) at the Teatro Costanzi, Rome.
*26 January* Caruso's La Scala début as Rodolfo in ***La Bohème***. He was suffering from laryngitis and the occasion was, in the words of La Scala's manager Gatti-Casazza, 'not lucky'.

## Louise

Charpentier's opera is set in the 'Republic of Montmartre' and tells the story of the unhappy love affair of a *grisette* and a Bohemian poet, opposed by the girl's parents. What distinguished the work from Puccini's *La Bohème* and similar operas was that it was set in the present day – in the year 1900 – and contained a large cast of local characters, including the young women who work with Louise at the dressmaker's workshop. The most celebrated numbers are the orchestral evocation of Paris at dawn, 'Paris s'éveille', which opens Act II, Louise's aria 'Depuis le jour' at the beginning of Act III and her crowning as 'muse of Montmartre' by the Pope of Fools – a ceremony that Charpentier had himself initiated in real life – which forms the climax to the act. Charpentier's socialism is blended with the sentiment of the story in the gently romantic style of his music, and, despite the fierce opposition of conservatives, the opera was a huge international success.

A Montmartre street scene, the convincingly realistic set for the original production of Gustave Charpentier's *Louise* at the Opéra-Comique in 1900.

Costume design by Edward Gordon Craig for the sorceress in Purcell's *Dido and Aeneas* in the production in 1900 by the Purcell Operatic Society at the Hampstead Conservatoire, five years after the opera's first modern staging.

*2 February* Première of ***Louise*** (Charpentier/composer) at the Opéra-Comique, Paris. The huge international success of the work was never matched by any of Charpentier's other works.
*May* The Moravian tenor Leo Slezak's first international engagement was as a guest artist from the Breslau opera at Covent Garden; he sang Lohengrin, which was performed without rehearsals.
*18 June* Revival of Gluck's ***Iphigénie en Tauride*** at the Opéra-Comique, Paris, with Rose Caron in the title role.
*27 August* Open-air première of ***Prométhée*** (Fauré/Lorrain and Hérold) in the Arènes, Béziers, the composer's first operatic work.
*3 November* Première of ***Skazka o Tsare Saltane*** [***The Tale of Tsar Saltan***] (Rimsky-Korsakov/Bel'sky after Pushkin) at the Private Russian Opera, Moscow (now run by its members, as Mamontov was in prison for fraud). A nationalist fairy-story opera, brilliantly orchestrated, the opera contains the composer's best known piece, 'The Flight of the Bumble Bee'.
*10 November* Première of ***Zazà*** (Leoncavallo/composer after Simon and Berton) at the Teatro Lirico, Milan. The opera was well received and widely performed, but Leoncavallo was never able to match the success of ***Pagliacci***.
*26 December* Metropolitan Opera première of Puccini's ***La Bohème*** with Melba as Mimì. The opera was performed at the Met in practically every subsequent season for over seventy years.

**1901** *17 January* Simultaneous premières of ***Le maschere*** (Mascagni/Illica) in Milan (La Scala), Rome (Teatro Costanzi), Venice (La Fenice), Turin (Teatro Regio), Genoa (Teatro Carlo Felice) and Verona (Teatro Filarmonico); and in Naples (San Carlo) two days later. The performance in Milan featured Caruso and was conducted by Toscanini, while that in Rome, conducted by the composer, was slightly more successful than the others, which were not well received. The *commedia dell'arte* subject made

Rupert Bunny's portrait of the Australian soprano Nellie Melba, painted in 1902, when she had achieved international stardom and was at the height of her powers.

the opera one of the earliest new works to be part of the neoclassical revival.
*27 January* Death of Verdi. At the funeral, Toscanini conducted the choir and orchestra of La Scala in a performance of 'Va pensiero' from ***Nabucco.***
*31 March* Première of ***Rusalka*** (Dvořák/Kvapil) at the Czech National Theatre, Prague, Dvořák's finest opera. The tragic story of a water sprite who becomes human, like Undine, was set in Bohemia, and the allusions to folk rhythms and melodies give the work a pronounced Czech character.
*13 April* Première of ***Lorenza*** (Mascheroni/Illica) at the Teatro Costanzi, Rome. The title role was composed for Bellincioni. Mascheroni was better known as a conductor, but he was also a singer and recorded an aria from his own opera in 1904.
*Summer* First Salzburg Festival of the twentieth century. Festivals had been held in Mozart's birthplace in 1877, 1879, 1887 and 1891, but they now began to be held more regularly, and from 1920 became an annual international event.
*15 October* Début of the American soprano Geraldine Farrar, as Marguerite in Gounod's ***Faust,*** in Berlin.
*20 November* Première of ***Grisélidis*** (Massenet/Silvestre and Morand) at the Opéra-Comique, Paris, with Bréval in the title role.
*21 November* Première of ***Feuersnot*** (Strauss/Wolzogen) at the Hofoper, Dresden, with Annie Krull as Diemuth. The work is a comedy with strong sexual overtones.

**1902** *4 January* Première of ***I Pirenei*** (Pedrell/Balaguer) at the Liceo, Barcelona; the first of a trilogy of Catalan nationalist operas (though sung in Italian), the other two parts of which, ***La Celestina*** and ***Raimondo Lulio,*** were not performed.
*18 February* Première of ***Le Jongleur de Notre-Dame*** (Massenet/Léna) at the Théâtre du Casino, Monte Carlo.
*11 March* Première of ***Germania*** (Franchetti/Illica) at La Scala, Milan, under Toscanini with Caruso as Frederick Loewe. The performance was heard by Fred Gaisberg of Victor Records, who made a series of recordings of Caruso in a hotel room converted into a studio.
*12 April* Première of ***Los amores de la Inés*** (de Falla and Vives/Dugi) at the Teatro Cómico, Madrid, one of five *zarzuelas* de Falla wrote with Vives and the only one to receive a performance.
*30 April* Première of ***Pelléas et Mélisande*** (Debussy/Maeterlinck) at the Opéra-Comique, Paris. The cast included Mary Garden (Mélisande), Jeanne Gerville-Réache, Jean Périer, Hector Dufranne (Golaud) and Jean Vieulle. Maeterlinck, who had wanted his companion Georgette Leblanc to play the title role, protested about the production. It was not performed elsewhere until 1907.
*14 May* Caruso's Covent Garden début as the Duke in ***Rigoletto.***
*6 November* Première of ***Adriana Lecouvreur*** (Cilea/Colautti after Scribe and Legouvé) at the Teatro Lirico, Milan, conducted by C. Campanini with a cast including Caruso, de Luca, Pandolfini and Ghibaudo. The opera remains Cilea's best known work.
*28 November* Première of ***Saul og David*** (Nielsen/Christiansen) at the Royal Theatre, Copenhagen, the Danish composer's first opera.
*25 December* Première of ***Kashchey bessmertny*** [***Kashchey the Immortal***] (Rimsky-Korsakov/composer after Petrovsky) by the Private Russian Opera in Moscow. The composer's stylistic chameleonism is shown by this Wagnerian essay, following hard on the heels of an *opera seria,* ***Servilia,*** which had been premièred in St Petersburg two months earlier.

Scene from the 1901 production of Isidoro de Lara's *Messaline* in Bordeaux in a painting by Toulouse-Lautrec. Messaline was the most successful of a string of operas written by the English-born composer and, two years later, became the first opera by an Englishman to be given at La Scala.

Mary Garden as Mélisande in the original production of *Pelléas et Mélisande*, 1902.

*'On hearing opera, the spectator is accustomed to experiencing two distinct sorts of emotion: on the one hand the musical emotion, and on the other the emotion of the characters – usually he experiences them in succession. I tried to ensure that the two were perfectly merged and simultaneous. Melody, if I dare say so, is anti-lyrical. It cannot express the varying states of the soul, and of life. Essentially it is suited only to the song that expresses a simple feeling…I have never allowed my music to precipitate or retard the changing feelings or passions of my characters for technical convenience. It stands aside as soon as it can, leaving them the freedom of their gestures, their utterances – their joy or their sorrow…'*

Debussy on *Pelléas et Mélisande*

# 1903
# 1907

# Revival and Rebellion

*As early operas began to be made more familiar by groups like the Schola Cantorum in Paris, many composers turned away from* verismo *towards eighteenth-century forms and styles or took refuge in the symbolic world of the fairy tale. Others clung to the fading tradition of romanticism, while the young rebels attacked it head on: Strauss's* Salome *became the operatic sensation of the decade.*

**DATES**

**1904**
Start of Russo-Japanese War
Films of *Le Barbier de Séville* and *La Damnation de Faust*

**1905**
Russian surrender of Port Arthur to the Japanese is followed by student unrest, a general strike and mutiny on the *Potemkin*
Fauve painters exhibit at the Paris Salon d'Automne

**1907**
Picasso paints *Les Demoiselles d'Avignon*

**1903** *7 January* Première of ***L'Etranger*** (d'Indy/composer) at the Théâtre de la Monnaie, Brussels. D'Indy's most important work for the stage is a symbolist drama impregnated with the musical and philosophical ideas of Wagner.
*20 March* Performance of ***Der Wald*** (Ethel Smyth/composer) at the Metropolitan Opera, New York (premièred the previous year at the Berlin Oper); for more than half a century ***Der Wald*** was the only opera by a woman to be performed at the Met.
*28 March* Revival of Rameau's ***Hippolyte et Aricie*** in Geneva under Jacques Dalcroze.
*15 November* Première of ***Tiefland*** (d'Albert/Lothar after Guimerà) at the New German Theatre, Prague, with Emmy Destinn in one of the roles she was to make famous – Marta, seduced by the landowner from the lowlands and avenged by the highland shepherd.
*23 November* Caruso's début at the Metropolitan Opera, New York, as the Duke in ***Rigoletto***, with Antonio Scotti in the title role and Sembrich as Gilda.
*27 November* Première (in German) of ***Le donne curiose*** (Wolf-Ferrari/Sugano after Goldoni) at the Residenztheater, Munich. The first Italian performance was at the Metropolitan Opera under Toscanini on 3 January 1912, and the first in Italy was at La Scala on 16 January 1913. The opera is lightly scored in keeping with its *commedia dell'arte* theme and characters, who include Harlequin, Columbine and Pantaloon. The composer's second opera after Goldoni, ***I quattro rusteghi***, received its first performance at the Hoftheater, Munich, on 19 March 1906.
*30 November* Première of ***Le Roi Arthus*** (Chausson/composer) at the Théâtre de la Monnaie, Brussels, staged four years after the death of the composer, who had been one of the leading Wagnerians in France.
*19 December* Première of ***Siberia*** (Giordano/Illica) at La Scala, Milan, conducted by C. Campanini, with Rosina Storchio, Giovanni Zenatello, Giuseppe de Luca and Antonio Pini-Corsi. The opera enjoyed international success, and Giordano became the first Italian composer since Verdi to have a work performed at the Paris Opéra.
*24 December* First performance of ***Parsifal*** at the Metropolitan Opera, New York, against the wishes of Cosima Wagner. The work was put on by Heinrich Conried in his first season as director of the Met, and he successfully defended a lawsuit brought by the Wagner family since the opera was not protected by copyright in the USA. The affair caused a huge furore, and the performances were a great success. European copyright ran out at midnight on 31 December 1913, and performances took place the next day in Barcelona (starting at the minute copyright expired), Berlin, Breslau, Bremen, Kiel, Prague (two performances, one in Czech, one in German), Budapest, Bologna, Rome and Madrid. La Scala followed (in Italian) on 9 January 1914 and Covent Garden twenty-four days later.

Lilli Lehmann, one of the great sopranos of the late nineteenth century and a leading light in the early Salzburg Mozart festivals, of which the most notable celebrated the 150th anniversary of Mozart's birth in 1906.

Caruso as Canio in *Pagliacci*, photographed by Mishkin in New York, one of the most famous images of the Metropolitan Opera's leading star. Following his début there in 1903 Caruso was to make a total of over 600 appearances at the Met, singing on the opening night every year (except 1906) until 1920, shortly before his death.

## Salome

Although there were problems of censorship in city after city where *Salome* was to be staged, the première in Dresden was a colossal success, and the opera was performed in fifty other German towns within two years. Heinrich Conried staged the American première at the Metropolitan Opera on 22 January 1907, but furious attacks in the press on the immorality of the piece and the threat of the opera company's landlords – supposedly led by J. P. Morgan – to revoke their lease forced cancellation of remaining performances, although the opera was put on two years later (in French) at Hammerstein's Manhattan Opera House with Mary Garden in the title role.

The reason for *Salome*'s success – scandal apart – was its astonishing score: it is musically as tightly constructed as any of Strauss's orchestral works (Fauré described the opera as 'a symphonic poem with vocal parts added'), and, as drama, it builds up relentlessly to a terrifying climax – not in the dazzling exoticism of the 'Dance of the Seven Veils' but in the final scene, introduced by dissonant woodwind trills, where Salome's desire for Jokanaan is consummated in her kissing the lips of his severed head.

Scene from the original Dresden production of Richard Strauss's *Salome* (1905).

Poster for the première of Puccini's *Madama Butterfly* at La Scala, Milan, 1904. Puccini had seen David Belasco's play (itself based on a magazine story by John Luther Long) in London in 1900 while preparing the English première of *Tosca*, and he subsequently did research into the melodic and instrumental characteristics of Japanese music.

**1904** *21 January* Première of ***Její pastorkyňa*** [***Her Stepdaughter***] (Janáček/composer after Preissová) at the National Theatre, Brno. It was revived as ***Jenůfa***, the name of its heroine, at the Czech National Theatre, Prague, on 26 May 1916. Janáček began work on the score in 1894, and it is the first of his operas to use the technique he described as 'musical life-drawing', allowing the musical rhythms and structures to be conditioned by the speech-patterns of the text.
*17 February* Première of ***Madama Butterfly*** (Puccini/Giacosa and Illica after Belasco) at La Scala, Milan, with Storchio, Zenatello and de Luca. The opera was a disaster: there was organized opposition, and Puccini was accused of recycling the music of ***La Bohème***. After he had revised the score, the new version was first performed at the Teatro Grande, Brescia, with Salomea Krusceniski as Butterfly on 28 May 1904.
*25 February* First modern performance of Monteverdi's ***Orfeo*** at the Schola Cantorum, Paris, in a concert version translated and arranged by Vincent d'Indy. An Italian version (by Giacomo Orefice) was performed in Mantua and elsewhere in Italy five years later. The first stage performance was given at the Théâtre Réjane, Paris, on 2 May 1911. Other versions were prepared by Carl Orff (Mannheim, 17 April 1925), Malipiero (Leningrad, spring 1929; also used for the first American staging at Northampton, Mass., on 12 May 1929) and Respighi (La Scala, Milan, 16 March 1935, and elsewhere).
*25 March* Première of ***Armida*** (Dvořák/Vrchlický) at the Czech National Theatre, Prague. The composer's last opera suffered from a highly unsatisfactory libretto, and the first production was so plagued by strikes that, despite an excellent score, the opera has never been successful.
*30 March* Première of ***Koanga*** (Delius/composer and Keary after Cable) in the Stadttheater, Elberfeld, in a German version by the composer. The opera, a tragic story set on a cotton plantation, was composed in 1897. The first performance of the original English version was at Covent Garden on 23 September 1935.
*30 November* Première of ***Risurrezione*** (Alfano/Hanau after Tolstoy), at the Teatro Vittore Emanuele, Turin. The opera had a wide international success, although Alfano is now known primarily as the man who completed Puccini's ***Turandot***.

**1905** *14 February* Première of ***Chérubin*** (Massenet/de Croisset and Cain) at the Théâtre du Casino, Monte Carlo, with Mary Garden, Lina Cavalieri and Maurice Renaud. The opera concerns new amorous adventures of Beaumarchais's character immortalized by Mozart.
*24 February* Revival (in concert form) of Monteverdi's ***L'incoronazione di Poppea*** at the Schola Cantorum, Paris, in a version prepared and conducted by d'Indy; The first modern stage performance took place at the Théâtre des Arts, Paris on 5 February 1913.
*28 June* Première of ***L'oracolo*** (Leoni/Zanoni after Fernald) at Covent Garden, London, conducted by Messager. The opera, set in San Francisco's Chinatown, was the one international success of the composer, who had settled in England in 1892. Scotti, who had sung the role of the sinister keeper of an opium-den in the première, persuaded Gatti-Casazza to stage it at the Metropolitan Opera in 1915.
*20 November* Revival of Beethoven's ***Leonore*** (the original version of ***Fidelio***) under Richard Strauss at the Opernhaus, Berlin.
*24 November* Revival of Lully's ***Armide*** (in concert version) by d'Indy at the Schola Cantorum, Paris; the first modern stage revival was in Monte Carlo on 6 April 1918.
*9 December* Première of ***Salome*** (Strauss/Wilde trans. Lachmann) at the Hofoper, Dresden, conducted by Schuch, with Marie Wittich in the title role.

# Gustav Mahler in Vienna

Mahler's tenure of the directorship of the Vienna Hofoper, from 1897 to 1907, set an entirely new standard for the performance and production of opera. He had already earned a reputation as a perfectionist in the opera houses of Budapest and Hamburg, but Vienna offered him both new challenges and new opportunities. Tradition had always been used as an excuse for bad habits, but Mahler was ruthless with any kind of slovenliness; equally, he was determined to work with a group of singers he had chosen himself and was not afraid to make enemies of those he dismissed – who included Marie Renard and Ernest Van Dyck – and their supporters. The ensemble he built up included the sopranos Marie Gutheil-Schoder, Selma Kurz (whose famous trill, developed by Mahler can be heard in her recordings of *Lucia*) and Anna Mildenburg, the tenors Erik Schmedes and Leo Slezak, the baritones Leopold Demuth and Friedrich Weidemann, and the basses Richard Mayr and Wilhelm Hesch. Mahler insisted that singers should follow the score, and did away with many of the cadenzas and embellishments that had become the norm, particularly in Mozart's operas.

He also reorganized rehearsals so that productions could be properly prepared and was equally uncompromising with his audience (though he was unsuccessful in abolishing the singers' claques), darkening the auditorium during performances and introducing many new works by composers who included Pfitzner, d'Albert, Wolf-Ferrari, Zemlinsky, Siegfried Wagner and Richard Strauss.

In 1903 he persuaded the Jugendstil artist Alfred Roller to design a new production of *Tristan und Isolde* (starring Mildenburg, Schmedes and Mayr), and the spare scenery with a symbolist use of colour and light created a new kind of *Gesamtkunstwerk*. Roller was engaged as head of design at the Hofoper, and highlights of his collaboration with Mahler included a Mozart cycle, *Das Rheingold* and *Die Walküre*, and, shortly before Mahler's resignation, Gluck's *Iphigénie en Aulide*.

Viennese intriguing finally forced Mahler to leave, and at the end of 1907 he took up an appointment at the Metropolitan Opera in New York. His illness and the much shallower cultural atmosphere in America inhibited his success there, but the musical, dramatic and artistic standards he set in Vienna have remained a benchmark for all conductors and directors of opera since his time.

Anna Mildenburg as Isolde in the Mahler/Roller production of Wagner's *Tristan und Isolde* at the Hofoper, Vienna, which opened on 21 February 1903 (painting by Vitežlav Mašek).

Roller's set for the graveyard scene in Mahler's production of Mozart's *Don Giovanni* at the Vienna Hofoper in December 1905. The towers on either side of the stage remained in place throughout the opera, taking on a different function in each scene.

Self-caricature of Caruso in the recording studio.

## Caruso's Victor recordings

In Fred Gaisberg's improvised recording studio in Milan in March 1902, for a fee of £100, Caruso recorded ten 10-inch sides of music (the first of nearly 250 in his career). Other recordings in Italy followed, and while he was in New York for the 1903 Met season the tenor signed an exclusive recording contract with the Victor Talking Machine Company. His voice was reproduced exceptionally faithfully on the primitive equipment, and the real success of operatic recording began with him – within ten years the Victor catalogue contained substantial excerpts from nearly 150 operas and a roster of practically all the greatest international operatic stars. In 1924 the founder-editor of *The Gramophone* wrote: 'People did not really begin to buy gramophones until the appearance of the Caruso records gave them an earnest of the gramophone's potentialities. We to-day...owe our good fortune to Caruso. Fifteen years ago when violin solos sounded like bluebottles on a window-pane, overtures like badly played mouth-organs, chamber music like amorous cats, brass bands like runaway steam rollers, and the piano like an old woman clicking her false teeth, Caruso's voice proclaimed a millennium and preserved our faith.'
Compton Mackenzie, *My Record of Music*, 1955.

*30 December* Première of ***Die lustige Witwe*** [***The Merry Widow***] (Lehár/Léon and Stein) at the Theater an der Wien, Vienna.

**1906** *24 January* Première of ***Skupoy ritsar*** [***The Miserly Knight***] (Rachmaninov/Pushkin) and ***Francesca da Rimini*** (Rachmaninov/M. Tchaikovsky after Dante) at the Bolshoi Theatre, Moscow.
*31 January* Première of ***The Pipe of Desire*** (Converse/Barton) in Boston. On 18 March 1910 it was the first American opera to be staged at the Met.
*16 April* Opening in San Francisco of a season by the Metropolitan Opera touring company (after performances in Philadelphia, Baltimore, Washington DC, Pittsburgh, Chicago, St Louis and Kansas City) with ***Die Königin von Saba***, followed the next night by ***Carmen*** with Olive Fremstad and Caruso. The following morning the city was devastated by an earthquake.
*11 November* Première of ***Maskarade*** (Nielsen/V. Andersen after Holberg) at the Royal Theatre, Copenhagen. The opera is an eighteenth-century pastiche.
*11 November* Première of ***Strandrecht*** [***The Wreckers***] (Smyth/composer) at the Neues Theater, Leipzig; the English stage première, under Thomas Beecham, was at His Majesty's Theatre, London, on 22 June 1909.
*26 November* The opening of the new season at the Metropolitan Opera, New York, marked the début there of Geraldine Farrar as Juliette in Gounod's ***Roméo et Juliette***. Farrar was to become the most popular American-born star at the Metropolitan until her retirement in 1922, with an entourage of fans who were known as Gerry-flappers. On 11 February she sang the title role in the New York première of ***Madama Butterfly*** with Caruso and Scotti.
*3 December* Opening of the first of Oscar Hammerstein's four seasons at the Manhattan Opera House with Bellini's ***I puritani***, conducted by Cleofonte Campanini, followed by ***Rigoletto*** and ***Faust***. Hammerstein aimed to counter the social exclusivity of the Metropolitan Opera, and during these years the rivalry was intense, with each company trying to secure the greatest stars. Those who sang for Hammerstein included Melba, Garden, Tetrazzini, McCormack, Ancona and Renaud, and the French repertory he pioneered, including ***Pelléas***, ***Louise*** and several Massenet operas, came as a revelation to New York opera-goers. During

Caricature of Mahler with three members of the Hofoper company, Selma Kurz, Erik Schmedes and Leo Slezak, in an advertisement for a music and record shop.

Rival sopranos: (left) Geraldine Farrar as Manon (Massenet), a role she first sang at the Met on 3 February 1909; and (far left) Luisa Tetrazzini as Philine in Thomas's *Mignon*, one of the operas in the Manhattan Opera House repertory the first season she sang there (and a role also sung the following year by Farrar at the Met).

A French recording studio in 1899, in which the trio from Gounod's *Faust* is being recorded with piano accompaniment.

the same period the Met could offer Sembrich, Farrar, Eames, Fremstad, Cavalieri, Destinn, Homer, Caruso, Slezak, Scotti, Amato and Plançon.

**1907** *18 January* Metropolitan Opera première of Puccini's ***Manon Lescaut***, with Cavalieri, Caruso and Scotti. The performance was directed by the composer, making his first visit to the US.
*20 February* Première of ***Kitezh*** [***Legend of the Invisible City of Kitezh and the Maiden Fevroniya***] (Rimsky-Korsakov/Bel'sky after various) at the Maryinsky Theatre, St Petersburg. The opera marked the composer's return to the Russian style after a number of unrewarding excursions in other directions, and was a tremendous success.
*21 February* Première of ***Romeo und Julia auf dem Dorfe*** [***A Village Romeo and Juliet***] (Delius/composer after Keller) at the Komische Oper, Berlin. The work is a pastoral tragedy of lovers from feuding families.
*30 March* ***Lohengrin***, performed in Melbourne, was the first opera sung in German in Australia.
*10 May* Première of ***Ariane et Barbe-bleu*** (Dukas/Maeterlinck) at the Opéra-Comique, Paris, with Georgette Leblanc, Maeterlinck's companion, as Ariane. This was Dukas's only opera and is a masterpiece of French post-Wagnerism. Toscanini included the opera in his repertory at the Met (from 29 March 1911) with Farrar in the leading role.
*6 July* Revival of Gluck's ***Armide*** at Covent Garden, London, conducted by Messager with Bréval and Léon Laffitte.
*15 October* Mahler conducted ***Fidelio*** as his last performance at the Hofoper, Vienna.
*20 November* Metropolitan Opera début of Fedor Chaliapin in the role of Mefistofele (Boito), in which his realism (particularly his oiled naked torso) were much criticized.
*25 November* First appearance of Mary Garden, a protégée of Sibyl Sanderson, at the Manhattan Opera House in the title role of Massenet's ***Thaïs***.
*December* First staged revival of Rameau's ***Dardanus*** in Dijon by the Schola Cantorum under d'Indy (following a concert performance in Paris in April).

# 1908 1914 A Blaze of Glory

*The last years before the outbreak of war belonged to Richard Strauss and Sergei Diaghilev. Two of Strauss's greatest operas,* Elektra *and* Der Rosenkavalier, *achieved immediate international success in the wake of his scandalous* Salome, *while the seasons promoted by Diaghilev in Paris and London introduced the brilliant colours of Russian opera to the west.*

**DATES**

**1909**
First film of *Carmen*
*August* *Setmana tràgica* in Barcelona, the brutal suppression of an anarchist uprising

**1912**
Start of Balkan War (to 1913)
The *Titanic* sinks on her maiden voyage

**1913**
Opening of Panama Canal
Armory Show introduces cubism to New York

**1914**
*28 June* Assassination of Archduke Franz Ferdinand, heir to Austrian throne
*4 August* Outbreak of First World War

**1908** *11 January* Duel between Vincent d'Indy and Albert Carré, director of the Opéra-Comique, following d'Indy's fierce criticism of Carré's revival of Gluck's ***Iphigénie en Aulide*** the previous month, with Bréval taking the title role; neither party was injured.
*15 January* New York début of the *coloratura* soprano Luisa Tetrazzini at the Manhattan Opera House as Violetta (***La traviata***). The growing success of Hammerstein's venture led the directors of the Met to appoint Gatti-Casazza as manager, with Toscanini as his chief conductor.
*23 January* Mahler conducted ***Don Giovanni*** for his début at the Met.
*13 May* Revival of Rameau's ***Hippolyte et Aricie*** in a version by d'Indy at the Opéra, Paris.
*19 May* The Diaghilev company staged Mussorgsky's ***Boris Godunov*** (the first performance of the opera outside Russia) at the Opéra, Paris, with Chaliapin as Boris.
*19 June* Première of ***Pohjan Neiti*** [***The Maid of Bothnia***] (Merikanto/Rytkönen after the *Kalevala*) in the open air in Viipuri. It was composed in 1898, the first opera to be written with a Finnish text.
*21 June* Death of Rimsky-Korsakov at Lyubensk, near St Petersburg.
*5 September* Opening of the Teatro Colón, Buenos Aires, with the première of Panizza's ***Aurora*** (libretto by Quesada trans. Illica).

Cover of the score of Rimsky-Korsakov's *Zolotoi petushok* [*The Golden Cockerel*]. Completed in 1907, the opera tells the story of a stupid tsar. The censors would not allow a performance in Rimsky-Korsakov's lifetime; he was out of favour for supporting the students during the unrest in 1905 which followed the war with Japan. Diaghilev's company performed the opera in Paris in 1913 as an *opéra dansé* four years after its Moscow première.

**1909** *25 January* Première of ***Elektra*** (Strauss/Hofmannsthal after Sophocles) at the Hofoper, Dresden, conducted by Ernst von Schuch. It was also staged the same year in Berlin, Vienna and Milan (La Scala).
*19 May* Start of Diaghilev's first season of opera and ballet at the Théâtre du Châtelet, Paris.
*7 October* Posthumous première of ***Zolotoi petushok*** [***The Golden Cockerel***] (Rimsky-Korsakov/Bel'sky after Pushkin) by the Private Russian Opera, Moscow.
*10 November* New York début of the Irish tenor John McCormack as Alfredo (***La traviata***) at the Manhattan Opera House.
*4 December* Première (in German) of ***Il segreto di Susanna*** (Wolf-Ferrari/Golisciani) at the Hofoper, Munich. The first performance in the original Italian of this popular satirical comedy was by Hammerstein's Chicago Opera Company at the Met on 14 March 1911.

Poster by Lovis Corinth for the original production of Richard Strauss's *Elektra*, 1909.

## Strauss and Hofmannsthal

The collaboration between Richard Strauss and Hugo von Hofmannsthal is quite exceptional in operatic history. Strauss had an instinctive theatrical sense, so effective that his music can conjure up every nuance of the drama even in a recording, yet Hofmannsthal – ten years younger than the composer – was in many ways the stronger partner in their relationship, reversing the usual roles of composer and librettist. *Elektra*, on which they first collaborated, was based on Hofmannsthal's adaptation of Sophocles' play and had been produced in the theatre (by Max Reinhardt) before Strauss suggested to the playwright that he should set it as an opera; although the composer shortened the text, it remains very close to the original play. Their work together on subsequent operas – *Der Rosenkavalier*, *Ariadne auf Naxos*, *Die Frau ohne Schatten*, *Die ägyptische Helene* and *Arabella* – was largely carried on through correspondence, and, while Strauss offered many suggestions to Hofmannsthal, the playwright took great pains to suppress what he felt was Strauss's tendency to vulgarity. There is a poignancy to the theme of Strauss's last opera, *Capriccio*, written more than twelve years after Hofmannsthal's death: do words or music come first?

Silhouette evoking the collaboration of Hofmannsthal and Strauss.

*8 December* Première of ***Le Cœur du moulin*** (Séverac/Magre) at the Opéra-Comique, Paris. Déodat de Séverac was a product of the Schola Cantorum; like his oratorio *Héliogabale*, written for outdoor performance at Béziers the following year, in which he included the penetrating reed-instruments of the Catalan *cobles* (traditional bands), his opera is imbued with the local colour of the Roussillon.

*23 December* Revival of Gluck's ***Orfeo ed Euridice*** (with insertions from other Gluck operas) at the Metropolitan Opera, New York, conducted by Toscanini, with sets by the French symbolist painter Pierre Puvis de Chavannes.

**1910** *1 February* Strauss's ***Elektra*** was staged in French by Hammerstein's company at the Manhattan Opera House. The title role was sung by Mariette Mazarin – who fainted after the performance but continued to sing the role until the end of the run. The company gave its final performances on 24 March – a matinée of ***Salome*** with Mary Garden and ***Elektra*** with Mazarin in the evening.

*19 February* Première of ***Don Quichotte*** (Massenet/Cain after Cervantes and Le Lorrain) at the Théâtre du Casino, Monte Carlo, with Lucy Arbell (Dulcinée) and Chaliapin. This was the composer's last great success and one of his most accomplished scores, with Spanish local colour and mock eighteenth-century music that provided outstanding set-pieces for the leading singers.

*February–March* First of three opera seasons put on during 1910 by the conductor Thomas Beecham. It took place at Covent Garden and was followed by one of *opéra-comique* at His Majesty's Theatre, then by an autumn season at Covent Garden – more than thirty operas in all. The first of the innovative programmes included Smyth's ***The Wreckers***, Delius's ***A Village Romeo and Juliet*** and Strauss's ***Elektra*** as well as ***Carmen*** and ***Tristan und Isolde***; among the *opéras-comiques* were ***Die Fledermaus***, ***Les Contes d'Hoffmann***, ***Werther***, ***Fra Diavolo***, Stanford's ***Shamus O'Brien***, works by Méhul, Auber and Massenet, and four Mozart operas (including ***Così fan tutte***). On Beecham's return to Covent Garden the season included Mozart, Beethoven, Rossini, Gounod, Verdi, Bizet, Offenbach, Johann Strauss, Wagner and, among the new works, d'Albert's ***Tiefland***, Debussy's ***Pelléas et Mélisande*** and Richard Strauss's ***Salome***.
*June* Visit of the Metropolitan Opera with Caruso and Toscanini to the Opéra, Paris, organized by the impresario Gabriel Astruc.
*3 November* The first resident company in Chicago opened its season at the Auditorium with ***Aida*** conducted by Cleofonte Campanini (who became artistic director of the company in 1913). The singers were essentially those who had worked for Hammerstein at the now defunct Manhattan Opera House.
*14 November* The Metropolitan Opera season opened with Gluck's ***Armide*** (the first performance in the USA) conducted by Toscanini with sets by Puvis de Chavannes. Olive Fremstad sang Armide and Caruso Renaud.
*20 November* Première of ***Macbeth*** (Bloch/Fleg after Shakespeare) at the Opéra-Comique, Paris, with Bréval as Lady Macbeth. Although it was Bloch's only opera, it is a work of considerable power that remains close in spirit and language to Shakespeare.
*2 December* Première of ***Kleider machen Leute*** (Zemlinsky/Feld after Keller) at the Volksoper, Vienna. The composer, Schoenberg's brother-in-law and a pioneer of new music, had been associated with Mahler as a conductor at the Hofoper, but after Mahler's resignation Zemlinsky moved to the Volksoper, where he staged this work of his own as well as the Viennese première of ***Salome*** among many other novelties.
*10 December* Première of ***La fanciulla del West*** (Puccini/Civinini and Zangarini after Belasco) at the Metropolitan Opera, New York (for whom it had been composed). The conductor was Toscanini, Belasco was co-producer, and the principals were Caruso, Destinn and Amato.
*28 December* Première of ***Die Königskinder*** (Humperdinck/Rosmer) at the Metropolitan Opera, New York. The original version of the work (composed as incidental music for Rosmer's play) had had its first performance in Munich on 23 January 1897.

Lucien Moratore and Lucienne Bréval as Ulysse and Pénélope in Fauré's *Pénélope* (1913), a chastely classical work of subtle beauty.

The Catalan contralto Maria Gay as Carmen, the role in which she made her début in Brussels in 1902 (at five days notice) and which she sang with tremendous passion at Covent Garden (from 1906), the Met (from 1908) and in Boston and Chicago. She was married to the tenor Giovanni Zenatello, who was often her Don José.

Caruso and Emmy Destinn in the original production of Puccini's *La fanciulla del West* in 1910. The work is based on Belasco's play *The Girl of the Golden West*, which Puccini had seen in 1907 during the preparations for the Met première of *Madama Butterfly*. The play began with a series of lantern slides evoking the forests and mountains of California, and the music which accompanied these included 'Old Dog Tray', which Puccini included in the opera.

**1911** *26 January* Première of ***Der Rosenkavalier*** (Strauss/Hofmannsthal) at the Hofoper, Dresden, conducted by Ernst von Schuch in a production by Max Reinhardt. It was heard in Nürnberg the following night, in Munich on 1 February, Basel on 15 February, Bremen on 28 February, Frankfurt and Milan (La Scala, in Italian) on 1 March, Prague on 4 March, Berlin on 4 April, Vienna on 8 April, and Budapest (in Hungarian) on 21 May.
*25 February* Première of ***Natoma*** (Herbert/Redding) at the Metropolitan Opera House, Philadelphia, with Garden and McCormack. It was heard the same night in the Ladbroke Hall, London – in order to establish copyright – and repeated two days later with the Philadelphia cast at the Met.
*Spring* Revival of Gagliano's ***Dafne*** (1608), restored by Professor von Glehn, in Moscow.
*18 May* Death of Mahler in Vienna.
*19 May* Première of ***L'Heure espagnole*** (Ravel/Franc-Nohain, i.e. Maurice Legrand) at the Opéra-Comique, Paris. Completed in 1909, the opera is a witty farce of amorous adventures and confusion.
*2 June* Première of ***Isabeau*** (Mascagni/Illica) at the Teatro Coliseo, Buenos Aires, conducted by the composer. Mascagni abandoned *verismo* in this work to present a 'dramatic legend'.
*14 October* Première of ***Conchita*** (Zandonai/Vaucaire and Zangarini after Louys) at the Teatro dal Verme, Milan, a colourful opera in which the heroine turns flamenco dancer.
*23 December* Première (in German) of ***I gioielli della Madonna*** (Wolf-Ferrari/Golisciani and Zangarini) at the Kurfürsten-Oper, Berlin, Wolf-Ferrari's only *verismo* tragic opera.
*27 December* Metropolitan Opera début of Tetrazzini as Lucia.
*Autumn* Oscar Hammerstein opened his first season at the London Opera House in Kingsway. The operas performed included Rossini's ***Guillaume Tell***, Donizetti's ***Lucia di Lammermoor***, the British première of Massenet's ***Don Quichotte*** and the première of Holbrooke's ***The Children of Don***; the enterprise was not a success and this was its only season.

**1912** *3 March* Open-air production of ***Aida*** at the Pyramids, Giza.
*14 March* Première of ***Mona*** (Parker/Hooker) at the Metropolitan Opera, New York, with a cast including Louise Homer, Riccardo Martin and Herbert Witherspoon. The work was the $10,000 prizewinner in the Met's competition for an opera in English by an American composer.
*15 June* Première of ***The Children of Don*** (Holbrooke/Ellis) at the London Opera House, the first part of the composer's Celtic trilogy ***The Cauldron of Annwen*** (see 1914, 1929).
*18 August* Première of ***Der ferne Klang*** (Schreker/composer) at the Opernhaus, Frankfurt. The mystic-erotic quality of the plot is reflected in the luxuriant chromaticism of the score, largely written in 1902–8. It was the first substantial opera by one of the most advanced and imaginative German composers.
*25 October* Première of the original version of ***Ariadne auf Naxos*** (Strauss/Hofmannsthal), following a performance of Molière's *Le Bourgeois gentilhomme* with incidental music by Strauss, to inaugurate the Kleines Haus of the new Hoftheater, Stuttgart. The production was by Max Reinhardt and Ariadne was sung by Maria Jeritza.
Revival of Staden's ***Seelewig*** (1644), the first extant German opera, mounted by Rudolf Schulz-Dornburg in Cologne.
Performance of Moniuszko's ***Halka*** in Crakow in Esperanto.

**1913** *27 February* Première of ***Cyrano de Bergerac*** (Damrosch/Henderson) at the Metropolitan Opera, New York, with Amato in the title role and

*'At first hearing the drama can get in the way of listening to the music, but at a second or third hearing the action is familiar and no longer surprises with the same intensity; then the music can be heard. This always happens for operas with exciting libretti.'*

Puccini (1912) on *La fanciulla del West*

## Diaghilev's opera productions

The Russian style had been taken up in Paris following the construction of the exotic Russian pavilion at the 1900 Exposition, so that the ground was well prepared when Diaghilev mounted an exhibition of Russian art at the Salon d'Automne in 1906 and, using the impresario Gabriel Astruc as an intermediary, put on a series of concerts of Russian music at the Opéra in 1907. These included operatic excerpts sung by the soprano Félia Litvinne, the tenor Dmitri Smirnov and the bass Fedor Chaliapin, and their reception was tumultuous. Diaghilev returned the following year with a programme that included one full-length opera, *Boris Godunov*, as a vehicle for Chaliapin. The success of these first two seasons was such that the following year he was able to bring over artists from the Imperial Ballet, as well as the Opera, for a season of fully staged works at the Théâtre du Châtelet, where the opera performances included Rimsky-Korsakov's *Pskovityanka* (retitled *Ivan the Terrible*) and a repeat of *Boris Godunov*, as well as single acts of *Knyaz Igor*, *Ruslan i Lyudmila* and Serov's *Judith*. Although the fame of his 'Ballets Russes' has eclipsed Diaghilev's reputation as an opera impresario, it was the operatic music – and especially Chaliapin's performances – that first established his reputation and introduced the great nineteenth-century Russian composers to the west. In 1913 and 1914 operas again figured large in Diaghilev's programmes both in Paris (in Astruc's new Théâtre des Champs-Elysées and the Opéra) and London (at Drury Lane, promoted by Beecham and his father), with, in addition to *Boris* and *Ivan*, complete performances of *Knyaz Igor* and productions of *Maiskaya noch* (see 1880), *Zolotoi petushok* (see 1909) and the première of Stravinsky's *Le Rossignol*.

Fedor Chaliapin (painted by Golovin in 1912) as the Tsar in Mussorgsky's *Boris Godunov*, the role in which he over-whelmed Paris and London during Diaghilev's pre-war seasons.

Frances Alda as Roxane. Alda (Frances Davies), a soprano from New Zealand, was the wife of Met director Gatti-Casazza.

*4 March* Première of ***Pénélope*** (Fauré/Fauchois) at the Théâtre du Casino, Monte Carlo, with Bréval in the title role.

*1 April* Première (in French) of ***La vida breve*** (de Falla/Fernández Shaw) at the Casino Municipal, Nice. The opera had won a prize in 1905 at the Academy of San Fernando, Madrid, but was not performed in Spain until 14 November 1914, at the Teatro de la Zarzuela, Madrid.

*10 April* Première of ***L'amore dei tre re*** (Montemezzi/Benelli) at La Scala, Milan, conducted by Serafin. The work achieved international recognition through its production at the Met under Toscanini on 2 January 1914 with a cast including Lucrezia Bori and Pasquale Amato, and the role of Fiora later became one of Mary Garden's greatest vehicles.

*May–June* A season of Russian opera and ballet was held at Drury Lane, London, promoted jointly by Diaghilev, Sir Joseph Beecham and Thomas Beecham. Chaliapin made a triumphant London début as Boris on 24 June.

*4 December* Première (in German) of ***L'amore medico*** (Wolf-Ferrari/Golisciani) at the Hofoper, Dresden. The Italian première was at the Met on 25 March 1914.

**1914** *4 February* Première of ***Las golondrinas*** [***The Swallows***] (Usandizaga/Martínez Sierra) at the Teatro Price, Madrid. The Basque composer José Maria Usandizaga had studied at the Schola Cantorum, and his second opera made a decisive break with the *zarzuela* tradition, but his brilliant promise was cut short by his early death in 1915.
*19 February* Première of ***Francesca da Rimini*** (Zandonai/Tito Ricordi after d'Annunzio) at the Teatro Regio, Turin. The musical form of Zandonai's most accomplished opera is conventional, but his use of orchestral colour (the scoring includes a lute) is highly imaginative.
*23 February* Posthumous première of ***Cléopâtre*** (Massenet/Payen) at the Théâtre du Casino, Monte Carlo.
*15 May* Première of ***Mârouf, savetier du Caire*** (Rabaud/Népoty after the *1001 Nights*) at the Opéra-Comique, Paris. The opera belongs to the tradition of orientalism, though there is a hint of modernism in its score.
*26 May* Première of ***Solovei*** [***Le Rossignol***] (Stravinsky/composer after Mitusov after H. C. Andersen) at the Opéra, Paris, conducted by Pierre Monteux, with sets designed by Alexander Benois. The first act had been composed in 1908–9 and the second and third were written in 1913–14.
*4 July* Première of ***Dylan: Son of the Wave*** (Holbrooke/Ellis) at Drury Lane, London; the second part of Holbrooke's Celtic trilogy.
*26 August* Première of ***The Immortal Hour*** (Boughton/'Fiona Macleod') at the Assembly Rooms, Glastonbury. Boughton's fairy opera was intended to inaugurate a British Bayreuth in a town full of mystic associations.

Poster for Zandonai's *Francesca da Rimini* (1914). The Ricordis had been anxiously looking for a successor to Puccini to sustain the fortunes of their publishing house and believed Zandonai could assume the mantle. They sent him to Spain to gain local colour for *Conchita* (1912), and Tito Ricordi himself adapted d'Annunzio's play for *Francesca da Rimini*.

Costume designs by Alfred Roller for Baron Ochs and the Feldmarschallin in the original production of *Der Rosenkavalier* (1911).

# 1915–1997

# THE AGE OF RECORDING

*Even before the introduction of electrical recording in the early 1920s, opera records had attracted many new devotees who had never heard a live performance in the opera house. As techniques improved and, more recently, film, television and video recordings were made, new standards for performance were established and an enormous repertory became available. As a result, in the opera house, new productions of established or of forgotten works have often replaced the staging of new compositions, so that the history of opera in the past eighty years is as much the history of performance as of operatic music.*

Set design by Josef Svoboda for the 1969 Boston revival of Luigi Nono's *Intolleranza 1960*, a work that suggests that the solidarity of working people will overcome the repression of capitalist society.

alla T
Cens

# The Age of Recording

Costume design for the title role, created by Peter Pears, of Benjamin Britten's *Peter Grimes*, first performed at Sadler's Wells Theatre, London, in 1945. Set in a Suffolk fishing village, the theme of the opera is 'innocence a prey to violence, the outsider a prey to society'.

THE SURVIVAL and renewal of opera after the First World War is something of a miracle, given the breakdown of the old social order which had for decades sustained opera houses around the world. Opera had, of course, survived revolutionary changes in the past, but over the next eighty years recovery was confused and difficult. Certainly the divide between the standard repertory and modern works widened considerably, and, with only occasional exceptions, the principal opera houses steered well clear of any new works of quality. Nevertheless, the stimulus of recorded performances did much to enhance interpretations of traditional opera, and in the chronicle that follows references to the careers of celebrated singers can be brought to life by listening to the recordings of their voices captured on disc.

Among composers a reaction had set in to both Wagnerism and *verismo* in the early years of the century, and the rediscovery of baroque operas contributed to yet another movement for reform, a renewal through classicism. Classical ideals, themes and forms were interpreted in many different ways, from Busoni's references to the *commedia dell'arte* to the classical miniatures of Milhaud or Stravinsky's *Histoire du soldat* (where the characters and voices are separated as in the Venetian madrigal operas written around 1600). Many composers preferred to work on a small scale. A succession of chamber operas was commissioned by Princesse Edmond de Polignac (Winaretta Singer, the sewing-machine heiress), from Stravinsky, de Falla, Satie and Milhaud. These then received public performances at the new festivals of contemporary music that began after the war. Their scale has made them unsuited to performance in the traditional opera house and – as is the case with many of the works written during this period for limited resources – they have never entered the main operatic repertory.

Richard Strauss, whose career spanned the war years, had moved from the erotic and symbolist violence of *Salome* and *Elektra* to the neo-baroque of *Der Rosenkavalier* and *Ariadne auf Naxos*; the sometimes wistful lyricism of his later operas constantly refers back to these two works. However, in *Die Frau ohne Schatten* the symbolism is interpreted in a more expressive way, and the work is one of many German operas of the period to use music to delve into the erotic mysteries of myth. The drive for innovation in German opera between the wars had tremendous energy, as much in production as in composition, culminating in Alban Berg's two great operatic masterpieces, *Wozzeck* and *Lulu*, which united classical forms, atonal techniques of composition and the most intense expressionism. The other great opera composer of this period, who wrote in a highly personal style, was the Moravian Leoš Janáček, who had begun composing in the 1890s but achieved international recognition only near the end of his life.

Dictatorships in Europe stifled experimentation and innovation, and while emigration enriched musical life in America and Britain, the provocative qualities of composers such as Hindemith and Weill in their native Germany were moderated after they had left. In Italy, after the death of Puccini, *verismo* lingered on, opposed by the rather sterile classicism of a group of composers who included Respighi, Pizzetti and Malipiero. In Russia, Prokofiev and Shostakovich wrote strikingly original operas, but few performances were possible in the conformist atmosphere of Soviet communism. In America, though many composers tried their hand at grand opera, the only works to have outlived their time were two operas by George Gershwin and Virgil Thomson, both of which stretched the definition of the medium. Musical comedy (by Berlin, Porter and Rodgers) was the American contribution of this period rather than opera. In Britain the revelation came at the end of the Second World War, when Benjamin Britten's *Peter Grimes* had its first performance. Not since the seventeenth century had an English composer written operatic music of international stature, and Britten's great natural musical gifts were matched by an instinctive understanding of dramatic requirements. Each of his operas offers new musical insights into character and the human situation, and taken together they are one of the most substantial bodies of work to enter the repertory during this whole period; although they are quite traditional in form, their outlook is coloured by the angst of the post-war world.

A far more drastically political viewpoint was embodied in many of the works to emerge from Germany and Italy. Henze and Zimmermann, Dallapiccola and Nono challenged the threats to human freedom, by war and intolerance, that the end of the war had done little to alleviate, but it was a challenge that remained largely confined by the limits of the avant garde. Major opera houses staged new works by Menotti, Barber, Walton, Tippett, Poulenc, Pizzetti and other composers whose operas retained traditional forms, and Schoenberg's monumental *Moses und Aron* was at last performed, but the opera-going public was more attracted by the rivalry of prima donnas Renata Tebaldi and Maria Callas, the reopening of Bayreuth or the latest revival of a forgotten romantic opera. It is hardly surprising that later composers such as Pousseur, Berio or Ligeti should take opera itself as the subject of their works.

Long-playing records went on sale at the beginning of the 1950s, and stereo sound was introduced only a few years later. This made it possible to listen at home to complete operas without changing sides every five minutes. Not only were the voices of the world's greatest singers reproduced with astonishing fidelity, but, with stereo, an imaginary performance, more faultless than any that might be heard in an opera house, could be re-created complete with production effects. Stage directors were now able to work on the assumption that many people in their audience would be familiar with the work being presented, and new productions were often presented as radical reinterpretations. Patrice Chéreau, Götz Friedrich, Jonathan Miller and, since the 1980s, Peter Sellars are among many who have revealed – or suggested – new meanings in the operas of Handel and Mozart, Wagner, Verdi and Puccini.

In the pluralistic climate of the postmodern era, therefore, the idea of opera as a closed form no longer seems to be valid, either for new works or, frequently, for old ones. Few opera houses remain content to stage traditional productions, with or without star casts, and the newly thought-out versions of familiar operas have been brought closer to contemporary works, more of which are themselves being performed alongside the traditional repertory. The works of Schnittke, Birtwistle, Weir, Glass or Adams are, in very different ways, again challenging audiences to accept the reform of an art form whose history shows that it is well able to withstand these periodic bouts of renewal.

Scene from Wieland Wagner's 1962 Bayreuth production of his grandfather's *Tristan und Isolde*, with Birgit Nilsson and Wolfgang Windgassen in the title roles. The reduction of all the composer's elaborate stage directions to these spare symbolic sets structured by effects of light was characteristic of all Wieland Wagner's productions from the reopening of Bayreuth in 1951, and they pioneered the creative reinterpretation of operas, often in defiance of the composer's own instructions.

# 1915 1918 Neoclassicism

*During the war years the search for new operatic forms led a number of composers – including Richard Strauss, Ferruccio Busoni and Hans Pfitzner – to develop a new kind of classicism that expressed modern ideals, rather than simply taking refuge from the overpowering influence of Wagner by imitating baroque and classical forms.*

**DATES**

**1916**
Battle of the Somme
Easter Rebellion in Dublin
Italy joins war against Germany
Dada movement founded in Zurich

**1917**
US joins war against Germany
*18 May* Première of *Parade* (Satie/Cocteau/Picasso) causes scandal in Paris
Publication of Purist manifesto by Le Corbusier and Ozenfant
*7 November* 'October Revolution' in Russia

**1918**
*9 November* November Revolution in Germany and proclamation of Bavarian Soviet Republic
*11 November* Armistice brings First World War to an end

**1915** *25 January* Première of ***Madame Sans-Gêne*** (Giordano/Simoni after Sardou and Moreau) at the Metropolitan Opera, New York, conducted by Toscanini, with Farrar, Martinelli and Amato. It was the conductor's last première before returning to Italy in April 1915.
*20 March* Première of ***Fedra*** (Pizzetti/d'Annunzio) at La Scala, Milan. It had been written in 1909–12 and a performance was planned at the Teatro Costanzi, Rome, for Carnival 1913, but ***Parisina*** (also with a d'Annunzio libretto) was preferred. The composer's return to classicism was an unexpected success.
*Spring* Première of ***The Enchanter*** (Holbrooke/composer) at the Auditorium, Chicago.
*26 September* Première of ***Mona Lisa*** (Schillings/Dovsky) at the Hoftheater (Kleines Haus), Stuttgart; performances were given the same year in Vienna and Berlin. The last opera by Schillings, who had been musical director of the Stuttgart opera house since 1908, ***Mona Lisa*** was one of the most popular German operas of the first half of the century.
Première of ***Treemonisha*** (Joplin/composer) with piano accompaniment in a rented theatre in Harlem, New York. This performance of Joplin's remarkable opera set on a plantation in Arkansas, written in 1908, went virtually unnoticed. It was not to have a proper staging until January 1972, first a partial performance at Morehouse College, Atlanta, and later at the Houston Grand Opera. The work mixes the familiar ragtime style of Joplin

Amelita Galli-Curci in the title-role of Delibes's *Lakmé*, a role in which she appeared in Chicago and on disc in 1917. She became the outstanding *coloratura* soprano of her generation making her career almost entirely in the USA, in Chicago, New York and the recording studio.

Geraldine Farrar as Carmen in Cecil B. De Mille's 1915 silent film.

with reminiscences of the European grand operas played in America around the turn of the century.

**1916** *28 January* Première of ***The Boatswain's Mate*** (Smyth/composer after Jacobs) by Beecham's company at the Shaftesbury Theatre, London, conducted by the composer.
*28 January* Première of ***Goyescas*** (Granados/Periquet y Zuaznabar) at the Metropolitan Opera House, New York, with Anna Fitziu (Fitzhugh – making her Met début), Flora Pepini, Martinelli, de Luca and Max Bloch. Part of the score was based on Granados's piano suite of the same title with texts written to fit the music.
*5 March* Première of ***Die toten Augen*** (d'Albert/Henry, trans. Ewers), at the Hofoper, Dresden. The opera was performed widely in Europe and in the USA.
*11 March* Première of ***Ho Protomastoras (The Master Builder)*** (Kalomiris/after Kazantzakis) at the Municipal Theatre, Athens. This was the first Greek opera, by a musician distinguished as both composer and teacher.
*28 March* Première of ***Violanta*** (Korngold/Müller) and ***Der Ring des Polykrates*** (Korngold/after Teweles) at the Nationaltheater, Munich, the first operas by the nineteen-year-old composer, presented as a double bill.
*4 October* Première of revised version of ***Ariadne auf Naxos*** (Strauss/Hofmannsthal) at the Hofoper, Vienna, conducted by Franz Schalk, with Jeritza again in the title role. Kurz sang Zerbinetta, and Lotte Lehmann was a last-minute substitute for Gutheil-Schoder in the role of the Composer.
*18 November* American début of Amelita Galli-Curci at the Auditorium, Chicago, as Gilda in ***Rigoletto***, the role in which she had made her stage début in Italy in 1907.
*5 December* Première of ***Sāvitri*** (Holst/composer) by the London School of Opera at Wellington Hall, London. The libretto of this chamber opera is based on the *Mahābharata.*

**1917** *30 January* Première of ***Eine florentinische Tragödie*** (Zemlinsky/after Wilde) at the Hoftheater (Kleines Haus), Stuttgart. This brooding story of infidelity avenged inspired a richly expressionist score.
*27 March* Première of ***La rondine*** (Puccini/Willner and Reichert adapted by Adami) at the Théâtre du Casino, Monte Carlo, with Tito Schipa as Ruggiero. The operetta had been commissioned for the Carltheater, Vienna, in 1913, when Puccini was there for the production

Anna Fitziu as Rosario in Granados's *Goyescas*. Granados stayed on in New York for the première of his opera and was drowned when the ship on which he was returning to Europe was torpedoed by a German submarine.

## Palestrina

Hans Pfitzner's opera (which he started in 1909) is an allegory of the dilemma facing a composer at a time when musical styles are changing. Pfitzner was himself involved in a fierce dispute with, among others, Busoni, whose aesthetic ideas he attacked in a work entitled 'Danger of Futurists'. *Palestrina* revolves around a decision to be made by the Pope and Cardinals at the Council of Trent about the kind of music the Church will approve. Cardinal Carlo Borromeo wants Palestrina to write a new polyphonic mass to persuade the Pope not to restrict church music to plainchant. Palestrina, fearing that 'God no longer speaks from his soul', refuses; he is sent to prison, where inspiration comes to him, and the Pope is persuaded. However, with conscious irony Pfitzner frames this plot with the story of Palestrina's pupil Silla, who is attracted by the simpler and more modern style of Florentine monody, the foundation of the operatic style. By the end of the opera he has left for Florence.

Thomas Mann wrote to Bruno Walter, who conducted the première: 'With its metaphysical atmosphere, its ethic of "cross, death and grave", its alliance of music, pessimism and humour (which I define to embrace the idea of humanity), it complies with my own personal deepest needs.'

Portrait of Ferruccio Busoni by the futurist painter Umberto Boccioni, *c.* 1910.

## Young Classicism

'In thinking about a twentieth-century masterwork, I have in mind something of which the dissimilarity to the Wagnerian masterwork is both substantial and, I believe, beneficial. I have in mind something extremely logical, formally balanced and clear; something at once rigorous and serene, no less intellectually taut than Wagner, but of a cooler, more refined and intellectual spirituality; something that does not seek greatness in Baroque ponderousness or beauty in intoxication. It seems to me there must be a new classicism.'
Thomas Mann, 'Concerning the Art of Richard Wagner', 1911

'By "Young Classicism" I mean the mastery, the sifting and the turning to account of all the gains of previous experiments and their inclusion in strong and beautiful forms. This art will be old and new at the same time at first...With "Young Classicism" I include the definite departure from what is thematic and the return to melody again as the ruler of all voices and all emotions (not in the sense of a pleasing motif) and as the bearer of the idea and the begetter of harmony, in short, the most highly developed (not the most complicated) polyphony.'
Ferruccio Busoni, letter to Paul Bekker, January 1920; translated by Rosomond Ley, 1957

'Your cry of distress against Wagnerian "music-making" went straight to my heart and opened the door to a completely new musical landscape in which, led by *Ariadne* and especially its new prologue, I hope to enter entirely into the domain of the un-Wagnerian comic opera, "affective opera" and "human opera".'
Richard Strauss to Hugo von Hofmannsthal, mid-August 1916

of ***La fanciulla del West*** – which was to cause the composer's patriotism to be questioned when Italy joined the war against Germany and Austria.
*30 April* Première of ***Lodoletta*** (Mascagni/Forzano after Ouida) at the Teatro Costanzi, Rome. The tender love story of an exiled French painter and a Dutch girl turns rather abruptly to tragedy in the melodramatic final act.
*11 May* Première of ***Arlecchino, oder Die Fenster*** (Busoni/composer) and ***Turandot*** (Busoni/composer after Gozzi) at the Stadttheater, Zurich. In their adoption of eighteenth-century conventions – the artificial orientalism of ***Turandot*** and the masked *commedia dell'arte* characters of ***Arlecchino*** – the two one-act operas were a conscious rejection of *verismo* as the basis for modern music-drama.
*12 June* Première of ***Palestrina*** (Pfitzner/composer) at the Prinzregententheater, Munich, with Karl Erb in the title role.
*26 October* Première of Cui's version of Mussorgsky's ***Sorochinskaya Yarmarka*** [***Sorochintsy Fair***] (libretto by the composer after Gogol), in Petrograd. The opera had first been perfomed privately in a concert version; then semi-publicly on 30 December 1911 at the Comedia Theatre, St Petersburg, in a version partly orchestrated by Lyadov; then in a bastard version by Sakhnovsky at the Free Theatre, Moscow, on 3 November 1913. A version by Tcherepnin was produced at Monte Carlo on 27 March 1923, but Mussorgsky's music, composed in 1877–80, is so fragmentary that it is impossible to prepare an 'authentic' version.

*24 November* Performance of Raymond Roze's ***Jeanne d'Arc*** in aid of the Red Cross at the Opéra, Paris, which had recently reopened with a production of ***Faust*** despite the continuing bombardment of the city.

**1918** *25 March* Death of Debussy, leaving incomplete his opera ***La Chute de la maison Usher*** (based on Poe's story), on which he had worked from 1908 to 1917.
*25 April* Première of ***Die Gezeichneten*** (Schreker/composer) at the Opernhaus, Frankfurt. Schreker's libretto (originally commissioned by Zemlinsky) recounts the tragedy of an ugly man, and his music creates an extraordinary world of sound to match the orgiastic expressionism of the text,
*24 May* Première of ***A Kékszakállú Herceg Vára*** [***Duke Bluebeard's Castle***] (Bartók/Balázs) at the Royal Opera, Budapest, Bartók's only opera. It had been completed in 1911, but was not performed for seven years. While rhythmically indebted to Hungarian folksong, the work owes its static, meditative character – there are only two singing characters – to Debussy's ***Pelléas et Mélisande.***
*10 June* Death of Arrigo Boito in Milan.
*28 September* Première of ***L'Histoire du soldat*** [***The Soldier's Tale***] (Stravinsky/Ramuz) in Lausanne, conducted by Ansermet. The work is an anti-opera, in the sense that there are only speaking and dancing roles, and the narrator and orchestra are on stage as well as the characters.
*15 November* Operatic début of Rosa Ponselle as Leonora in the Metropolitan Opera's first production of Verdi's ***La forza del destino***, with Caruso as Alvaro. Ponselle and her sister Carmela had previously appeared in vaudeville as the Ponzillo Sisters. On 28 December she sang Rezio in Weber's ***Oberon***, which escaped the ban on German opera because of its English libretto.
*14 December* Première of ***Il trittico*** at the Metropolitan Opera House, New York: ***Il tabarro*** (Puccini/Adami after Gold), a *verismo* melodrama with Claudia Muzio (as Giorgetta), Adamo Didur and Luigi Montesanto; ***Suor Angelica*** (Puccini/Forzano), a sentimental opera set in a nunnery, with Farrar in the title role; and ***Gianni Schicchi*** (Puccini/Forzano after Dante), a comic masterpiece in which de Luca sang the title role and Didur again appeared. The trilogy was repeated at the Teatro Costanzi, Rome, four weeks later, with the Canadian tenor Edward Johnson, billed as 'Eduardo di Giovanni', replacing Didur.

Poster for Puccini's *Suor Angelica*, the second part of *Il trittico*.

Scene from *Gianni Schicchi*, the last opera in Puccini's *Il trittico*, in the original production at the Metropolitan Opera, New York, 1918.

# 1919–1925 After the War

*The high romanticism of nineteenth-century opera survived in the great opera houses, but in recent compositions the divergent trends of classicism, expressionism and Freudian symbolism produced works with a far more modern intensity. Outstanding among new operas was* Wozzeck *by the young Viennese composer Alban Berg.*

**DATES**

**1919**
*5–11 January* Spartacist Rising in Berlin
Establishment of the League of Nations
Foundation of the Bauhaus at Weimar by Walter Gropius
**1920**
End of Civil War in Russia
**1922**
Fascists come to power in Italy with Mussolini as dictator
Assassination of Walter Rathenau, German foreign minister, by nationalists
**1923**
French ocupation of the Ruhr to force Germany to pay war debts; period of massive inflation in Germany
*7–8 November* Hitler's 'beer-cellar putsch' in Munich

**1919** *10 October* Première of ***Die Frau ohne Schatten*** (Strauss/Hofmannsthal) at the Staatsoper, Vienna, conducted by Franz Schalk, with Jeritza as the Empress, Mayr as Barak and Lehmann as his wife. This symbolic opera exploring the themes of marriage and fertility was the most ambitious and most profound of the collaborations between Hofmannsthal and Strauss. The composer had recently been appointed co-director of the Staatsoper (with Schalk), a position he held until 1924.
*21 October* Première of ***Fennimore and Gerda*** (Delius/composer after Jacobsen) at the Opernhaus, Frankfurt. Delius's last opera had been written in 1908–13 and was not performed in England until 1968.

Lotte Lehmann as the wife of Barak the Dyer in the original Vienna production of Strauss and Hofmannsthal's *Die Frau ohne Schatten* at the Staatsoper in 1919.

**1920** *21 January* Première of ***Der Schatzgräber*** (Schreker/composer) at the Opernhaus, Frankfurt; the composer's most successful opera, it received over fifty performances. The mystifying, symbolic libretto is balanced by luxuriant harmony and orchestration.
*January–February* The enterprising season given by the Chicago Opera Association at the Lexington Theater, New York, included ***L'amore dei tre re*** (Montemezzi) with Garden as Fiora – one of her finest roles; ***Falstaff*** (Verdi); ***L'Heure espagnole*** (Ravel); ***Linda di Chamounix*** (Donizetti) with Galli-Curci; and ***Norma*** (Bellini) with Rosa Raïsa.
*28 January* First modern revival of Peri's ***Euridice*** by the Associazione Scarlatti at the Politeama, Naples; the performance was repeated at the Pitti Palace, Florence (where the work had been first performed in 1600) on 29 December 1923.
*14 February* Première (concert performance) of ***Socrate*** (Satie/from Cousin's translation of Plato's *Dialogues*), a 'symphonic drama' for four sopranos and small orchestra, at the Société Nationale de Musique, Paris. The first staged performance took place in the private theatre of Princesse Edmond de Polignac (to whom the work is dedicated) before 1925, and the first public staged performance (in Czech) in Prague in May 1925 during the ISCM festival.
*5 April* Revival of Blow's masque ***Venus and Adonis*** (see 1684) at Glastonbury, the same company later performing it at the Old Vic, London.
*23 April* Première of ***Výlety páně Broučkovy*** [***The Excursions of Mr Brouček***] (Janáček/Dyk and Procházka after Čech) at the Czech National Theatre, Prague; a comic opera in two parts, with the self-important Mr 'Beetle' visiting first the moon and then Prague during the Hussite wars.
*5 June* Revival of ***The Beggar's Opera*** (see 1728) at the Lyric Theatre, Hammersmith, a production which ran for 1,463 consecutive performances.
*9 June* Première of ***La Légende de Saint-Christophe*** (d'Indy/composer) at the Opéra, Paris. The temptations of the legendary saint satirize many of d'Indy's special aversions, from Massenet's ***Thaïs*** to scientists and freemasons.

Maria Jeritza as Jenůfa in the production of Janáček's opera at the Vienna Hofoper in 1918.

Elisabeth Rethberg as Cio-Cio San in Puccini's *Madama Butterfly*, a role she recorded in 1922 with Richard Tauber as Pinkerton. Toscanini described her as 'the perfect soprano'.

*26 June* A production of Handel's ***Rodelinda*** (see 1725) in Göttingen, in a German version by the art-historian Oskar Hagen with expressionist sets by Paul Thiersch, was the first opera of the 'Handel Renaissance'. It was followed in Göttingen by ***Ottone*** (1921), ***Giulio Cesare*** (1922), ***Serse*** (1924), ***Ezio*** (1926) and ***Radamisto*** (1927).
*30 November* Première of ***Die Vögel*** (Braunfels/composer) at the Nationaltheater, Munich, a satirical opera based on Aristophanes' *The Birds*, which enjoyed great success in Germany.
*4 December* Première of ***Die tote Stadt*** (Korngold/Schott after Rodenbach) at the Stadttheater, Hamburg, and the Stadttheater, Cologne. The principal action of the opera is a sensuous dream through which the hero learns to accept the death of his beloved wife.
*24 December* Caruso's swansong, as Eleazar in Halévy's ***La Juive*** at the Met.

**1921** *2 May* Première of ***Il piccolo Marat*** (Mascagni/Forzano and Targioni-Tozzetti) at the Teatro Costanzi, Rome. It became the composer's most successful opera after ***Cavalleria rusticana.*** After Mussolini's coup, Mascagni became an official Fascist composer.
*4 June* Première of ***Mörder, Hoffnung der Frauen*** (Hindemith/Kokoschka), with a libretto by the expressionist painter, and ***Das Nusch-Nuschi*** (Hindemith/Blei), an erotic comedy for Burmese marionettes, as a double bill at the Landestheater, Stuttgart.
*21 June* Première of ***Le Roi David*** (Honegger/Morax) at the Théâtre Jorat, Mézières, a *psaume dramatique* indebted to Handel's oratorios and Bach's cantatas.

*'I was protesting against the picturesque in Russian music and against those who failed to see that the picturesque is produced by very small tricks.'*

Stravinsky on *Mavra*

Set design by the Polish cubist Leopold Survage for the original production of Stravinsky's *Mavra* at the Paris Opéra, 1922.

*2 August* Death of Caruso.
*23 November* Première of ***Kát'a Kabanová*** (Janáček/Červinka) at the National Theatre, Brno. The story of the illicit love and eventual suicide of a woman tortured by her mother-in-law, taken from Ostrovsky's *The Storm*, inspired one of Janáček's most powerful scores.
*10 December* Première of ***La leggenda di Sakuntala*** (Alfano/composer) at the Teatro Comunale, Bologna, conducted by Serafin. The opera, based on an Indian legend, enjoyed great international success in the 1920s and was revived in Rome in 1952.
*26 December* Production of Verdi's ***Falstaff*** in which Toscanini cast Mariano Stabile as the hero. Stabile's interpretation of the role became one of the outstanding performances of the century.
*30 December* Première (in French) of ***Lyubov k tryom apel'sinam*** [***The Love for Three Oranges***] (Prokofiev/composer after Meyerhold) at the Auditorium, Chicago, an opera commissioned in 1918 by Campanini (who was succeeded in 1921 by Mary Garden as 'directa' of the Chicago Opera Company). Based on one of Gozzi's fables, the opera's mixture of symbolism and satire provoked fierce criticism.

**1922** *26 March* Première of ***Sancta Susanna*** (Hindemith/Stramm) at the Opernhaus, Frankfurt, performed on a triple bill with his other two operas (see 1921). Like those, it is a product of the erotic fantasy of expressionism.
*22 April* Farewell performance of Farrar in the title role of ***Zazà*** (see 1900) at the Met. The house 'dissolved in tears. You could hear the weeping rise in great waves and flood onto the stage.'
*18 May* Première of ***Renard*** (Stravinsky/composer), at the Opéra, Paris, on the opening night of Diaghilev's new season. The work, described as a 'burlesque ballet with songs', is based on Russian folktales and had been commissioned by the Princesse de Polignac. It was designed to be performed by mute actors (Stravinsky specified 'clowns, dancers or acrobats') on a trestle stage in front of the orchestra, in which the singers were also to be placed.
*28 May* Première of ***Der Zwerg (Der Geburtstag der Infantin)*** (Zemlinsky/Klaren after Wilde) at the Neues Theater, Cologne. The painful contrast of beauty and ugliness – in appearance and in character – is brilliantly

Beniamino Gigli as Lyonel in Flotow's *Martha*, a role he interpreted at the Met in 1923 with Frances Alda, Kathleen Howard and Giuseppe de Luca. Gigli made his Met début in the 1920–1 season and he and Martinelli were soon to share the mantle of Caruso, Gigli excelling in lyrical roles, and Martinelli in more dramatic ones.

captured in Zemlinsky's colourful expressionist score.
*3 June* Première of ***Mavra*** (Stravinsky/Kochno after Pushkin) by Diaghilev's company at the Opéra, Paris, with Oda Slobodskaya singing the leading role of Parasha. In this comic work the composer consciously evoked the Russia of Glinka, Pushkin and Tchaikovsky.
*August* Four of the Vienna Staatsoper's Mozart productions were performed at the Salzburg Festival, which had been revived two years earlier by Max Reinhardt. The first Festspielhaus was built in 1927.
*Summer* An open-air opera season, put on by Gaetano Merola in Stanford University Football Stadium with performances of ***Carmen***, ***Pagliacci*** and ***Faust***, started a revival of opera in San Francisco.
*16 December* Première of ***Debora e Jaele*** (Pizzetti/composer) at La Scala, Milan, conducted by Toscanini, the work which most effectively carries out the composer's intention of replacing the popular emotionalism of Puccini with a new classically based operatic style.

**1923** *6 January* ***Hänsel und Gretel*** from Covent Garden was the first opera to be broadcast complete. The same opera was the first to be broadcast in the USA (on 25 December 1931).
*14 May* Première of ***The Perfect Fool*** (Holst/composer after Shakespeare) at Covent Garden, London, a satire on grand opera with Wagner as its main target, though there are also references to ***La traviata*** and ***Faust***.
*1 June* Première of ***Padmâvati*** (Roussel/Laloy) at the Opéra, Paris. The theme of this 'opera-ballet' had preoccupied the composer since visiting India in 1909, and he made use of Hindu modes in the score.
*25 June* Première of ***El retablo de maese Pedro*** (de Falla/composer after

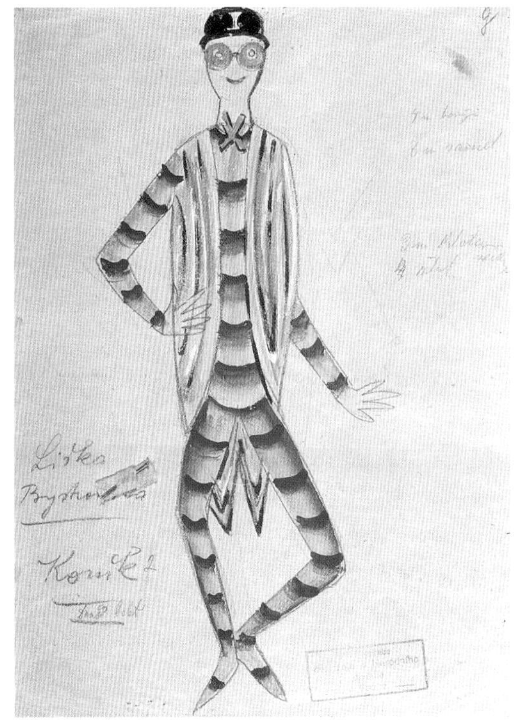

Costume design (the caterpillar) for the original production of Janáček's *The Cunning Little Vixen*, 1924.

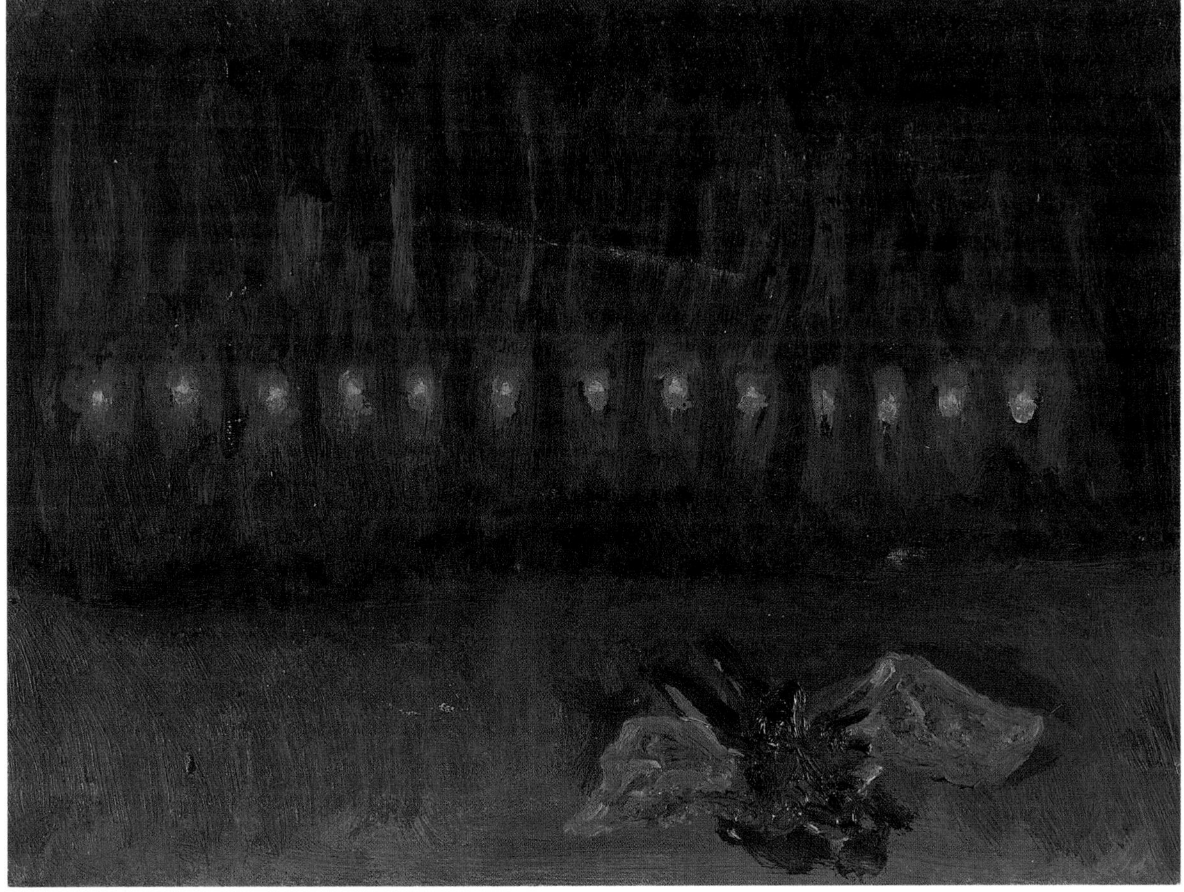

Schoenberg's own set for the first scene of *Die glückliche Hand,* first produced in 1924. The hero lies on his back trapped beneath the bat-winged monster, while the voices of the chorus behind him represent his inner voices.

Alban Berg (front) with three of the cast of the 1930 production of *Wozzeck* in Vienna: (from left) Georg Maikl (Captain), Josef von Monowarda (Wozzeck) and Hermann Wiedemann (Doctor). Marie was sung by Rosa Pauly.

## Wozzeck

The play by Georg Büchner (1813–37) was based on the documentary records of a soldier executed for the murder of his wife, despite doubts about his mental competence. It was never published in the author's brief lifetime and was reconstructed from his manuscript during the 1870s, though not staged until November 1913 in Munich. It was put on in Vienna a few months later, and Alban Berg, who saw it there, was overwhelmed by the power of the drama, in which the real events are seen through the disturbed mind of Wozzeck. When Berg began his setting, at the end of the war, he retained all the words of Büchner's text, simply omitting a few scenes and rearranging the others into three groups of five. The music itself was then given a highly formal structure – five character pieces (suite, rhapsody, march and lullaby, passacaglia, rondo); a five-movement symphony; and six inventions (the additional one an orchestral epilogue that precedes the final scene) – although the composer wrote that 'there must not be anyone in the audience who, from the moment when the curtain rises until it descends for the last time, notices anything of these various fugues, inventions, suites and sonata movements, variations and passacaglias. Nobody must be filled with anything except the idea of the opera.' In fact, the brutality and pathos of the drama is matched by music of great beauty untouched by any false note of sentimentality, and Berg's opera has remained the outstanding example of musical drama in the twentieth century.

Cervantes) at the house of the Princesse de Polignac in Paris, with Wanda Landowska playing the featured harpsichord part. The work, about Don Quixote's encounter with marionettes, had been conceived as a puppet-opera (with the human characters twice the size of the marionettes) but was eventually performed by singers and masked mimes.

**1924** *1 May* Posthumous première of ***Nerone*** (Boito/composer) at La Scala, Milan, under Toscanini.
*14 May* Covent Garden début of Lauritz Melchior, one of the century's greatest Heldentenors, as Siegmund; he made his Bayreuth début as Parsifal later in the year. Originally a baritone, Melchior had first appeared with the Royal Danish Opera in 1913. On 21 May a performance of ***Der Rosenkavalier*** under Bruno Walter with Lehmann (making her Covent Garden début), Delia Reinhardt and Elisabeth Schumann was described by Ernest Newman as 'so near perfection that I should probably be suspected of exaggeration if I praised it as it deserved'. Lehmann had previously sung the roles of both Sophie and Octavian, but this was her first Marschallin.
*6 June* Première of ***Erwartung*** (Schoenberg/Marie Pappenheim) at the New German Theatre, Prague. This Freudian monodrama, composed in 1909, was performed at the end of the second ISCM festival by Gutheil-Schoder with Zemlinsky as conductor.
*17 June* Performance of ***La Juive*** in Jerusalem in Hebrew.
*4 July* Première of ***Hugh the Drover, or Love in the Stocks*** (Vaughan Williams/Child) at the Royal College of Music, London; the first professional performance was given ten days later by the British National Opera Company at Her Majesty's Theatre. The work, a ballad opera which incorporates folksongs, was completed in 1914.
*14 October* Première of ***Die glückliche Hand*** (Schoenberg/composer) at the Volksoper, Vienna. This expressionist opera – an allegory of the isolation of man in industrial society – had been written and published eleven years earlier.
*3 November* Tullio Serafin made his début at the Metropolitan Opera House, conducting the opening-night performance of ***Aida*** with Rethberg (also making her Met début) and Martinelli. Serafin conducted the Met opening night each year until 1933.
*4 November* Première of ***Intermezzo*** (Strauss/composer) at the Staatsoper, Dresden, under Fritz Busch, with Lehmann and Joseph Correck. The incidents in the opera are quasi-autobiographical: the original sets re-created 'with photographic accuracy' Strauss's villa in Garmisch, while Correck as Hofkapellmeister Storch was made up to look just like the composer.

*6 November* Première of ***Příhody lišky bystroušky*** [***The Cunning Little Vixen***] (Janáček/composer after Těsnohlídek) at the National Theatre, Brno. It was repeated at the third ISCM festival in Prague the following year. The disarming mixture of human and animal characters is used not for parody or comic effect but to underline the universality of freedom, love, death and renewal.
*29 November* Death of Puccini in Brussels.

**1925** *21 March* Première of ***L'Enfant et les sortilèges*** (Ravel/Colette) at the Théâtre du Casino, Monte Carlo. The score, influenced by American popular music and jazz, is both witty and lyrical and perfectly matches the story of a child, the toys and animals he has mistreated, and his redemptive act of kindness.
*16 May* Revival of Monteverdi's ***Il ritorno di Ulisse in patria***, adapted and orchestrated by Vincent d'Indy, at the Petit Scène, Paris.
*21 May* Posthumous première of ***Doktor Faust*** (Busoni/composer) at the Staatsoper, Dresden, under Fritz Busch with Robert Burg in the title role; the final monologue was composed by Philipp Jarnach. Based not on Goethe but on the ancient puppet play, the opera uses abstract musical forms (variations and the suite) and was the summation of Busoni's musical philosophy.
*5 August* Death of Erik Satie, leaving an unfinished opera, ***Paul et Virginie*** (libretto by Cocteau and Radiguet after Bernardin de Saint-Pierre).
*5 November* Première of the trilogy ***L'Orfeide*** (Malipiero/composer) at the Stadttheater, Düsseldorf. The polemical work uses antique musical forms, the characters of *commedia dell'arte* and the figure of Orpheus to explore the conflict between operatic convention and reality.
*26 November* First modern revival of ***L'italiana in Algeri*** (see 1813) to inaugurate the Teatro di Torino, Turin. It was conducted by Vittorio Gui, and Isabella was sung by Supervia, who later sang the role at the Opéra-Comique (1933) and Covent Garden (1935).
*December* Première of ***Šárka*** (Janáček/Zeyer) at the National Theatre, Brno; the composer's first opera, written in 1887–8 and revised in 1924–5.
*14 December* Première of ***Wozzeck*** (Berg/reduction of Büchner's play) at the Staatsoper, Berlin, under Erich Kleiber. The opera had been completed in 1921.

Poster for the fifth performance of Boito's posthumous opera *Nerone* cancelled out of respect for Puccini, who had died that day. The original cast included the Polish soprano Rosa Raïsa, star of Chicago Opera Company from 1916 into the 1930s, and Marcel Journet, one of the finest basses of the twentieth century.

## The Handel renaissance

Following the revival of Italian and French baroque operas since the turn of the century, the work of Handel aroused special interest in post-war Germany. His music exhibited the formal qualities admired by the 'young classicists', while the conventional plots of his operas provided an opportunity for symbolic productions in the spirit of expressionism – and he was a German composer (even if almost all his operas had been written in Italian for the London stage). The initiative begun by Oskar Hagen in Göttingen, which developed there into an annual festival, had wider repercussions, so that *Giulio Cesare* (as *Julius Cäsar*) received 222 performances in 34 different towns. This was the opera that inaugurated the most interesting series of Handel productions (which included staged oratorios as well as operas), put on in Münster (Westphalia) under the motto '*Spiel und Feier*' (Performance and Celebration) by the team of Rudolf Schulz-Dornburg (conductor), Hanns Niedecken-Gebhard (stage director), Hein Heckroth (designer) and Kurt Jooss (choreographer), which – although they have been anathematized by modern proponents of 'authenticity' – epitomized the idealism of the Weimar Republic.

Scene from the Göttingen festival production of Handel's *Radamisto*, first staged in June 1927 by Niedecken-Gebhard, Schulz-Dornburg and Heckroth.

# 1926 1932 Opera in the Weimar Republic

*The attempt to match new operas and new productions to the ideals of post-war Europe created a strong reaction against the traditional romantic repertoire and its bourgeois audience. Many works were either very brief or employed limited instrumental resources, so that from an intensely creative period comparatively few works have remained in the standard repertory.*

**DATES**

**1926**
General Strike in England

**1929**
*29 October*
New York stock market crash provokes world-wide economic and political crisis

Costume designs for the Russian première of Prokofiev's *The Love for Three Oranges* in Leningrad in 1926.

**1926** *24 March* Première of ***Tre commedie goldoniane (La bottega del caffè, Sior Todero brontolon, Le baruffe chiozzotte)*** (Malipiero/composer after Goldoni) at the Hessisches Landestheater, Darmstadt. This brilliant evocation of eighteenth-century Venice is one of Malipiero's most attractive works.
*27 March* Première of ***Der Protagonist*** (Weill/Kaiser) at the Staatsoper, Dresden, conducted by Fritz Busch; Weill's first opera.
*25 April* Posthumous première of ***Turandot*** (Puccini completed by Alfano/Adami and Simoni after Gozzi) at La Scala, Milan, conducted by Toscanini, with the title role created by Rosa Raïsa.
*7 May* Première of ***Les Malheurs d'Orphée*** (Milhaud/Lunel) at the Théâtre de la Monnaie, Brussels. The work, whose brevity is an ironic comment on romantic opera, is scored for fifteen instruments. It was dedicated to the Princesse de Polignac.
*8 June* Farewell performance of Melba at Covent Garden as Mimì in ***La Bohème.***
*19 June* Première of ***Król Roger*** (Szymanowski/composer and Iwaszkiewicz) at the Wielki Teatr, Warsaw. The opera, which transfers Euripides' *Bacchae* to medieval Sicily, had been written in 1920–4.
*16 October* Première of ***Háry János*** (Kodály/Paulini and Harsányi after Garay) at the Royal Opera, Budapest; a ballad opera in which the characters, including Napoleon and Marie Louise, are brought to life in the vivid imagination of a boastful peasant veteran.

Cover of the score of Puccini's *Turandot*, 1926.

*9 November* Première of ***Cardillac*** (Hindemith/Lion after Hoffmann) at the Staatsoper, Dresden, conducted by Fritz Busch, with Robert Burg in the title role. The polyphonic writing, the separation of individual numbers and the stylization of the dramatic roles show the influence of the Handel revival, while Hoffmann's rapacious and murderous goldsmith is used to represent capitalism.
*18 December* Première of ***Več Makropoulos*** [***The Makropoulos Case***] (Janáček/composer after Karel Čapek) at the National Theatre, Brno with sets by Josef Čapek. The strangely dramatic plot concerns the daughter of a Prague alchemist who, having lived for 300 years thanks to drinking an elixir of life, is confronted by characters connected to her past life and finally accepts death.

**1927** *8 January* Première of ***Penthesilea*** (Schoeck/composer after Kleist) at the Staatsoper, Dresden, conducted by Fritz Busch, the composer's most important opera. In its original form the orchestration omitted strings, but it was later 'normalized'.
*28 January* Première of ***Angélique*** (Ibert/Nino) at the Théâtre Bériza, Paris. The work, based on the old legend of the man who puts his shrewish wife up for sale only to have her returned by every purchaser, including the devil, is a *tour de force* of French comic opera.
*10 February* Première of ***Jonny spielt auf*** (Křenek/composer) at the Stadttheater, Leipzig. By far the most popular 'new' opera of the period (it was translated into eighteen languages), the work presents the interaction of an intellectual composer, a beautiful prima donna, a virtuoso violinist and a jazz saxophonist with an appropriate mixing of musical styles.
*17 February* Première of ***The King's Henchmen*** (Taylor/Millay) at the Metropolitan Opera House, New York, conducted by Serafin. The cast included Florence Easton, Lawrence Tibbett and Edward Johnson. It was the first opera by a composer described by Virgil Thomson as one of those 'who went right on as if the twentieth century did not exist'.
*27 April* Première of ***Švanda dudák*** [***Schwanda the Bagpiper***] (Weinberger/Kareš) at the Czech National Theatre, Prague. The plot involves two figures of Czech folklore, the piper Švanda (joy) and Babinsky, a Robin Hood figure, who outwits the devil. The score incorporates Bohemian folksong but is through-composed, with a celebrated fugue when the heroes play cards with the devil in hell.

Set design by Gustav Olah for the first production of Kodály's *Háry János* in Budapest, 1926. The music of the opera is based on Hungarian folksongs, 'gems', as the composer said, 'of which the settings alone are mine'.

*30 May* Première of ***Oedipus Rex*** (Stravinsky/Cocteau after Sophocles), at the Théâtre Sarah Bernhardt, Paris. The composer used Latin for the text of his opera-oratorio because he wanted to work in 'a medium not dead but turned to stone', to distance the audience from the action. The first stage productions were at the Vienna Staatsoper on 23 February 1928 and two days later at the Kroll Theater, Berlin, on a bill with ***Mavra*** and the ballet *Petrushka*.
*17 July* Premières of the four short operas ***Hin und Zurück*** (Hindemith/Schiffer), ***Die Prinzessin auf der Erbse*** (Toch/Elkan after H. C. Andersen), ***Kleine Mahagonny*** (Weill/Brecht) and ***L'Enlèvement d'Europe*** (Milhaud/Hoppenot) at the Baden-Baden chamber music festival. Hindemith gave geometrical form to the cabaret-style words and music, with the action reversing from its point of crisis (like a film winding back) and the music subject to strict counterpoint. Milhaud's work was the first of his *opéras-minutes* (instant operas), while Weill's *Songspiel* was set on a boxing-ring stage using projections of satirical drawings and texts by the young designer Caspar Neher.
*18 November* Première of ***La campana sommersa*** (Respighi/Guastalla) at the Stadttheater, Hamburg – a worldwide success. At the Met première, on 24 November 1928, conducted by Serafin, the cast included Rethberg, Martinelli, de Luca and Pinza, and the composer commented: 'In heaven itself I could not wish for such a production.'
*19 November* Inauguration of the Kroll Opera, Berlin, directed by Klemperer, with a performance of ***Fidelio*** with Rosa Pauly as Leonore.
*16 December* Première of ***Le pauvre matelot*** (Milhaud/Cocteau) at the

Set design by Josef Čapek for the original production of Janáček's *The Makropoulos Case*.

The Kroll Theater, Berlin, where Otto Klemperer was music director from 1927 to 1931.

## The Kroll Theater, Berlin

After a period of chaotic intrigue in the Berlin state theatres, which forced the resignation of the reactionary and incompetent Max von Schillings (see 1915), Otto Klemperer was in September 1926 appointed director of the city's third opera house, located in the recently refurbished Kroll Theater. He had previously held appointments in Cologne and Wiesbaden but was ambitious for a post in which he could exercise artistic autonomy. One of his first acts was to appoint Zemlinsky and Fritz Zweig as staff conductors and for four seasons, despite frequent failures and setbacks, he pursued a strikingly adventurous artistic policy. This was demonstrated more in the style of productions than in performances of new music: although Stravinsky, Hindemith and Křenek were featured, Klemperer withdrew from productions of both Weill's *Kleine Mahagonny* and Schoenberg's *Von Heute auf Morgen*. In many ways his inspiration was Mahler, and his intention was to build up an ensemble of repertory singers (international stars were largely reserved for the Staatsoper), with full preparation of new productions, to give a consistently high standard of performance.
The ideal was 'to make good theatre. Not avant-garde theatre, but good theatre.' However, the anti-realist productions, some in modern dress, several with the 'cubist' sets of Ewald Dülberg and others designed by Moholy-Nagy, Schlemmer and de Chirico, provoked fierce hostility from reactionary critics, who attacked the whole enterprise as Jewish *Kulturbolschewismus*. After they had forced the closure of the company Klemperer wrote prophetically: 'Whenever this approach to opera is revived, it will have to start where we have been obliged to leave off. They may shut one theatre, but the idea underlying it cannot be killed.'

Opéra-Comique, Paris. The text and music of this short opera are an ironic comment on the old operatic themes of constancy, friendship and murder.
*28 December* Première of ***Antigone*** (Honegger/Cocteau) at the Théâtre de la Monnaie, Brussels. Cocteau's modernized version of Sophocles' play had originally been produced in Paris in 1922 with incidental music by Honegger, who transformed it into an opera five years later.

**1928** *18 February* Première of ***Der Zar lässt sich photographieren*** (Weill/Kaiser) at the Neues Theater, Leipzig. Weill's comic opera includes the specially composed 'Tango Angèle' played on an on-stage gramophone.
*20 April* Premières (in German) of ***L'Abandon d'Ariane*** and ***La Déliverance de Thésée*** (Milhaud/Hoppenot) at Wiesbaden; two *opéras-minutes*, which were later performed together with their companion ***L'Enlèvement d'Europe*** (see 1927).
*16 May* Première of ***Fra Gherardo*** (Pizzetti/composer) at La Scala, Milan, conducted by Toscanini. The powerful story of sin and expiation is carried forward in a style of dramatic recitative.
*6 June* Première of ***Die ägyptische Helene*** (Strauss/Hofmannsthal) at the Staatsoper, Dresden, conducted by Fritz Busch and with Rethberg in the name part. Three days later the opera was performed in Vienna (Strauss had promised it to both houses), conducted by the composer, with Jeritza whom both composer and librettist had originally envisaged as Helen. She also sang the role at the Met on 6 November.
*12 August* Death of Janáček in Ostrava.
*31 August* Première of ***Die Dreigroschenoper*** (Weill/Brecht after Gay, Villon and Kipling) at the Theater am Schiffbauerdamm, Berlin, designed by Neher and with Lotte Lenya (Weill's wife) as Jenny Diver. The work, derived from ***The Beggar's Opera***, featured cabaret and operetta artists rather than opera singers and was as sharply satirical – and widely successful – as its eighteenth-century predecessor.

**1929** *15 January* New staging of the original version of ***Der fliegende Holländer*** at the Kroll Theater, Berlin, under Klemperer with spare, geometric sets by Dülberg and an anti-romantic, realistic presentation. The revolutionary nature of the brilliantly coordinated production enraged conservative critics, one of whom called it 'a total destruction of Wagner's work, a basic falsification of his creative intentions'.
*1 February* Première of ***Bronwen*** (Holbrooke/Ellis) in Huddersfield; the third and final part of ***The Cauldron of Annwen*** (see 1912, 1914).
*21 March* Première of ***Sir John in Love*** (Vaughan Williams/composer after Shakespeare) at the Royal College of Music, London.
*29 April* Première of ***Igrok*** [***The Gambler***] (Prokofiev/composer after Dostoevsky) at the Théâtre de la Monnaie, Brussels. The work had been written in 1915–16 and reached rehearsal at the Maryinsky Theatre but was withdrawn after an artistic disagreement.
*May–June* Opera productions at a star-studded Berlin Festival included six performances by the La Scala company under Toscanini, six Strauss operas conducted by the composer, performances of ***Tristan*** and ***Figaro*** under Furtwängler, the ***Ring*** and ***Doktor Faust*** under Blech, ***Andrea Chenier*** under Szell and ***La clemenza di Tito*** and ***Don Pasquale*** under Kleiber.
*8 June* Première of ***Neues vom Tage*** (Hindemith/Schiffer) at the Kroll Theater, Berlin, under Klemperer. Hindemith's *Gebrauchsoper* contained a notorious scene with the heroine in a bathtub singing in a flood of cotton soapsuds. The Kroll's other productions during the festival were ***Don Giovanni***, ***Der fliegende Holländer*** and a Křenek triple bill.

**1930** *18 January* Première of ***Nos*** [***The Nose***] (Shostakovich/composer after Gogol) at the Maly Theatre, Leningrad.

Lawrence Tibbett as Jonny in the final scene of the New York production, designed by Joseph Urban, of Křenek's *Jonny spielt auf* staged in January 1929.

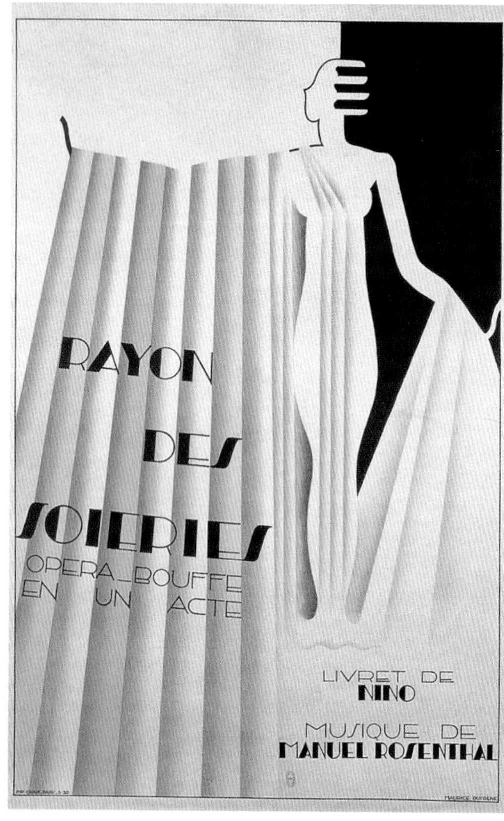


Poster for *Rayon des soieries*, an *opéra-bouffe* by Ravel's pupil Manuel Rosenthal.

*1 February* Première of ***Von Heute auf Morgen*** (Schoenberg/'Max Blonda', i.e. Gertrud Schoenberg) at the Opernhaus, Frankfurt. Schoenberg's contribution to the current genre of socially satirical short operas is remarkable for its complex and witty score.
*9 March* Première of ***Aufstieg und Fall der Stadt Mahagonny*** (Weill/Brecht and composer) at the Neues Theater, Leipzig. In the most 'operatic' of the collaborations between Brecht, Weill and Neher (whose designs were an integral part of the work) American popular music is used to suggest moral degradation.
*12 April* Posthumous première of ***Z mrtvého domu*** [***From the House of the Dead***] (Janáček/composer after Dostoevsky) at the National Theatre, Brno. The work was completed by B. Bakala (music) and O. Zitek (text).
*5 May* Première (in German) of ***Christophe Colomb*** (Milhaud/Claudel) at the Staatsoper, Berlin, conducted by Erich Kleiber. In contrast to Milhaud's *opéras-minutes*, the work is on a colossal scale, interspersing film sequences (one of the earliest appearances of film in opera) with stage scenes.
*25 May* Première (in German) of ***Transatlantic: the People's Choice*** (Antheil/composer) at the Opernhaus, Frankfurt. The composer of the *Ballet mécanique* (for sixteen pianolas to accompany a film) wrote an outrageous jazzy score for this satire on an American presidential election.
*3 June* Première of ***Rayon des soieries*** (Rosenthal/Nino) at the Opéra-Comique, Paris.
*21 June* Unofficial début of Jussi Björling in the role of the lamplighter in ***Manon Lescaut*** at the Royal Opera, Stockholm.
*23 June* Première of ***Der Jasager*** (Weill/Brecht) at the Central Institute for Education, Berlin, directed by the student Kurt Drateck. This school opera is based on the Japanese Noh play *Taniko*. The same year Hindemith composed ***Wir bauen eine Stadt*** (libretto by Seitz), an opera for children written as a model of *Gebrauchsmusik*, music for ordinary use in which anyone can participate.
*4 November* Opening of the new Civic Opera House in Chicago with ***Aida***. The first new opera performed there (on 10 December) was Hamilton Forrest's soon-to-be-forgotten ***Camille***, commissioned by Garden, who sang the title role.

**1931** *3 January* Met début of Lily Pons as Lucia, with Gigli, de Luca and Pinza.

Janáček in 1926; portrait by Gustav Böhm.

## Leoš Janáček

Janáček's operatic procedure is rooted in Czech nationalist music, but differs radically from that of his great predecessors Smetana and Dvořák. The music itself is derived from the rhythms and inflexions of the language – on which, along with the sounds of animals and birds, Janáček had been collecting notes since the 1880s – and he did not imitate folk music so much as absorb it into his musical vocabulary. In the same way, the action of his operas, though clearly located in Czechoslovakia or Russia, is not confined by either time or place and has a universality that few composers in the twentieth century have matched. While *Jenůfa* and *Kát'a Kabanová* treat familiar operatic subject matter, both *The Cunning Little Vixen* and *The Makropoulos Case* offer highly unusual approaches to the questions of mortality and renewal, but are also astonishingly effective in the theatre. The composer's last opera, based on Dostoevsky's *From the House of the Dead*, is one of music's most uplifting explorations of imprisonment and freedom.

Lotte Lenya as Jenny in *Mahagonny*, the role she played in the 1931 Berlin production of the opera conducted by Zemlinsky, after which it was banned in Germany by the Nazis.

Caspar Neher's design for a scenic projection for the final scene of the Weill-Brecht opera *Aufstieg und Fall der Stadt Mahagonny* first produced in Leipzig in 1930.

*'The new operatic theatre which is developing today has an epic character. Its function is to report rather than portray. Its concern is not to construct a plot around moments of suspense but to tell the story of people, of their actions and motives. The purpose of music in this new operatic theatre is not to inflate the plot from inside, to smooth out transitions, emphasize the action, exaggerate passions. The music goes its own long and tranquil way, does not come in until the static moments in the plot, and can therefore (if it is matched by the right subject matter) retain its absolute concertante quality.'*

Kurt Weill

*January* Opening of Sadler's Wells Theatre for productions by the Vic-Wells Opera founded by Lilian Baylis. The company moved to the Coliseum in 1965 and in 1974 became the English National Opera.
*7 February* Première of ***Peter Ibbetson*** (Taylor/composer and Collier after Du Maurier) at the Metropolitan Opera House, New York. Serafin conducted and the leading roles were taken by Lucrezia Bori, Johnson and Tibbett. It received a rapturous reception and on 26 December 1933 became the first American opera to open a Met season.
*15 May* Première of ***Torneo notturno*** (Malipiero/composer) at the Nationaltheater, Munich. The opera, a succession of seven nocturnes which document the struggle between the desperate man and the carefree man, marks the ultimate refinement of the composer's operatic style.
*17 May* Première (in German) of the first part of ***Matka*** [***The Mother***] (Hába/composer) at the Staatstheater am Gärtnerplatz, Munich; a quarter-tone opera composed in 1927–9.

**1932** *14 February* Première of ***Der gewaltige Hahnrei*** [***The Magnificent Cuckold***] (Goldschmidt/after Crommelynck) in Mannheim. A new production planned by Carl Ebert for Berlin was cancelled after the Nazis seized power.
*17 March* Première of ***La donna serpente*** (Casella/Lodovici after Gozzi) at the Opera, Rome; a work which demonstrates the composer's mastery of orchestral colouring, polyphonic writing and vocal virtuosity. His archaizing ***La favola d'Orfeo*** (libretto by Pavolini after Poliziano) was premièred six months later at the Teatro Goldoni, Venice.
*26 April* NBC broadcast of the first opera written for radio: ***The Willow Tree*** by Charles Wakefield Cadman, a composer who had studied and absorbed Native American music.
*15 October* Inauguration of the Memorial Opera House, San Francisco, with a performance of ***Tosca*** starring Claudia Muzio.

# 1933–1944 Opera in the Shadow of War

*As Nazism took over in Germany, many composers and performers emigrated, while throughout the operatic world the spirit of experimentation began to be replaced with a return to tradition, even as a means to convey political criticism. Nevertheless, in Germany and Soviet Russia works were often suppressed by the authorities if they failed to conform to the aesthetic norms of the totalitarian régimes.*

**1933** *7 January* Première of ***The Emperor Jones*** (Gruenberg/composer and Kathleen de Jaffa after O'Neill) at the Metropolitan Opera House, New York, conducted by Serafin.
*7 March* At a performance of ***Rigoletto*** in Dresden Fritz Busch, a noted anti-Nazi, was forced to leave the rostrum after almost all seats in the house had been bought by the Brownshirts. Busch left Germany for good in June.
*22 April* Opening of the first Maggio Musicale in Florence with a performance of ***Nabucco*** under Gui, with Cigna as Abigaille and Stignani as Fenena.
*7 June* Première of ***Die sieben Todsünden der Kleinbürger*** (Weill/Brecht) at the Théâtre des Champs-Elysées, Paris. This *opéra-ballet* was based on a scenario by Edward James and Boris Kochno and was choreographed by George Balanchine. The leading role is divided between a singer and dancer – performed at the première by Lotte Lenya and Tilly Losch.
*1 July* Première of ***Arabella*** (Strauss/Hofmannsthal) at the Staatsoper, Dresden.
*30 December* The first commercially sponsored broadcast from the Metropolitan Opera was ***Mignon*** with Bori, Pons, Swarthout and Schipa; the sponsor was Lucky Strike.

**1934** *13 January* Première of ***La favola del figlio cambiato*** (Malipiero/Pirandello) at the Landestheater, Braunschweig. The anti-clerical and anti-monarchical satire led to a hostile reception at the work's Italian première in Rome on 24 March, and the Fascist authorities insisted on its withdrawal after the performance. With his next opera, ***Giulio Cesare*** (1936), based on Shakespeare's play, Malipiero remained on safer ground.
*20 January* Première of ***Giuditta*** (Lehár/Knepler and Löhner) at the Staatsoper, Vienna, conducted by the composer, with Jarmila Novotná and Richard Tauber in the leading roles. The expansion of the operetta form for a production designed for the Staatsoper rather stretched Lehár's abilities, but it was, nevertheless, a great popular success.
*22 January* Première of ***Ledi Makbet Mtsenskovo uezda [Lady Macbeth of the Mtsensk District] (Katerina Ismailova)*** (Shostakovich/composer and Preis after Leskov) at the Maly Theatre, Leningrad. It was produced shortly afterwards in Moscow by Eisenstein, but in January 1936 was condemned by Pravda for its 'western modernism'.
*23 January* Première of ***La fiamma*** (Respighi/Guastalla) at the Opera, Rome, conducted by the composer. The libretto, which tells of witchcraft in Byzantine Ravenna, was set with enormous care by Respighi, and the opera enjoyed considerable initial success, though the music is too rooted in convention for this to have lasted.
*8 February* Première of ***Four Saints in Three Acts*** (Thomson/Stein) to inaugurate the Avery Memorial Theater, Hartford, Ct. Despite the intentional provocation of the work and its production, it enjoyed a highly

**DATES**

**1933**
*30 January* Hitler becomes German Chancellor
F. D. Roosevelt inaugurated as 32nd American President
**1934**
Start of Stalin's purges in the Soviet Union
**1935**
Italian invasion of Abyssinia
**1936**
*July* Start of the Spanish Civil War (to 1939), with both the left-wing Republicans and Franco's Falangists receiving outside assistance
Abdication crisis in Britain. Edward VIII, who had succeeded George V, is replaced as king in December by his brother George VI
**1937**
International exhibition in Paris, dominated by the huge German and Soviet pavilions. The Spanish Republican pavilion shows Picasso's *Guernica*
**1938**
*13 March* Annexation of Austria by Nazi Germany
*29 September* Munich Agreement allows Germany to annex areas of Czechoslovakia
Racial laws come into effect in Italy
**1939**
*15 March* Germany occupies the rest of Czechoslovakia
*August* Pact between Germany and Russia
*1 September* German occupation of Poland, followed two days later by the declaration of war against Germany by Britain and France
**1940**
By May German forces have overrun Denmark, Norway, Holland and Belgium; the USSR has occupied Finland
*21 June* Armistice between Germany and France leaving the country partitioned
**1941**
*22 June* German forces invade Russia; siege of Leningrad begins (to 1944)
*7 December* Japanese attack on Pearl Harbor brings the USA into the war
**1942**
Siege of Stalingrad
**1943**
*July* Allied invasion of Italy and fall of Mussolini
**1944**
*6 June* Allied landings in Normandy
*July* Failed attempt by German officers to assassinate Hitler
*25 August* Liberation of Paris

Scene from the original production of Gershwin's *Porgy and Bess*. The title roles were sung by Todd Duncan and Anne Brown, supported by Abbie Mitchell, Bubbles, Warren Coleman, Edward Matthews and James Rosamond Johnson.

*'You must never forget when you write about George Gershwin that the rest of us were songwriters. George was a composer.'*

Irving Berlin

## American opera

Despite the fact that by the turn of the century New York's Metropolitan Opera had become the showcase for international opera, the search for a local masterpiece had met with no success. However, it was during the 1930s that the influence of contemporary developments in European music began to be felt in the USA, and although the furthest the Met went was the staging of the Russian-American Louis Gruenberg's *The Emperor Jones*, two composers produced significant works in the mid-thirties – Virgil Thomson's *Four Saints in Three Acts* and George Gershwin's *Porgy and Bess* – while Aaron Copland, Gian-Carlo Menotti and Douglas Moore also made their operatic débuts. Thomson's opera (which sets Gertrude Stein's libretto in its entirety, including the stage directions), is derived from the transparency of Milhaud's 'instant operas' blended with traditional American thematic material, but the success on Broadway of the unconventional production indicated that opera might exist outside the 'grand opera' strait-jacket. Gershwin succeeded brilliantly in bridging the gap between the American musical and the operatic stage, although the achievement has never been repeated so effectively.

Two other developments were more marginal: while George Antheil was in Paris he was close to Ezra Pound and helped with the orchestration of Pound's first opera, *Le Testament,* based on texts by François Villon. This work, broadcast during the 1930s by the BBC is of great interest, written in an individual declamatory style derived from pre-Renaissance music. By contrast, Marc Blitzstein's *The Cradle Will Rock* was a fiercely political music-drama in the Weill-Brecht vein developed by John Houseman and Orson Welles under the Federal Theater Project – so controversial that the Government closed the theatre before its first performance.

Lawrence Tibbett as Brutus Jones in the original production of Louis Gruenberg's *The Emperor Jones*, based on Eugene O'Neill's play, at the Metropolitan Opera in January 1933.

Scene from the original production of *Four Saints in Three Acts*, 1934, Virgil Thomson's setting of Gertrude Stein's libretto. It was staged for the 'Friends and Enemies of Modern Music' by Frederick Ashton and John Houseman, with cellophane scenery designed by Florine Stettheimer. The opera was cast entirely with African-American singers, though this was for purely aesthetic, not political, reasons: they found black performers 'more beautiful and more expressive'.

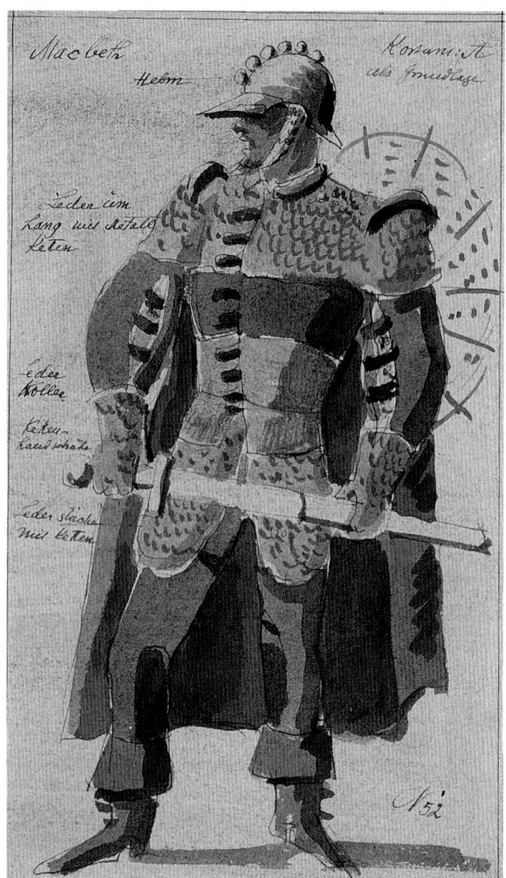


A costume design by Caspar Neher for the Glyndebourne production of *Macbeth*, which opened on 21 May 1938, the British première of Verdi's opera. It was produced by Carl Ebert and conducted by Fritz Busch, and the cast included Vera Schwarz, Francesco Valentino, David Franklin (who appeared in eight Glyndebourne seasons from 1936 to 1958) and David Lloyd.

## Opera festivals: Salzburg, Florence and Glyndebourne

The first regular summer opera festival (the season when opera houses were closed) was instituted in 1876 by Wagner at Bayreuth, but Salzburg followed with several festivals in the late nineteenth century, which became more regular in the years before the First World War. Under the direction of Max Reinhardt from 1920, they allowed summer visitors to hear fine productions – with an emphasis on Mozart – from the Vienna and Munich opera houses, with guest conductors who included Strauss, Schalk, Walter and Krauss. Toscanini's appearance there from 1935 to 1937 added works by Beethoven, Verdi and Wagner.

Florence instituted its Maggio Musicale in 1933, initially as a biennial festival. Revivals of Renaissance operas and new works by contemporary composers were performed there as well as operas from the standard nineteenth-century repertory.

The festival at Glyndebourne had a quite different background. John Christie, who was married to the singer Audrey Mildmay, decided to build a small theatre in the grounds of his Sussex home where operas could be performed on an intimate scale, and he took on three distinguished refugees from the Nazis to realize his idea: Carl Ebert, in charge of productions; Fritz Busch, as musical director; and Rudolf Bing, as general manager. An experimental production of Pergolesi's *La serva padrona* was put on in March 1934, and during the first season, two months later, two Mozart operas, *Le nozze di Figaro* and *Così fan tutte*, were staged with singers of international repute. The success of this quixotic venture was ensured by the high standards of performance, and further productions in the years before the war included three more Mozart operas, *Die Zauberflöte*, *Die Entführung aus dem Serail* and *Don Giovanni*, as well as Donizetti's *Don Pasquale* and Verdi's *Macbeth*. During the war Rudolf Bing organized a touring production of *The Beggar's Opera,* which received 42 performances in theatres around Britain and a further 84 at the Haymarket Theatre, London, with a cast that included Roy Henderson, Michael Redgrave and Audrey Mildmay.

Design by V. V. Dmitriev for the original Leningrad production of Shostakovich's *Lady Macbeth of the Mtsensk District* in January 1934. Although it was condemned two years later by the Soviet authorities, the opera enjoyed considerable success abroad, with productions in the USA (in Cleveland and then at the Met) and in Stockholm in 1935, in Prague, Zurich, Copenhagen, Ljublana and London (a concert performance) in 1936, in Zagreb in 1937 and in Bratislava in 1938.

Viorica Ursuleac (Arabella) and Alfred Jerger (Mandryka) in the original production of *Arabella*, which Hofmannsthal had based on his novella *Lucidor*. The bittersweet Viennese love story, set in 1860, inspired some of Strauss's most sensuously romantic music. Although the opera is dedicated to Fritz Busch and the director of the Dresden Staatsoper, Alfred Reucker, both had been forced to leave Germany, and the première was conducted by Clemens Krauss, Ursuleac's lover and later husband.

Gina Cigna as Abigaille in Verdi's *Nabucco*, the role she played in the production of the opera at the first Maggio Musicale in Florence in 1933.

successful six-week run on Broadway after Hartford and was produced in Chicago in the autumn.

*10 February* Première of ***Merry Mount*** (Hanson/Stokes after Hawthorne) at the Metropolitan Opera, New York, conducted by Serafin. Not for the first time, Tibbett was required to rescue an uninspired American opera with a virtuoso performance.

*24 March* Première of ***Il dibuk*** (Rocca/Simoni after Anski) at La Scala, Milan. This dramatic opera, based on Jewish folklore, about the possession of a young man by his dead lover, was a great success though soon suppressed by the racial laws in Italy. There were, however, productions in New York, Chicago and Detroit.

*13 April* ***The Threepenny Opera*** (an English version of Weill's ***Die Dreigroschenoper***) opened at the Empire Theater, New York, with Lotte Lenya and Louis Armstrong.

*28 May* Official opening of the first Glyndebourne Festival with a performance of ***Le nozze di Figaro*** conducted by Busch and produced by Ebert. It was followed the next night by their ***Così fan tutte.*** The casts included Ina Souez (Fiordiligi), Audrey Mildmay (Susanna), Luise Helletsgruber (Cherubino and Dorabella), Aulikki Rautawaara (the Countess), Irene Eisinger (Despina), Roy Henderson (the Count), Willi Domgraf-Fassbänder (Figaro and Guglielmo), John Brownlee (Don Alfonso) and Heddle Nash (Ferrando and Don Basilio).

*18 September* Première of ***Osud*** [***Fate***] (Janáček/Bartošová and composer) on Brno Radio. The stage première was given at the National Theatre, Brno, in October 1958. The work had been written in 1903–7, but after more than one production had been aborted before 1914, the composer set the work aside. The libretto is based on personal events that were taking place in the composer's life as composition progressed, and the time-sequences in the opera present considerable production difficulties, but it is a fine and highly characteristic example of Janáček's work.

**1935** *16 January* Première of ***Nerone*** (Mascagni/Targioni-Tozzetti after Cossa) at La Scala, Milan; an opera intended as a tribute to Mussolini.

*22 May* Première of ***Die Zaubergeige*** (Egk/Andersen and composer) at the Opernhaus, Frankfurt. This was Egk's first staged opera – ***Columbus*** (1933) had only received a radio performance – and was based on the tradition of Bavarian puppet theatre.

*24 June* Première of ***Die schweigsame Frau*** (Strauss/Zweig after Ben Jonson) at the Staatsoper, Dresden, with Maria Cebotari as Aminta. The opera fell victim to Nazi 'political correctness'; Zweig's name was dropped from the programme, upon which Strauss resigned his position as head of the Reichsmusikkammer. The opera was revived in Zurich on 16 May 1936 and in Prague on 3 June 1937.

*Summer* In the production of ***Fidelio*** conducted by Toscanini at the Salzburg Festival Lehmann sang Leonore, considered by many to be her greatest role.

*30 September* Première of ***Porgy and Bess*** (Gershwin/DuBose Heyward and Ira Gershwin after play by DuBose and Dorothy Heyward after DuBose Heyward's novel) at the Colonial Theater, Boston. Over 120 performances followed at the Alvin Theater, New York (opening on 10 October), before the production went on tour. The work belongs to the genre of folk opera, although it is based on American commercial music rather than folksong.

*22 October* Première of ***Tikhy Don*** [***Quiet Flows the Don***] (Dzerzhinsky/composer after Sholokhov) at the Maly Theatre, Leningrad. This orthodox Soviet opera was dedicated to Shostakovich, who helped to arrange its performance.

*24 December* Death of Alban Berg in Vienna.

**1936** *12 February* Première of ***Il campiello*** (Wolf-Ferrari/Ghisalberti after Goldoni) at La Scala, Milan. The opera which follows the little events taking place in a small Venetian square (*campiello*) has music of great freshness and charm.
*13 March* Première of ***Oedipe*** (Enescu/Fleg after Sophocles) at the Opéra, Paris; a grand romantic opera incorporating Romanian folk material in the score.
*2 November* Opening of the visiting season at Covent Garden by the Dresden Staatsoper with a performance of ***Der Rosenkavalier***, using the original 1911 sets and costumes, conducted by Karl Böhm.

**1937** *18 March* Première of ***Veselohra na mostě*** [***Comedy on the Bridge***] (Martinů/composer after Klicpera), on Czech Radio, Prague. The second of the composer's radio operas, the action takes place on a bridge between two villages at war, and the trivial comic events of the plot are overshadowed by the constant military presence. The first staged performance was at the State Theatre, Ostrava, on 9 January 1948.
*1 April* Première (in English) of ***Amelia al ballo*** [***Amelia Goes to the Ball***] (Menotti/composer) at the Philadelphia Academy of Music; after this preview the production was staged at the New Amsterdam Theater, New York, and the following year at the Metropolitan Opera. The work, which belongs within the Italian lyric tradition, established Menotti's reputation.
*21 April* Première of ***The Second Hurricane*** (Copland/Denby), an opera for music schools, at the Grand Street Playhouse, New York. The production by Orson Welles placed the orchestra on a platform behind the two on-stage choruses with the conductor facing the audience.
*19 May* Première of ***Il deserto tentato*** (Casella/Pavolini) at the Teatro Comunale, Florence; an operatic allegory referring to the conquest of Abyssinia.
*2 June* Posthumous première of ***Lulu*** (Berg/composer after Wedekind) at the Stadttheater, Zurich. The opera was almost complete at the composer's death, but since neither Schoenberg nor Webern was willing to prepare a final version, his widow allowed only the first two acts to be performed. The work uses both complex structural techniques and multiple serialism, but – as with ***Wozzeck*** – Berg's instincts as an operatic composer transcended the need for formal analysis, producing one of the most powerful operatic scores of the twentieth century. The version completed by Friedrich Cerha was first performed at the Opéra, Paris, on 24 February 1979.
*8 June* Première of ***Carmina Burana*** (Orff/medieval songs) at the Staatsoper, Frankfurt. All three parts of Orff's ***Trionfi*** triptych of 'scenic cantatas', including ***Catulli Carmina*** (premièred in Leipzig on 6 November 1943) and ***Trionfo di Afrodite*** were first performed together in Milan on 13 February 1953, conducted by Herbert von Karajan.
*16 June* Première of ***The Cradle Will Rock*** (Blitzstein/composer) at the Venice Theater, New York.
*1 December* Première of ***Riders to the Sea*** (Vaughan Williams/composer after Synge) at the Royal College of Music, London. The composer had started work on the opera in 1925, and the use of folksong is more fully integrated into the symphonic structure of the score than in any of his other operatic works.
*17 December* Met début of Zinka Milanov – who was to become the company's leading soprano during the 1940s – as Leonora (***Il trovatore***).

**1938** *16 March* Première of ***Julietta: Snář*** [***Julietta: The Book of Dreams***] (Martinů/composer after Neveux) at the National Theatre, Prague, with settings by František Muzika. The composer described Neveux's surrealist

Nuri Hadzič as Lulu and Albert Emmerich as the Lion-Tamer in the original production of the first two acts of Berg's *Lulu* at the Zurich Stadttheater in June 1937.

Marc Blitzstein rehearsing the cast of *The Cradle Will Rock*, his explosively political 'play in music' dedicated to Brecht. After two successful dress rehearsals of Orson Welles's sumptuous production for the Federal Theater Project, the theatre was closed by the Government on the evening of the planned première. At the very last minute Welles moved the audience to the Venice Theater, where for two weeks Blitzstein gave performances playing the piano and singing all the roles, with members of the cast joining in from the auditorium.

The Norwegian soprano Kirsten Flagstad as Isolde, a role she first sang in Oslo in 1932. The following year she made her international début as Sieglinde in the Bayreuth *Ring* directed by Heinz Tietjen, and this was also the role in which she made her Met début on 2 February 1935. Flagstad was the principal Wagnerian soprano at the New York opera house until her return to Norway, after singing Isolde on 12 April 1941.

Giovanni Martinelli as Otello. His interpretation of the role was one of the highlights of the 1937 'Coronation' season at Covent Garden, for which Sir Thomas Beecham assembled a series of brilliant and star-studded productions with singers who included Tibbett as Scarpia; Eva Turner as Turandot; Lubin as Dukas's Ariane and Gluck's Alceste; Maggie Teyte as Eurydice; and, in Wagner, Leider, Flagstad, Kerstin Thorborg, Melchior, Lorenz, Ludwig Weber and Herbert Janssen.

play – his wonderfully sensitive setting of it delighted the playwright – as 'not a philosophical dissertation, but an extraordinarily beautiful and poetic fantasy in the form of a dream'.

*12 May* Concert première of ***Jeanne au bûcher*** (Honegger/Claudel) by the Basel Kammerchor conducted by Paul Sacher. The first stage production of this 'dramatic oratorio', in which virtually all the singing roles are assigned to the celestial characters, was in Zurich in 1942, but there were frequent officially supported performances in France during the war.

*28 May* Première of ***Mathis der Maler*** (Hindemith/composer) at the Stadttheater, Zurich. The theme of the opera, based on the life of the painter Grünewald, is the role of the independent artist in time of war, and it remained Hindemith's most profound statement of his musical and political beliefs. The first performance in Germany was given under Ferdinand Leitner in Stuttgart in 1946.

*22 June* Première of ***Karl V*** (Křenek/composer) at the New German Theatre, Prague. This large-scale twelve-note opera had been commissioned for Vienna, but was banned by the Nazis; it presents a utopian vision of a peaceful Europe united by the Catholic dynasty of the Habsburgs, though at its conclusion the Emperor Charles V confesses on his deathbed the failure of his vision.

*24 July* Première of ***Friedenstag*** (Strauss/Gregor and Zweig) at the Nationaltheater, Munich, conducted by Krauss, with Ursuleac, Hans Hotter, Julius Patzak and Ludwig Weber. The libretto, dramatically highly unsatisfactory, is a plea for peace and toleration; it elicited one of Strauss's least characteristic operatic scores. The production marked the start of Hotter's international career.

*15 October* Première of ***Daphne*** (Strauss/Gregor) at the Staatsoper, Dresden, conducted by Karl Böhm (to whom it is dedicated) and with Margarete Teschemacher in the title role – on a double bill with ***Friedenstag***. The work is in the lyrical vein which characterizes the best of Strauss's late compositions.

Sergei Eisenstein, one of the first film directors to turn also to opera production, rehearsing a group of Valkyries in a scene from Act III of *Die Walküre* at the Bolshoi Theatre, Moscow, in 1943.

Benjamin Britten and W. H. Auden in America, where both had moved in 1939. Their collaboration on *Paul Bunyan* marked Britten's début as an operatic composer and Auden's as a librettist.

**1939** *28 January* Première of ***Die Bürger von Calais*** (Wagner-Régeny/Neher) at the Staatsoper, Berlin, conducted by Karajan. The production was also designed by Neher, who wrote four libretti for the composer. Other productions followed in Germany, but the anti-romantic Handelian style was unsuited to the climate of approaching war.
*5 February* Première of ***Der Mond*** (Orff/composer after the brothers Grimm) at the Nationaltheater, Munich.
*18 May* Première of ***The Devil and Daniel Webster*** (Moore/Benét) at the Martin Beck Theater, New York; this folk opera was the third of Moore's operas.

**1940** *13 April* Première of ***Romeo und Julia*** (Sutermeister/composer after Shakespeare), conducted by Böhm, at the Staatsoper, Dresden; the Swiss composer's first opera.
*18 May* Première of ***Volo di notte*** (Dallapiccola/composer after Saint-Exupéry) at the Teatro della Pergola, Florence, during the Maggio Musicale. Dallapiccola's first opera, which has spoken dialogue and incorporates wordless vocalization into the serially composed score, was derived from material written for his *Tre laudi*, giving a religious dimension to the story of a night pilot who runs out of fuel.
*30 June* Première of ***Semyon Kotko*** (Prokofiev/Katayev and composer) at the Stanislavsky Theatre, Moscow. The work was dropped from the repertory the following year for political reasons and not revived until 1959.
*24 August* The season at the Paris Opéra opened with Berlioz's ***La Damnation de Faust***, to an audience largely made up of German officers and Spanish Falangists. The box office receipts were ten times those of 5 June, just before the German occupation of the city.
*November* Professional début of Maria Kalegeropoulos (Callas) at the National Lyric Theatre, Athens, in Suppé's light opera ***Boccaccio.***
*28 December* Revival of ***La Fille du régiment*** at the Metropolitan Opera House, New York, starring Lily Pons. She had learned to play the drum and appeared in press photographs wearing military uniform, being appointed an honorary member of a US army regiment. The production was used to open the 1942–3 season.

**1941** *5 May* Première of ***Paul Bunyan*** (Britten/Auden) at Columbia University, New York. The satirical ballad opera, designed for high school performance, is based on the story of the giant American folk hero.
*22 May* Wagner's birthday was celebrated in Paris, in the presence of his daughter-in-law Winifred, with an outstanding performance of ***Tristan und Isolde*** at the Opéra conducted by Karajan, with Lubin and Lorenz in the title roles.
*28 May* Première of the revised version of Alfano's ***L'ombra di Don Giovanni*** (1914) as ***Don Juan de Mañara*** at the Teatro della Pergola, Florence, during the Maggio Musicale.

**1942** *15 March* Death of Zemlinsky in Larchmont, N.Y. He had emigrated in 1938, never completing the orchestration of ***Der König Kandaules***, composed in 1935–6, though his rendering of the classical myth as an allegory of the new order in music is exceptionally effective. His last opera, ***Circe***, begun in America, remained a fragment.
*May* Dallapiccola's realization of Monteverdi's ***Il ritorno di Ulisse in patria*** was produced at the Maggio Musicale in Florence. Orff's versions of Monteverdi's ***Ballo delle ingrate*** and ***Orfeo*** (both later revised) received their first performances the same year at Karlsruhe and Mannheim.
*28 October* Première of ***Capriccio*** (Strauss/composer and Krauss) at the Nationaltheater, Munich, conducted by Krauss.

Scene from the original production of *Capriccio*, Richard Strauss's last opera, performed at the Nationaltheater, Munich, in October 1942. The Countess was played by Viorica Ursuleac and Olivier by Hans Hotter. The work had its origins in *Prima la musica e poi le parole*, the opera by G. B. Casti and Salieri (see 1786), and is a discourse on the relationship of music and text in opera. Its transparent, lyrical score matches the conversational style of the libretto.

*November* Italian première of ***Wozzeck*** at the Opera, Rome, conducted by Serafin and with Gobbi in the title role.

**1943** *20 February* Première of ***Die Kluge*** (Orff/composer after the brothers Grimm) at the Opernhaus, Frankfurt. The bullying figure of the King seems to be an obviously totalitarian figure, although performances of the work were not banned.
*23 September* First performance of the children's opera ***Brundibár*** [***The Bumble Bee***] (Krása/after Hoffmeister) in the concentration camp at Terezín (Theresienstadt).
*2 December* Première of ***Carmen Jones***, in New York, a musical by Oscar Hammerstein II using Bizet's music, set in the American south: Carmen works in a parachute factory, José is a black corporal and Escamillo a prizefighter.

**1944** *June* Strauss's eightieth birthday was celebrated at the Staatsoper, Vienna, with productions of several of his operas. These included ***Ariadne auf Naxos***, conducted by Böhm, with Maria Reining, Max Lorenz and Irmgard Seefried; and ***Salome***, conducted by Strauss. The title role of the latter opera was sung for the first time by Ljuba Welitsch (at Strauss's request); he had admired her performance as the Composer in an earlier performance of ***Ariadne auf Naxos***.
*16 August* Dress rehearsal of ***Die Liebe der Danae*** (Strauss/Gregor) at the Festspielhaus, Salzburg, conducted by Krauss, with Ursuleac as Danae and Hotter as Jupiter. The opera had been completed in June 1940, but Strauss had been reluctant to allow its performance. In the event, German reverses in the war led to the cancellation of all public performances of the opera, and it was not officially premièred until 1952 (again at Salzburg), four years after the composer's death.
*October* Dress rehearsal of ***Der Kaiser von Atlantis*** (Ullmann/Kien) at the Terezín concentration camp, although performances were forbidden after the polemical nature of the work became clear: Death has gone on strike and will allow no one to die, and this dreadful situation is only resolved when Kaiser Überall, who has declared total war, agrees to be the first to go. Both composer and librettist died later in the year in Auschwitz.

# 1945 / 1953 The New Order

*As opera houses reopened after the war, the way was open for new composers, new singers and new styles of production: Benjamin Britten and Hans Werner Henze both began their operatic careers; the dramatic interpretations of Maria Callas began to turn attention back to the romantic repertoire; while Walter Felsenstein in East Berlin and the Wagner brothers in Bayreuth were among those who simplified and modernized the presentation of opera for post-war audiences.*

Kathleen Ferrier as Orpheus in the 1947 Glyndebourne production of Gluck's *Orfeo ed Euridice*, which was conducted by Ernest Ansermet, directed by Ebert and designed by Neher. Orpheus was the last role the great mezzo sang in her brief operatic career, at Covent Garden on 6 February 1953.

**1945** *7 June* Première of ***Peter Grimes*** (Britten/Slater after Crabbe) at Sadler's Wells Theatre, London, conducted by Reginald Goodall, with Peter Pears in the title role and Joan Cross as Ellen.

**1946** *5 May* Première of ***Obruchenie v monastire*** [***Betrothal in a Monastery***] (Prokofiev/composer and Mendel'son after Sheridan's *The Duenna*) at the National Theatre, Prague; the Russian première was in November at the Kirov Theatre, Leningrad. The work, a romantic comedy with music of transparent charm, had been written for Stanislavsky's Moscow Opera Theatre in 1940, but public performances were prevented by the war.
*8 May* Première of ***The Medium*** (Menotti/composer) at Columbia University, New York, the first of the melodramatic operas which made Menotti famous. He later directed the film version of the opera.
*12 June* Première of ***Voina i mir*** [***War and Peace***] (Prokofiev/composer and Mendel'son after Tolstoy) at the Maly Theatre, Leningrad. Only eleven scenes from the opera were given. A planned performance of the second part of the opera three years later was prevented by the Zhdanov decree (see 1948), and the whole opera, a lyrical work in the tradition of the grand Russian historical works of the previous century, was not given until 1957, following several partial performances.
*12 July* Première of ***The Rape of Lucretia*** (Britten/Duncan after Obey) at Glyndebourne, conducted by Ansermet. The burden of post-war taxation made it impossible for John Christie to continue financing Glyndebourne himself, and a joint company was set up with Britten's English Opera Group which performed the new opera at Glyndebourne (the only production that year) and then on tour in Britain and Holland.
*16 December* Première of ***Street Scene*** (Weill/Rice and Hughes) at the Shubert Theatre, Philadelphia. This powerful realization of Elmer Rice's play, set among down-and-outs in New York, is characteristic of the mixture of liberal opinions and imaginative musical ideas that moulded all of Weill's American works.

**1947** *18 February* Première of ***The Telephone*** (Menotti/composer) at the Heckscher Theater, New York, presented as a comic curtain-raiser to ***The Medium*** (see 1946).
*4 March* Première of ***Die Flut*** (Blacher/von Cramer) at the Staatsoper, Dresden. The work was written for Berlin Radio (broadcast on 20 December 1946) for a ten-piece orchestra and employed metrical as well as tonal serialism.

Scene from the first stage production of Dallapiccola's *Il prigioniero* at the Maggio Musicale, Florence, in 1950. (The first concert performance of the work, written in 1944–8, had been given on RAI on 1 December 1949.) The opera is set in sixteenth-century Spanish Flanders, where the prisoner's torturers hold out hopes of freedom only for these to be dashed in the crushingly pessimistic conclusion.

*6 October* Première of ***Regina*** (Blitzstein/composer after Hellman) at the Première Shubert Theater, New Haven, Ct. Based on Lillian Hellman's play *Little Foxes*, it is the most successfully 'operatic' of the composer's stage works.

**1950** *1 March* Première of ***The Consul*** (Menotti/composer) at the Shubert Theater, Philadelphia. In Menotti's cold-war *verismo* opera, which enjoyed great international success, a man and his wife are thwarted in their attempt to escape from a police state.
*10 May* Première of ***Bolivar*** (Milhaud/after Supervielle) at the Opéra, Paris.
*18 May* Première of ***The Jumping Frog of Calaveras County*** (Foss/Karsavina after Mark Twain) at the University of Indiana Theater, Bloomington, an entertaining short opera written at the start of Foss's career as a composer.
*20 May* Première of ***Il prigioniero*** (Dallapiccola/composer) at the Teatro Comunale, Florence, during the Maggio Musicale, following a radio performance on RAI on 1 December 1949. The score combines serial technique with an expressive vocal line.
*6 November* Opening of the first season at the Metropolitan Opera, New York, under the directorship of Rudolf Bing with Verdi's ***Don Carlos***, directed by the Shakespearean specialist Margaret Webster. Bing's reign was to be characterized by high performance standards but great conservatism in the repertory.

Scene from Milhaud's *Bolivar* at the Opéra, Paris, with sets designed by Fernand Léger. The third of the composer's operas to treat an epic South American theme, following *Christophe Colomb* (see 1930) and *Maximilien* (1932), it was composed in 1943, while Milhaud was living in exile in the USA.

**1951** *17 March* Première of ***Die Verurteilung des Lukullus*** (Dessau/Brecht) at the Admiralspalast, East Berlin. The opera was taken off after this trial performance at government request because of its strong pacifism, and it reopened in revised form at the Staatsoper on 12 October. Dessau's later operas included ***Einstein*** (1974), on the theme of atomic weapons.
*26 April* Première of ***The Pilgrim's Progress*** (Vaughan Williams/composer after Bunyan) at Covent Garden, London. Composed over a period of thirty years, the work is described as a 'morality'. In response to his critics

The first scene of Stravinsky's *The Rake's Progress* at La Fenice, Venice, with Elisabeth Schwarzkopf, Thomas Rounseville, Otakar Kraus and Raphaël Arié.

Scene from the 1957 Berlin Festival production of Blacher's *Abstracte Oper I*, first performed four years earlier.

Vaughan Williams wrote: 'It's not like the operas they are used to, but it's the sort of opera I wanted to write, and there it is.'
*June* First staging of Haydn's ***L'anima del filosofo*** (cut and titled ***Orfeo ed Euridice***) at the Maggio Musicale, Florence, conducted by Kleiber, with Callas and Christoff. The opera had been written for London in 1791 but was not performed.
*30 July* Wieland Wagner's production of ***Parsifal*** conducted by Knappertsbusch, with which the Wagner Festival at Bayreuth reopened, marked the start of the Wieland/Wolfgang Wagner régime there.
*11 September* Première of ***The Rake's Progress*** (Stravinsky/Auden and Kallman) at La Fenice, Venice, conducted by the composer. Based on Hogarth's cycle of paintings, the opera is full of ironical references to eighteenth-century music.
*1 December* Première of ***Billy Budd*** (Britten/Forster and Crozier after Melville) at Covent Garden, conducted by the composer, with Peter Pears as Captain Vere. The opera, which portrays a struggle between the forces of good and evil, is the most forcefully dramatic and one of the greatest of all Britten's compositions.
*24 December* Première of ***Amahl and the Night Visitors*** (Menotti/composer) on an NBC telecast; the first stage performance was at the University of Indiana Theater, Bloomington, on 21 February 1952. Inspired by an *Adoration of the Magi* by Bosch, this was the first opera written for television, and has taken its place alongside ***Hänsel und Gretel*** as Christmas operatic entertainment for children.

**1952** *17 February* Première of ***Boulevard Solitude*** (Henze/Weil after Jokisch) at the Landestheater, Hanover. Henze's third opera, influenced by the Viennese school as well as by popular music and jazz, is a modern version of the Manon Lescaut theme.
*April–May* The Maggio Musicale in Florence included five operas by Rossini: ***Armida*** (with Callas), ***Le Comte Ory***, ***Tancredi***, ***La pietra del paragone*** (with Giulietta Simionato) and ***Guillaume Tell*** (with Tebaldi, Baum and Rossi-Lemeni).
*12 June* Première of ***Trouble in Tahiti*** (Bernstein/composer), at Brandeis University; a satire on suburban sentimentality that was later incorporated into ***A Quiet Place*** (see 1983). It was followed two days later by the première of ***The Threepenny Opera***, Marc Blitzstein's version of Weill's ***Die Dreigroschenoper*** reorchestrated for an eight-man band. Its professional run, starring Weill's widow, Lotte Lenya, began at the Theater de Lys, New York, on 10 March 1954. It was revived the following year and ran for 2,611 continuous performances, grossing more than $2.5m at the box office.
*July* Revival of Handel's ***Giulio Cesare*** (in a nineteenth-century version) in the ruins of the Teatro Grande, Pompeii, starring Renata Tebaldi and Cesare Siepi.
*14 August* Posthumous première of ***Die Liebe der Danae*** (Strauss/Gregor after Hofmannsthal) in the Festspielhaus, Salzburg, conducted by Krauss.
*28 October* Covent Garden début of Joan Sutherland as the First Lady in ***Die Zauberflöte***. Eleven days later she sang Clotilde in ***Norma*** in the production conducted by Gui that starred Callas and Ebe Stignani.
During 1952–3 an all-black American company, led by Leontyne Price and William Warfield toured European capitals, including Berlin, Vienna and London, with a production of ***Porgy and Bess***. Price's success launched her international operatic career.

**1953** *13 February* Première of ***Trionfo di Afrodite*** (Orff/classical texts) at La Scala, Milan, under Karajan, with Schwarzkopf and Gedda; the third of

The Temple of the Grail in Wieland Wagner's production of *Parsifal* at the first post-war Bayreuth Festival in 1951. The production stripped the stage of all realistic props, using illuminated space to emphasize the symbolic action of Wagner's music drama.

Orff's ***Trionfi*** (see 1937), which were performed as a trilogy.

*8 June* Première of ***Gloriana*** (Britten/Plomer) at Covent Garden, London, conducted by John Pritchard, with a cast including Joan Cross (Queen Elizabeth), Jennifer Vyvyan, Monica Sinclair, Peter Pears (Earl of Essex) and Geraint Evans. 'The Philistines ran riot, and the opera hardly had a chance.'

*23 June* Première of ***Dekabristy*** [***The Decembrists***] (Shaporin/Rozhdestvensky after Tolstoy) at the Bolshoi Theatre, Moscow. The work, which had occupied the composer since the 1920s, is the outstanding Soviet opera.

*17 August* Première of ***Der Prozess*** (Einem/Blacher and von Cramer after Kafka) at the Festspielhaus, Salzburg. The opera by the newly appointed director of the Salzburg Festival conveys the real and surreal nightmare of Kafka's novel.

*25 September* Georg Solti made his American début conducting a performance of ***Elektra*** at the San Francisco Opera with Inge Borkh (also making her US début) in the title role and Schöffler as Orest.

*17 October* Première of ***Abstracte Oper I*** (Blacher/Egk) at the Nationaltheater, Mannheim, following a radio performance on Hesse Radio on 28 June. The work has no plot and the 'words' consist of meaningless combinations of vowels and consonants.

# 1954–1960 Grand Opera Reborn

*As revivals of nineteenth-century operas became increasingly extravagant, several new operas conceived on a grand scale were staged, making considerable demands on the musical and dramatic gifts of singers and instrumentalists and on the financial resources of opera houses.*

Julius Patzak in the title role of Pfitzner's *Palestrina* in the Vienna Staatsoper production at the Theater an der Wien in 1954, before the reopening of the opera house on the Ringstrasse. Patzak was one of the leading singers in a company that maintained the ensemble tradition into the post-war period.

**1954** *1 April* Première of ***The Tender Land*** (Copland/Everett after Agee) at the City Center, New York. The work is a lyrical setting of a mid-western story.
*14 September* Première of ***The Turn of the Screw*** (Britten/Piper after James) at La Fenice, Venice, during the Venice Festival, by the English Opera Group directed by the composer.
*3 December* Première of ***Troilus and Cressida*** (Walton/Hassall after Chaucer) at Covent Garden, London. Walton's only full-length opera had been commissioned by the BBC in 1947 and enjoyed immediate success thanks to the bittersweet lyricism of its music.
*7 December* The season at La Scala, Milan, opened with Visconti's first opera production: ***La Vestale*** (Spontini) with Callas in the title role.
*27 December* Première of ***The Saint of Bleecker Street*** (Menotti/composer) at the Broadway Theater, New York, in a production by Lincoln Kirstein conducted by Thomas Schippers. It is a *verismo* grand opera about a child saint in New York's Little Italy.

**1955** *7 January* Marian Anderson became the first black singer to appear at the Met, as Ulrica in a production of ***Un ballo in maschera*** conducted by Mitropoulos with Milanov, Peters, Tucker and Warren.
*27 January* Première of ***The Midsummer Marriage*** (Tippett/composer) at Covent Garden, London, conducted by John Pritchard; Tippett's first opera.
*2 February* Première of ***David*** (Milhaud/Lunel) at La Scala, Milan; originally performed in a concert version at the King David Festival, Jerusalem, on 1 June 1954.
*24 February* Première of ***Susannah*** (Floyd/composer) at Florida State University, Tallahassee, with Phyllis Curtin. This version of the biblical story of Susanna and the elders, set in the mountains of Tennessee, has homespun music based on a variety of American sources, including reels, blues and hymn tunes.
*14 September* Stage première of ***Ognennyi angel*** [***The Fiery Angel***] (Prokofiev/Bryusov) at La Fenice, Venice. Fragments of the work, which had been written in 1922–5, were played in Paris on 14 June 1928 after a planned performance in 1926 under Walter had fallen through. The opera, based on a symbolist novel, relates the story of a sexual hysteric.
*15 October* Reopening of the Hamburg Staatsoper with a performance of ***Die Zauberflöte***. Two days later the première of ***Pallas Athene weint*** (Křenek/composer) was given, with a cast including Helga Pilarczyk and Hermann Prey, and Egk's ***Irische Legende***, premièred a few weeks earlier at the Salzburg Festival, was also included in the opening festival week.
*5 November* Reopening of the Vienna Staatsoper (a new theatre inside an exterior rebuilt to the original designs) with ***Fidelio*** conducted by Karl Böhm. The performance was relayed to the street through loudspeakers.
*December* Opening of La Piccola Scala, a 600-seat theatre, with a performance of Cimarosa's ***Il matrimonio segreto*** conducted by Sanzogno with a cast led by Sciutti, Simionato and Luigi Alva.

Jennifer Vyvyan as the Governess and Peter Pears as Quint in the original English Opera Group production of Britten's *The Turn of the Screw* at Venice in 1954. Using the modest resources of a thirteen-piece orchestra, Britten created a menacing sense of the evil that corrupts the two children in Henry James's ghost story.

Scene from Tippett's *The Midsummer Marriage* at Covent Garden in 1955, where the cast included Joan Sutherland, Adele Leigh, Oralia Dominguez, Edith Coates, Richard Lewis, Otakar Kraus and John Lanigan. The opera, which has been described as a Jungian *Die Zauberflöte*, typifies the composer's idealistic attitude to opera, in contrast to the natural operatic gifts of Britten or the craftsmanship of Walton.

**1956** *1 February* Première of ***Le Fou*** (Landowski/composer) in Nancy. The theme is the crisis of conscience of an atomic scientist, and the work combines pre-recorded music accompanied by Ondes Martenot (to express the inner thoughts of the characters) with the live performance on stage.
*10 March* Première of ***L'ipocrita felice*** [***The Happy Hypocrite***] (Ghedini/Antonicelli after Beerbohm) at La Piccola Scala, Milan, with Sciutti and Gobbi. The original radio version of the opera, titled ***Lord Inferno***, won the Prix Italia in 1952 for its prolific operatic composer.
*17 June* Première of ***Der Sturm*** [***The Tempest***] (Martin/after Shakespeare) at the Staatsoper, Vienna, conducted by Ansermet and with Anton Dermota and Christa Ludwig in the leading roles. Following the tradition of *singspiel*, the musical items are connected with spoken dialogue and are accompanied by a small orchestra. Ariel's role is given to a dancer, with his words sung by the chorus.
*7 July* Première of ***The Ballad of Baby Doe*** (Moore/Latouche) at the Opera House, Central City, Colorado. Telling the true story of a Central City cabaret singer and her silver magnate husband, who are eventually ruined and die, the work is in the style of a folk opera. A revised version was premièred at the New York City Opera on 3 April 1958, with Beverly Sills in the name part. For some twenty years the work was performed widely in the USA and earned a reputation as the 'great American opera'.
*1 September* Herbert von Karajan took over as director of the Vienna Staatsoper following an interregnum after the resignation of Böhm. He had already been appointed artistic director of the Salzburg Festival, where he put in hand the construction of a new Festspielhaus.
*23 September* Première of ***König Hirsch*** [***King Stag***] (Henze/von Cramer after Gozzi) at the Städtische Oper, Berlin, with Sándor Kónya and Helga Pilarczyk. The work is Henze's 'tribute to Naples', in which he combined atonal techniques with traditional musical forms and folksong to create a personal and extremely effective musical language.
*29 October* Met début of Maria Callas in the title role of Bellini's ***Norma*** (with Barbieri, Siepi and del Monaco), followed on 15 November by her appearance as Tosca. She sang at the Met for only two seasons, falling out with Bing when she refused to sing Lady Macbeth in the 1958–9 season.

*29 October* Première of ***Candide*** (Bernstein/various) at the Colonial Theater, Boston. The work underwent repeated revisions, and a final version was recorded by the composer in 1989.

**1957** *26 January* Première (in Italian) of ***Les Dialogues des carmélites*** (Poulenc/composer after Bernanos) at La Scala, Milan, conducted by Nino Sanzogno. The French première was given on 21 June and included new orchestral music to adapt to the production by Maurice Jacquemont; Denise Duval sang Blanche de la Force and Régine Crespin La Nouvelle Prieure. At the US première of the opera in San Francisco the same year (and in the NBC telecast on 8 December) the latter role was taken by Leontyne Price; at the Covent Garden première under Kubelik on 18 January 1958 it was sung by Sutherland.
*19 March* Revival of Handel's ***Alcina*** at St Pancras Town Hall, London, by the Handel Opera Society conducted by Charles Farncombe, with Sutherland, John Carvalho (male soprano) and Monica Sinclair. The Society's annual performances pioneered more authentic interpretations of Handel's operas.
*14 April* Revival of Donizetti's ***Anna Bolena*** at La Scala, conducted by the Donizetti-specialist Gavazzeni and directed by Visconti. The cast included Callas as Anna (which some considered her finest role), Simionato, Gianni Raimondi, Nicola Rossi-Lemeni and Plinio Clabassi.
*9 May* Première of ***Der Revisor*** (Egk/after Gogol) in the Schlosstheater, Schwetzingen. The comic opera, with a score full of quotations from operatic precursors, is extremely effective, and within a year productions were given throughout Germany and at the Venice Festival.
*22 May* Première of ***Una domanda di matrimonio*** (Chailly/Fino and Vertone after Chekhov) at La Piccola Scala, Milan; the highly successful operatic début of Chailly, who later became artistic director of La Scala.
*6 June* Première of ***Moses und Aron*** (Schoenberg/composer) at the Stadttheater, Zurich, conducted by Hans Rosbaud. The first complete performance, attended by Schoenberg's widow and daughter, had been on 12 March 1954 on Nordwestdeutscher Rundfunk, Hamburg, with the same conductor and Helmut Krebs singing the role of Aron.
*6 June* Revival of the complete version of both parts of Berlioz's ***Les Troyens*** at Covent Garden, in a production by John Gielgud conducted by

Scene from the original Zurich production of Schoenberg's *Moses und Aron*.

## Moses und Aron

The origins of Schoenberg's unfinished opera go back to drafts for the text of an oratorio, *Der biblische Weg*, made in 1926, which gave a political dimension to the Jewish quest for a promised land. Over the next few years the composer rewrote the work into its present form, and by March 1932 he had completed the music for the first two acts, the second of which contains a vast orgiastic scene of worship of the golden calf; this, as Schoenberg himself said, is the most operatic scene in the work. The libretto for the final act was written in the USA in 1935, but the music was never composed, and, shortly before his death in 1951, Schoenberg agreed that the work might be staged with the last act spoken (though it is generally omitted altogether in performance).

The opera is written in strict serial technique and is scored for a large orchestra and chorus with solo singers in the orchestra as well as on stage. The role of Moses, the spokesman of God, is written to be performed entirely in *Sprechgesang*, while his 'mouthpiece', Aron, is sung by a tenor. Although a fragment, *Moses und Aron* is one of the composer's greatest achievements – a stage work of enormous power and technical mastery.

In the text of *Der biblische Weg* the composer wrote: 'For me Moses and Aron signify two activities of the same man – of a statesman, whose two souls know nothing of one another: the purity of his mind is untroubled by the public actions that he takes; and these are not weakened by consideration of any unsolved problems that may be presented by his mind.' It is Moses' tragedy that the words God has spoken to him are traduced by Aron, and his final words at the end of Act II are: 'Unrepresentable God! Inexpressible, many-sided idea, can you allow it to be explained like this?...Then it was all madness that I believed, and can and may not be spoken. O word, word that I lack!' It was surely Schoenberg's close identification with his character's mental struggle, as much as the circumstances of his own exile, that made it impossible for him to complete the music.

Scene from Hindemith's *Die Harmonie der Welt*. The opera is based on the life of the astronomer Kepler (the title is that of his greatest work) and both the subject and the traditional musical forms used – the work ends with a massive passacaglia – exemplify Hindemith's ideas of the unity of music and the universe.

Kubelik with Blanche Thebom as Dido and Jon Vickers as Aeneas. This production was Kubelik's greatest achievement as music director of Covent Garden and was described by a French critic at the time as 'probably the most important operatic event in the world since the end of the war'.

*8 June* Première of ***Bluthochzeit*** (Fortner/García Lorca trans. Beck) at the new Städtische Oper in Cologne. The work is derived from instrumental music composed (in serial technique) since 1948 for Lorca's *Bodas de sangre* and in its final form contains long passages of dialogue. It demonstrates the composer's belief that the starting point for a renewal of musical theatre must not be opera but 'the conquest of the dramatic work by musicians'.

*3 July* Inauguration of the Santa Fe Opera, founded by John O'Hea Crosby as the first US summer repertory company, with a production of ***Madama Butterfly***. The highlight of the first season was ***The Rake's Progress***, conducted by Robert Craft and prepared under Stravinsky's supervision, who described it as 'the finest *Rake* I have seen'. Performances were in English and Crosby planned to stage one new work each season.

*11 August* Première of ***Die Harmonie der Welt*** (Hindemith/composer), at the Prinzregententheater, Munich, conducted by the composer.

Visconti's sumptuous production of Verdi's *Don Carlos* at Covent Garden in May 1958. The cast included Gré Brouwenstein, Fedora Barbieri, Jon Vickers, Tito Gobbi and Boris Christoff.

## Visconti and Zeffirelli as opera producers

The production of Verdi's *Don Carlos* staged for the centenary of Covent Garden in May 1958 was described by a critic at the time as 'one of the finest operatic productions ever seen or heard at Covent Garden.' Much of its success was due to its production by the film director Luchino Visconti. Visconti's grandfather and uncle had both been *sovrintendenti* at La Scala, but his interest in opera was seriously awakened when he saw Callas in *Norma* in Rome. He got to know the soprano and did much to develop her dramatic ability in a series of productions in Milan, starting in 1954: Spontini's *La Vestale*, Gluck's *Iphigénie en Tauride*, Verdi's *La traviata*, Donizetti's *Anna Bolena* and Bellini's *La sonnambula.* Visconti's style of direction required singers who were also actors and could reveal the drama inherent in the composer's score – the cast of his Covent Garden *Don Carlos* contained some of the finest singing actors of the period, including Gré Brouwenstein, Jon Vickers, Tito Gobbi and Boris Christoff – while at the same time he used the visual effects of sets, costumes and lighting to establish a mood for each scene. The same year Visconti began his association with the first Spoleto 'Festival of Two Worlds', where he collaborated with the conductor Thomas Schippers on a number of productions, including, in 1959, the first revival of Donizetti's *Le Duc d'Albe* since 1882. Visconti continued to direct operas into the 1970s.

Franco Zeffirelli, Visconti's colleague in films, also worked extensively in opera: the first of his many productions at La Scala dated from 1952, and his collaboration with the conductor Carlo Maria Giulini was especially effective. There was sometimes a tendency in his work for the drama to be overwhelmed by lavish sets, costumes and crowd scenes, but his work with Joan Sutherland at the beginning of her career (*Lucia di Lammermoor* at Covent Garden in 1959 and *Alcina* at La Fenice in 1960) was highly acclaimed.

Scene from Zeffirelli's production of Peri's *Euridice*, which was revived during the 1960 Maggio Musicale in the gardens of the Pitti Palace, Florence, where the work had first been performed in 1600.

Virginia Copeland as Annina during the filming of Menotti's *The Saint of Bleecker Street* by BBC Television.

Nicola Rossi-Lemeni as St Thomas in the original production of Pizzetti's *Assassinio nella cattedrale* at La Scala, 1958.

Scene from the original production of Karl-Birger Blomdahl's space opera *Aniara* in Stockholm, 1959. It was one of the productions the Swedish Opera brought to the Edinburgh Festival that summer.

*19 August* Première of ***West Side Story*** (Bernstein/Laurents and Sondheim) at the National Theater, Washington DC.
*8 November* Première of the full version of Prokofiev's ***War and Peace*** (see 1946) at the Stanislavsky Theatre, Moscow.
*22 November* The first production (following a Callas concert the previous evening) at the new Dallas Civic Opera was ***L'italiana in Algeri***, conducted by Rescigno (the company's music director), with Simionato as Isabella. The following year a 'Callas in Dallas' season included ***La traviata*** directed by Franco Zeffirelli and Cherubini's ***Medée***, in which Jon Vickers also made his US début, while Teresa Berganza (another American début) sang Isabella in a revival of ***L'italiana***. Singers who subsequently made their American stage débuts in Dallas included Denise Duval, Montserrat Caballé and Gwyneth Jones.

**1958** *15 January* Première of ***Vanessa*** (Barber/Menotti) at the Metropolitan Opera, New York, conducted by Mitropoulos and designed by Cecil Beaton, with Eleanor Steber in the title role. Barber's music remains within the romantic tradition of grand opera, and ***Vanessa*** was the only American opera to be performed at the Met at this period.
It was performed the following August at the Salzburg Festival.
*1 March* Première of ***Assassinio nella cattedrale*** [***Murder in the Cathedral***] (Pizzetti/Eliot trans. Castelli) at La Scala, Milan, with the role of St Thomas sung by Rossi-Lemeni. The opera was the crowning achievement of Pizzetti's long operatic career. The following January a special performance was given for Pope John XXIII in the Vatican, supposedly the first opera ever to have been performed there.
*June* The Spoleto 'Festival of Two Worlds' was inaugurated with Verdi's ***Macbeth***, directed by Visconti, conducted by Schippers and with Irene Jordan as Lady Macbeth.
*18 June* Première of ***Noye's Fludde*** (Britten/Chester Miracle Play) in Orford church. Written for children (apart from the roles of Noah and his wife), the opera has become one of the most successful works of its kind.
*25 October* Stage première of Janáček's ***Osud*** [***Fate***] (see 1934) in a festival at the National Theatre, Brno, to celebrate the thirtieth anniversary of the composer's death, during which all his operas were performed.

**1959** *5 February* A new production of Verdi's ***Macbeth*** (intended for Callas) opened at the Met, directed by Ebert and designed by Neher, with

Leonie Rysanek, Bergonzi, Warren and Hines. The first night was interrupted by cries of 'Viva Callas!'
*6 February* Première of ***La Voix humaine*** (Poulenc/Cocteau) at the Opéra-Comique, Paris. The conductor was Georges Prêtre and the only role was sung by Denise Duval, for whom it had been composed.
*17 February* Joan Sutherland sang her first Lucia at Covent Garden in a production by Zeffirelli with Serafin conducting. The BBC changed its announced schedule to broadcast the opera complete. Sutherland made her début at the Met in the same role on 29 November 1961, five years after Callas had first been heard in the role there.
*31 May* Première of ***Aniara*** (Blomdahl/Lindegren) at the Royal Opera, Stockholm. The opera, about the voyage of a spaceship lost on a journey to Mars, includes three recorded tapes – with spoken voices, *musique concrète* and electronic music – in its score.
*11 June* The second Spoleto 'Festival of Two Worlds' opened with a revival (in Italian) at the Teatro Nuovo of Donizetti's ***Le Duc d'Albe*** under Visconti's direction, with the original 1882 sets and the score re-edited by Thomas Schippers to be as close to Donizetti's original as possible. On 17 June the Festival staged the première of ***A Hand of Bridge*** (Barber/Menotti) at the Teatro Caio Melisso.
*10 July* Revival of ***Il mondo della luna*** (Haydn/Goldoni) at the Stadsschouwburg, Amsterdam, in a version realized by H. C. Robbins Landon and conducted by Giulini. The work had been performed in Schwerin in 1932, but this new production initiated a revival of Haydn's operas for the stage: it was followed in September by a performance of ***L'infedeltà delusa*** in Budapest and the following year of ***La fedeltà premiata*** in London.
*18 December* Met début of Birgit Nilsson, who had been a member of the Royal Opera in Stockholm since 1946, as Isolde.

**1960** *19 February* Joan Sutherland made her Italian début in Handel's ***Alcina*** at La Fenice, Venice, in a lavishly baroque production by Zeffirelli. Sutherland made her US début in the same production in Dallas under Rescigno on 16 November.
*4 March* Leonard Warren died on the stage of the Metropolitan Opera singing the role of Carlo in ***La forza del destino***, having just completed the recitative and aria 'Morir!...Tremenda cosa...Urna fatale'. It was his 636th performance at the Met, where he had sung twenty-two roles.
*22 May* Première of ***Der Prinz von Homburg*** (Henze/Bachmann after Kleist) at the Staatsoper, Hamburg; one of the most Italianate of Henze's scores, it is lightly orchestrated and mixes a variety of compositional techniques.
*11 June* Première of ***A Midsummer Night's Dream*** (Britten/Pears and composer after Shakespeare) at the Jubilee Hall, Aldeburgh, conducted by the composer, with the English Opera Group company. The Covent Garden première, in which Russell Oberlin replaced Alfred Deller as Oberon, was conducted by Solti on 2 February 1961.
*24 July* Bayreuth début of Anja Silja as Senta in ***Der fliegende Holländer***. Silja became Wieland Wagner's lover and muse.
*24 August* Performance of Bellini's ***Norma*** in the Greek Theatre at Epidaurus, conducted by Serafin and with Callas in the title role.
*8 October* Opening of the new Leipzig Opernhaus with a 'socialist' performance of ***Die Meistersinger***, in which Sachs and Beckmesser are reconciled at the end of the work.
*7 December* Opening of the season at La Scala, Milan, with a production of Donizetti's ***Poliuto*** with Callas, Corelli and Bastianini. Tickets were reported to have changed hands for as much as $800.

Cocteau's cover for the score of Poulenc's *La Voix humaine*. Cocteau's text had been written as a mono-drama in 1930, and the opera consists of a telephone conversation (only the woman is heard) in which two lovers break off their affair. It continues, on an intimate scale, the exploration of the female psyche that Poulenc had undertaken in *Les Dialogues des carmélites*.

## Les Dialogues des carmélites

The première of Poulenc's opera at La Scala in January 1957 was followed by performances the same year in Paris, Cologne (as part of the opening season in the new Städtische Oper), San Francisco and Trieste. Productions in London, Vienna and other major operatic centres soon followed, and *Les Dialogues des carmélites* became by far the most celebrated new work of these years. The subject of the opera is the martyrdom in 1794 of thirteen Carmelite nuns who refuse to accept the secularization order of a French revolutionary tribunal, and its themes are the psychology of fear and its conquest through religious faith.

Poulenc, known for the wit and *esprit* of his earlier works, had turned increasingly to religious themes, but his musical precedents were operatic: Monteverdi, Verdi, Mussorgsky and Debussy. The work is unusual in that all the principal roles are written for women's voices – straining the resources of most opera houses – and these are blended and contrasted in Poulenc's masterly orchestration, reaching a tragic climax in the final 'Salve Regina' which is accompanied by the repeated sound of the guillotine blade falling.

Scene from the première at La Scala of Poulenc's *Les Dialogues des carmélites*.

# 1961 / 1975 Opera and Anti-Opera

*Although traditional opera was given new energy by a rising generation of outstanding singers, many composers questioned the very nature of the operatic medium, putting its values in doubt, breaking down its structures and parodying its famous composers. Others again built on the serial method of composition and the highly structured closed forms that had been developed by Berg, enriching them with electronic and other new techniques.*

**DATES**

**1961**
J. F. Kennedy inaugurated as US President
Construction of Berlin Wall
First manned space flights
**1962**
Cuban missile crisis
**1963**
Martin Luther King arrested after leading civil rights march
Start of major US military involvement in Vietnam (to 1975)
Assassination of J. F. Kennedy
**1967**
Arab-Israeli Six-Day War
**1968**
Martin Luther King assassinated
Student revolt in Paris
Prague 'Spring' defeated by Russian invasion of Czechoslovakia
**1970**
Richard Nixon inaugurated as US President
**1974**
*9 August* Nixon resigns US presidency after Watergate revelations
**1975**
Death of General Franco and accession of Juan Carlos I as King of Spain

**1961** *27 January* Met débuts of Leontyne Price and Franco Corelli in ***Il trovatore***, with Robert Merrill.
*21 February* Joan Sutherland and Marilyn Horne made their New York débuts in a New York Opera Society concert performance of ***Beatrice di Tenda*** conducted by Rescigno at the Town Hall.
*13 April* Première of ***Intolleranza 1960*** (Nono/various) at La Fenice, Venice. The work is written for a large orchestra and chorus and also includes an electronic score. Its theme is the rediscovery of humanity by a miner who is arrested, tortured and brainwashed but finds solidarity and love among his fellow-prisoners, before the earth is submerged in a flood that promises renewal.
*April* Professional début of Luciano Pavarotti in ***La Bohème*** in Reggio Emilia.
*20 May* Première (in German) of ***Elegy for Young Lovers*** (Henze/Auden and Kallman) at the Schlosstheater, Schwetzingen, in which Henze used tuned percussion instruments to characterize each of his alienated characters.
*9 June* Posthumous première of ***Řecke Pašije*** [***The Greek Passion***] (Martinů/composer after Kazantzakis) at the Stadttheater, Zurich, conducted by Paul Sacher.
*23 July* Opening of the Bayreuth Festival with ***Tannhäuser*** performed by a cast including Wolfgang Windgassen, Victoria de los Angeles, Dietrich Fischer-Dieskau and Josef Greindl, with Grace Bumbry as Venus.
Début of Placido Domingo as Alfredo in ***La traviata*** in Monterrey, Mexico. He made his Met début in 1966.

**1962** *7 January* Montserrat Caballé's début at the Liceo, Barcelona, in the Spanish première of ***Arabella***. Her professional début had been at the Stadttheater, Basel, on 17 November 1956.
*29 May* Première of ***King Priam*** (Tippett/composer) at the Coventry Festival, produced by San Wanamaker for the Covent Garden company. Based on the *Iliad*, the opera explores the effects of violence on human relationships, defining the different characters with their own individual groups of accompanying instruments.
*18 June* Première of ***Atlantida*** (de Falla/composer after Verdaguer) at La Scala, Milan. The score of this epic work was completed by Hallfter, and a concert performance of excerpts had been given the previous November at the Liceo, Barcelona.
*12 August* Première of ***Don Perlimpin*** (Maderna/composer after García Lorca) on RAI. The work is a tape montage in which the principal roles are taken by instruments rather than voices.
Début of Gwyneth Jones in Zurich; her first appearance at Covent Garden followed in 1963.

Birgit Nilsson as Brünnhilde and Hans Hotter as Wotan in *Die Walküre*. Both artists were oustanding interpreters of these roles and were leading members of the cast of the complete Decca *Ring*.

Georg Solti and John Culshaw in discussion during the recording of *Die Götterdämmerung* in 1964.

Scene from a production of Martinů's *The Greek Passion*, 1961, at the National Theatre, Prague. Based on Kazantzakis's novel, *Christ Recrucified*, the tragic opera is set in a Greek village, where a passion play is being prepared. Martinů incorporated Greek Orthodox chants into his score.

## Recording the Ring

The first complete recording of Wagner's *Ring* changed opera as much as Caruso's first records had done. From the outset it had been envisaged not to provide a 'record' of a performance but to create a new aural production of the work, making full use of the effects that had been made possible by the recent introduction of stereo sound. While traditional 'realistic' Wagner productions were clearly a thing of the past, the poverty of Wieland Wagner's first post-war *Ring* production convinced the young Decca producer John Culshaw, who had been sent to Bayreuth in 1951 to try – unsuccessfully – to make a live recording, that a fully produced staging in sound could come closer to the composer's intentions. Working with Georg Solti, he began to assemble a 'dream cast', with some great singers taking roles they had never played on stage (Flagstad's Fricka in *Das Rheingold* and Fischer-Dieskau's Gunther in *Die Götterdämmerung*, for example), and going to great lengths both to match the precise sounds Wagner called for (whether anvils, steerhorns or vocal transformations) and to follow every one of his stage directions. He was aided by a chief engineer, Gordon Parry, who was a passionate Wagnerian, and a team that included Erik Smith, Christopher Raeburn and James Brown. From the appearance of the first opera, *Das Rheingold*, in 1959, their innovative methods began to be copied, and it was undoubtedly the creation of such 'ideal' aural productions that encouraged directors to mount the innovative stage productions which became the dominant characteristic of opera in the last quarter of the twentieth century.

**1963** *6 May* Première of ***Passaggio*** (Berio/Sanguineti) at La Piccola Scala, Milan. The female protagonist, a role written for Cathy Berberian, is presented as an object of the audience's fantasies.

**1964** *12 June* Première of ***Curlew River*** (Britten/Plomer) in Orford church. The first of Britten's three 'parables for church performance', it is based on a Japanese Noh play. While the instrumental sonority shows oriental influence, the vocal lines, as in the other parables, ***The Burning Fiery Furnace*** (1966) and ***The Prodigal Son*** (1968) are more indebted to medieval plainchant.
*24 July* Première of ***Don Rodrigo*** (Ginastera/Casona) at the Teatro Colón, Buenos Aires, the work which was the spectacular opening of Ginastera's operatic career.
*6 October* Première of ***Hyperion*** (Maderna/composer after Hölderlin) at La Fenice, Venice, a lyric spectacle that allows for the aleatoric assembling of its component parts, in which the leading role is given to the flautist.

**1965** *15 February* Première of ***Die Soldaten*** (Zimmermann/composer after Lenz) at the Städtische Oper, Cologne.
*February* Pavarotti made his US début in Miami, supporting Sutherland's Lucia, following which he toured Australia with the soprano.
*7 April* Première of ***Der junge Lord*** (Henze/Bachmann after Hauff) at the Deutsche Oper, Berlin; a black comedy set in *buffo* style.
*5 July* Callas made her last stage appearance, as Tosca at Covent Garden.
*19 November* Completion by Decca of the first complete recording of Wagner's ***Der Ring des Nibelungen***, a project which had been begun on 24 September 1958.
Radio première of ***Laborintus II*** (Berio/Sanguineti), on ORTF, Paris, a work composed for the 700th anniversary of the birth of Dante. The composer stated: 'Laborintus is a dramatic work and can be considered as a representation, as a history, an allegory, a document, a dance etc. So that it can be performed in a school, in a theatre, on television, in the open air.'

**1966** Revival of Bellini's ***I Capuleti e i Montecchi*** at La Scala, Milan, in a new version by Abbado with the role of Romeo rewritten for tenor. The lovers were played by Giacomo Aragall and Renata Scotto, with Pavarotti as Tebaldo making his La Scala début.

Scene from the original Salzburg production of Henze's *Die Bassariden*, 1966, with a libretto by W. H. Auden and Chester Kallman based on Euripides' *The Bacchae*. The conflict between the rational (identified by the composer with socialism) and ecstatic irrationality (capitalism) is conveyed in an expressive idiom contained in quasi-symphonic forms – a sonata movement, a scherzo, an adagio and intermezzo, and a final passacaglia.

*6 August* Première of ***Die Bassariden*** (Henze/Auden and Kallman) at the Festspielhaus, Salzburg.
*16 September* Inauguration of the new Metropolitan Opera in the Lincoln Center, New York, with the première of ***Antony and Cleopatra*** (Barber/Zeffirelli after Shakespeare), directed by Zeffirelli, with Leontyne Price and Justino Diaz in the title roles.
*16 September* A new production at the New York City Opera of Handel's ***Giulio Cesare***, with Beverly Sills as Cleopatra, eclipsed the old-fashioned romanticism of Barber's opera. Sills's success in Handel's florid music led to her playing three Tudor heroines of romantic opera in subsequent seasons: Rossini's ***Elisabetta, regina d'Inghilterra*** and Donizetti's ***Maria Stuarda*** and ***Anna Bolena***.
*19 October* Première of ***Aventures*** and ***Nouvelles Aventures*** (Ligeti/composer) at the Staatstheater, Stuttgart. The works are Dadaist happenings, related to contemporary performance art; their music is defined by the 'surface of timbres', and intervals and rhythms are suppressed.

**1967** *19 May* Première of ***Bomarzo*** (Ginastera/Mujica Laínez) in Washington DC. The opera was inspired by the grotesque baroque garden of the Orsini family near Rome, and the vivid score (which employs tone rows, quarter-tones and chord clusters, and includes improvisational and aleatoric episodes) matches the eroticism of the action, which led to the banning of the opera in the composer's native Argentina until 1972.
*3 June* Première of ***The Bear*** (Walton/Dehn after Chekhov) at the Jubilee Hall, Aldeburgh; a witty comedy which is the best of Walton's operas.
*23 September* Première of ***Louis Riel*** (Somers/Moore and Languirand) by the Canadian Opera, Toronto. The work, which enjoyed great success, is written in three languages, English, French and Cree, and the score combines Native American music collected by Marius Barbeau with popular and electronic music.

Joan Sutherland in the title role of Massenet's *Esclarmonde*, with Huguette Tourangeau as Parséis, in 1974 in San Francisco, where the opera was revived for her. She later sang in productions in New York and London.

Filming of Britten's *Owen Wingrave* by BBC Television at the Maltings, Snape, in November 1970. The leading roles were sung by Benjamin Luxon, Janet Baker and Nigel Douglas.

**1968** *8 June* Première of ***Punch and Judy*** (Birtwistle/Pruslin) at the Jubilee Hall, Aldeburgh; the composer's first opera (which takes its place in the succession of operatic puppet plays) touches the vein of violence that characterizes Birtwistle's operas.
*29 September* Première of ***Ulisse*** (Dallapiccola/composer after Homer) at the Deutsche Oper, Berlin, a complex and highly structured serial composition, which – as a meditation on man's knowledge of himself and of God – was designed as a final account of Dallapiccola's life's work.

**1969** *15 January* Première of ***Votre Faust*** (Pousseur/Butor) at La Piccola Scala, Milan. A composer makes a pact with the devil to write a Faust opera – with various possible outcomes that are decided by the audience.
*8 May* Première of ***Down by the Greenwood Side*** (Birtwistle/Nyman) at the Festival Pavilion, Brighton.
*20 June* Première of ***Diably z Loudon*** [***The Devils of Loudon***] (Penderecki/Whiting after Huxley) at the Staatsoper, Hamburg, with

Tatiana Troyanos as Mère Jeanne. The religious and sexual hysteria conveyed in the tragic story is given heightened tension by the composer's setting, which makes use of a wide variety of vocal techniques, accompanied by the instrumental colour created by using small groups from the large orchestra.

**1970** *12 August* Première of ***Opera*** (Berio/composer and others) at the Santa Fe Opera. The theme of loss – with references both to the sinking of the *Titanic* and Orpheus' loss of Euridice – is used to draw parallels between opera and the capitalist state. A revised version was produced at the Maggio Musicale, Florence, in 1977.
*2 December* Première of ***The Knot Garden*** (Tippett/composer) at Covent Garden, London, conducted by Colin Davis and directed by Peter Hall. The characters of the opera act out parts of Shakespeare's *Tempest* as a form of therapy. The music incorporates blues, which the composer considered, rather than Schoenberg's twelve-note method, 'the most fundamental musical form of our time'.
*19 December* Official début of José Carreras as Gennaro in Donizetti's ***Lucrezia Borgia*** at the Liceo, Barcelona. In 1957 he had appeared there as the boy (El trujamán) in de Falla's ***El retablo de maese Pedro.***

**1971** *25 April* Première of ***Staatstheater*** (Kagel/composer) at the Staatsoper, Hamburg. All the resources of the opera and ballet companies are deployed in a meaningless way, and the sounds of household utensils – including a chamber pot and enema equipment – are introduced.
*16 May* Première of ***Owen Wingrave*** (Britten/Piper after James) on BBC TV (recorded in the Maltings, Snape, 22–30 November 1970); the first stage production took place at Covent Garden on 10 May 1973. The work was commissioned for television in 1967, and although the political events that took place during its composition made its anti-war sentiment highly topical, it was not very well received.
*23 May* Première of ***Der Besuch der alten Dame*** (Einem/after Dürrenmatt) at the Staatsoper, Vienna. The cast was led by Christa Ludwig and also included Eberhard Wächter and Hans Hotter. The work had an immediate international success, with productions in 1971–3 in Zurich, Berlin, Glyndebourne and San Francisco (directed by Francis Ford Coppola).
*14 October* Première of ***Postcard from Morocco*** (Argento/Donahue) by the Center Opera Company, Minneapolis, which the composer had founded in 1963 with John Olin-Scrymgeor. The work is an eclectic, accessible chamber opera (for seven singers and eight instrumentalists), with many references to past operatic styles and techniques.

**1972** *28 January* Stage première of Joplin's ***Treemonisha*** (see 1915) at Morehouse College, Atlanta; it was later staged at the Houston Grand Opera (during their 1975 spring festival on 23 May), with Willard White, in an arrangement and orchestration by Gunther Schuller.
*12 July* Première of ***Taverner*** (Maxwell Davies/composer) at Covent Garden, London, with Ragnar Ulfung in the title role. The score incorporates some of Taverner's own music, and the second part (in which the hero has become the villain) is a musical parody of the first.
*7 September* Première of ***Lorenzaccio*** (Bussotti/composer after Musset) at La Fenice, Venice. This 'danced romantic melodrama' has an extravagance, both in the elaboration of the stage spectacle and the exploitation of vocal technique, characteristic of its Florentine composer.

**1973** *16 March* Première of ***Satyricon*** (Maderna/composer and Strasfogel after Petronius) in Scheveningen by the Nederlandse Operastichting van Amsterdam, conducted by the composer. In this work, performed shortly

Luciano Berio, whose wife, the soprano Cathy Berberian, was the inspiration for many of his vocal and operatic works.

## Anti-Opera

In the revolutionary climate of the 1960s and 1970s the museum atmosphere of the world's opera houses seemed to many young composers to be matched by the reactionary nature of most new opera and of the medium itself. Music theatre, however, remained an area of great importance to the contemporary composer aiming to engage an audience in his work, and several composers confronted opera on its own terms, while using electronic, aleatoric and other new musical techniques. Luciano Berio, an outstanding composer for the voice whose early musical career was as a conductor in provincial opera houses, made opera itself the subject of several works, while works by Ligeti, Maderna, Pousseur and Kagel also called the operatic medium into question. In Germany, Henze and Zimmermann retained the traditional form, but used opera to convey a political message in musical and dramatic terms.

*'The most elegant solution to the problem of opera is to blow up the opera houses... Opera is the area before all others in which things have stood still.'*

Pierre Boulez in *Der Spiegel*, 1967

before the composer's death, techniques of musical collage combine motifs of widely different origin.
*4 May* Première of ***Gilgamesh*** (Nørgård/composer) in Århus. The Danish composer's opera 'in six days and seven nights' uses six instrumental and vocal groups as well as electronic tape, and embraces and integrates a wide range of musical styles.
*16 June* Première of ***Death in Venice*** (Britten/Piper after Mann) at the Maltings, Snape, during the Aldeburgh Festival. Britten's last opera has two main singing roles, written for Peter Pears (as Aschenbach, a role sung almost entirely in unaccompanied recitative) and John Shirley-Quirk, while the forces of destruction are represented by dancers. It is one of Britten's most subtle, complex and effective scores.
*2 October* Opening of the Sydney Opera House.
Rolf Liebermann, who as artistic director of the Hamburg Staatsoper since 1959 had commissioned a succession of avant-garde operas, moved to the Opéra in Paris, where his outstanding achievement was the production of the complete version of Berg's ***Lulu*** in 1979.

**1974** *26 February* Première of ***Kentervil'skoe prividenie*** [***The Canterville Ghost***] (Knaifel/Kramarova) in Leningrad, a strongly humorous work by a younger contemporary of Schnittke.
*27 September* Première of ***Rites of Passage*** (Sculthorpe/composer) at the Sydney Opera House; the work had been commissioned for the opening of the opera house in 1973 but, in the event, it was not performed until the following year.

**1975** *4 April* Première of ***Al gran sole carico d'amore*** (Nono/composer and Lyubimov) at the Teatro Lirico, Milan, by the La Scala company under Abbado. The work has no plot and is a collage of musical elements relating to the class struggle.
*2 September* Première of ***Viimeistet kiusaukset*** [***The Last Temptations***] (Kokkonen/after L. Kokkonen) at the Finnish National Opera, Helsinki, with Martti Talvela as the preacher Paavo Ruotsalainen. The work achieved huge success in Finland, where it was adopted as the national opera, and was well received abroad.
*16 December* Public première of Ullmann's ***Der Kaiser von Atlantis*** (see 1944) at the Bellevue Theater, Amsterdam.

Maria Callas in Zeffirelli's triumphant Covent Garden production of *Tosca*, with which she returned to the stage (with Gobbi as her Scarpia) in January 1964 after a retirement of several years with vocal problems. In May–June she sang Norma at the Paris Opéra, and her Tosca was repeated the following year in London, Paris and New York, but at the last of a series of Normas at the Opéra on 29 May 1965 Callas collapsed, and her final appearance was a single performance as Tosca at Covent Garden on 5 July.

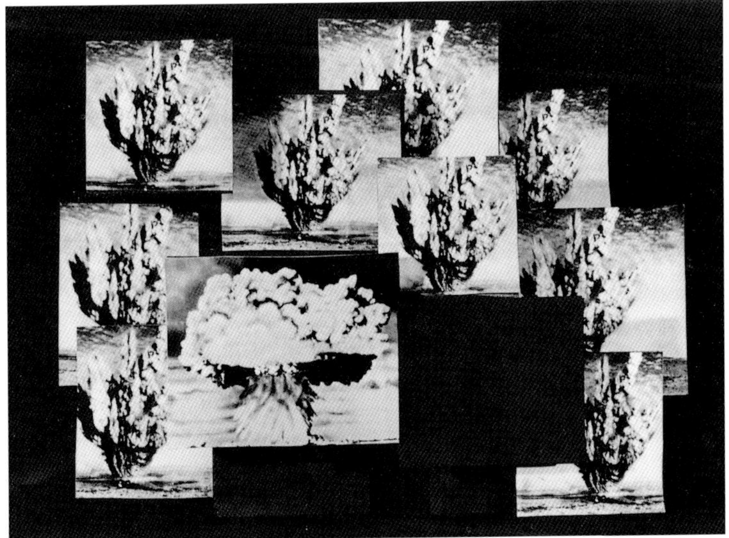

Josef Svoboda's set design for the 1969 Munich production of Bernd-Alois Zimmermann's *Die Soldaten*, originally staged in Cologne in 1965. The work, which is strongly indebted to Berg's operas, entails the use of multi-level stages as well as film, and the serial composition is fashioned within baroque forms, although they incorporate 'collages' of quoted material, including pop music and jazz as well as Bach chorales.

# 1976 / 1997 Postmodernism

*Many characteristics of postmodernism are evident in the new operas written during this period and in the radical productions of works from the historical repertory: eclecticism, pastiche and the collage of several layers of musical material; the anti-narrative sequencing of stage events; relativism in political and spiritual ideals; and an increasingly reverent attitude towards popular culture.*

**DATES**

**1976**
Death of Mao Zedong
**1979**
Margaret Thatcher becomes British prime minister (to 1990)
**1982**
Iran–Iraq War (to 1988)
**1983**
Identification of AIDS virus
**1985**
Gorbachev becomes leader of USSR
**1990**
Demolition of Berlin Wall and reunification of Germany
**1991**
Break-up of USSR
Start of civil war in Yugoslavia (to 1997)
**1994**
Democratic elections in South Africa

Scene from the original Royal Swedish Opera production of György Ligeti's *Le grand macabre*, 1978. The work – derived from both Brueghel and Jarry – is an opera about opera, viewing its erotic, political and metaphysical aspects through a veil of irony. The music is appropriately eclectic, mixing sound clusters with academic counterpoint and classical arias, quoting composers from Monteverdi to Verdi.

**1976** *12 July* Première of ***We Come to the River*** (Henze/Bond) at Covent Garden, London. The collaboration with the playwright Edward Bond was an example of the extreme politicization of Henze's compositions at this period.
*25 July* Première of ***Einstein on the Beach*** (Glass/Wilson) at the Avignon Festival.
*Summer* Pierre Boulez was invited to conduct and Patrice Chéreau to direct the centenary production of the ***Ring*** at Bayreuth.
*4 December* Death of Benjamin Britten.

**1977** *17 June* Première of ***The Martyrdom of St Magnus*** (Maxwell Davies/composer after George Mackay Brown) in St Magnus Cathedral, Kirkwall; an epic subject treated with modest resources, each singer taking several roles, accompanied by a small group of instrumentalists.
*7 July* Première of ***The Ice Break*** (Tippett/composer) at Covent Garden, London, conducted by Davis and directed by Wanamaker. A banal setting is used for the exploration of fundamental human themes – questions of the survival of life amid the violence of the modern world, of imprisonment and freedom of thought, of racism and tolerance.
*29 September* Première of ***Toussaint*** (Blake/Ward) at the English National Opera, London; an epic work which draws on both the music of Elizabethan England and that of Haitian popular tradition.

Scene from the centenary production of Wagner's *Der Ring des Nibelungen* at Bayreuth in 1976, conducted by Boulez and directed by Chéreau. Much controversy was excited by the politicization of the work, which was performed in nineteenth-century costume and transmitted worldwide on television. The singers included Gwyneth Jones as Brünnhilde, Donald McIntyre as Wotan and Manfred Jung as Siegfried.

**1978** *12 April* Première of ***Le grand macabre*** (Ligeti/Meschke and composer after Ghelderode) at the Royal Opera, Stockholm, directed by Michael Meschke, former director of the Stockholm Puppet Theatre, and including Elisabeth Söderström, Kerstin Meyer and Sven-Erik Vikström among the cast.
*9 July* Première of ***Lear*** (Reimann/composer after Shakespeare) at the Nationaltheater, Munich. The work was dedicated to Dietrich Fischer-Dieskau and was performed by him and Julia Varady. The composition requires a huge orchestra with a colourful percussion section.
*30 November* Première of ***Punainen viiva*** [***The Red Line***] (Sallinen/composer after Kianto) at the Finnish National Opera, Helsinki. A tragic opera by the leader of the new Finnish operatic movement which contrasts the reality of the lives of poor people with the false optimism offered by priests or politicians.

**1979** *24 February* Production of Berg's ***Lulu*** (see 1937), completed by Friedrich Cerha, at the Opéra, Paris.
*8 March* Première of ***Jakob Lenz*** (Rihm/composer and Fröhling after Büchner) at the Staatsoper, Hamburg. In his second 'chamber opera', a musical study of the psychotic romantic poet Lenz, Rihm contrasts the closed forms of the baroque with the violence of expressionist music-theatre.

Teresa Stratas as Lulu in the first complete production of Berg's opera (completed by Friedrich Cerha) at the Paris Opéra in 1979. The work was conducted by Boulez and directed by Chéreau, and the cast also included Yvonne Minton, Kenneth Riegel, Franz Mazura, Robert Tear and Toni Blankenheim.

Scene from the Philip Glass/Robert Wilson *Einstein on the Beach* in the original production at the 1976 Avignon Festival.

## Philip Glass

Glass's music is minimalist in the sense that small fragments of rhythmic and harmonic material – frequently triads, static chords that do not require resolution – are repeated, varied, expanded and contracted to create a trance-like sense of timelessness. Glass's first opera, *Einstein on the Beach*, was a collaboration with the performance artist Robert Wilson, whose work is also concerned with changing an audience's perception of time. This anti-narrative, postmodern style of music theatre characterizes Glass's later operas, although these are more 'performable', in that they do not require Wilson's vast array of production effects. They are also less radical in having storylines – if not always time-linear plots – and using language (although parts of *Satyagraha* are sung in Sanskrit and *Akhnaten* uses Hebrew and ancient Egyptian as well as English), and they are written for the vocal and instrumental resources of the opera house. With *Akhnaten* the composer also introduced a more chromatic, directional element into his music. Glass has been extremely prolific, continuing to write works for the opera house and pursuing his 'theatre of images' in collaboration with Wilson.

**1980** *2 September* Première of ***The Lighthouse*** (Maxwell Davies/composer) at the Moray House Gymnasium, Edinburgh, during the Edinburgh Festival. Three singers and a small group of instrumentalists create music-theatre of exceptional dramatic power. The US première was in Boston in 1983 directed by Peter Sellars.
*5 September* Première of ***Satyagraha: M. K. Gandhi in South Africa*** (Glass/DeJong and composer) by the Netherlands Opera at the Stadsschouwburg, Rotterdam. The commission for the opera specified that it should be composed for traditional operatic vocal resources, and the composer used an orchestra (strings, woodwind and organ) of instruments common to western and Indian music.
*28 November* Première (in French) of ***Where the Wild Things Are*** (Knussen/Sendak) at the Théâtre de la Monnaie, Brussels; a fantasy opera based on Maurice Sendak's children's book.

**1981** *3 April* Première of ***Donnerstag*** (Stockhausen/composer) at La Piccola Scala, Milan; the first part of ***Licht***, a projected seven-part work, each part being a sequence of free-standing movements. ***Samstag***, ***Montag***, ***Dienstag*** and ***Freitag*** followed in 1984, 1988, 1992 and 1996. The whole work is planned to have the nature of a universal sacred performance.

**1982** *9 March* Première of ***La vera storia*** (Berio/Calvino) at La Scala, Milan, conducted by the composer. The work is an operatic analysis of the plot of ***Il trovatore.***

**1983** *2 June* Première of ***The English Cat*** (Henze/Bond after Balzac) at the Schlosstheater, Schwetzingen, a black comedy in the form of a ballad opera scored for chamber orchestra extended by a large group of percussion instruments.
*17 June* Première of ***A Quiet Place*** (Bernstein/Wadsworth) at the Houston Grand Opera. The opera followed (and in later versions incorporated) the earlier ***Trouble in Tahiti*** (see 1952).
*28 November* Première of ***Saint-François d'Assise*** (Messiaen/composer) at the Opéra, Paris. The composer's last major work incorporates much of his lifelong study of birdsong.

> *'Something tremendously powerful was lost when composers moved away from tonal harmony and regular pulses…*
> *Among other things the audience was lost.'*
>
> John Adams

**1984** *24 March* Première of ***Akhnaten*** (Glass/composer, Goldman, Israel and Riddell) at the Staatstheater (Kleines Haus), Stuttgart. The US première was at the Houston Grand Opera on 12 October, with Christopher Robson in the hermaphrodite title role.
*1 April* Première of ***Erszebet*** (Chaynes/Janvier) at the Opéra, Paris, with Christiane Ede-Pierre, to whom the work is dedicated, as the notorious child-murderess revered by the surrealists. The extreme violence of the score matches the opera's subject.
*7 July* Première of ***Kuningas lähtee Ranskaan*** [***The King Goes Forth to France***] (Sallinen/Haavikko) at the Savonlinna Festival, a 'fairy tale for adults'. Performances in Germany, USA and Britain followed in 1986–7.
*7 August* Première (in German) of ***Un re in ascolto*** (Berio/composer) at the Kleines Festspielhaus, Salzburg. The 'listening king' is an opera director auditioning singers.
*25 September* Première of ***Prometeo*** (Nono/Cacciari) in Venice. The work, which creates a new ambience for opera in a physical and metaphysical sense, demands a specially constructed 'auditorium' which effects a new relationship between singers, instrumentalists and audience.

**1985** *19 April* Première (in German) of ***Behold the Sun*** (Goehr/McGrath and composer) at the Deutsche Oper am Rhein, Duisburg. The opera is concerned with the same events as Meyerbeer's ***Le Prophète.***
*Summer* Sellars directed Handel's ***Giulio Cesare in Egitto*** at the PepsiCo Summerfare Festival, Purchase, N.Y. This was followed in 1986 by the first of his acclaimed Mozart opera productions, ***Così fan tutte.***

**1986** *1 March* Première of ***Voss*** (Meale/Malouf) by the Australian Opera at the Adelaide Festival. The opera by Australia's leading avant-garde composer was based on Patrick White's celebrated novel.
*15 March* Première of ***L'Ecume des jours*** (Denisov/composer after Vian) at the Opéra-Comique, Paris. The idiom of the Siberian composer is tonal with a pronounced jazz influence; his next opera, ***Les quatre filles***, was a setting of Picasso's surreal play *Les quatre petites filles.*
*21 May* Première of ***The Mask of Orpheus*** (Birtwistle/Zinovieff) at the English National Opera, London.
*7 August* Première of ***Yan Tan Tethera*** (Birtwistle/Harrison) at the Queen Elizabeth Hall, London.

**1987** *8 July* Première of ***A Night at the Chinese Opera*** (Weir/composer after Chi Chun-Hsiang) at the Everyman Theatre, Cheltenham. Although the work is based on a medieval Chinese play and the reduced orchestra parallels Chinese sonority, the vocal and instrumental writing follow the speech patterns of the English text.
*22 October* Première of ***Nixon in China*** (Adams/Goodman), at the Houston Grand Opera, directed by Peter Sellars. Traditional operatic formulae were reinterpreted in Alice Goodman's political text, John Adams's neo-romantic minimalist music and Peter Sellars's arresting production.

**1988** *17 June* Première of ***Greek*** (Turnage/after Berkoff) at the Carl-Orff Saal, Munich. The opera, based on the Oedipus myth but set in the East End of London, was commissioned for Munich by Henze and was acclaimed as a major work by a new operatic composer.
*18 September* Première of ***Resurrection*** (Maxwell Davies/composer) at the Staatstheater, Darmstadt. In this vastly ambitious indictment of conformism the hero is an inert dummy, whose brain, heart and genitals are operated upon to bring him to life. The musical resources required for the eclectic score include an on-stage rock group and a marching band as well as singers and orchestra.

François Le Roux as Gawain and John Tomlinson as the Green Knight in the original production of Birtwistle's *Gawain* at Covent Garden in 1991.

## Harrison Birtwistle

The focus of Birtwistle's works of music theatre is the relationship of words, music and gesture. The survival of ancient ritual in myth, folklore or children's games provided a fruitful alternative to the linear unfolding of a plot, while the fragmentation of Stravinsky's *Histoire du soldat*, in which the instrumentalists play as important a role as the singers, was a modern example drawn on by Birtwistle as early as *Punch and Judy* (1968). In *Yan Tan Tethera* (1986), the ritual and refrain that had been part of the fabric of his previous operas became the actual stuff of the 'plot', for ritual also uncovers the violence, linked to the goodness and badness of the human psyche, which is a fundamental element in each of these works. The most complex musically is *The Mask of Orpheus* (1986), in which the electronic element of the score is of great importance among the layers of music, but in *Gawain* (1991) and *The Second Mrs Kong* (1994), the one a clearly articulated version of the medieval tale, the other a fantasy set in the world of the dead, the experience of the previous works seems to have been assimilated, so that the richness of Birtwistle's approach is more immediately accessible to the audience. After seeing *The Mask of Orpheus* Michael Tippett wrote: 'I could only marvel at the way it...so courageously, so tenaciously regenerated an art-form often regarded these days as dead.'

Costume design by Gianni Versace for the 1995 Covent Garden production of Richard Strauss's *Capriccio*, which starred Kiri te Kanawa as the Countess and William Shimell and David Rendall as the rival poet and composer.

*19 November* Première of ***The Aspern Papers*** (Argento/composer after James) at the Civic Opera, Dallas, with Elisabeth Söderström and Frederike von Stade. The work, written in Argento's accessibly popular style was also widely seen on PBS TV.
*6 December* Première of ***Busqueda*** (MacMillan/trans. Markus) in Edinburgh. The work is a setting of letters from mothers to their children who 'disappeared' in Argentina, interlayered with sections of the Latin Mass.

**1989** *20 May* Première of ***Le Maître et Marguerite*** (Höller/after Bulgakov) at the Opéra, Paris, the last new work to be staged there before the company moved to the new house at the Bastille. The music of this powerful adaptation of Bulgakov's novel by a pupil of Zimmermann was described by its composer as a 'gigantic passacaglia'.
*27 October* Première of ***New Year*** (Tippett/composer after H. G. Wells) at the Houston Grand Opera. Tippett's last opera characteristically gives primal myth a space-age setting.

**1990** *5 May* Première of ***Das verratene Meer*** (Henze/Treichel after Mishima) at the Deutsche Oper, Berlin, a highly theatrical opera with a sumptuously orchestrated score.
*Summer* Concert by the Three Tenors – Pavarotti, Domingo and Carreras – in the Baths of Caracalla, Rome, during the soccer World Cup, when Pavarotti's recording of 'Nessun dorma' from ***Turandot*** was used as a theme tune. The Three Tenors reappeared at the 1994 World Cup in Los Angeles.

**1991** *19 March* Première of ***The Death of Klinghoffer*** (Adams/Goodman), at the Théâtre de la Monnaie, Brussels, directed by Peter Sellars. The story of the hijacking of the cruise ship *Achille Lauro* is made into an intense drama of ideas, underlined by the power of orchestral and vocal resources deployed by the composer.
*30 May* Première of ***Gawain*** (Birtwistle/Harsent) at Covent Garden, conducted by Elgar Howarth.

Scene from the Finnish National Opera's 1990 production of John Adams's *Nixon in China* (1987). The roles of Nixon (baritone), Pat Nixon (soprano) and Mao (Heldentenor) were sung by Heikki Keinonen, Raili Viljakainen and Anssi Hirvonen.

Scene from the production of Berlioz's *Les Troyens* staged in 1990 at the new home of the Paris Opéra at the Bastille, which opened in 1989. The role of Cassandre was sung by Grace Bumbry and that of Didon by Shirley Verrett.

*Autumn* Première of ***Backanterna*** [***The Bacchae***] (Börtz/Bergman after Euripides) at the Royal Opera, Stockholm, directed by Ingmar Bergman. The fiercely expressionistic score, which gives primacy to the voices, makes this an especially effective version of Euripides' play.
*19 December* Première of ***The Ghosts of Versailles*** (Corigliano/Hoffman after Beaumarchais) at the Metropolitan Opera, New York, conducted by James Levine, with a cast including Stratas and Horne. It was commissioned for the Met's centenary and was the first new work performed there for a quarter of a century. The plot involves the characters of Beaumarchais's Figaro plays, Louis XVI and Marie Antoinette.

**1992** *9 February* Première of ***Die Eroberung von Mexico*** (Rihm/after Artaud and Paz) at the Staatsoper, Hamburg. The epic theme is treated with all the musical and spatial resources available in the opera house.
*13 April* Première of ***Zhizn s idiotom*** [***Life with an Idiot***] (Schnittke/Erofeyev) by the Netherlands Opera at the Muziektheater, Amsterdam. In his first opera Schnittke employed his polystylistic approach, a kind of musical collage, to match the disturbing satire of the dissident writer Victor Erofeyev's story.
*11 May* Premières of ***Snatched by the Gods*** (Vir/Radice after Tagore) and ***Broken Strings*** (Vir/Rudkin) at the Muziektheater, Amsterdam, as a double bill.
*19 June* Première of ***Mary of Egypt*** (Taverner/Mother Tekla) at the Maltings, Snape. The work is influenced by the wide range of the

Dale Duesing, Howard Haskin and Teresa Ringholz in the original production of Alfred Schnittke's *Life with an Idiot*, conducted by Mstislav Rostropovich for the Netherlands Opera in 1992.

composer's associations, from pop music to Greek Orthodoxy.
*12 October* Première of ***The Voyage*** (Glass/Hwang) at the Metropolitan Opera, New York, directed by Pountney. The work, composed for the quincentenary of Columbus's voyage, is on a grand-opera scale.

**1994** *24 October* Première of ***The Second Mrs Kong*** (Birtwistle/Hoban) at Glyndebourne following the first summer season in the new, enlarged opera house.
*2 November* Première of ***Rosa*** (Andriessen/Greenaway) at the Muziektheater, Amsterdam. Cinematic sex and violence are graphically portrayed by Andriessen whose 1989 music-theatre work ***De Materie*** (a collaboration with Robert Wilson) showed that his eclectic idiom, with its roots in popular music, was highly effective in a dramatic context.

**1995** *22 June* Première of ***Faust*** (Schnittke/Morgener and composer) at the Staatsoper, Hamburg. The multi-layered score successfully evokes the terror of the ancient folktale on which the libretto is based. Four weeks earlier the Vienna Staatsoper had premièred Schnittke's ***Gesualdo*** (libretto by Bletschacher), based on the character of Carlo Gesualdo, Prince of Venosa, madrigalist and murderer.
*1 July* Première of ***Powder Her Face*** (Adès/Henscher) by the Almeida Opera at Cheltenham, with Jill Gomez as the Duchess; the first opera by an exceptionally gifted young composer.
*26 July* Première of ***Palatsi*** [***The Palace***] (Sallinen/Dische and Enzensberger after Kupiscinski) at the Savonlinna Festival, with Tom Krause. The richly eclectic score accompanies action that uses the characters of Mozart's ***Die Entführung*** in a parable of Europe after the collapse of communism.

**1996** *29 January* La Fenice in Venice is destroyed by fire.
*2 March* Met début of Cecilia Bartoli as Despina in ***Così fan tutte***. She had made her international début at the Paris Opéra as Cherubino (***Le nozze di Figaro***) in 1991.
*7 May* Première of ***Marco Polo*** (Tan Dun/Griffiths) in Munich, with a score that mixes oriental instruments and Chinese operatic techniques with western methods of composition.

**1997** *11 January* Première of ***Venus und Adonis*** (Henze/Treichel) at the Staatsoper, Munich. The work incorporates unseen madrigalists in a tribute to the Renaissance origins of opera.

# GLOSSARY

**aleatoric** Term for music in which the sequence of elements is in part random or dictated by chance.
**aria** Individual number in an opera for a solo singer composed in a closed musical form.
***arioso*** Setting of words with orchestral accompaniment where, although it is not composed as a closed form, the melodic nature of the vocal line is closer to that of an **aria** than to **recitative**.
**ballad opera** Dramatic work in which the dialogue is interspersed with musical numbers based on ballads, popular songs, or familiar **arias** and choruses.
***ballet de cour*** French court entertainment of the Renaissance and subsequent periods in which an allegorical scenario is enacted in a series of danced episodes.
***ballet héroïque*** See ***tragédie-lyrique***.
**baritone** See **voice**.
**bass** See **voice**.
***bel canto*** Style of singing in which a legato vocal line is pre-eminent, allowing the singer every opportunity for virtuoso ornamentation. It was particularly characteristic of ***castrati*** in the 18th century and of Italian singers of the romantic period.
***buffo*** Comic. A *buffo* role in an opera was frequently assigned to a bass voice, with fast-moving vocal patter in both arias and ensembles. See also ***opera buffa***.
***castrato*** Male singer castrated before puberty to preserve the unbroken voice, which was then trained to allow the production of an instrument capable both of a wide dynamic range and of considerable agility.
**chest voice** See **voice**.
***coloratura*** Brilliant passage-work, with scales, arpeggios, trills and other flourishes, generally written for the high register of the soprano voice. Also used to describe the character of a voice trained or particularly suited to this style of singing.
***comédie-ballet*** Precursor of ***opéra-comique***, in which musical episodes were inserted into the action of a spoken comedy. The term is used almost exclusively to refer to the collaborations between Lully and Molière in 1661–71.
***comédie larmoyante*** Sentimental drama in which the heroine (generally) overcomes perils and obstacles to find true love.
***comédie-lyrique*** Genre which adopts the conventions (including the classical characters) of ***tragédie-lyrique*** to comic material. The principle example is Rameau's *Platée*.
***commedia dell'arte*** Popular Italian comedy of traditional origin, with acrobatic, mimetic and musical elements, played by a group of stock characters, including Harlequin and Columbine. It was an important element in the origins of both ***opera buffa*** and ***opéra-comique*** and was often alluded to in early 20th-century operas to evoke the atmosphere of old Italian comedy.
***commedia in musica*** Comic opera; the precursor of ***opera buffa***.
**concerted finale** Ensemble number at the end of an act which is longer and has a more complex and developed structure than other operatic numbers. It offered a model for the first composers of **through-composed** operas.
**contralto** See **voice**.
**countertenor** See **voice**.
***dramma giocosa*** See ***opera semiseria***.
***en travesti*** Describes a female singer performing a male role. Generally (as with Cherubino in *Le nozze di Figaro* or Octavian in *Der Rosenkavalier*), such roles were written to be sung by women, but in modern times many male ***castrato*** roles have been played by female singers *en travesti*. In the past tenor or baritone roles were occasionally transposed to allow them to be sung by a woman.
***entrée*** See ***opéra-ballet***.
**falsetto** (head voice) See **voice**.
***grand opéra*** Opera with lavish theatrical effects, particularly French operas of the first half of the 19th century (by Meyerbeer et al.)
***intermedio*** One of a set of episodes of musical drama, usually of allegorical character, performed between other elements of a court festivity, generally to celebrate a dynastic marriage.
***intermezzo*** Comic operatic drama performed as episodes between the acts of a serious opera; an important precursor of ***opera buffa***.
**leitmotif** Thematic fragment associated with a particular character, event or concept in an opera, woven into its musical fabric. It serves both as a unifying element and to make the narrative explicit in the music itself.
**madrigal opera** Musical drama in which the words are sung as polyphonic madrigals while the action is mimed on stage.
**masque** English musical court entertainment of the Tudor and Stuart period. The term is also used for the musical interludes in a **semi-opera**.
***melodrama, mélodrame*** Spoken dramatic text whose effect is heightened by music played to accompany the words.
**mezzo-soprano** See **voice**.
**obbligato** Instrumental solo prominently featured with the voice in an **aria**.
***opéra-ballet*** Form similar to ***tragédie-lyrique***, from which it is distinguished by the fact that the separate acts do not form a complete drama but are separate episodes (***entrées***) linked by a common theme. (The element of ballet is as important to both.)
***opera ballo*** Early Italian form of music drama which mixed singing and dance.
***opéra-bouffe*** French translation of ***opera buffa***, used especially for Offenbach's parodies and for 20th-century works of similar character.
***opera buffa*** Italian comic opera.
***opéra-comique*** French opera with spoken dialogue, not necessarily of comic character.
**opera-oratorio** Term used to describe Handel's late oratorios (secular as well as religious), which are operatic in character, although not staged in his own time; or to refer to more recent sacred dramatic works intended for theatrical performance.
***opera semiseria*** Sentimental music drama, the equivalent of French ***comédie larmoyante***, often with spoken dialogue. As genres became more fluid in the later 18th century, several terms (***dramma giocosa*** among others) were used to define operas in which serious and comic material were mixed.
***opera seria*** Principal form of Italian opera current from the mid-17th century to the late 18th. It consisted almost entirely of a sequence of formal arias joined by ***secco* recitative** (***scene***), and the rules of its composition, both words and music, were rigidly defined.
***opérette, operetta*** Light opera of comic, romantic or satirical character.
**oratorio** Sacred work cast in quasi-dramatic form. As generally understood, the term refers to works never intended for the theatre, although the earliest oratorios, later sacred works written for performance during Lent, and a number of 20th-century oratorios were envisaged for stage performance.
**passacaglia** Extended musical form characterized by the insistent repetition of a bass line of extreme harmonic and rhythmic simplicity.
***pasticcio*** Opera in which the libretto is set by more than one composer (and often compiled from existing music).
***pastorale*** Opera (or other musical work) with an antique pastoral setting.
**prima donna** Singer of the principal female role in an opera (especially in ***opera seria***) or the principal female singer in an opera company.
**recitative** Setting of words in an opera (generally dialogue or the introduction to an **aria**) closely following the patterns of speech. It may be accompanied simply by the continuo (***secco* recitative**) or by the orchestra.
**reminiscence motif** Musical phrase associated with a particular character or event in an opera which is reintroduced in order to recall its original context. It was the origin of the Wagnerian **leitmotif**, which is more fully integrated in the musical texture.
**rescue opera** Opera whose plot relates the danger-fraught rescue from captivity of hero or heroine, generally by a devoted spouse.
***scena*** Musical item made up of an introductory **recitative** and extended **aria** which was the principal component of both baroque opera and the contemporary unstaged ***serenata*** or cantata.
***secco* recitative** See **recitative**.
**semi-opera** Term applied specifically to Purcell's stage works consisting of spoken drama interspersed with musical **masques**.
***serenata*** Dramatic poem made up of a sequence of ***scene*** set to music for performance at court, either staged or unstaged.
***singspiel*** German opera with spoken dialogue, derived from English **ballad opera** and French ***opéra-comique***.
**soprano** See **voice**.
**tenor** See **voice**.
**through-composed** Term for an opera which is not composed of individual 'numbers' linked by dialogue or **recitative**, but where the composition is continuous throughout each act.
***tragédie en musique*** See ***tragédie-lyrique***.
***tragédie-ballet*** See ***tragédie-lyrique***
***tragédie-lyrique*** French equivalent of ***opera seria***, current from the mid-17th century. The principal differences from its Italian counterpart were the more declamatory style of **recitative**, derived from French theatrical practice, and the importance given to dance, which was integrated into the dramatic action (e.g. to depict a dream). Ballet in the early period was not considered a separate category although distinctions might be drawn between *tragédie-lyrique, tragédie en musique, tragédie-ballet*, ***opéra-ballet***, *ballet héroïque*, etc.
***verismo, vérisme*** Realist movements in literature in the later 19th century which affected both opera libretti and the style of their setting – music that is direct, unadorned and emotionally highly charged.
**voice** The normal compass of the trained human voice is 2–3 octaves. Voices are classified according to the position of this compass on the overall scale (in which middle C is indicated by c′, the octaves above by c′′ and c′′′, and the octaves below by c and C), although their range frequently extends further. The standard range of a soprano is b–c′′′; of a mezzo-soprano a–a′′; of a contralto g–g′′; of a tenor c–c′′; of a baritone F–g′; and of a bass D–f′. The physical method of producing the sound may vary between different parts of a singer's compass, and the compass of a male voice can be extended upwards by the use of falsetto or 'head voice' (when the vocal cords vibrate only at their edges) as opposed to the normal 'chest voice'. Countertenors and modern male sopranos, who often sing roles originally assigned to ***castrati***, have developed this particular part of their vocal range.
***volksoper*** Light opera of specifically popular character.
***zarzuela*** Traditional Spanish operatic form with spoken dialogue and dance as well as singing.

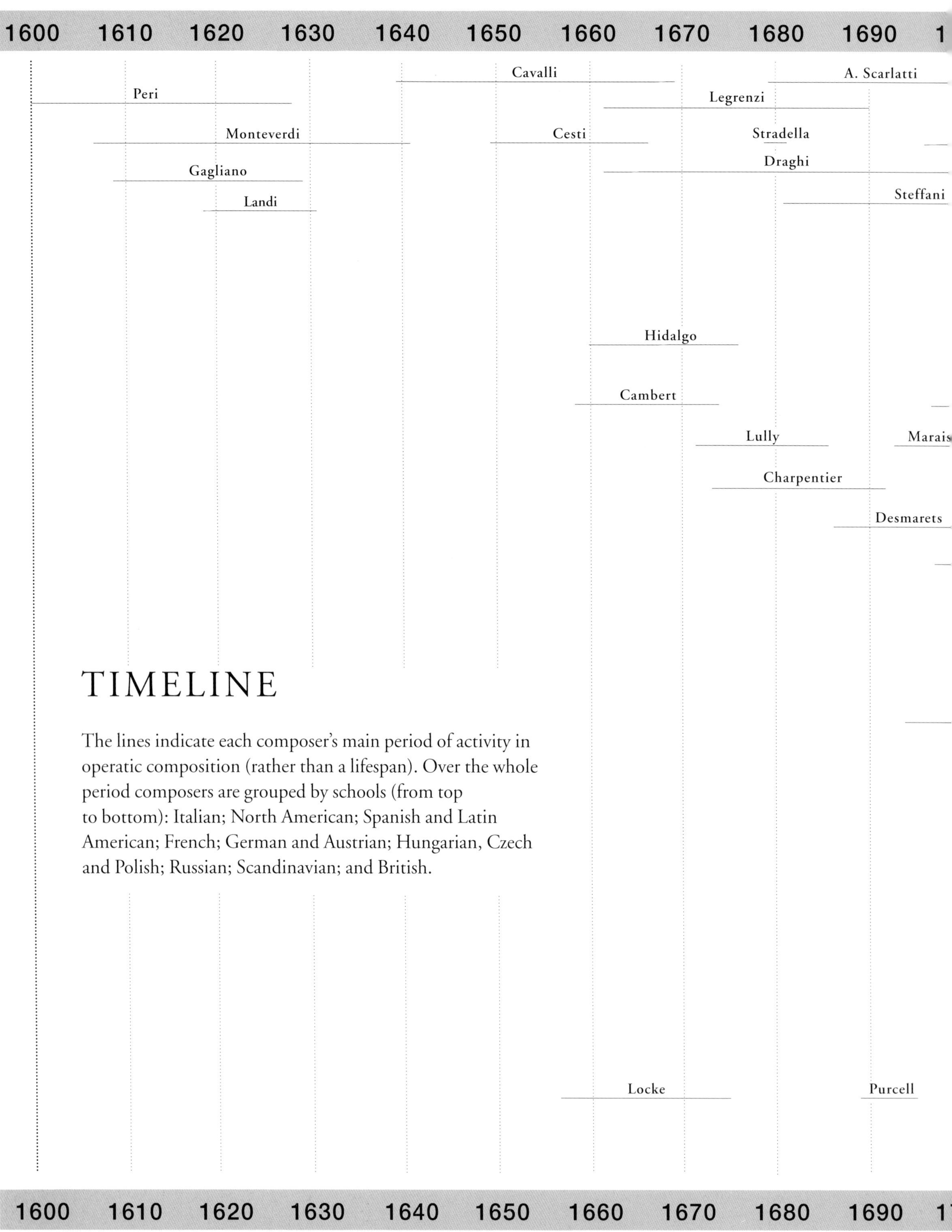


# TIMELINE

The lines indicate each composer's main period of activity in operatic composition (rather than a lifespan). Over the whole period composers are grouped by schools (from top to bottom): Italian; North American; Spanish and Latin American; French; German and Austrian; Hungarian, Czech and Polish; Russian; Scandinavian; and British.

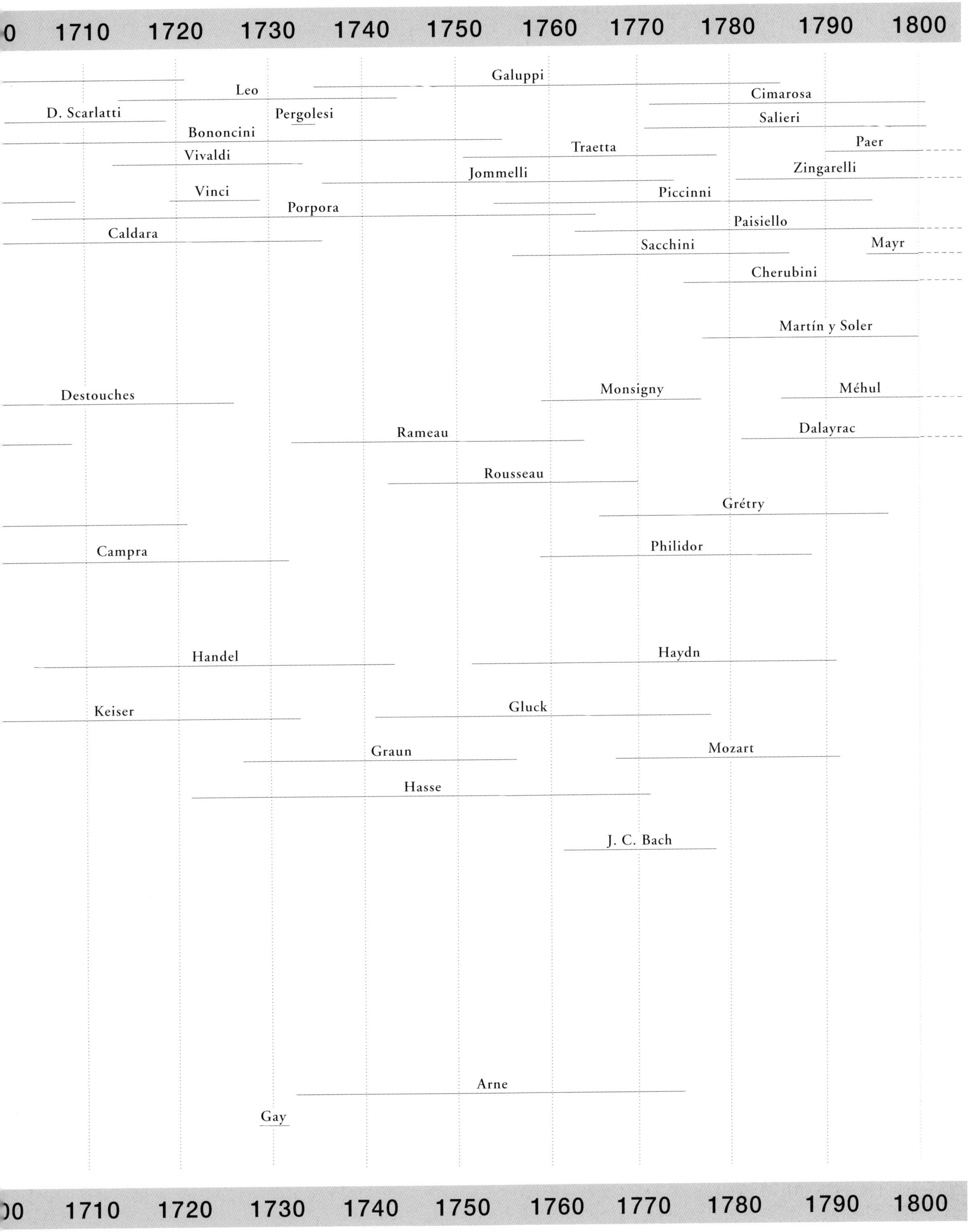

0 1710 1720 1730 1740 1750 1760 1770 1780 1790 1800

Galuppi

Leo

Cimarosa

D. Scarlatti

Pergolesi

Salieri

Bononcini

Paer

Traetta

Vivaldi

Zingarelli

Jommelli

Vinci

Piccinni

Porpora

Paisiello

Caldara

Mayr

Sacchini

Cherubini

Martín y Soler

Destouches

Monsigny

Méhul

Rameau

Dalayrac

Rousseau

Grétry

Campra

Philidor

Handel

Haydn

Keiser

Gluck

Graun

Mozart

Hasse

J. C. Bach

Arne

Gay

00 1710 1720 1730 1740 1750 1760 1770 1780 1790 1800

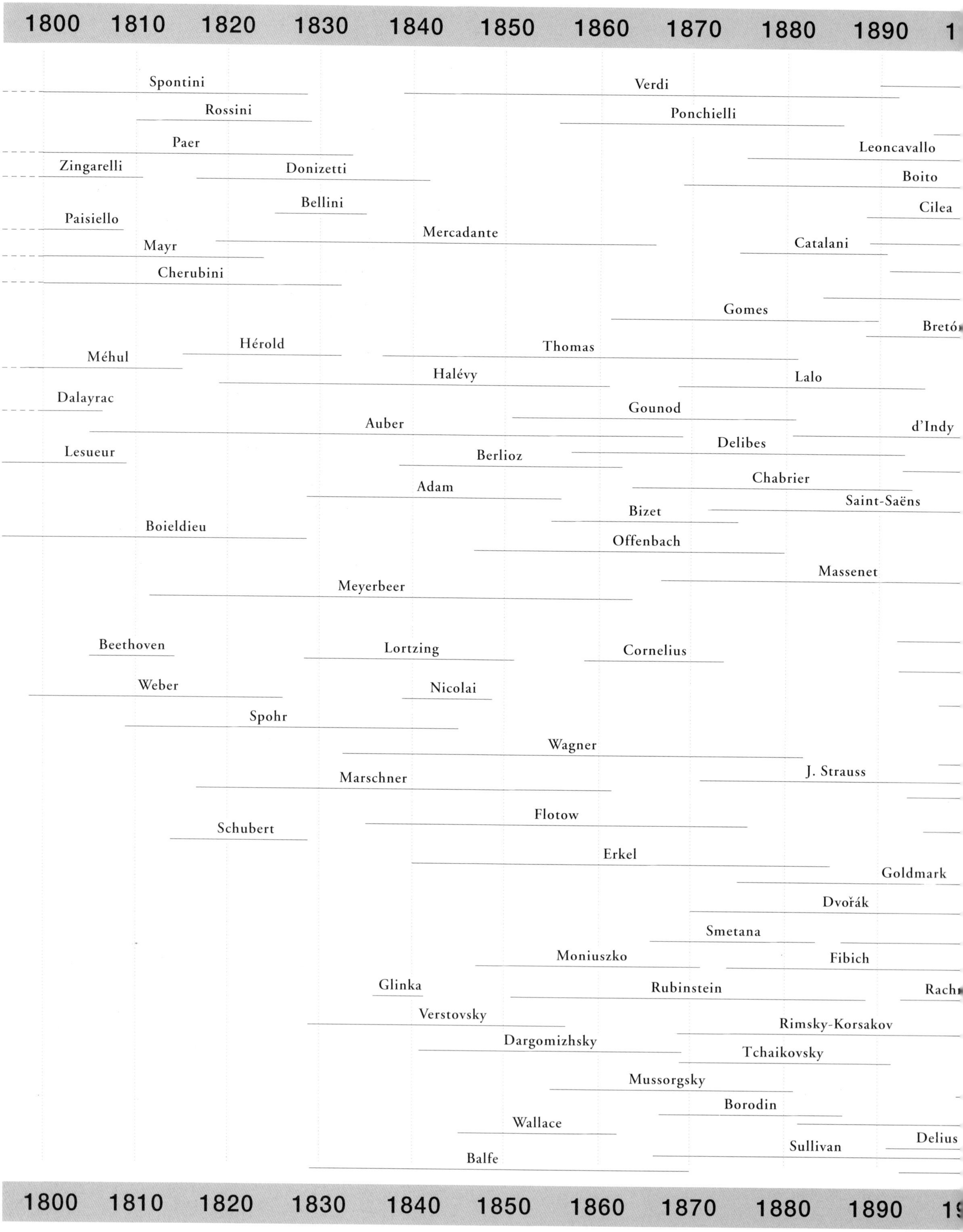

1800 1810 1820 1830 1840 1850 1860 1870 1880 1890 1

Spontini
Verdi
Rossini
Ponchielli
Paer
Leoncavallo
Zingarelli
Donizetti
Boito
Bellini
Cilea
Paisiello
Mercadante
Catalani
Mayr
Cherubini
Gomes
Bretó
Hérold
Thomas
Méhul
Halévy
Lalo
Dalayrac
Gounod
Auber
d'Indy
Delibes
Lesueur
Berlioz
Chabrier
Adam
Saint-Saëns
Bizet
Boieldieu
Offenbach
Massenet
Meyerbeer
Beethoven
Lortzing
Cornelius
Weber
Nicolai
Spohr
Wagner
J. Strauss
Marschner
Flotow
Schubert
Erkel
Goldmark
Dvořák
Smetana
Moniuszko
Fibich
Glinka
Rubinstein
Rach
Verstovsky
Rimsky-Korsakov
Dargomizhsky
Tchaikovsky
Mussorgsky
Borodin
Wallace
Delius
Sullivan
Balfe

1800 1810 1820 1830 1840 1850 1860 1870 1880 1890 19

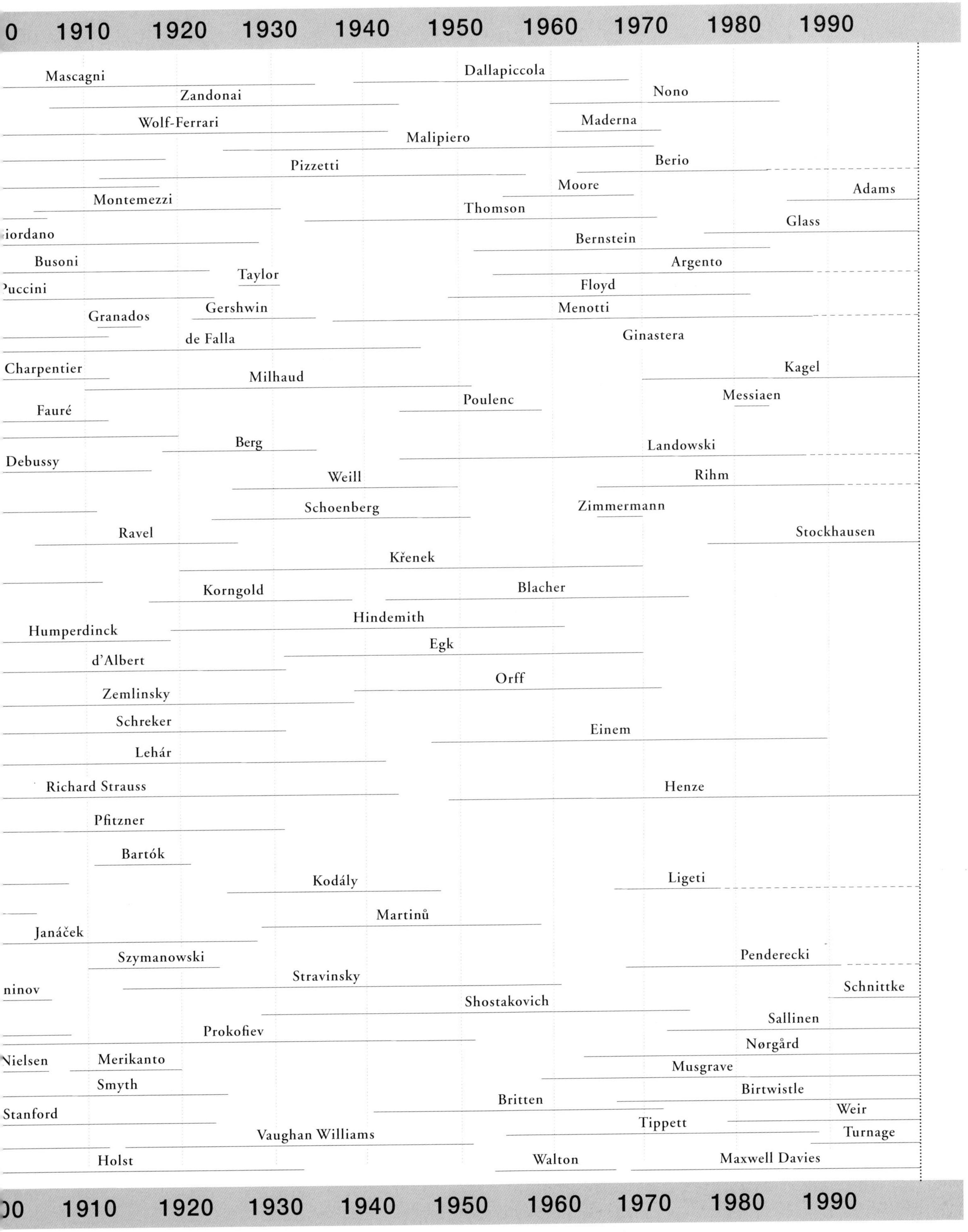

0 1910 1920 1930 1940 1950 1960 1970 1980 1990

Mascagni
Dallapiccola
Zandonai
Nono
Wolf-Ferrari
Maderna
Malipiero
Berio
Pizzetti
Moore
Adams
Montemezzi
Thomson
Glass
iordano
Bernstein
Busoni
Argento
Taylor
Floyd
'uccini
Gershwin
Menotti
Granados
de Falla
Ginastera
Charpentier
Kagel
Milhaud
Messiaen
Poulenc
Fauré
Berg
Landowski
Debussy
Rihm
Weill
Schoenberg
Zimmermann
Ravel
Stockhausen
Křenek
Korngold
Blacher
Hindemith
Humperdinck
Egk
d'Albert
Orff
Zemlinsky
Schreker
Einem
Lehár
Richard Strauss
Henze
Pfitzner
Bartók
Kodály
Ligeti
Martinů
Janáček
Penderecki
Szymanowski
Stravinsky
Schnittke
ninov
Shostakovich
Sallinen
Prokofiev
Nørgård
Nielsen
Merikanto
Musgrave
Smyth
Birtwistle
Britten
Weir
Stanford
Tippett
Turnage
Vaughan Williams
Holst
Walton
Maxwell Davies

)0 1910 1920 1930 1940 1950 1960 1970 1980 1990

# OPERA PREMIÈRES

* inauguration of new theatre
† posthumous première

## ITALY

### Florence

PITTI PALACE
1600 *Euridice* (Peri)

TEATRO DELLA PERGOLA
1658 *L'Hipermestra* (Cavalli)
1847 *Macbeth* (Verdi)
1940 *Volo di notte* (Dallapiccola)

TEATRO COMUNALE
1950 *Il prigioniero* (Dallapiccola)

### Rome

TEATRO DELLE DAME
1760 *Cecchina* (Piccinni)

TEATRO VALLE
1779 *L'italiana in Londra* (Cimarosa)
1817 *La Cenerentola* (Rossini)

TEATRO ARGENTINA
1816 *Il barbiere di Siviglia* (Rossini)
1844 *I due Foscari* (Verdi)

TEATRO APOLLO
1853 *Il trovatore* (Verdi)
1859 *Un ballo in maschera* (Verdi)

TEATRO COSTANZI
1890 *Cavalleria rusticana* (Mascagni)
1900 *Tosca* (Puccini)

### Naples

TEATRO SAN BARTOLOMEO
1733 *La serva padrona* (Pergolesi)

TEATRO SAN CARLO
*1737 *Achille in Sciro* (Sarro)
1815 *Elisabetta* (Rossini)
1818 *Mosè in Egitto* (Rossini)
1819 *La donna del lago* (Rossini)
1835 *Lucia di Lammermoor* (Donizetti)
1837 *Roberto Devereux* (Donizetti)
1840 *Saffo* (Pacini)
1849 *Luisa Miller* (Verdi)

TEATRO DEL FONDO
1816 *Otello* (Rossini)

### Venice

TEATRO SAN CASSIANO
*1637 *L'Andromeda* (Manelli)
1644 *L'Ormindo* (Cavalli)
1649 *Il Giasone* (Cavalli)

TEATRO SS. GIOVANNI E PAOLO
1640 *Il ritorno di Ulisse in patria* (Monteverdi)
1642 *L'incoronazione di Poppea* (Monteverdi)

TEATRO SAN GIOVANNI GRISOSTOMO
1707 *Il Mitridate Eupatore* (A. Scarlatti)
1709 *Agrippina* (Handel)
1730 *Artaserse* (Hasse)

TEATRO LA FENICE
1813 *Tancredi* (Rossini)
1823 *Semiramide* (Rossini)
1833 *Beatrice di Tenda* (Bellini)
1844 *Ernani* (Verdi)
1851 *Rigoletto* (Verdi)
1853 *La traviata* (Verdi)
1857 *Simon Boccanegra* (Verdi)
1951 *The Rake's Progress* (Stravinsky)
1954 *The Turn of the Screw* (Britten)
1955 *Ognennyi angel* (Prokofiev)
1961 *Intolleranza 1960* (Nono)

TEATRO SAN BENEDETTO
1813 *L'italiana in Algeri* (Rossini)

### Milan

TEATRO REGIO DUCALE
1770 *Mitridate* (Mozart)

LA SCALA
*1778 *Europa riconosciuta* (Salieri)
1814 *Il turco in Italia* (Rossini)
1817 *La gazza ladra* (Rossini)
1829 *La straniera* (Bellini)
1831 *Norma* (Bellini)
1833 *Lucrezia Borgia* (Donizetti)
1835 *Maria Stuarda* (Donizetti)
1839 *Oberto* (Verdi)
1842 *Nabucco* (Verdi)
1868 *Mefistofele* (Boito)
1876 *La gioconda* (Ponchielli)
1887 *Otello* (Verdi)
1889 *Edgar* (Puccini)
1892 *La Wally* (Catalani)
1893 *Falstaff* (Verdi)
1896 *Andrea Chenier* (Giordano)
1904 *Madama Butterfly* (Puccini)
1913 *L'amore dei tre re* (Montemezzi)
†1926 *Turandot* (Puccini)
1957 *Les Dialogues des carmélites* (Poulenc)
1958 *Assassinio nella cattedrale* (Pizzetti)
†1962 *Atlantida* (de Falla)
1982 *La vera storia* (Berio)

TEATRO CARCANO
1830 *Anna Bolena* (Donizetti)
1831 *La sonnambula* (Bellini)

TEATRO DELLA CANOBBIANA
1832 *L'elisir d'amore* (Donizetti)

TEATRO DAL VERME
1892 *Pagliacci* (Leoncavallo)

TEATRO LIRICO
1898 *Fedora* (Giordano)
1902 *Adriana Lecouvreur* (Cilea)

## FRANCE

### Paris

OPÉRA [JEU DE PAUME]
*1671 *Pomone* (Cambert)
[PALAIS-ROYAL]
*1674 *Alceste* (Lully)
1686 *Armide* (Lully)
1693 *Médée* (Charpentier)
1706 *Alcione* (Marais)
1733 *Hippolyte et Aricie* (Rameau)
1735 *Les Indes galantes* (Rameau)
1737 *Castor et Pollux* (Rameau)
1739 *Dardanus* (Rameau)
[PALAIS-ROYAL: NEW HOUSE]
1774 *Iphigénie en Aulide* (Gluck)
1777 *Armide* (Gluck)
1778 *Roland* (Piccinni)
1779 *Iphigénie en Tauride* (Gluck)
[PORTE SAINT-MARTIN]
1787 *Tarare* (Salieri)
[SALLE MONTANSIER]
1807 *La Vestale* (Spontini)
[SALLE LE PELETIER]
1828 *La Muette de Portici* (Auber)
1828 *Le Comte Ory* (Rossini)
1829 *Guillaume Tell* (Rossini)
1831 *Robert le diable* (Meyerbeer)
1835 *La Juive* (Halévy)
1836 *Les Huguenots* (Meyerbeer)
1838 *Benvenuto Cellini* (Berlioz)
1840 *La Favorite* (Donizetti)
1849 *Le Prophète* (Meyerbeer)
1855 *Les Vêpres siciliennes* (Verdi)
†1865 *L'Africaine* (Meyerbeer)
1867 *Don Carlos* (Verdi)
1868 *Hamlet* (Thomas)
[SALLE GARNIER]
1894 *Thaïs* (Massenet)
1914 *Solovei* (Stravinsky)
1922 *Renard* and *Mavra* (Stravinsky)
1923 *Padmâvati* (Roussel)
1979 *Lulu* (Berg), complete
1983 *Saint-François d'Assise* (Messiaen)

THÉÂTRE FEYDEAU
1797 *Médée* (Cherubini)

OPÉRA-COMIQUE [SALLE FAVART]
1807 *Joseph en Egypte* (Méhul)
[SALLE FEYDEAU]
1825 *La Dame blanche* (Boieldieu)
[SALLE VENTADOUR]
1830 *Fra Diavolo* (Auber)
1831 *Zampa* (Hérold)
[SECOND SALLE FAVART]
1840 *La Fille du régiment* (Donizetti)
1866 *Mignon* (Thomas)
1875 *Carmen* (Bizet)
†1881 *Les Contes d'Hoffmann* (Offenbach)
1883 *Lakmé* (Delibes)
1884 *Manon* (Massenet)
[THIRD SALLE FAVART]
1900 *Louise* (Charpentier)
1902 *Pelléas et Mélisande* (Debussy)
1907 *Ariane et Barbe-bleu* (Dukas)
1947 *Les Mamelles de Tirésias* (Poulenc)
1959 *La Voix humaine* (Poulenc)

THÉÂTRE-ITALIEN [SALLE FAVART]
1835 *I puritani* (Bellini)
[SALLE VENTADOUR]
1843 *Don Pasquale* (Donizetti)

BOUFFES-PARISIENS
1858 *Orphée aux enfers* (Offenbach)

THÉÂTRE-LYRIQUE
1859 *Faust* (Gounod)
1863 *Les Pêcheurs de perles* (Bizet)
1863 *Les Troyens à Carthage* (Berlioz)
1867 *Roméo et Juliette* (Gounod)

### Versailles

THÉÂTRE DE LA GRANDE ÉCURIE
1745 *Platée* (Rameau)

### Fontainebleau

1752 *Le Devin du village* (Rousseau)
1771 *Zémire et Azor* (Grétry)

### Nice

CASINO MUNICIPAL
1913 *La vida breve* (de Falla)

## MONACO

### Monte Carlo

THÉÂTRE DU CASINO
†1893 *La Damnation de Faust* (Berlioz)
1910 *Don Quichotte* (Massenet)
1913 *Pénélope* (Fauré)
1925 *L'Enfant et les sortilèges* (Ravel)

## BELGIUM

### Brussels

THÉÂTRE DE LA MONNAIE
1881 *Hérodiade* (Massenet)
1886 *Gwendoline* (Chabrier)
1903 *L'Etranger* (d'Indy)
1903 *Le Roi Arthus* (Chausson)
1926 *Les Malheurs d'Orphée* (Milhaud)
1991 *The Death of Klinghoffer* (Adams)

## ENGLAND

### London

JOSIAS PRIEST'S SCHOOL
1684 *Venus and Adonis* (Blow), 2nd performance
1689 *Dido and Aeneas* (Purcell)

DORSET GARDENS THEATRE
1691 *King Arthur* (Purcell)
1692 *The Fairy Queen* (Purcell)

QUEEN'S/KING'S THEATRE
1711 *Rinaldo* (Handel)
1720 *Radamisto* (Handel)
1723 *Flavio* (Handel)
1724 *Giulio Cesare in Egitto* (Handel)
1725 *Rodelinda* (Handel)
1733 *Orlando* (Handel)
1738 *Serse* (Handel)
1745 *Hercules* (Handel)

LINCOLN'S INN FIELDS THEATRE
1728 *The Beggar's Opera* (Pepusch et al.)

COVENT GARDEN
1735 *Alcina* (Handel)
1744 *Semele* (Handel)
1762 *Love in a Village* (Arne)
1826 *Oberon* (Weber)
[NEW THEATRE]
1951 *The Pilgrim's Progress* (Vaughan Williams)
1951 *Billy Budd* (Britten)
1954 *Troilus and Cressida* (Walton)
1955 *The Midsummer Marriage* (Tippett)
1972 *Taverner* (Maxwell Davies)
1991 *Gawain* (Birtwistle)

SADLER'S WELLS THEATRE
1945 *Peter Grimes* (Britten)

ENGLISH NATIONAL OPERA
1986 *The Mask of Orpheus* (Birtwistle)

**Glyndebourne**
OPERA HOUSE
1946 *The Rape of Lucretia* (Britten)
1947 *Albert Herring* (Britten)

**Aldeburgh**
JUBILEE HALL
1960 *A Midsummer Night's Dream* (Britten)

**Snape**
THE MALTINGS
1973 *Death in Venice* (Britten)

## GERMANY

**Berlin**
KÖNIGLICHES OPERNHAUS
*1742 *Cleopatra e Cesare* (Graun)
[NEW HOUSE]
1849 *Die lustigen Weiber von Windsor* (Nicolai)
1895 *Der Evangelimann* (Kienzl)
[STAATSOPER]
1925 *Wozzeck* (Berg)

SCHAUSPIELHAUS
*1821 *Der Freischütz* (Weber)

KOMISCHE OPER
1907 *Romeo und Julia auf dem Dorfe* (Delius)

THEATER AM SCHIFFBAUERDAMM
1928 *Die Dreigroschenoper* (Weill)

**Munich**
RESIDENZTHEATER
1781 *Idomeneo* (Mozart)

HOFOPER
1865 *Tristan und Isolde* (Wagner)
1868 *Die Meistersinger* (Wagner)
1869 *Das Rheingold* (Wagner)
1870 *Die Walküre* (Wagner)
1909 *Il segreto di Susanna* (Wolf-Ferrari)
[NATIONALTHEATER]
1939 *Der Mond* (Orff)
1942 *Capriccio* (R. Strauss)

PRINZREGENTENTHEATER
1917 *Palestrina* (Pfitzner)

**Leipzig**
STADTTHEATER
1828 *Der Vampyr* (Marschner)
1837 *Zar und Zimmermann* (Lortzing)
1927 *Jonny spielt auf* (Křenek)

NEUES THEATER
1906 *Strandrecht* (Smyth)
1930 *Aufstieg und Fall der Stadt Mahagonny* (Weill)

**Dresden**
HOFOPER
1842 *Rienzi* (Wagner)
1843 *Der fliegende Holländer* (Wagner)
1845 *Tannhäuser* (Wagner)
1905 *Salome* (R. Strauss)
1909 *Elektra* (R. Strauss)
1911 *Der Rosenkavalier* (R. Strauss)
[STAATSOPER]
†1925 *Doktor Faust* (Busoni)
1926 *Cardillac* (Hindemith)
1933 *Arabella* (R. Strauss)

**Weimar**
HOFTHEATER
1850 *Lohengrin* (Wagner)
†1854 *Alfonso und Estrella* (Schubert)
1858 *Der Barbier von Bagdad* (Cornelius)
1877 *Samson et Dalila* (Saint-Saëns)
1893 *Hänsel und Gretel* (Humperdinck)

**Baden-Baden**
STADTTHEATER
1862 *Béatrice et Bénédict* (Berlioz)

**Bayreuth**
FESTSPIELHAUS
1876 *Siegfried* (Wagner)
1876 *Die Götterdämmerung* (Wagner)
1882 *Parsifal* (Wagner)

**Karlsruhe**
HOFTHEATER
†1890 *Les Troyens* (Berlioz)

**Stuttgart**
HOFTHEATER (KLEINES HAUS)
*1912 *Ariadne auf Naxos*, original version (R. Strauss)

**Cologne**
STÄDTISCHE OPER
1957 *Bluthochzeit* (Fortner)
1965 *Die Soldaten* (Zimmermann)

**Hamburg**
STAATSOPER
1960 *Der Prinz von Homburg* (Henze)
1969 *Diably z Loudon* (Penderecki)
1971 *Staatstheater* (Kagel)
1979 *Jakob Lenz* (Rihm)
1995 *Faust* (Schnittke)

## SWITZERLAND

**Zurich**
STADTTHEATER
1917 *Arlecchino* and *Turandot* (Busoni)
†1937 *Lulu* (Berg), incomplete
1938 *Mathis der Maler* (Hindemith)
†1957 *Moses und Aron* (Schoenberg)

## AUSTRIA

**Vienna**
BURGTHEATER
1762 *Orfeo ed Euridice* (Gluck)
1767 *Alceste* (Gluck)
1782 *Die Entführung aus dem Serail* (Mozart)
1786 *Le nozze di Figaro* (Mozart)
1790 *Così fan tutte* (Mozart)
1792 *Il matrimonio segreto* (Cimarosa)

THEATER AUF DER WIEDEN
1791 *Die Zauberflöte* (Mozart)

THEATER AN DER WIEN
1805 *Leonore* (Beethoven)
1874 *Die Fledermaus* (J. Strauss)
1905 *Die lustige Witwe* (Lehár)

KÄRNTNERTORTHEATER
1814 *Fidelio* (Beethoven)
1823 *Euryanthe* (Weber)
1842 *Linda di Chamounix* (Donizetti)
1847 *Martha* (Flotow)

HOFOPER
1875 *Die Königin von Saba* (Goldmark)
1892 *Werther* (Massenet)
[STAATSOPER]
1919 *Die Frau ohne Schatten* (R. Strauss)

VOLKSOPER
1924 *Die glückliche Hand* (Schoenberg)

## HUNGARY

**Eszterháza**
OPERA HOUSE
1775 *L'incontro improvviso* (Haydn)
1777 *Il mondo della luna* (Haydn)
1779 *La vera costanza* (Haydn)
[NEW HOUSE]
*1781 *La fedeltà premiata* (Haydn)

**Budapest**
ROYAL OPERA
1918 *A Kékszakállú Herceg Vára* (Bartók)
1926 *Háry János* (Kodály)

## RUSSIA

**St Petersburg/Leningrad**
HERMITAGE THEATRE
1782 *Il barbiere di Siviglia* (Paisiello)

BOLSHOI THEATRE
*1836 *Zhizn za tsarya* (Glinka)
1842 *Ruslan i Lyudmila* (Glinka)
1862 *La forza del destino* (Verdi)

MARYINSKY THEATRE
†1872 *Kamenny Gost* (Dargomizhsky)
1873 *Pskovityanka* (Rimsky-Korsakov)
1874 *Boris Godunov* (Mussorgsky)
1875 *Demon* (Rubinstein)
1880 *Maiskaya noch* (Rimsky-Korsakov)
1882 *Snegurochka* (Rimsky-Korsakov)
1890 *Knyaz Igor* (Borodin)
1890 *Pikovaya dama* (Tchaikovsky)

MALY THEATRE (LENINGRAD)
1934 *Ledi Makbet Mtsenskovo uezda* (Shostakovich)
1946 *Voina i mir* (Prokofiev)

**Moscow**
IMPERIAL COLLEGE OF MUSIC
1879 *Evgeny Onegin* (Tchaikovsky)

PRIVATE RUSSIAN OPERA
1898 *Sadko* (Rimsky-Korsakov)
1899 *Tsarskaya nevesta* (Rimsky-Korsakov)
1900 *Skazka o Tsare Saltane* (Rimsky-Korsakov)
†1909 *Zolotoi petushok* (Rimsky-Korsakov)

## CZECH REPUBLIC

**Prague**
NATIONAL THEATRE
1787 *Don Giovanni* (Mozart)
1791 *La clemenza di Tito* (Mozart)
[ESTATES THEATRE]
1816 *Faust* (Spohr)

PROVISIONAL CZECH THEATRE
1866 *Prodaná nevěsta* (Smetana)

CZECH NATIONAL THEATRE
*1881 *Libuše* (Smetana)
1899 *Čert a Káča* (Dvořák)
1920 *Výlety páně Broučkovy* (Janáček)
1927 *Švanda dudák* (Weinberger)
[NATIONAL THEATRE]
1938 *Julietta: Snář* (Martinů)

NEW GERMAN THEATRE
1903 *Tiefland* (d'Albert)
1924 *Erwartung* (Schoenberg)

**Brno**
NATIONAL THEATRE
1904 *Její pastorkyňa* (Janáček)
1921 *Káťa Kabanová* (Janáček)
1924 *Příhody lišky bystroušky* (Janáček)
1926 *Več Makropoulos* (Janáček)
†1930 *Z mrtvého domu* (Janáček)

**Terezín (Theresienstadt)**
CONCENTRATION CAMP
1943 *Brundibár* (Krása)
1944 *Der Kaiser von Atlantis* (Ullmann)

## UNITED STATES

**New York**
METROPOLITAN OPERA
1910 *La fanciulla del West* (Puccini)
1916 *Goyescas* (Granados)
1918 *Il trittico* (Puccini)
[AT LINCOLN CENTER]
*1966 *Antony and Cleopatra* (Barber)

COLUMBIA UNIVERSITY
1946 *The Medium* (Menotti)
1947 *The Mother of Us All* (Thomson)

**Chicago**
AUDITORIUM
1921 *Lyubov k tryom apel'sinam* (Prokofiev)

**Hartford**
AVERY MEMORIAL THEATER
*1934 *Four Saints in Three Acts* (Thomson)

**Bloomington**
UNIVERSITY OF INDIANA
1952 *Amahl and the Night Visitors* (Menotti)

**Central City**
OPERA HOUSE
1956 *The Ballad of Baby Doe* (Moore)

**Santa Fe**
OPERA
1970 *Opera* (Berio)

**Minneapolis**
CENTER OPERA COMPANY
1971 *Postcard from Morocco* (Argento)

**Houston**
GRAND OPERA
1983 *A Quiet Place* (Bernstein)
1987 *Nixon in China* (Adams)

## SWEDEN

**Stockholm**
ROYAL OPERA
1959 *Aniara* (Blomdahl)
1978 *Le grand macabre* (Ligeti)

## NETHERLANDS

**Amsterdam**
MUZIEKTHEATER
1992 *Zhizn s idiotom* (Schnittke)

# BIOGRAPHIES OF 100 SINGERS

**MARIETTA ALBONI** (Maria Anna Marzia Alboni), 1826–94. Italian dramatic contralto. Début: Bologna, 1842, in title role of Pacini's *Saffo* after studying there with Mombelli and Rossini. La Scala début: 1843, as Orsini (one of her many roles *en travesti*) in *Lucrezia Borgia*. Sang in St Petersburg with Viardot, Rubini and Tamburini, 1844–5. Starred in opening seasons of Royal Italian Opera at Covent Garden, 1847–8 (fees £2,000 per season), and of Italian Opera at Astor Place Theatre, New York, 1852. Repertory: Rossini, Donizetti, Verdi and Mozart (Cherubino).

**VICTORIA DE LOS ANGELES** (Victoria Gómez Cima), b. 1923. Lyric soprano, born in Barcelona. Début: Barcelona (Liceo), 1945, as the Countess (*Le nozze di Figaro*). First appearances at the Paris Opéra in 1949 (Marguerite); at Covent Garden in 1950 (Mimì); the Met in 1951 (Marguerite); and Bayreuth (Elisabeth) in 1961. Notable recordings as Dido, Rosina, Carmen, Mimì, Butterfly. Outstanding in Spanish roles.

**MADELEINE-SOPHIE ARNOULD**, 1740–1802. Soprano, born in Paris. Début at the Opéra: 1757, in Mouret's *Les Amours des dieux*; she remained the leading singer there until 1778. She was celebrated for her roles in Rameau's operas, especially *Castor et Pollux*, although Burney complained of her 'vocal outrages'. She created Monsigny's *Aline* and principal roles in Gluck's first Paris operas (1774), *Iphigénie en Aulide* and *Orphée et Euridice*. She was a fine actress and celebrated wit, remarking: 'To go to the opera is to go to the devil. But so what? It is my destiny.'

**DAME JANET BAKER**, b. 1933. English mezzo-soprano. Début: Oxford, 1956, in Smetana's *Kiss*; she also sang in the Glyndebourne chorus that year. In 1959 she was in the cast (with Sutherland) of Handel's *Rodelinda* at Sadler's Wells. She joined the English Opera Group in 1962, singing Dido at Aldeburgh that year, and was in the original cast of *Owen Wingrave* (1971). Her repertory included baroque opera (notably *Calisto* at Glyndebourne, 1970), *bel canto* and contemporary works. She retired from the stage in 1982.

**CECILIA BARTOLI**, b. 1966. Mezzo-soprano, born in Rome. Début: Verona, 1987, as King Alboino in Ciampi's *Bertoldo* (following a juvenile appearance as the Shepherd Boy in *Tosca* in Rome in 1975). Since then, she has specialized in Rossini and Mozart roles, making débuts in 1991 at the Opéra (Cherubino) and La Scala (in *Le Comte Ory*) and in 1996 at the Met (Despina). She has made several outstanding recordings.

**GEMMA BELLINCIONI**, 1864–1950. Italian dramatic soprano, taught by her father, a celebrated *buffo* bass. Début: Naples, 1879; La Scala début: 1886. Best known for her interpretation of *verismo* roles, creating both Santuzza (*Cavalleria rusticana*) and Fedora. At the end of her career she specialized in the role of Salome: she gave the Italian première under Strauss in 1906 and sang the role over 100 times before her retirement in 1911.

**FRANCESCO BENUCCI**, *c.* 1745–1824. Italian bass. He sang in Pistoia in 1769 and was the leading character *buffo* bass in Venice, 1778–9, and Milan, 1779–82. In 1784 he was one of the principals of the new Italian Opera in Vienna, where he was a favourite of Mozart's, creating the roles of Figaro, and Guglielmo (*Così fan tutte*); he was also the first Leporello in Vienna. In 1792 he created Count Robinson in Cimarosa's *Il matrimonio segreto*. He returned to Italy after 1795.

**CATHY BERBERIAN**, 1925–83. American mezzo-soprano. She specialized in contemporary music, developing not only a vocal range of over 3 octaves but also an extensive repertory of unconventional pitched and unpitched vocal sounds. She was married, 1950–66, to Luciano Berio, who wrote many scores for her.

**TERESA BERGANZA**, b. 1935. Mezzo-soprano, born in Madrid. Début: Aix-en-Provence Festival, 1957, as Dorabella. In 1958 she sang Cenerentola in the Palazzo Reale, Naples, and Isabella (*L'italiana in Algeri*) in Dallas. Her repertory included Rossini, Mozart, Handel and much Spanish music, including *zarzuelas*.

**JUSSI BJÖRLING**, 1911–60. Swedish lyric tenor. Son of an operatic tenor, he sang (as a treble) in a quartet with his father and two brothers from 1916, touring the USA in 1919–21. Official début: Royal Opera, Stockholm, 1930, as Don Ottavio (*Don Giovanni*). US début: Chicago, 1937, as the Duke (*Rigoletto*). He was engaged by the Met for the 1938–9 season, where his first role was Rodolfo. In the Italian repertory, in which he specialized, he was the outstanding singer of his era, making many recordings.

**FAUSTINA BORDONI**, 1700–81. Venetian mezzo-soprano of aristocratic birth, who studied with Benedetto Marcello. Début: Venice, 1716, in Pollarolo's *Ariodante*, after which she became known as 'la nuova sirena'. In 1718–19 she made several appearances with Cuzzoni, later her rival in London. In 1724 she joined the court opera in Vienna, where Handel heard her and engaged her for his company in London. In 1730 she married Hasse, and they worked together in Dresden, 1731–63, then Vienna, returning to Venice in 1773. A fine actress, she was noted for her breath control, her tasteful ornamentation and her perfect intonation.

**LUCIENNE BRÉVAL** (Bertha Schilling), 1869–1935. Swiss dramatic soprano, active principally in Paris, where she studied at the Conservatoire. Début: Paris Opéra, 1892, as Sélika (*L'Africaine*). She was the first French Brünnhilde in *Siegfried* and *Die Götterdämmerung* (1902) and created the title roles in Massenet's *Grisélidis* (1901), Dukas's *Ariane et Barbe-bleu* (1907), Février's *Monna Vanna* (1909), and Fauré's *Pénélope* (1913). She was also a noted interpreter of Gluck's heroines in the revivals of his operas in Paris and London in 1906–7.

**MONTSERRAT CABALLÉ**, b. 1933. Soprano, born in Barcelona. Début: Basel, 1956, as the First Lady (*Die Zauberflöte*), then as Mimì. Her Barcelona (Liceo) début was in 1962 as Arabella. Her US début was at Carnegie Hall, 1965, replacing Marilyn Horne in a concert performance of *Lucrezia Borgia*, and as a result of her success several Donizetti operas were revived for her. Her Met début took place the same year as Marguerite. Her other roles have included Donna Anna, Norma, Violetta, Aida, Tosca, Salome, Elektra and Marie (*Wozzeck*).

**MARIA CALLAS** (Maria Anna Sofia Cecilia Kalogeropoulos), 1923–77. Greek-American dramatic soprano, born in New York. Her family returned to Greece, and her first major role was Tosca in Athens, 1942. On her return to New York, 1945, she was offered a contract by the Met but went instead to Italy, where she made her début in Verona, 1947, in *La gioconda*. Under the guidance of Serafin and Visconti she became the outstanding operatic actress of her time, especially noted for her interpretations of dramatic romantic heroines. She retired from the stage in 1965. At her death a radio commentator noted: 'If an orgasm could sing, it would sound like Maria Callas.'

**EMMA CALVÉ** (de Roquer), 1858–1942. French soprano, a pupil of Mathilde Marchesi (who had studied with Manuel Garcia, jun.). Début: Brussels, 1881, as Marguerite. Massenet wrote Sapho and Anita (*La Navarraise*) for her, and she created Suzel (*L'amico Fritz*), but was most celebrated for her legendary, earthy interpretation of Carmen, of which she left several recordings (1902 etc.). She sang Carmen at the Met from 1893, where her Santuzza and Juliette were also celebrated.

**JOSÉ CARRERAS**, b. 1946. Lyric tenor, born in Barcelona. Official début (following juvenile appearances): Barcelona Liceo, 1970, as Gennaro (*Lucrezia Borgia*). He opened the 1972 season at the Teatro Regio, Parma, as Rodolfo and made his US début, at the New York City Opera, as Pinkerton the same year. Performances at Covent Garden, the Vienna Staatsoper, the Met, La Scala and Salzburg followed, 1974–6, principally in Verdi and Puccini roles, which, with Don José, have remained his core repertory.

**ENRICO CARUSO**, 1873–1921. Tenor, born in Naples. Débuts: Naples (Teatro Nuovo), 1894, in *L'amico Francesco*; La Scala, 1899; Covent Garden, 1902; Met, 1903. His first great success was in Cilea's *L'arlesiana*, and he later created the tenor roles in *Fedora*, *Adriana Lecouvreur*, *Germania* and *La fanciulla del West*, building up a repertory of some 50 roles. He settled in New York in 1903, singing regularly at the Met until shortly before his death. A great recording artist, he was the archetypal tenor of the twentieth century.

**ANGELICA CATALANI**, 1780–1849. Italian soprano. Début: Venice (La Fenice), 1800, in Mayr's *Lodoïska*. She performed at La Scala in 1801 and in 1806 sang for Napoleon at Saint-Cloud and made her London début. She was hugely successful there (earning £16,000 in one year), but artistically insensitive, including her favourite bravura showpieces in whatever work she happened to be singing. From 1814 to 1817 she took over management of the Théâtre des Italiens, Paris, but this enterprise was a failure. Her final appearance was in 1828 at the York Festival.

**CATERINA CAVALIERI** (Franziska Kavalier), 1760–1801. Viennese soprano. Début: Vienna (Kärntnertor-theater), 1775, in Anfossi's *La finta giardiniera*. She subsequently studied with Salieri and became his mistress. She sang Sophie in *Die Bergknappen* at the opening of the Nationalsingspiel, 1778, and was admired by Mozart, who wrote several pieces for her. She was the original Constanze (*Entführung*), the first Viennese Donna Elvira, and sang the Countess in the 1790 revival of *Le nozze di Figaro*. She retired from the stage in 1793.

**FEDOR IVANOVICH CHALIAPIN**, 1873–1938. Russian bass, born in Kazan. Débuts: Ufa, 1890, in *Halka*; Tblisi, 1893, in *Aida*; Maryinsky Theatre, St Petersburg, 1895, as Méphistophélès in *Faust*. He built up an extensive repertory of Russian, French and Italian works, singing with the Russian Private Opera, 1896–9. His début outside Russia was at La Scala, 1901, as Boito's Mefistofele, and his Met début in 1908 as Leporello. He was the sensation of Diaghilev's pre-war seasons in Paris and London. He performed many of his finest roles (Boris, Méphistophélès, Mefistofele, King Philip) at the Met after 1921. One of the greatest recording artists of the pre-electric era.

**LAURE CINTI (-DAMOREAU)**, 1801–63. Soprano, born in Paris. Début: Paris (Théâtre des Italiens), 1816, in *Una cosa rara*. She sang at the Opéra for ten years

(1825–35), taking part in the première of Auber's *La Muette de Portici*, Rossini's principal French operas and Meyerbeer's *Robert le diable*. She then moved to the Opéra-Comique, 1836–41, starring in a succession of Auber premières. She had complete mastery of florid vocal technique and, after her retirement, became a professor of singing at the Conservatoire.

**ISABELLA COLBRAN**, 1785–1845. Dramatic *coloratura* soprano, born in Madrid. The daughter of a Spanish court musician, she made her stage début in Spain in 1806. She performed in Bologna (1807) and Milan (1808) before Barbaia engaged her in 1811 for Naples, where she became his mistress (and the King's). An excellent actress, she was celebrated for her performances in Spontini's *La Vestale*, Mayr's *Saffo* and, after the composer's arrival in Naples in 1815, many Rossini roles. She married Rossini in 1822 and, after touring with his company to Vienna, Paris and London, retired from the stage in 1823.

**RÉGINE CRESPIN**, b. 1927. French soprano, born in Marseille. Début: Mulhouse, 1950, as Elsa (*Lohengrin*), a role she repeated for her Opéra début the following year. She created the role of the Nouvelle Prieure in Poulenc's *Les Dialogues des carmélites*, 1957. She sang Kundry at Bayreuth in 1958–60 and was an outstanding Marschallin at Glyndebourne in 1959–60, the role she sang at her Met début in 1962.

**FRANCESCA CUZZONI**, 1698–1770. Contralto, born in Parma. Débuts: before 1716; Venice, 1718, in Pollarolo's *Ariodante* (with Faustina Bordoni). She was celebrated for the intensity of her pathetic singing and was hired, unheard, by Handel for the Royal Academy of Music at a salary of £2,000. Her first appearance in *Ottone* in January 1723 re-established the composer's pre-eminence in London, and she remained a leading member of the company until its closure in 1728, which was precipitated by her undignified rivalry with Faustina. Her later career was marked by extravagance, debt and hardship.

**HARICLEA DARCLÉE** (Hariclea Haricly), 1868–1939. Romanian soprano, born in Bucharest. She studied with J. B. Faure and made her début at the age of 20, replacing Patti as Juliette at the Opéra. She sang in St Petersburg and Nice and made a brilliant début at La Scala, 1890, as Climène in *Le Cid*, going on to create the title roles in *La Wally* (1892), *Iris* (1898) and *Tosca* (1900). From 1893 to 1910 she performed on the operatic circuit, retiring in 1918. The versatility of her voice allowed her repertory to range from *coloratura* parts (Gilda) to Wagner heroines and other dramatic roles.

**GIUSEPPE DE LUCA**, 1876–1950. Baritone, born in Rome. Début: Piacenza, 1897, as Valentin (*Faust*). He created the principal baritone roles in *Adriana Lecouvreur* (1902) and *Madama Butterfly* and sang for 8 seasons at La Scala from 1908. He starred at the Teatro Colón, Buenos Aires, and sang in Barcelona, Vienna, Moscow and St Petersburg before making his Met début in 1915 as Figaro (*Il barbiere di Siviglia*). He remained the regular Verdi baritone at the Met for 20 years, forming a great partnership with Martinelli (well documented by recordings) and also created the roles of Paquiro (*Goyescas*) and Gianni Schicchi. He made his stage farewell there in 1940 as Rigoletto.

**EMMY DESTINN** (Kittl), 1878–1930. Dramatic soprano, born in Prague. Début: Berlin (Kroll Theater), 1898, as Santuzza. She was a member of the Berlin Hofoper to 1908, making guest appearances in Bayreuth (début as Senta, 1901), where she was sponsored by Cosima Wagner, and Covent Garden (début, 1904, as Donna Anna), where she became a great favourite. She was chosen by Strauss to sing Salome in Berlin and Paris. In 1908 she made her Met début, where she partnered both Slezak and Caruso, performing with the latter in the première of *La fanciulla del West* (1910). She returned there for one post-war season before her retirement from the stage in 1920.

**PLACIDO DOMINGO**, b. 1941. Tenor, born in Madrid. At the age of 9, he went to Mexico with his parents, who were *zarzuela* singers. As a child he performed in *zarzuelas*, in which he also made his professional début (as a baritone) in 1957. His first major tenor role was Alfredo (*La traviata*) in 1960, and in 1962–5 he was a member of the opera company in Tel Aviv. His US début was at the New York City Opera in Ginastera's *Don Rodrigo*, 1966, and he first sang at the Met in 1968, at La Scala in 1969 and at Covent Garden in 1971. By 1977 he had already sung 1,209 performances in 74 roles, and he has continued to expand his singing repertory while also performing as a conductor and working as artistic director of the Washington Opera.

**JULIE DORUS-GRAS** (Julie-Aimée-Josèphe Van Steenkiste), 1805–96. Soprano, born in Valenciennes. Début: Brussels (Théâtre de la Monnaie), 1825. She sang Elvira in the performances of *La Muette de Portici* which sparked the 1830 revolution there. From 1831 she sang at the Paris Opéra, creating many roles, including Eudoxie (*La Juive*), Alice (*Robert le diable*), Marguerite de Valois (*Les Huguenots*) and Teresa (*Benvenuto Cellini*). In 1847 she sang Lucia at Drury Lane, under Berlioz.

**GILBERT-LOUIS DUPREZ**, 1806–96. Tenor and composer, born in Paris. Début: Paris (Théâtre de l'Odéon), 1825, as Almaviva (*Il barbiere di Siviglia*). Soon after this he went to Italy for further training, succeeding Nourrit as principal tenor at the Opéra in 1836. His robust technique, with a high C produced from the chest, was not to Rossini's taste, but suited the dramatic tenor roles in the new style of romantic opera, many of which (including Edgardo in *Lucia di Lammermoor*, 1835) he created. After 1847 he retired from the stage to teach singing and compose.

**MARGARITA DURASTANTI**, *fl.* 1700–34. Italian soprano. She was in Rome in 1707–8, when Handel composed *serenate* for her. She created the title role in his *Agrippina* (1709) in Venice, where she was prima donna at the Teatro San Giovanni Grisostomo until 1712. She was engaged in Parma, Naples and Dresden before joining Handel's Royal Academy of Music for its first performance in 1720, continuing to sing in the composer's operas until 1734.

**SIR GERAINT EVANS**, 1922–92. Welsh baritone. He joined the Covent Garden company in 1948, singing Figaro there in 1949. From 1950 to 1961 he sang regularly at Glyndebourne. He created many parts in British operas (particularly the works of Britten) but was best known for his characterizations of Figaro, Leporello, Papageno, Beckmesser and Falstaff, roles that were the basis of his international career (débuts at La Scala, 1960; Vienna, 1961; and Salzburg, 1962). During the 1970s he turned successfully to opera production and TV master-classes.

**CORNÉLIE FALCON**, 1814–97. Dramatic soprano, born in Paris. Début: Paris Opéra, 1832, as Isabelle (*Robert le diable*), after which she created powerful roles such as Rachel (*La Juive*) and Valentine (*Les Huguenots*), partnering Nourrit, her teacher. In 1837 she lost her voice and was forced to retire the following year. The great dramatic soprano roles in romantic opera are still known as *falcon* roles in her honour.

**FARINELLI** (Carlo Broschi), 1705–82. Italian *castrato* soprano. A pupil of Porpora, he made his operatic début in Rome in 1722 in his master's *Eomene*. Following a contest with the rival *castrato* Bernacchi in 1727 he took lessons in *coloratura* technique from his adversary, so that by the time he arrived in London in 1734 to sing for the Opera of the Nobility he had perfected his art and was received with unparalleled adulation. He was in Spain from 1737 to 1758, then lived in retirement in Bologna.

**GERALDINE FARRAR**, 1882–1967. American soprano, the daughter of a professional baseball player. Début (after study with Lilli Lehmann): Berlin Hofoper, 1901, as Marguerite. She sang at Monte Carlo for three seasons, 1903–6, then returned to the USA, where she became a favourite performer at the Met, 1906–22. Her most successful roles were Butterfly (she partnered Caruso in the US première, 1907) and Carmen, which she also played in two silent movies (1915, 1919). She created the title role of *Suor Angelica* in 1918. She made many recordings for Victor, later introducing the celebrated Metropolitan Opera radio broadcasts.

**JEAN-BAPTISTE FAURE**, 1830–1914. French baritone. Début: Paris (Opéra-Comique), 1852, in Massé's *Galathée*. He remained the leading baritone at the Opéra-Comique (also singing at the Opéra and at Covent Garden) until his retirement in 1876, with a wide repertory of roles (several of which he created), including Figaro (Mozart), Don Giovanni, Iago (Rossini), Assur (*Semiramide*), Guillaume Tell, Méphistophélès, Nélusko (*L'Africaine*), Peter the Great (*L'Etoile du nord*), Lothario (*Mignon*) and Hamlet – his last role on stage. He taught singing at the Conservatoire from 1857.

**DIETRICH FISCHER-DIESKAU**, b. 1925. German baritone. Operatic début: Berlin (Städtische Oper), 1948, as Posa (*Don Carlos*). Following that, he developed a wide repertory of roles in the operas of Mozart, Gluck, Verdi, Wagner, Strauss, Busoni, Berg, Hindemith and others, while maintaining a career as a peerless concert singer. He created roles in several new operas, including Henze's *Elegy for Young Lovers* and Reimann's *Lear* (in which he was partnered by his wife, Julia Varady). He has also become a distinguished conductor.

**KIRSTEN FLAGSTAD**, 1895–1962. Norwegian dramatic soprano. Début: Oslo (National Theatre), 1912, as Nuri (*Tiefland*). She remained with the National Opera Company until the start of her international career: at Bayreuth (1933–4); the Met (début as Sieglinde, 1935); and Covent Garden (début as Isolde, 1936). Isolde was her most famous role, which she sang at the Met until 1941, returning in 1951 and giving her farewell performance there the following year. Many of her superb Wagner performances (as well as her interpretations of Dido and Leonore) are preserved on recordings. She was director of the Norwegian Opera 1958–60.

**FILIPPO GALLI**, 1783–1853. Italian bass, born in Rome. He began his career as a tenor (début in Naples, 1801), but resumed it, after an illness, as a bass (début in Venice, 1812). Rossini created several of his finest bass roles for him, and Henry VIII in Donizetti's *Anna Bolena* was also written for him. During the mid-1830s he sang with the Mexico City Opera.

**AMELITA GALLI-CURCI**, 1889–1963. Italian soprano, born in Milan. Début: Trani, 1906, as Gilda, the role in which she also made her débuts in Rome (Teatro Costanzi, 1910) and in the USA (Chicago Opera, 1916), where she went after Italy had joined the war. She was one of the outstanding stars in Chicago until 1924, and at the Met from 1921 (début as Violetta) to 1930. One of the finest recording artists of the pre-electric period.

**MANUEL DEL POPOLO VICENTE GARCIA** (sen.), 1775–1832. Tenor, composer, teacher and manager, born in Seville. He made his mark as a singer and composer in Spain from 1798 and sang with success in Paris from 1808 to 1811. He was then engaged by Barbaia for Naples, where he created several roles for Rossini, including (in Rome) Almaviva in *Il barbiere di Siviglia*. He returned to Paris in 1816, going on to London because of Catalani's disastrous management of the Théâtre-Italien, but coming back again in 1819. In 1825 he took his family and a small group of other singers to New York, where they put on the celebrated season at the Park Theatre, then continued to Mexico. He was back in Paris in 1829, active as a teacher: his pupils included Nourrit, as well as his son Manuel and daughter Pauline, both of whom were among the most influential singing teachers of the century.

**MARY GARDEN**, 1874–1967. Soprano, born in Aberdeen but taken to the USA as a child. Débuts: Paris, 1896; Opéra-Comique, 1900, in mid-performance as Louise, replacing Marthe Rioton who was taken ill. In 1902 she created Mélisande there; the director, Albert Carré, was threatened with legal action and a duel by Maeterlinck (who wanted his lover, Georgette Leblanc, to have the part). Garden returned to New York in 1907, singing for Hammerstein, first with the Manhattan Opera (début as Thaïs), where until 1910 she was the leading soprano in French roles, and then with the Chicago Opera. She remained with the Chicago company, of which she was appointed 'directa' in 1921–2, until 1930.

**BENIAMINO GIGLI**, 1890–1957. Italian lyric tenor. Début: Rovigo, 1914, as Enzo (*La gioconda*). His first role with the Met was Faust (*Mefistofele*) in 1920 and he sang with the company until 1934, specializing in Verdi and Puccini. He had a particularly mellifluous voice and made many recordings. He retired from the stage in 1956.

**TITO GOBBI**, 1915–84. Italian baritone. Débuts: Gubbio, 1935, as Rodolfo (*La sonnambula*); La Scala, 1942, as Belcore (*L'elisir d'amore*); USA (San Francisco Opera), 1948; Met, 1956, as Scarpia. He was the outstanding singer-actor of his generation, with a voice that, though not large, was capable of an extraordinary range of expression in a repertory of around 100 roles, of which Scarpia and Iago were among the finest. He made 26 films and retired from the stage in 1979.

**GIULIA GRISI**, 1811–69. Dramatic soprano born in Milan. Début: Milan, 1828, as Emma (*Zelmira*). Two years later Bellini wrote the role of Giulietta for her and in 1831 she created Adalgisa (to Pasta's Norma). She was soon to assume the mantle of Pasta, who had been one of her teachers, though Grisi's style was purer, if less expressive. In 1832 she broke her contract with Milan and made her Paris début (Théâtre-Italien) as Semiramide. She was one of the celebrated quartet (with Rubini, Tamburini and Lablache) who took part in the première of *I puritani* in 1835 there. In 1844 she married Mario (who had replaced Rubini in the quartet) and they performed together in Paris (to 1849), London (to 1861) and the USA (1854).

**HANS HOTTER**, b. 1909. German bass-baritone and opera producer. Début: Troppau, 1930. This was followed by engagements in Prague (1932–4), Hamburg (1934–45), Munich (from 1934), Berlin (from 1939) and Vienna (from 1939). He made his Met début in 1950 as the Holländer and was the outstanding Wotan in the post-war seasons at Bayreuth. His repertory of nearly 120 roles included many in operas by 20th-century German composers, as well as those in more familiar works by Wagner, Verdi, Mozart, Strauss and Puccini, to which his voice and presence always brought great dignity. Among his many productions (the first – *Siegfried* – in Strasbourg, 1954) his *Ring* cycles at Covent Garden (1961–4) were outstanding. He retired from the stage in 1972 and became a notable teacher.

**MARIA JERITZA** (Jedlitzka), 1887–1982. Soprano, born in Brno. Débuts (after singing in the chorus of the Brno Opera): Olomouc, 1910, as Elsa; Vienna (Volksoper), 1911, as Elisabeth (*Tannhäuser*). She joined the Hofoper at the request of Emperor Franz Josef, who had seen her play Rosalinde (*Die Fledermaus*) in Ischl. She created Strauss's Ariadne (Stuttgart, 1912) and the Empress (*Die Frau ohne Schatten*) (Vienna, 1919), and Marietta (Hamburg, 1920) in Korngold's *Die tote Stadt*. At the Met, 1921–32, she was unrivalled in German roles and as Tosca and Turandot.

**LUIGI LABLACHE**, 1794–1858. Neapolitan bass. Début: Naples (Teatro San Carlino), 1812, as *buffo* bass in Fioravanti's *La molinara*. He later sang heroic roles, in Palermo, Naples and at the Théâtre-Italien, Paris. In 1830 he made his début in London, where he was to be a great favourite, in *Il matrimonio segreto*, and in 1836–7 he was singing master to Princess Victoria just before she became queen. He was a member of the 'Puritani Quartet' (see Grisi) and, with his powerful but flexible voice and enormous stature, was a towering figure in the world of music.

**LILLI LEHMANN**, 1848–1929. German soprano. Début: Prague, 1868, as First Boy in *Die Zauberflöte*. In 1870 her brilliant *coloratura* singing won her an engagement at the Berlin Hofoper, which became a life contract in 1876. That year she sang Woglinde, Helmwige and the Wood Bird in the first Bayreuth *Ring*, having been coached in the roles by Wagner the previous summer. In 1880 she made her London début (Violetta at Her Majesty's), and she sang Isolde in the English première of *Tristan und Isolde* (Covent Garden, 1884). In 1885 she broke her contract with Berlin to sing in New York (Isolde), where she appeared for several seasons, having been banned from the stage in Germany. She returned to Bayreuth to sing Brünnhilde in the complete *Ring* cycle in 1896. In all, she performed 170 roles in 119 operas. She was later an outstanding teacher.

**LOTTE LEHMANN**, 1888–1976. German lyric-dramatic soprano. Début: Hamburg, 1910, as Second Boy in *Die Zauberflöte*. She was engaged for twenty years at the Vienna Hofoper, where she was known especially for her interpretation of Richard Strauss roles, several of which she created. She later sang in the USA (début, 1930, in Chicago as Sieglinde), becoming a US citizen in 1945. After retiring from the stage, she became a highly influential singing teacher.

**NICOLAS LEVASSEUR**, 1791–1871. French dramatic bass. Opéra début: 1813, in Grétry's *La Caravane de Caire*. He sang in London in 1815 and joined the Paris Théâtre-Italien in 1819, where his first role was the Count (*Le nozze di Figaro*). However, he came to prominence as a result of his performance in Meyerbeer's *Margherita d'Anjou* at La Scala in 1820 and was subsequently to take leading roles in the romantic operas of Rossini, Donizetti, Halévy and Meyerbeer at the Opéra for over 25 years.

**ROSALIE LEVASSEUR**, 1749–1826. French soprano. She was engaged at the Paris Opéra from 1766 to 1785. In 1774 she took the role of Amor in Gluck's *Orphée et Euridice* (in which the heroine was sung by Arnould). Thereafter she was chosen by the composer for the title roles in his subsequent operas in preference to Arnould, creating the roles of Alceste, Armide and Iphigénie (en Tauride).

**JENNY LIND**, 1820–87. Swedish soprano. Début: at the Swedish court, 1838, as Agathe (*Der Freischütz*). She came to Paris in 1841 and studied with Manuel Garcia, jun., singing at the Opéra the following year, though without securing an engagement. In 1844–6, as she toured Germany and Austria, her reputation began to soar, and her London début in 1847, as Alice in *Robert le diable*, was sensational: the compass of her voice and its astonishing purity and agility were unprecedented. She remained on the operatic stage only two more years, turning in 1849 to concert singing. In the words of a later commentator: 'Her private life was unusually serene, impeccable and generous.'

**FÉLIA LITVINNE** (Françoise-Jeanne Schütz), 1861–1936. Dramatic soprano, born in St Petersburg. She studied with Maurel and Viardot. Début: Paris (Théâtre-Italien), 1883. She sang for Mapleson at the New York Academy in 1885 and two years later sang Brünnhilde in the first French *Walküre* at the Théâtre de la Monnaie, Brussels. She also sang Wagnerian roles at the Met, where she made her début (in *Les Huguenots*) in 1896. From 1890 she was engaged by the Imperial Theatres in Moscow and St Petersburg, joining Diaghilev's company in 1907 in Paris, where she was later to settle.

**PAULINE LUCCA**, 1841–1908. Viennese soprano. Début: Olomouc, 1859, as Elvira (*Ernani*). After Meyerbeer had heard her sing Norma in Prague she was engaged in Berlin, where she was romantically linked with the Emperor, but broke her life contract with the Hofoper to sing at the New York Academy in 1872. She was a member of the Vienna Hofoper from 1874 to 1889, where her roles included Carmen, Mignon, Cherubino and Zerlina (in both *Don Giovanni* and *Fra Diavolo*). Her ferocious temperament made her an outstanding Carmen, and she was the first to sing the role, in 1882, at Covent Garden, where she had first appeared, partnering Mario, in the 1860s.

**MARIA MALIBRAN**, 1808–36. Dramatic contralto (extending to the soprano register), born in Paris. The daughter of Manuel Garcia, sen. Following a juvenile appearance at the age of 5 (in Paer's *Agnese*) and studies with her father, she made her début in London in 1825 as Rosina (*Il barbiere di Siviglia*). Later that year she became the star of her father's company in New York, remaining there until 1827. She made her Paris début (Théâtre-Italien) in 1828 as Semiramide, and for the next eight years her passionate and unpredictable performances captivated Europe. She died in Manchester after a riding accident.

**MARIO** (Giovanni Mario, cavaliere di Candia), 1810–83. Tenor, of noble Sardinian birth. Débuts: Paris (Opéra), 1838, in *Robert le diable*, coached by the composer; London (Her Majesty's), 1839, as Gennaro (*Lucrezia Borgia*) with Grisi, who became his stage partner for 22 years and later his wife. He joined the Théâtre-Italien the same year, appearing in 1843 in the première of *Don Pasquale*, with Grisi, Tamburini and Lablache, with whom he formed a new 'Puritani Quartet'. He was later a noted interpreter of Gounod's Roméo and Faust and of several Verdi roles, including Alfredo, Manrico and Riccardo (*Un ballo in maschera*).

**GIOVANNI MARTINELLI**, 1885–1969. Italian tenor. Début: Milan (Teatro dal Verme), 1910, as Ernani; Puccini heard his performance and engaged him for the European première of *La fanciulla del West*. He made his Covent Garden début in *Tosca* in 1912 and his US début in the same role in Philadelphia in 1913, appearing at the Met later that year as Rodolfo. He remained one of the company's principal tenors until 1946 (his last role was Pollione to Milanov's Norma). He was an oustanding recording artist, and many of his performances, including complete recordings of *La gioconda* and *Otello* (possibly his finest role) have been preserved. His final stage appearance was as the Emperor in *Turandot* with the Seattle Opera in 1967.

**AMALIE MATERNA**, 1844–1918. Austrian soprano. Her first stage appearances were in operetta in Graz (1865) and at the Vienna Carltheater; her Hofoper début was in 1869. She sang the first Amneris and first Queen of Sheba (Goldmark) in Vienna, but her fame rests on her Wagner performances in Vienna, Bayreuth – where she was the first Brünnhilde and created the role of Kundry – and New York, where she appeared in 1884–5 and 1894. She retired from the stage in 1902 to teach.

**VICTOR MAUREL**, 1848–1923. French baritone, born in Marseille. Débuts: Paris Opéra, 1868, as Raoul (*Les Huguenots*); La Scala, 1870, in *Il Guarany*. He first sang at the New York Academy in 1873, the year of his Covent Garden début, and from that time appeared in the world's operatic capitals, though he remained on the staff of the Paris Opéra from 1879 to 1894. His repertory included Mozart and Rossini, Gounod and Meyerbeer, Wagner and Verdi – for whom he created both Iago and Falstaff – and he was also the first Tonio in *Pagliacci*. In 1909 he retired to teach singing in New York.

**DAME NELLIE MELBA** (Helen Mitchell Armstrong), 1861–1931. Australian *coloratura* soprano, born near Melbourne, from which she took her stage name. She studied with Marchesi and made her début in Brussels (Théâtre de la Monnaie) in 1887 as Gilda. This led to her engagement the following year at Covent Garden (her first role was Lucia), and appearances at the Opéra and the Met (where she partnered the de Reszke brothers). She was the star of the first season of Hammerstein's Manhattan Opera in 1906–7. Her repertory was limited, but her effortless singing of highly decorated vocal lines was outstanding. In 1922 she founded the British National Opera Company and then organized a company to tour Australia. Her gala farewell at Covent Garden took place in 1926.

**LAURITZ MELCHIOR**, 1890–1973. Danish Heldentenor. Début: Copenhagen (Royal Opera), 1913, as a baritone in *Pagliacci*. He first appeared as a tenor in 1918 and his Covent Garden début in 1924 led to an invitation from Cosima and Siegfried Wagner to sing Parsifal that year at Bayreuth. He was the outstanding Heldentenor of his era, and many of his performances are preserved on record.

**IVAN MEL'NIKOV**, 1832–1906. Russian baritone. Début: St Petersburg, 1867, in *I puritani*. He took part in the premières of many Russian operas written between 1870 and 1890, singing in all but one of Tchaikovsky's operas and also creating the roles of Don Carlos (*The Stone Guest*), Boris Godunov, the Charcoal Burner (*Maiskaya noch*) and Prince Igor. He retired from the stage in 1890.

**ANNA MILDER (-HAUPTMANN)**, 1785–1838. Austrian soprano, born in Constantinople. She was discovered by Schikaneder, who introduced her to Salieri, from whom she learned to sing opera. She made her début in Vienna in 1803 and in 1805 sang the title role in the first version of Beethoven's *Leonore*. The following year Cherubini wrote *Faniska* for her. In 1812 she gave outstanding performances in Gluck's operas in Berlin, her Iphigénie (en Tauride) being especially admired. She returned to Vienna to sing the title role in the revised version of Beethoven's opera, *Fidelio*, in 1814. She retired from the stage in 1836.

**NICOLINI** (Nicolò Grimaldi), 1673–1732. Neapolitan *castrato* contralto. He made his operatic début in 1697 in Naples, where he became associated with the works of Alessandro Scarlatti. From 1708 to 1716 he was in London, where his performances were the chief reason for the vogue for Italian opera. He created Handel's Rinaldo there in 1711. He was an accomplished actor and Addison considered him 'perhaps the greatest performer in dramatic music that ever appeared upon a stage'.

**ALBERT NIEMANN**, 1831–1917. German dramatic tenor. Début: Dessau, 1849. He studied in Paris with Duprez and was engaged in Hanover, 1860–6, and at the Berlin Hofoper, 1866–88. He sang the title role in the Paris performances of *Tannhäuser* in 1861 and took the role of Siegmund in the first Bayreuth *Ring*. He sang at the Met, 1886–8, and took part in the American premières of both *Tristan und Isolde* (as Tristan) and *Die Götterdämmerung* (as Siegfried). He retired in 1889.

**BIRGIT NILSSON**, b. 1918. Swedish dramatic soprano. Début: Stockholm (Royal Opera) as Agathe (*Der Freischütz*). The following year she sang Lady Macbeth there under Fritz Busch. Elektra (Glyndebourne, 1951) was her first major role outside Sweden. Her early international performances in Wagner were at Bayreuth (Elsa, 1954; Isolde, 1957 and 1959); Covent Garden (Brünnhilde, 1957); and the Met (Isolde, 1958). She went on to become the finest Wagner soprano of the post-war period. Other roles in which she was particularly admired include Puccini's Tosca and Turandot and Strauss's Salome and Elektra.

**CHRISTINE NILSSON**, 1843–1921. Swedish soprano. Début: Paris (Théâtre-Lyrique), 1864, as Violetta. She sang there for four years, then at the Opéra until 1870. She sang at the New York Academy and in London during the years 1870–4, returning to New York as one of the stars of the first season of the Metropolitan Opera in 1883–4. Her voice had a compass of two and a half octaves, but she was more successful in the lyric roles of Gounod and Thomas than in dramatic parts.

**ADOLPHE NOURRIT**, 1802–39. French tenor, born in Montpellier. He studied with Garcia, sen., and with his father, whom he succeeded as principal tenor at the Paris Opéra in 1826. He had made his début there in 1821 as Pylade (*Iphigénie en Tauride*). He was a highly intelligent musician (also a composer and teacher at the Conservatoire) and created many of the leading roles in French romantic opera, including Robert (le diable), Raoul de Nevers, Comte Ory, Arnold (*Guillaume Tell*), Masaniello (*La Muette de Portici*) and Eléazar (*La Juive*). He left the Opéra in 1837 and sang in Italy for two years, but succumbed to depression caused by ill health and committed suicide in Naples.

**GIUDITTA PASTA** (Negri), 1797–1865. Dramatic soprano, born in Milan. Her initial appearance in 1816 at the Théâtre-Italien in Paris was not a success and she made a second début in 1821. Her greatest fame came with the operas written for her in the early 1830s: Donizetti's *Anna Bolena* and Bellini's *La sonnambula* and *Norma*, which gave full scope to her great vocal compass and powerful dramatic gifts. However, these were unable to compensate for the deterioration of her voice, and she was replaced in public favour by Malibran and Grisi.

**ADELINA PATTI**, 1843–1919. Italian-American *coloratura* soprano, born in Madrid. Débuts: New York (Academy of Music), 1859, as Lucia; London (Covent Garden), 1861, as Amina (*La sonnambula*); Paris (Théâtre-Italien), 1862, as Amina. The ideal soprano of the Victorian era, Patti employed her amazing vocal technique, with a sweet, pure and even voice, in a repertory of no more than thirty roles, which she sang for 35 years, retiring from the stage to her fairytale Welsh castle in 1895.

**LUCIANO PAVAROTTI**, b. 1935. Tenor, born in Modena. Début: Reggio Emilia, 1961, as Rodolfo. He sang Alfredo at Covent Garden in 1965, making his US début in 1966, after which he joined Joan Sutherland in a tour of romantic opera performances. Although his repertory has widened, the brilliance of his voice, with its ringing high Cs, is particularly well suited to roles originally sung by Nourrit and Duprez.

**FANNY PERSIANI**, 1812–67. Italian *coloratura* soprano, the daughter and pupil of the tenor Niccolò Tacchinardi. Début: Livorno, 1832. She possessed a brilliant vocal technique which was the inspiration for the roles Donizetti wrote for her: Lucia di Lammermoor (1835) and Linda di Chamounix (1842). She sang at the Théâtre-Italien in 1837 and in London from 1838, where her husband, the composer Giuseppe Persiani, bought the lease of Covent Garden in 1846. In 1849 she gave a series of farewell performances at the theatre and retired to Paris.

**OSIP AFANASYEVICH PETROV**, 1806–78. Russian bass-baritone. Stage début: 1826. He was discovered and immediately engaged by an official of the Imperial Theatres, who saw him performing in 1830 on a country stage. He made his début in St Petersburg as Sarastro, going on to create many of the principal male roles in Russian opera: Glinka's Susanin and Ruslan; Dargomizhsky's Miller (*Rusalka*) and Leporello; Oziya and Vladimir in Serov's *Judith* and *Rogneda*; Varlaam in *Boris Godunov*; Ivan the Terrible in *Pskovityanka*; Prince Gudal in Rubinstein's *Demon* and Maya in Tchaikovsky's *Vakula the Smith*. He gave his last performance the day before he died.

**EZIO PINZA**, 1892–1957. Italian bass. Début: Soncino (Cremona), 1914, as Oroveso (*Norma*). He sang in Rome from 1920 and from 1922 at La Scala, where he was selected by Toscanini to sing the title role of Boito's *Nerone* in 1924. He made his Met début in 1926 in *La Vestale* and sang there until 1948, his Don Giovanni, Méphistophélès and Boris being particularly celebrated. He began a second career in musical comedy, earning a huge new audience for his singing in Rodgers and Hammerstein's *South Pacific* in 1949.

**LILY PONS**, 1898–1976. French *coloratura* soprano. Début: Mulhouse, 1928, as Lakmé, which became her most famous role. She was taken up by Maria Gay and Giovanni Zenatello, who arranged for her to sing at the Met, where she had a sensational début as Lucia in 1931, supported by Gigli, de Luca and Pinza. She remained in the USA, appearing on radio and making movies in Hollywood, and continued to sing at the Met into the 1950s.

**ROSA PONSELLE** (Ponzillo), 1897–1981. Italian-American soprano. Début: New York (Met), 1918, as Leonora (*La forza del destino*), sponsored by Caruso, having previously appeared in vaudeville with her sister. She proved to be an outstanding singer, principally in the Italian and French repertories, and was a leading member of the company until 1936, also appearing at Covent Garden, where she made her début in 1929 as Norma. Her final performance at the Met before her retirement was as Carmen in February 1937.

**LEONTYNE PRICE**, b. 1927. African-American soprano. In 1952 she was invited by Virgil Thomson, who had heard her sing Alice Ford at the Juilliard Opera Workshop, to sing in a revival of his *Four Saints in Three Acts*. She subsequently joined the European tour of a production of *Porgy and Bess*. In 1955 she played Tosca in a TV production of the opera and her first major international role was Aida: at the San Francisco Opera, 1957; in Vienna (under Karajan) and at Covent Garden, 1958; and at La Scala, 1959. She made her Met début in 1961 as Leonora (*Il trovatore*). The richness and expressive quality of her voice made her an ideal exponent of the great dramatic soprano roles, including Leonora (*La forza del destino*), Carmen and Tosca.

**EDOUARD DE RESZKE** (Mieczislaw), 1853–1917. Polish bass, born in Warsaw. Début: Paris (Théâtre-Italien), 1876, as Amonasro, in the first Paris production of *Aida*, directed by Verdi. From 1880 to 1884 he sang with the Italian Opera, London, returning to Paris where he created Don Diègue in *Le Cid* in 1885. He made his US début in 1891 in Chicago, going on to sing in New York. An exceptional actor, excelling in both serious and comic music, his greatest role was Méphistophélès.

**JEAN DE RESZKE** (Mieczislaw), 1850–1925. Polish tenor, born in Warsaw, elder brother of Edouard. Débuts: Venice, 1874, as a baritone in the role of Alfonso (*La Favorite*); Madrid, 1879, as a tenor in the title role of *Robert le diable*. His earliest success was in Paris in the operas of Massenet, as Jean in *Hérodiade*, 1884, and in the title of *Le Cid*, which he created in 1885. He sang from 1887 in London (Drury Lane) and from 1891 at the Met, where he excelled as Don José, as Tristan and in other Wagner roles. The chief tenor of his generation, he retired to Paris in 1902 to nurture the next generation with his teaching.

**ELISABETH RETHBERG** (Lisbeth Sättler), 1894–1976. German soprano. Début: Dresden, 1915, in *Der Zigeunerbaron*. She was engaged at the Dresden opera until 1922, when she made her début at the Met as Aida. She remained with the company until 1942, singing Wagnerian roles as well as works from the French and Italian repertory and – in rivalry with Jeritza – the heroines of Richard Strauss's operas.

**GIOVANNI BATTISTA RUBINI**, 1794–1854. Italian tenor. Début: Pavia, 1814. Barbaia heard him in Venice and engaged him for Naples, where his first role was Lindoro (*L'italiana in Algeri*) in 1815. He was mostly assigned lighter comic roles and did not portray the great romantic heroes until he was engaged at the Théâtre-Italien, Paris, in 1825. He was enormously successful there, especially in the works of Bellini (he was a member of the original 'Puritani Quartet'; see Grisi), and amassed a huge fortune. From 1831 to 1843 he sang in Paris and London and in 1843 went on tour with Liszt. He is reputed to have been the first tenor to employ vibrato and the sob.

**WILHELMINE SCHRÖDER-DEVRIENT**, 1804–60. German soprano, born in Hamburg, the daughter of an actress and a baritone. Début: Vienna (Kärntnertortheater), 1821, as Pamina (*Die Zauberflöte*). The following year she sang Agathe (*Der Freischütz*) under Weber and Leonore in the presence of Beethoven. From 1823 to 1847 she sang in Dresden, with an interval in 1830–2, when she enjoyed spectacular success in Paris. In the 1840s she created three important Wagner roles: Adriano Colonna (*Rienzi*, 1842), Senta (*Der fliegende Holländer*, 1843) and Venus (*Tannhäuser*, 1845).

**ELISABETH SCHWARZKOPF**, b. 1915. German soprano. Début: Berlin (Städtische Oper), 1938. After the war she became celebrated, particularly as a Mozart singer, in Vienna and Salzburg, also creating the role of Anne Trulove in Stravinsky's *The Rake's Progress* (Venice, 1951). She also made many appearances at Covent Garden. Her operatic début in the USA was as the Marschallin at the San Francisco Opera in 1955, the role she chose for her Met début in 1964, though she had appeared in New York as early as 1958 in an American Opera Society performance of Handel's *Giulio Cesare*. A highly accomplished musician, her portrayal of Mozart and Strauss heroines had a dignity unequalled in its time.

**MARCELLA SEMBRICH** (Praxede Marcelline Kochańska), 1858–1935. Polish (Galician) *coloratura* soprano. Débuts: Athens, 1877, as Elvira (*I puritani*); London, 1880, as Lucia; New York (Met), 1883, as Lucia. This first season at the Met – in which she also sang Violetta, Gilda, Amina, Elvira (*I puritani*), Ophélie, Marguerite (*Les Huguenots*), Harriet (*Martha*), Rosina and Zerlina – was so disastrous financially that she did not return until 1898, but from 1901 to 1909 she sang there regularly. After her retirement she taught singing at the Curtis Institute, Philadelphia, and the Juilliard School, New York.

**SENESINO** (Francesco Bernardi), *c.* 1680–1758. Italian *castrato* contralto, born in Siena. He studied in Bologna with Bernacchi and sang in Venice in 1707–8. By 1719 he was a member of the Dresden court opera, where Handel heard him in Lotti's *Teofane* and engaged him for his Royal Academy of Music. Senesino was the male principal of the company for 15 seasons until he defected in 1733 to the rival Opera of the Nobility, creating roles in virtually all Handel's operas of this period.

**LEO SLEZAK**, 1873–1946. Moravian tenor. Début: Brno, 1896, as Lohengrin. He was a member of the Breslau opera until he was engaged by Mahler for the Vienna Hofoper, where he was a principal tenor from 1901 to 1926. A fine Wagnerian singer, he also excelled in dramatic roles in the Italian repertory, notably Canio, Manrico and Otello, the role in which he made his Met début in 1909. He sang at the Met for three seasons and, with his huge figure, his warmth and musicianship, endeared himself to the New York public as much to the Viennese. His memoirs are the best and wittiest to have been written by a singer.

**ELISABETH SÖDERSTRÖM**, b. 1927. Swedish soprano. Début: Drottningholm, 1947, as Bastienne. She joined the Swedish Royal Opera and made her Glyndebourne début in 1957 as the Composer (*Ariadne*). For her Met début, 1959, she sang Susanna, and Mozart and Strauss were pillars of her inter-national career. She has also created roles in several contemporary operas, including Ligeti's *Le grand macabre* and Argento's *The Aspern Papers*. A great singing actress, she has been a superb interpreter of the heroines of Janáček's operas, many of she recorded under Sir Charles Mackerras.

**HENRIETTE SONTAG**, 1806–54. *Coloratura* soprano, born in Koblenz. After appearing in many juvenile roles, she made her adult début in Prague, 1821, in Boieldieu's *Jean de Paris*. She was engaged at the Kärntnertortheater the following year, and in 1823 created the role of Weber's Euryanthe. Débuts in Berlin (1825, as Isabella in *L'italiana in Algeri*) and at the Théâtre-Italien, Paris (1826, as Rosina), followed, but she interrupted her career when she married in 1828. She resumed her career in 1849, touring in England, USA and Mexico, where she died of cholera. Her final role was Lucrezia Borgia.

**CONCHITA SUPERVIA**, 1895–1936. *Coloratura* mezzo-soprano, born in Barcelona. Début: Buenos Aires (Teatro Colón), 1910. The following year she sang Octavian in the first Italian *Rosenkavalier* in Rome. In 1912 she played Carmen in Bologna, singing with the Havana Opera in 1914 and in Chicago in 1915–16. She was outstanding in travesty roles (Hänsel, Cherubino), but her finest achievement was the revival of Rossini's great mezzo heroines, especially Cenerentola.

**DAME JOAN SUTHERLAND**, b. 1926. Australian soprano, born in Sydney. Débuts: Sydney, 1951; Covent Garden, 1952, as the First Lady (*Die Zauberflöte*). Working with her husband, Richard Bonynge, she developed a brilliantly flexible vocal technique, allowing her to give masterly performances both of baroque and of romantic opera. Having sung several Handel heroines with the Handel Opera Society in the late 1950s, she was a devastating Alcina in Zeffirelli's sumptuous Venice production in 1960, which followed their much acclaimed collaboration on *Lucia di Lammermoor* at Covent Garden the previous year. Her performances, in partnership with such artists as Pavarotti and Marilyn Horne, were captured in a series of outstanding recordings.

**FRANCESCO TAMAGNO**, 1851–1903. Italian tenor. He joined the opera chorus in his native Turin in 1870, graduating to second tenor roles three years later, but his offical début was in Palermo in 1874 as Riccardo (*Un ballo in maschera*). This was followed in 1877 by his début at La Scala, where, during the 1880s, he sang a series of Verdi heroes: Gabriele (1881, in the revised *Simon Boccanegra*); Don Carlos (1884, in the revised opera); and Otello (1887). This earned him an international reputation and he sang Otello and other heroic roles, including Radames, Vasco de Gama, Arnold and Samson, at Covent Garden and the Met in 1894–5.

**ANTONIO TAMBURINI**, 1800–76. Italian lyric bass. Début: Cento, 1818. He was engaged by Barbaia for La Scala, Milan, in 1824 and sang in many premières of operas by Donizetti and Bellini, earning particular acclaim for his role in *La straniera*, 1829. From 1832 to 1841 he was engaged at the Théâtre-Italien in Paris and became a member of the 'Puritani Quartet', performing in the major operatic centres of Europe.

**RENATA TEBALDI**, b. 1922. Italian soprano. Début: Rovigo, 1944, as Elena (*Mefistofele*). In 1946 she was chosen by Toscanini to take part in the concert for the reopening of La Scala, and she became the leading soprano of the company. She made her Met début in 1955 as Desdemona. Her rather static stage presence contrasted with that of Callas, leading to a rivalry which was fanned by the press. Her glorious voice, preserved in many recordings, was perfectly suited to the Italian repertory.

**DAME KIRI TE KANAWA**, b. 1944. New Zealand soprano. Début: London (Covent Garden), 1970, as a Flower Maiden (*Parsifal*) . Soon after this she sang the Countess (*Le nozze di Figaro*) there, the role in which she made her US début at Sante Fe in 1973. Her Met début followed in 1974, when she took over the role of Desdemona from Teresa Stratas. She has been the leading soprano at Covent Garden for over 25 years, and is particularly successful in the lyric roles of Mozart, Verdi and Strauss.

**LAWRENCE TIBBETT**, 1896–1960. American baritone, born in Bakersfield, Ca. His operatic début at the Hollywood Bowl in 1923 was soon followed by his first major role, as Valentin to Chaliapin's Méphisto at the Met. His Met reputation was established with his interpretation of Ford in *Falstaff*, 1925, which eclipsed the rest of the cast (including Scotti, Gigli and Bori). He created roles in several American and other new operas, but also pursued a career in light opera, radio and movies. He retired from the operatic stage in 1950.

**THERESE TIETJENS**, 1831–77. German soprano. Début: Hamburg, 1849, as Lucrezia Borgia, which was also to be the last role she sang. From 1858 she appeared principally in London, though she also sang at the New York Academy, and her great dramatic gifts in a wide range of roles made her the leading prima donna of the period. She continued to perform until shortly before her death.

**PAULINE VIARDOT**, 1821–1910. Mezzo-soprano and teacher, born in Paris, the daughter of Manuel Garcia, sen. She studied the piano with Liszt and singing with her parents, making her operatic début in Brussels in 1837 as Rossini's Desdemona. In 1839 she was engaged at the Théâtre-Italien by its manager, Louis Viardot, whom she married. At the Opéra she created the roles of Fides (*Le Prophète*, 1849) and Sapho (1851) and was particularly acclaimed in the title roles of Gluck's *Orphée* and *Alceste*, revived by Berlioz in 1859 and 1861. She retired in 1863 and became, like her brother, an extremely influential singing teacher, as well as giving help and encouragement to many musicians.

**JON VICKERS**, b. 1926. Canadian heroic tenor. Début: Toronto Opera Festival, 1952, as the Duke (*Rigoletto*). At his Covent Garden début, 1957, he sang King Gustav in a restored version of *Un ballo in maschera*, and the following year was a superb Enée in the great production of *Les Troyens*. Débuts followed at Bayreuth (Siegmund, 1958), Vienna (Canio, 1959) and the Met (Canio, 1960). One of the great Wagnerian tenors of the age and an unrivalled Florestan, he has also been acclaimed in the French repertory and for his intensely moving portrayal of Peter Grimes.

# DISCOGRAPHY

There are countless books and catalogues (several listed in the Bibliography on p. 240) which offer details and recommendations on preferred opera recordings. The aim of the list which follows is a little different; it is a selection of recordings of complete operas from the earliest works up to the 1990s which preserve performances of some of the greatest conductors and singers of the past fifty years and illustrate changing styles of interpretation. Inevitably, some favourite operas and performances will have been omitted in order to include a wide variety of artists in little over one hundred recordings – to offer a brief chronicle of recorded opera since the advent of stereophonic sound. A handful of outstanding pre-stereo recordings have been included, but great voices from the early years of recording are generally best heard in the compilations that are widely available. Operas are listed in order of their first performance, and the date of the recording follows the details of orchestra and conductor.

1600 PERI ***Euridice*** Ensemble Arpeggio, Roberto De Caro (1992)
*Euridice/Tragedia/Proserpina:* Gloria Banditelli; *Orfeo:* Gian Paolo Fagotto; *Aminta/Radamanto:* Mario Cecchetti; *Arcetro:* Giuseppe Zambon; *Caronte:* Sergio Foresti; *Dafne:* Rossana Bertini; *Venere:* Monica Benvenuti; *Plutone:* Furio Zanasi

1607 MONTEVERDI ***Orfeo*** New London Consort, Philip Pickett (1991)
*Orfeo:* John Mark Ainslie; *Euridice:* Julia Gooding; *La Musica/Proserpina/Messenger:* Catherine Bott; *Hope:* Christopher Robson; *Apollo:* Andrew King; *Plutone:* Michael George; *Caronte:* Simon Grant

1642 MONTEVERDI ***L'incoronazione di Poppea*** Concentus Musicus Wien, Nicolaus Harnoncourt (1974)
*Poppea:* Helen Donath; *Nerone:* Elisabeth Söderström; *Ottavia:* Cathy Berberian; *Ottone:* Paul Esswood; *Seneca:* Giancarlo Luccardi; *Drusilla:* Rotraud Hansmann; *Nurse:* Maria Minetto; *Arnalta:* Carlo Gaifa; *Lucano:* Philip Langridge

1651 CAVALLI ***Calisto*** London Philharmonic Orchestra, Raymond Leppard (1971)
*Calisto:* Ileana Cotrubas; *Diana:* Janet Baker; *Endimione:* James Bowman; *Linfea:* Hugues Cuénod; *Pane:* Federico Davià; *Mercurio* Peter Gottlieb; *Giove:* Ugo Trama; *Giunone:* Teresa Kubiak; Glyndebourne Festival Chorus

1656 CESTI ***Orontea*** Giacinta Instrumental Ensemble, René Jacobs (1982)
*Orontea:* Helga Müller-Molinari; *Love:* Cettina Cadelo; *Silandra:* Isabelle Poulenard; *Giacinta:* Jill Feldman; *Ceronte:* Gregory Reinhart; *Alidoro:* René Jacobs; *Corindo:* David James; *Gelone:* Gastoni Sarti; *Philosophy:* Andrea Bierbaum

1676 LULLY ***Atys*** Arts Florissants Orchestra, William Christie (1987)
*Atys:* Guy de Mey; *Sangaride/Iris:* Agnès Mellon; *Cybèle:* Guillemette Laurens; *Célénus:* Jean-François Gardeil; *Time:* Bernard Delétré; *Flore:* Monique Zanetti; *Melpomène:* Arlette Steyer; *Sleep:* Gilles Ragon; Arts Florissants Chorus

1689 PURCELL ***Dido and Aeneas*** Academy of Ancient Music, Christopher Hogwood (1992)
*Dido:* Catherine Bott; *Aeneas:* John Mark Ainsley; *Belinda:* Emma Kirkby; *Sorceress:* David Thomas; Academy of Ancient Music Chorus

1693 CHARPENTIER ***Médée*** Arts Florissants Orchestra, William Christie (1994)
*Médée:* Jill Feldman; *Créon:* Jacques Bona; *Créuse:* Agnès Mellon; *Jason:* Gilles Ragon; *Oronte:* Philippe Cantor; *Nérine:* Sophie Boulin; Arts Florissants Chorus

1724 HANDEL ***Giulio Cesare*** Concerto Köln, René Jacobs (1991)
*Giulio Cesare:* Jennifer Larmore; *Cleopatra:* Barbara Schlick; *Cornelia:* Bernarda Fink; *Sesto:* Marianne Rørholm; *Tolomeo:* Derek Lee Ragin; *Achille:* Furio Zanasi

1731 HASSE ***Cleofide*** Cappella Coloniensis, William Christie (1987)
*Cleofide:* Emma Kirkby; *Erissena:* Agnès Mellon; *Poro:* Derek Lee Ragin; *Alessandro:* Dominique Visse; *Gandarte:* Randall Wong; *Timagene:* David Cordier

1733 PERGOLESI ***La serva padrona*** English Chamber Orchestra, Antoni Ros Marbà (1973)
*Serpina:* Carmen Bustamante; *Uberto:* Renato Capecchi

1734 VIVALDI ***L'Olimpiade*** Clemencic Consort, René Clemencic (1990)
*Clistene:* Andrew Walker Schultze; *Aristea:* Lucia Meeuwsen; *Argene:* Elisabeth von Magnus; *Megacle:* Mieke van der Sluis; *Licida:* Gérard Lesne; *Aminta:* Aris Christofellis; *Alcandro:* William Oberholtzer; La Cappella Choir

1735 HANDEL ***Alcina*** London Symphony Orchestra, Richard Bonynge (1962)
*Alcina:* Joan Sutherland; *Ruggiero:* Teresa Berganza; *Bradamante:* Monica Sinclair; *Oronte:* Luigi Alva; *Morgana:* Graziella Sciutti; *Oberto:* Mirella Freni; *Melisso:* Ezio Flagello

1737 RAMEAU ***Castor et Pollux*** Concentus Musicus Wien, Nicolaus Harnoncourt (1972)
*Castor/Love:* Zeger Vandersteene; *Pollux:* Gérard Souzay; *Télaïre/Minerve:* Jeanette Scovotti; *Phébé:* Norma Lerer; *Jupiter:* Jacques Villisech; *Mars:* Rolf Leanderson; *Vénus:* Märta Schéle; *High Priest:* Sven-Erik Alexandersson; Stockholm Chamber Choir

1760 PICCINNI ***Cecchina (La buona figliuola)*** Pro Arte Orchestra, Bruno Campanella (1990)
*Cecchina:* Maria Angeles Peters; *Marchese della Conchiglia:* Giuseppe Morino; *Tagliaferro:* Bruno Praticò; *Cavaliere Armidoro:* Alessandra Ruffini; *Marchesa Lucinda:* Gabriella Morigi; *Mengotto:* Pietro Spagnoli; *Paoluccia:* Sara Mingardo; *Sandrina:* Maria Cristina Zanni

1762 GLUCK ***Orfeo ed Euridice*** English Baroque Soloists, John Eliot Gardiner (1991)
*Orfeo:* Derek Lee Ragin; *Euridice:* Sylvia McNair; *Amor:* Cyndia Sieden; Monteverdi Choir

1772 MOZART ***Lucio Silla*** Concentus Musicus Wien, Nicolaus Harnoncourt (1989; live)
*Lucio Silla:* Peter Schreier; *Giunia:* Edita Gruberová; *Cecilio:* Cecilia Bartoli; *Lucio Cinna:* Yvonne Kenny; *Celia:* Dawn Upshaw; Arnold Schönberg Choir

1779 GLUCK ***Iphigénie en Tauride*** La Scala Orchestra, Riccardo Muti (1992)
*Iphigénie:* Carol Vaness; *Pylade:* Gösta Winbergh; *Oreste:* Thomas Allen; *Diane:* Sylvie Brunet; *Thoas:* Giorgio Surian; La Scala Chorus

1781 MOZART ***Idomeneo*** English Baroque Soloists, John Eliot Gardiner (1990; live)
*Idomeneo:* Anthony Rolfe Johnson; *Idamante:* Anne Sofie von Otter; *Ilia:* Sylvia McNair; *Electra:* Hillevi Martinpelto; *Arbace:* Nigel Robson; *High Priest:* Glenn Winslade; *Oracle:* Cornelius Hauptmann; Monteverdi Choir

1782 MOZART ***Die Entführung aus dem Serail*** Bavarian Radio Symphony Orchestra, Eugen Jochum (1965)
*Constanze:* Erika Köth; *Belmonte:* Fritz Wunderlich; *Blonde:* Lotte Schädle; *Pedrillo:* Friedrich Lenz; *Osmin:* Endre Koréh; Bavarian State Opera Chorus

1782 HAYDN ***Orlando Paladino*** Lausanne Chamber Orchestra, Antal Dorati (1976)
*Angelica:* Arleen Auger; *Eurilla:* Elly Ameling; *Alcina:* Gwendoline Killebrew; *Orlando:* George Shirley; *Medoro:* Claes Hakon Ahnsjö; *Rodomonte:* Benjamin Luxon; *Pasquale:* Domenico Trimarchi

1786 MOZART ***Le nozze di Figaro*** London Philharmonic Orchestra, Georg Solti (1981)
*Figaro:* Samuel Ramey; *Susanna:* Lucia Popp; *Count Almaviva:* Thomas Allen; *Countess Almaviva:* Kiri te Kanawa; *Cherubino:* Frederike von Stade; *Marcellina:* Jane Berbié; *Bartolo:* Kurt Moll; *Don Basilio:* Robert Tear; *Don Curzio:* Philip Langridge; *Antonio:* Giorgio Tadeo; *Barberina:* Yvonne Kenny; London Opera Chorus

1787 MOZART ***Don Giovanni*** Philharmonia Orchestra, Carlo Maria Giulini (1959)
*Don Giovanni:* Eberhard Wächter; *Donna Anna:* Joan Sutherland; *Donna Elvira:* Elisabeth Schwarzkopf; *Zerlina:* Graziella Sciutti; *Don Ottavio:* Luigi Alva; *Leporello:* Giuseppe Taddei; *Masetto:* Piero Cappuccilli; *Commendatore:* Gottlob Frick; Philharmonia Chorus

1790 MOZART ***Così fan tutte*** Glyndebourne Festival Orchestra, Fritz Busch (1935)
*Fiordiligi:* Ina Souez; *Dorabella:* Luise Helletsgruber; *Ferrando:* Heddle Nash; *Guglielmo:* Willi Domgraf-Fassbänder; *Don Alfonso:* John Brownlee; *Despina:* Irene Eisinger; Glyndebourne Festival Chorus

1791 MOZART ***Die Zauberflöte*** Vienna Philharmonic Orchestra, Wilhelm Furtwängler (1951; live)
*Pamina:* Irmgard Seefried *Queen of the Night:* Wilma Lipp *Tamino:* Anton Dermota *Papageno:* Erich Kunz *Sarastro:* Josef Greindl *Sprecher:* Paul Schöffler *Monostatos:* Peter Klein Vienna State Opera Chorus

1792 CIMAROSA ***Il matrimonio segreto*** English Chamber Orchestra, Daniel Barenboim (1975/6)
*Geronimo:* Dietrich Fischer-Dieskau; *Elisetta:* Julia Varady; *Carolina:* Arleen Auger; *Fidalma:* Júlia Hamari; *Count Robinson:* Alberto Rinaldi; *Paolino:* Ryland Davies

1807 SPONTINI ***La Vestale*** La Scala Orchestra, Riccardo Muti (1993; live)
*Licinio:* Anthony Michaels Moore; *Giulia:* Karen Huffstodt; *Cinna:* J. Patrick Raftery; *Pontifex Maximus:* Dimitri Kavrakos; *Chief Vestal:* Denyce Graves; La Scala Chorus

1813 ROSSINI ***L'italiana in Algeri*** Vienna Philharmonic Orchestra, Claudio Abbado (1987)
*Isabella:* Agnes Baltsa; *Lindoro:* Frank Lopardo; *Taddeo:* Enzo Dara; *Mustafà:* Ruggiero Raimondi; *Elvira:* Patrizia Pace; *Zulma:* Anna Gonda; *Haly:* Alessandro Corbelli; Vienna State Opera Chorus

1814 BEETHOVEN ***Fidelio*** Philharmonia Orchestra, Otto Klemperer (1962)
*Leonore:* Christa Ludwig; *Florestan:* Jon Vickers; *Don Pizarro:* Walter Berry; *Rocco:* Gottlob Frick; *Marzelline:* Ingeborg Hallstein; *Jaquino:* Gerhard Unger; *Don Fernando:* Franz Crass; Philharmonia Chorus

1816 ROSSINI ***Il barbiere di Siviglia*** Bologna Teatro Comunale Orchestra, Giuseppe Patanè (1988)
*Figaro:* Leo Nucci; *Rosina:* Cecilia Bartoli; *Count Almaviva:* William Matteuzzi; *Doctor Bartolo:* Enrico Fissore; *Don Basilio:* Paata Burchuladze; Bologna Teatro Comunale Chorus

1817 ROSSINI ***La Cenerentola*** London Symphony Orchestra, Claudio Abbado (1971)
*Angelina:* Teresa Berganza; *Don Ramiro:* Luigi Alva; *Dandini:* Renato Capecchi; *Don Magnifico:* Paolo

Montarsolo; *Clorinda:* Margherita Guglielmi; *Tisbe:* Laura Zannini; *Alidoro:* Ugo Trama; Scottish Opera Chorus

**1821 WEBER *Der Freischütz*** Bavarian Radio Symphony Orchestra, Eugen Jochum (1959)
*Agathe:* Irmgard Seefried; *Max:* Richard Holm; *Ännchen:* Rita Streich; *Kaspar:* Kurt Böhme; *Ottakar:* Eberhard Wächter; *Hermit:* Walter Kreppel; Bavarian Radio Chorus

**[1821] SCHUBERT *Alfonso und Estrella*** Berlin State Opera Orchestra, Otmar Suitner (1978)
*Alfonso:* Peter Schreier; *Estrella:* Edith Mathis; *Froila:* Dietrich Fischer-Dieskau; *Mauregato:* Hermann Prey; *Adolfo:* Theo Adam; Berlin Radio Chorus

**1829 ROSSINI *Guglielmo Tell*** National Philharmonic Orchestra, Riccardo Chailly (1978/9)
*Guglielmo Tell:* Sherrill Milnes; *Arnoldo:* Luciano Pavarotti; *Matilde:* Mirella Freni; *Gualtiero:* Nicolai Ghiaurov; *Melchthal:* John Tomlinson; *Jemmy:* Della Jones; *Edwige:* Elizabeth Connell; *Leutoldo:* Richard Van Allan; *Gessler:* Ferruccio Mazzoli; *Rodolfo:* Piero de Palma; *Un pescatore:* Cesar Antonio Suarez; Ambrosian Opera Chorus

**1830 AUBER *Fra Diavolo*** Monte Carlo Philharmonic Orchestra, Marc Soustrot (1983/4)
*Fra Diavolo:* Nicolai Gedda; *Zerline:* Mady Mesplé; *Lorenzo:* Thierry Dran; *Lady Pamela:* Jane Berbié; *Lord Cockburn:* Remy Corazza; *Mathéo:* Jules Bastin; Jean Laforge Choral Ensemble

**1830 DONIZETTI *Anna Bolena*** London Symphony Orchestra, Julius Rudel (1972)
*Anna Bolena:* Beverly Sills; *Enrico VIII:* Paul Plishka; *Giovanna Seymour:* Shirley Verrett; *Riccardo Percy:* Stuart Burrows; *Rochefort:* Robert Lloyd; *Smeton:* Patricia Kern; John Alldis Choir

**1831 BELLINI *Norma*** London Symphony Orchestra, Richard Bonynge (1964)
*Norma:* Joan Sutherland; *Adalgisa:* Marilyn Horne; *Pollione:* John Alexander; *Oroveso:* Richard Cross; *Clotilde:* Yvonne Minton; *Flavio:* Joseph Ward; London Symphony Chorus

**1832 DONIZETTI *L'elisir d'amore*** English Chamber Orchestra, Marcello Viotti (1992)
*Adina:* Mariella Devia; *Nemorino:* Roberto Alagna; *Belcore:* Pietro Spagnoli; *Dulcamara:* Bruno Praticò; *Gianetta:* Francesca Provvisionato; Tallis Chamber Choir

**1833 DONIZETTI *Lucrezia Borgia*** National Philharmonic Orchestra, Richard Bonynge (1977)
*Lucrezia:* Joan Sutherland; *Gennaro:* Giacomo Aragall; *Orsini:* Marilyn Horne; *Alfonso:* Ingvar Wixell; *Liverotto:* Graham Clark; *Gazella:* Lieuwe Visser; *Petrucci:* John Bröcheler; *Vitelozzo:* Piero de Palma; *Gubetta:* Richard Van Allan; *Rustighello:* Graeme Ewer; *Astolfo:* Nicola Zaccaria; London Opera Chorus

**1835 BELLINI *I puritani di Scozia*** La Scala Orchestra, Tullio Serafin (1953)
*Elvira:* Maria Callas; *Arturo:* Giuseppe di Stefano; *Riccardo:* Rolando Panerai; *Giorgio:* Nicola Rossi-Lemeni; *Gualtiero:* Carlo Forti; *Enrichetta:* Aurora Cattelani; La Scala Chorus

**1835 DONIZETTI *Lucia di Lammermoor*** Maggio Musicale Fiorentino Orchestra, Tullio Serafin (1953)
*Lucia:* Maria Callas; *Edgardo:* Giuseppe di Stefano; *Enrico:* Tito Gobbi; *Raimondo:* Raffaele Arié; *Alisa:* Anna Maria Canali; *Arturo:* Valiano Natali; *Normanno:* Gastone Sarti; Maggio Musicale Fiorentino Chorus

**1836 MEYERBEER *Les Huguenots*** New Philharmonia Orchestra, Richard Bonynge (1969)
*Marguerite:* Joan Sutherland; *Valentine:* Martina Arroyo; *Urbain:* Huguette Tourangeau; *Comte de Saint-Bris:* Gabriel Bacquier; *Comte de Nevers:* Dominic Cossa; *Cossé:* Joseph Ward; *Méru:* John Gibbs; *Thoré:* John Noble; *Tavannes:* John Wakefield; *De Retz:* Glynne Thomas; *Raoul de Nangis:* Anastasios Vrenios; *Marcel:* Nikola Ghiuselev; *Maurevert:* Clifford Grant; *Léonard:* Janet Coster; *Maids of Honour:* Kiri te Kanawa, Josephte Clément; *Gypsies:* Arleen Auger, Maureen Lehane, Alan Opie; Ambrosian Opera Chorus

**1842 GLINKA *Ruslan i Lyudmila*** Kirov Orchestra, Valery Gergiev (1995; live)
*Ruslan:* Vladimir Ognovienko; *Lyudmila:* Anna Netrebko; *Svetosar:* Mikhail Kit; *Ratmir:* Larissa Diadkova; *Farlaf:* Gennady Bezubenkov; *Gorislava:* Galina Gorchakova; *Finn:* Konstantin Pluzhnikov; *Naina:* Irina Bogachova; *Bayan:* Yuri Marusin; Kirov Chorus

**1843 WAGNER *Der fliegende Holländer*** Bayreuth Festival Orchestra, Hans Knappertsbusch (1955; live)
*Holländer:* Hermann Uhde; *Senta:* Astrid Varnay; *Daland:* Ludwig Weber; *Erik:* Wolfgang Windgassen; *Mary:* Elisabeth Schärtel; *Steuermann:* Josef Traxel; Bayreuth Festival Chorus

**1845 WAGNER *Tannhäuser*** (Paris version, 1861) Vienna Philharmonic Orchestra, Georg Solti (1970)
*Tannhäuser:* René Kollo; *Elisabeth:* Helga Dernesch; *Wolfram von Eschenbach:* Victor Braun; *Venus:* Christa Ludwig; *Landgraf Hermann:* Hans Sotin; *Walther von der Vogelweide:* Werner Hollweg; *Biterolf:* Manfred Jungwirth; *Hienrich der Schreiber:* Kurt Equiluz; *Reinmar von Zweter:* Norman Bailey; Vienna Boys' Choir and Vienna State Opera Chorus

**1847 FLOTOW *Martha*** Munich Radio Orchestra, Heinz Wallberg (1977)
*Lady Harriet Durham:* Lucia Popp; *Nancy:* Doris Soffel; *Lionel:* Siegfried Jerusalem; *Plunkett:* Karl Ridderbusch; *Sir Tristram Mickleford:* Siegmund Nimsgern; *Sheriff:* Peter Lika; Bavarian Radio Chorus

**1850 WAGNER *Lohengrin*** Bavarian Radio Symphony Orchestra, Rafael Kubelik (1971)
*Lohengrin:* James King; *Elsa:* Gundula Janowitz; *Ortrud:* Gwyneth Jones; *Telramund:* Thomas Stewart; *König Heinrich:* Karl Ridderbusch; Bavarian Radio Chorus

**1851 VERDI *Rigoletto*** La Scala Orchestra, Tullio Serafin (1955)
*Rigoletto:* Tito Gobbi; *Gilda:* Maria Callas; *Duke:* Giuseppe di Stefano; *Sparafucile:* Nicola Zaccaria; *Maddalena:* Adriana Lazzarini; *Monterone:* Plinio Clabassi; La Scala Chorus

**1853 VERDI *Il trovatore*** RCA Victor Orchestra, Renato Cellini (1952)
*Manrico:* Jussi Björling; *Leonora:* Zinka Milanov; *Conte di Luna:* Leonard Warren; *Azucena:* Fedora Barbieri; *Ferrando:* Nicola Moscona; Robert Shaw Chorale

**1853 VERDI *La traviata*** Royal Opera House Orchestra, Georg Solti (1994; live)
*Violetta:* Angela Gheorghiu; *Alfredo:* Frank Lopardo; *Germont:* Leo Nucci; *Flora:* Leah-Marion Jones; Royal Opera House Chorus

**1857 VERDI *Simon Boccanegra*** Metropolitan Opera House Orchestra, Ettore Panizza (1939; live)
*Simon Boccanegra:* Lawrence Tibbett; *Amelia:* Elisabeth Rethberg; *Gabriele:* Giovanni Martinelli; *Fiesco:* Ezio Pinza; *Paolo:* Leonard Warren; Metropolitan Opera Chorus

**1859 GOUNOD *Faust*** Welsh National Opera Orchestra, Carlo Rizzi (1993)
*Faust:* Jerry Hadley; *Marguerite:* Cecilia Gasdia; *Méphistophélès:* Samuel Ramey; *Valentin:* Alexander Agache; *Siebel:* Susanne Mentzer; *Marthe:* Brigitte Fassbänder; *Wagner:* Philippe Fourcade; Welsh National Opera Chorus

**1862 VERDI *La forza del destino*** London Symphony Orchestra, James Levine (1976)
*Leonora:* Leontyne Price; *Don Alvaro:* Placido Domingo; *Don Carlo:* Sherrill Milnes; *Padre Guardiano:* Bonaldo Giaiotti; *Preziosilla:* Fiorenza Cossotto; *Fra Melitone:* Gabriel Bacquier; *Marchese:* Kurt Moll; *Trabuco:* Michel Sénéchal; John Alldis Choir

**[1863] BERLIOZ *Les Troyens*** Montreal Symphonic Orchestra, Charles Dutoit (1993)
*Enée:* Gary Lakes; *Cassandre:* Deborah Voigt; *Didon:* Françoise Pollet; *Chorèbe:* Gino Quilico; *Anna:* Hélène Perraguin; *Narbal:* Jean-Philippe Courtis; *Iopas:* Jean-Luc Maurette; *Hylas:* John Mark Ainsley; *Panthée:* Michel Philippe; *Ascagne:* Catherine Dubosc; *Shade of Hector:* Marc Belleau; *Priam:* René Schirrer; *Sinon:* Gregory Cross; Montreal Symphony Orchestra Chorus

**1865 WAGNER *Tristan und Isolde*** Berlin Philharmonic Orchestra, Herbert von Karajan (1971/2)
*Tristan:* Jon Vickers; *Isolde:* Helga Dernesch; *Brangäne:* Christa Ludwig; *King Mark:* Karl Ridderbusch; *Kurwenal:* Walter Berry; *Melot:* Bernd Weikl; *Shepherd/Sailor:* Peter Schreier; *Helmsman:* Martin Vantin; Chorus of Deutsche Oper, Berlin

**1866 SMETANA *The Bartered Bride*** Czech Philharmonic Orchestra, Zdeněk Košler (1980/1)
*Mařenka:* Gabriela Beňačková; *Jeník:* Petr Dvorský; *Vašek:* Miroslav Kopp; *Kečal:* Richard Novák; *Krušina:* Jindřich Jindrák; *Háta:* Marie Mrázová; *Micha:* Jaroslav Horácek; *Ludmila:* Marie Veselá; *Esmeralda:* Jana Jonášová; *Circus Master:* Alfréd Hampel; *Indian:* Karel Hanuš; Czech Philharmonic Chorus

**1867 VERDI *Don Carlo*** Rome Opera Orchestra, Gabriele Santini (1954)
*Don Carlo:* Mario Filippeschi; *Elisabetta:* Antonietta Stella; *Eboli:* Elena Nicolai; *Rodrigo:* Tito Gobbi; *Philip II:* Boris Christoff; *Grand Inquisitor:* Giulio Neri; Rome Opera Chorus

**1867 GOUNOD *Roméo et Juliette*** Royal Opera House Orchestra, Charles Mackerras (1993)
*Roméo:* Roberto Alagna; *Juliette:* Leontina Vaduva; *Frère Laurent:* Robert Lloyd; *Mercutio:* François le Roux; *Stéphano:* Anna Maria Panzarella; *Capulet:* Peter Sidhom; *Gertrud:* Sarah Walker; *Tybalt:* Paul Charles Clarke; Royal Opera House Chorus

**1868 BOITO *Mefistofele*** London Symphony Orchestra, Julius Rudel (1973)
*Mefistofele:* Norman Treigle; *Faust:* Placido Domingo; *Margherita:* Montserrat Caballé; *Elena:* Josella Ligi; Ambrosian Opera Chorus

**1868 WAGNER *Die Meistersinger von Nürnberg*** Bavarian Radio Orchestra, Rafael Kubelik (1967)
*Hans Sachs:* Thomas Stewart; *Walther von Stolzing:* Sandor Konya; *Eva:* Gundula Janowitz; *Pogner:* Franz Crass; *Beckmesser:* Thomas Hemsley; *David:* Gerhard Unger; *Magdalena:* Brigitte Fassbänder; Bavarian Radio Chorus

**1871 VERDI *Aida*** Rome Opera Orchestra, Georg Solti (1961)
*Aida:* Leontyne Price; *Amneris:* Rita Gorr; *Radamès:* Jon Vickers; *Amonasro:* Robert Merrill; *Ramfis:* Giorgio Tozzi; *King of Egypt:* Plinio Clabassi; Rome Opera Chorus

**1874 MUSSORGSKY *Boris Godunov*** Washington National Symphony Orchestra, Mstislav Rostropovich (1987)
*Boris Godunov:* Ruggiero Raimondi; *Grigory (Dmitry):* Vyacheslav Polozov; *Marina/Hostess:* Galina Vishnevskaya; *Pimen:* Paul Plishka; *Varlaam:* Romuald Tesarowicz; *Shuisky:* Kenneth Riegel; *Missail:* Misha Raitzin; *Rangoni:* Nikita Storozhev; *Simpleton:* Nicolai Gedda; Chevy Chase School Chorus with Oratorio Society and Choral Arts Societies of Washington

**1875 BIZET *Carmen*** London Symphony Orchestra, Claudio Abbado (1977/8)
*Carmen:* Teresa Berganza; *Don José:* Placido Domingo; *Micaela:* Ileana Cotrubas; *Escamillo:* Sherrill Milnes; *Frasquita:* Yvonne Kenny; Ambrosian Singers

**1875 GOLDMARK *Die Königin von Saba*** Hungarian State Opera Orchestra, Ádám Fischer (1980)
*King Solomon:* Sándor Sólyom-Nagy; *High Priest:* József Gregor; *Sulamith:* Veronika Kincses; *Assad:* Siegfried Jerusalem; *Queen of Sheba:* Klára Takács; Hungarian State Opera Chorus

**1876 PONCHIELLI *La gioconda*** Metropolitan Opera Orchestra, Ettore Panizza (1939; live)
*La gioconda:* Zinka Milanov; *Enzo Grimaldo:* Giovanni Martinelli; *Barnaba:* Carlo Morelli;

*La cieca:* Anna Kaskas; *Alvise:* Nicola Moscona; *Laura:* Bruna Castagna; Metropolitan Opera Chorus

1876 WAGNER ***Der Ring des Nibelungen*** Vienna Philharmonic Orchestra, Georg Solti (1958–65)
*Wotan (Rheingold):* George London; *Wotan (Walküre)/The Wanderer (Siegfried):* Hans Hotter; *Fricka (Rheingold):* Kirsten Flagstad; *Fricka (Walküre):* Christa Ludwig; *Freia/Gutrune:* Claire Watson; *Donner:* Eberhard Wächter; *Froh:* Waldemar Kmentt; *Loge:* Set Svanholm; *Erda (Rheingold):* Jean Madeira; *Erda (Siegfried):* Marga Höffgen; *Alberich:* Gustav Neidlinger; *Mime (Rheingold):* Paul Kuen; *Mime (Siegfried):* Gerhard Stolze; *Fasolt:* Walter Kreppel; *Fafner:* Kurt Böhme; *Siegmund:* James King; *Sieglinde:* Régine Crespin; *Brünnhilde:* Birgit Nilsson; *Hunding/Hagen:* Gottlob Frick; *Siegfried:* Wolfgang Windgassen; *Woodbird:* Joan Sutherland; *Gunther:* Dietrich Fischer-Dieskau; *Waltraute (Walküre):* Brigitte Fassbänder; *Waltraute (Götterdämmerung):* Christa Ludwig; Vienna State Opera Chorus

1877 SAINT-SAËNS ***Samson et Dalila*** Paris Opéra Orchestra, Georges Prêtre (1962)
*Samson:* Jon Vickers; *Dalila:* Rita Gorr; *High Priest:* Ernest Blanc; *Abimélech/Old Hebrew:* Anton Diakov; René Duclos Chorus

1879 TCHAIKOVSKY ***Evgeny Onegin*** Paris Orchestra, Semyon Bychkov (1990)
*Onegin:* Dmitri Hvorostovsky; *Tatyana:* Nuccia Focile; *Lensky:* Neil Shicoff; *Olga:* Olga Borodina; *Prince Gremin:* Alexander Anisimov; St Petersburg Chamber Choir

1881 OFFENBACH ***Les Contes d'Hoffmann*** Staatskapelle Dresden, Jeffrey Tate (1992)
*Hoffmann:* Francisco Araiza; *Olympia:* Eva Lind; *Giulietta:* Cheryl Studer; *Antonia:* Jessye Norman; *Nicklausse/Muse:* Anne Sofie von Otter; *Lindorf/Coppélius/Dappertutto/Dr Miracle:* Samuel Ramey; *Voice of Antonia's Mother:* Felicity Palmer; Leipzig Radio Chorus

1882 WAGNER ***Parsifal*** Bayreuth Festival Orchestra, Hans Knappertsbusch (1962; live)
*Parsifal:* Jess Thomas; *Amfortas:* George London; *Gurnemanz:* Hans Hotter; *Kundry:* Irene Dalis; *Klingsor:* Gustav Neidlinger; *Titurel:* Martti Talvela; Bayreuth Festival Chorus

1884 MASSENET ***Manon*** Opéra-Comique Orchestra, Pierre Monteux (1955)
*Manon:* Victoria de los Angeles; *Chevalier des Grieux:* Henri Legay; *Lescaut:* Michel Dens; *Comte des Grieux:* Jean Borthayre; *de Brétigny:* Jean Vieuille; *Guillot de Morfontaine:* René Hérent; *Poussette:* Liliane Berton; *Javotte:* Raymonde Notti; *Rosette:* Marthe Serres; Opéra-Comique Chorus

1887 VERDI ***Otello*** NBC Symphony Orchestra, Arturo Toscanini (1947; live)
*Otello:* Ramon Vinay; *Desdemona:* Herva Nelli; *Iago:* Giuseppe Valdengo; *Cassio:* Virginio Assandri; *Roderigo:* Leslie Chabay *Emilia:* Nan Merriman; *Lodovico:* Nicola Moscona; *Montano:* Arthur Newman; NBC Symphony Chorus

1890 MASCAGNI ***Cavalleria rusticana*** La Scala Orchestra, Pietro Mascagni (1940)
*Santuzza:* Lina Bruna Rasa; *Turiddu:* Beniamino Gigli; *Alfio:* Gino Bechi; *Lola:* Maria Marcucci; *Mamma Lucia:* Giulietta Simionato; La Scala Chorus

1892 LEONCAVALLO ***Pagliacci*** La Scala Orchestra, Herbert von Karajan (1965)
*Canio:* Carlo Bergonzi; *Nedda:* Joan Carlyle; *Tonio:* Giuseppe Taddei; *Silvio:* Rolando Panerai; *Beppe:* Ugo Benelli; La Scala Chorus

1893 VERDI ***Falstaff*** RCA Italiana Opera Orchestra, Georg Solti (1963)
*Falstaff:* Geraint Evans; *Ford:* Robert Merrill; *Alice:* Ilva Ligabue; *Nanetta:* Mirella Freni; *Fenton:* Alfredo Kraus; *Mistress Quickly:* Giulietta Simionato; *Meg Page:* Rosalind Elias; RCA Italiana Opera Chorus

1896 PUCCINI ***La Bohème*** RCA Victor Symphony Orchestra, Thomas Beecham (1956)
*Mimì:* Victoria de los Angeles; *Rodolfo:* Jussi Björling; *Musetta:* Lucine Amara; *Marcello:* Robert Merrill; *Schaunard:* John Reardon; *Colline:* Giorgio Tozzi; *Benoit/Alcindoro:* Fernando Corena; RCA Victor Chorus

1896 GIORDANO ***Andrea Chenier*** Accademia di Santa Cecilia Orchestra, Gianandrea Gavazzeni (1957)
*Andrea Chenier:* Mario del Monaco; *Maddalena:* Renata Tebaldi; *Carlo Gerard:* Ettore Bastianini; *Incredibile:* Mariano Caruso; *Countess de Coigny:* Maria Teresa Mandalari; *Bersi:* Fiorenza Cossotto; *Mathieu:* Fernando Corena; Accademia di Santa Cecilia Chorus

1899 RIMSKY-KORSAKOV ***The Tsar's Bride*** Bolshoi Theatre Orchestra, Fuat Mansorov (1973)
*Sobakin:* Evgeny Nestorenko; *Marfa:* Galina Vishnevskaya; *Griaznoy:* Vladimir Valaitis; *Skuratov:* Boris Morozov; *Likov:* Vladimir Atlantov; *Liubasha:* Irina Arkhipova; *Bomelius:* Andrei Sokolov; *Saburova:* Eleonora Andreevna; *Duniasha:* Galina Borisova; Bolshoi Theatre Chorus

1900 PUCCINI ***Tosca*** La Scala Orchestra, Victor de Sabata (1953)
*Tosca:* Maria Callas; *Cavaradossi:* Giuseppe di Stefano; *Scarpia:* Tito Gobbi; *Angelotti:* Franco Calabrese; La Scala Chorus

1900 CHARPENTIER ***Louise*** New Philharmonia Orchestra, Georges Prêtre (1976)
*Louise:* Ileana Cotrubas; *Julien:* Placido Domingo; *Father:* Gabriel Bacquier; *Mother:* Jane Berbié; *Noctambulist/King of Fools:* Michel Sénéchal; *Irma:* Lyliane Guitton; *Camille:* Eliane Manchet; Ambrosian Opera Chorus

1902 DEBUSSY ***Pelléas et Mélisande*** Orchestre de la Suisse Romande, Ernest Ansermet (1964)
*Pelléas:* Camille Maurane; *Mélisande:* Erna Spoorenberg; *Golaud:* George London; *Arkel:* Guus Hoekman; Chorus of the Grand Théâtre, Geneva

1904 JANÁČEK ***Jenůfa*** Vienna Philharmonic Orchestra, Charles Mackerras (1982)
*Jenůfa:* Elisabeth Söderström; *Laca:* Wieslaw Ochman; *Kostelnička:* Eva Randová; *Števa:* Petr Dvorský; *Karolka:* Lucia Popp; *Grandmother Burya:* Marie Mrázová; *Stárek:* Václav Zítek; Vienna State Opera Chorus

1904 PUCCINI ***Madama Butterfly*** Vienna Philharmonic Orchestra, Herbert von Karajan (1974)
*Butterfly:* Mirella Freni; *Pinkerton:* Luciano Pavarotti; *Sharpless:* Robert Kerns; *Suzuki:* Christa Ludwig; *Goro:* Michel Sénéchal; Vienna State Opera Chorus

1905 STRAUSS ***Salome*** Metropolitan Opera Orchestra, Fritz Reiner (1952; live)
*Salome:* Ljuba Welitsch; *Jokanaan:* Hans Hotter; *Herod:* Set Svanholm; *Herodias:* Elisabeth Höngen

1909 STRAUSS ***Elektra*** Vienna Philharmonic Orchestra, Giuseppe Sinopoli (1995)
*Elektra:* Alessandra Marc; *Klytemnestra:* Hanna Schwarz; *Chrysothemis:* Deborah Voigt; *Aegist:* Siegfried Jerusalem; *Orest:* Samuel Ramey; Vienna State Opera Konzertvereinigung

1911 STRAUSS ***Der Rosenkavalier*** Vienna Philharmonic Orchestra, Erich Kleiber (1954)
*Feldmarschallin:* Maria Reining; *Octavian:* Sena Jurinac; *Baron Ochs:* Ludwig Weber; *Sophie:* Hilde Gueden; *Faninal:* Alfred Poell; *Italian Tenor:* Anton Dermota; *Annina:* Hilde Rössl-Majdan; *Valzacchi:* Peter Klein; Vienna State Opera Chorus

1913 DE FALLA ***La vida breve*** London Symphony Orchestra, García Navarro (1978)
*Salud:* Teresa Berganza; *Paco:* José Carreras; *Carmela:* Paloma Pérez Iñigo; *Grandmother:* Alicia Nafé; *Uncle Sarvaor:* Juan Pons; *Manuel:* Ramon Contreras; Ambrosian Opera Chorus

1913 MONTEMEZZI ***L'amore dei tre re*** London Symphony Orchestra, Nello Santi (1976)
*Fiora:* Anna Moffo; *Archibaldo:* Cesare Siepi; *Manfredo:* Pablo Elvira; *Avito:* Placido Domingo; Ambrosian Opera Chorus

1916 STRAUSS ***Ariadne auf Naxos*** Philharmonia Orchestra, Herbert von Karajan (1954)
*Ariadne:* Elisabeth Schwarzkopf; *Composer:* Irmgard Seefried; *Zerbinetta:* Rita Streich; *Bacchus:* Rudolf Schock; *Music Master:* Karl Dönch; *Harlequin:* Hermann Prey; *Dancing Master:* Hugues Cuénod

1917 PFITZNER ***Palestrina*** Bavarian Radio Symphony Orchestra, Rafael Kubelik (1972)
*Palestrina:* Nicolai Gedda; *Pope Pius IV:* Karl Ridderbusch; *Morone:* Bernd Weikl; *Novagerio:* Heribert Steinbach; *Borromeo:* Dietrich Fischer-Dieskau; *Count Luna:* Hermann Prey; *Ighino:* Helen Donath; *Silla:* Brigitte Fassbander; Bavarian Radio Chorus; Tulz Boys' Choir

1918 BARTÓK ***Duke Bluebeard's Castle*** Berlin Philharmonic Orchestra, Bernard Haitink (1995; live)
*Bluebeard:* John Tomlinson; *Judith:* Anne Sofie von Otter

1919 STRAUSS ***Die Frau ohne Schatten*** Vienna Philharmonic Orchestra, Georg Solti (1989–91)
*Empress:* Julia Varady; *Emperor:* Placido Domingo; *Dyer's Wife:* Hildegard Behrens; *Barak:* José Van Dam; *Nurse:* Reinhild Runkel; Vienna Boys' Choir and State Opera Chorus

1921 JANÁČEK ***Kát'a Kabanová*** Vienna Philharmonic Orchestra, Charles Mackerras (1976–8)
*Kát'a:* Elisabeth Söderström; *Boris:* Petr Dvorský; *Kabanicha:* Nedĕžda Kniplová; *Tichon:* Vladimir Krejčik; *Varvara:* Libuše Márová; *Dikoj:* Dalibor Jedlička; Vienna State Opera Chorus

1924 JANÁČEK ***The Cunning Little Vixen*** Vienna Philharmonic Orchestra, Charles Mackerras (1981)
*Vixen:* Lucia Popp; *Fox:* Eva Randová; *Dog:* Libuše Márová; *Cock:* Gertrud Jahn; *Hen/Woodpecker/Innkeeper's wife:* Ivana Mixová; *Badger/Parson:* Richard Novák; *Owl/Forester's Wife:* Eva Zikmundová; *Forester:* Dalibor Jedlička; *Schoolmaster:* Vladimir Krejčik; *Innkeeper:* Beno Blachut; *Harašta:* Václav Zítek; Bratislava Children's Choir and Vienna State Opera Chorus

1925 BUSONI ***Doktor Faust*** Bavarian Radio Symphony Orchestra, Ferdinand Leitner (1969)
*Doktor Faust:* Dietrich Fischer-Dieskau; *Mephistopheles:* William Cochran; *Duke of Parma:* Anton de Ridder; *Duchess of Parma:* Hildegard Hillebrecht; *Wagner:* Karl Christian Kohn; *Girl's Brother/Scientist:* Franz Grundheber; Bavarian Radio Chorus

1925 BERG ***Wozzeck*** Vienna Philharmonic Orchestra, Christoph von Dohnányi (1979)
*Wozzeck:* Eberhard Wächter; *Marie:* Anja Silja; *Drum-major:* Hermann Winkler; *Andres:* Horst Laubenthal; *Captain:* Heinz Zednik; *Doctor:* Alexander Malta; *Margret:* Gertrude Jahn; Vienna State Opera Chorus

1926 PUCCINI ***Turandot*** London Philhamonic Orchestra, Zubin Mehta (1972)
*Turandot:* Joan Sutherland; *Calaf:* Luciano Pavarotti; *Liù:* Montserrat Caballé; *Ping:* Tom Krause; *Pang:* Pier Francesco Poli; *Pong:* Piero de Palma; *Timur:* Nicolai Ghiaurov; *Emperor:* Peter Pears; John Alldis Choir

1926–7 MILHAUD ***Les Malheurs d'Orphée*** and ***Le pauvre matelot*** Paris Opéra Orchestra, Darius Milhaud (1956)
*Orphée:* Jean Cussac; *Eurydice:* Jacqueline Brumaire. *The Wife:* Jacqueline Brumaire; *The Sailor:* Jean Giraudeau; *His Father-in-Law:* Xavier Depraz; *His Friend:* André Vessières

1933 STRAUSS ***Arabella*** Vienna Philharmonic Orchestra, Georg Solti (1957)
*Arabella:* Lisa della Casa; *Zdenka:* Hilde Gueden; *Mandryka:* George London; *Waldner:* Otto Edelmann; *Adelaide:* Ira Malaniuk; *Matteo:* Anton Dermota; *Elemer:* Waldemar Kmentt; *Dominik:* Eberhard Wächter; *Lamoral:* Harald Pröglhöf; *Fiakermilli:* Mimi Coertse; Vienna State Opera Chorus

1934 **SHOSTAKOVICH** ***Lady Macbeth of the Mtsensk District*** London Philharmonic Orchestra, Msistislav Rostropovich (1978)
*Katerina Izmailova:* Galina Vishnevskaya; *Sergei:* Nicolai Gedda; *Boris Izmailov:* Dimiter Petkov; *Zinovi Izmailov:* Werner Krenn; *Shabby Peasant:* Robert Tear; *Aksinya:* Taru Valjakka

1935 **GERSHWIN** ***Porgy and Bess*** London Philharmonic Orchestra, Simon Rattle (1988)
*Porgy:* Willard White; *Bess:* Cynthia Haymon; *Clara:* Harolyn Blackwell; *Serena:* Cynthia Clarey; *Sporting Life:* Damon Evans; *Maria:* Marietta Simpson; *Crown:* Gregg Baker; *Jake:* Bruce Hubbard; Glyndebourne Festival Chorus

1937 **BERG** ***Lulu*** Paris Opéra Orchestra, Pierre Boulez (1979)
*Lulu:* Teresa Stratas; *Dr Schön:* Franz Mazura; *Alwa Schön:* Kenneth Riegel; *Countess Geschwitz:* Yvonne Minton; *Painter/Negro:* Robert Tear; *Schigolch:* Toni Blankenheim; *Animal Trainer:* Gerd Nienstedt

1938 **MARTINŮ** ***Julietta*** Prague National Theatre Orchestra, Jaroslav Krombholc (1964)
*Julietta:* Maria Tauberová; *Michel:* Ivo Žídek; Prague National Theatre Chorus

1938 **HINDEMITH** ***Mathis der Maler*** Bavarian Radio Symphony Orchestra, Rafael Kubelik (1979)
*Mathis:* Dietrich Fischer-Dieskau; *Albrecht:* James King; *Lorenz von Pommersfelden:* Gerd Feldhoff; *Capito:* Manfred Schmidt; *Riedinger:* Peter Meven; *Schwalb:* William Cochran; *Truchsess von Waldburg:* Alexander Malta; *Sylvester von Schaumberg:* Donald Grobe; *Ursula:* Rose Wagemann; *Regina:* Urszula Koszut; *Countess Helfenstein:* Trudeliese Schmidt Bavarian Radio Chorus

1945 **BRITTEN** ***Peter Grimes*** Royal Opera House Orchestra, Colin Davis (1978)
*Peter Grimes:* Jon Vickers; *Ellen Orford:* Heather Harper; *Bulstrode:* Norman Bailey; *Auntie:* Elizabeth Bainbridge; *Bob Boles:* John Dobson; *Swallow:* Forbes Robinson; *Mrs Sedley:* Patricia Payne; Royal Opera House Chorus

1951 **STRAVINSKY** ***The Rake's Progress*** Royal Philharmonic Orchestra, Igor Stravinsky (1964)
*Tom Rakewell:* Alexander Young; *Anne Trulove:* Judith Raskin; *Nick Shadow:* John Reardon; *Baba the Turk:* Regina Sarfaty; Sadler's Wells Opera Chorus

1953 **EINEM** ***Der Prozess*** Vienna Philharmonic Orchestra, Karl Böhm (1953; live)
*Josef K:* Max Lorenz; *Deputy Director/Student:* Peter Klein; *Albert K:* Endre Koréh; *Frau Grubach:* Polly Batic; *Solicitor:* Alfred Poell; *Titorelli:* László Szemere; *Magistrate/Hit Man:* Oskar Czerwenka; *Franz/Office Manager:* Walter Berry; *Willem/Bailiff:* Alois Pernerstorfer; *Fräulein Bürstner/Bailiff's Wife:* Lisa della Casa; Vienna State Opera Chorus

1955 **TIPPETT** ***The Midsummer Marriage*** Royal Opera House Orchestra, Colin Davis (1970)
*Mark:* Alberto Remedios; *Jennifer:* Joan Carlyle; *King Fisher:* Raimund Herincx; *Bella:* Elizabeth Harwood; *Jack:* Stuart Burrows; *Sosostris:* Helen Watts; Royal Opera House Chorus

1956 **MOORE** ***The Ballad of Baby Doe*** New York City Opera Orchestra, Emerson Buckley (1959)
*Baby Doe:* Beverly Sills; *Horace:* Walter Cassel; *Augusta:* Frances Bible; *Bryan:* Joshua Hecht; New York City Opera Chorus

1957 **POULENC** ***Les Dialogues des carmélites*** Paris Opéra Orchestra, Pierre Dervaux (1958)
*Blanche de la Force:* Denise Duval; *Mme Lidoine:* Régine Crespin; *Mme de Croissy:* Denise Scharley; *Soeur Constance:* Liliane Berton; *Mère Marie:* Rita Gorr; *Marquis de la Force:* Xavier Depraz; *Chevalier de la Force:* Paul Finel; Paris Opéra Chorus

1960 **BRITTEN** ***A Midsummer Night's Dream*** London Symphony Orchestra, Benjamin Britten (1966)
*Oberon:* Alfred Deller; *Tytania:* Elizabeth Harwood; *Lysander:* Peter Pears; *Demetrius:* Thomas Hemsley; *Hermia:* Josephine Veasey; *Helena:* Heather Harper; *Theseus:* John Shirley-Quirk; *Helena:* Helen Watts; *Bottom:* Owen Brannigan; *Quince:* Norman Lumsden; *Flute:* Kenneth Macdonald; *Snug:* David Kelly; *Snout:* Robert Tear; Downside and Emanuel Schools Boys' Choirs

1961 **NONO** ***Intolleranza 1960*** Stuttgart Opera Orchestra, Bernhard Kontarsky (1993; live)
*An Emigrant:* David Rampy; *His Companion:* Urszula Koszut; *A Woman:* Kathryn Harries; *An Algerian:* Jerrold van der Schaaf; *A Tortured Prisoner:* Wolfgang Probst; *Policemen:* Joseph Dieken, Christian Hoening, Carsten Otto, Hermann Wenning; Stuttgart Opera Chorus

1966 **HENZE** ***Die Bassariden*** Berlin Radio Symphony Orchestra, Gerd Albrecht (1986)
*Dionysus/Voice:* Kenneth Riegel; *Pentheus:* Andreas Schmidt; *Cadmus:* Michael Burt; *Tiresias:* Robert Tear; *Captain:* William Murray; *Agave:* Karan Armstrong; *Autonoe:* Celina Lindsley; *Beroe:* Ortrun Wenkel; South German Radio Chorus

1978 **LIGETI** ***Le grand macabre*** Austrian Radio Symphony Orchestra, Elgar Howarth (1987; live)
*Gepopo/Venus:* Eirian Davies; *Clitoria:* Penelope Walmsley-Clark; *Spermando:* Olive Fredricks; *Prince Go-Go:* Kevin Smith; *Mescalina:* Christa Puhlmann-Richter; *Piet the Pot:* Pater Haage; *Nekrotzar:* Dieter Weller; *Astradamors:* Ude Krekow; Arnold Schönberg Choir

1983 **MESSIAEN** ***Saint-François d'Assise*** Paris Opéra Orchestra, Seiji Ozawa (1983; live)
*L'Ange:* Christiane Eda-Pierre; *Saint-François:* José Van Dam; *The Leper:* Kenneth Riegel; *Frère Léon:* Michel Philippe; *Frère Massée:* Georges Gautier; *Frère Elie:* Michel Sénéchal; *Frère Bernard:* Jean-Philippe Courtis; Paris Opéra Chorus

1984 **GLASS** ***Akhnaten*** Stuttgart Opera Orchestra, Dennis Russell Davies (1987)
*Akhnaten:* Paul Esswood; *Nefertiti:* Milagr Vargas; *Queen Tye:* Melinda Liebermann; *Horemheb:* Tero Hannula; *Amon High Priest:* Helmut Holzapfel; *Aye:* Cornelius Hauptmann; *Scribe:* David Warrilow; Stuttgart Opera Chorus

1986 **BIRTWISTLE** ***The Mask of Orpheus*** BBC Symphony Orchestra, Andrew Davis and Martyn Brabbins (1996)
*Orpheus: Man:* Jon Garrison; *Orpheus: Myth/Hades:* Peter Bronder; *Euridice: Woman:* Jean Rigby; *Euridice: Myth/Persephone:* Anne-Marie Owens; *Aristaeus: Man:* Alan Opie; *Aristaeus: Myth:* Omar Ebrahim; *Oracle of the Dead/Hecate:* Marie Angel; BBC Singers

1991 **ADAMS** ***The Death of Klinghoffer*** Lyon Opera Orchestra, Kent Nagano (1992)
*Leon Klinghoffer:* Sanford Sylvan; *Omar:* Stephanie Friedman; *Captain:* James Maddalena; *First Officer:* Thomas Hammons; *Molqi:* Thomas J. Young; *Mamoud:* Eugene Perry; *Marilyn Klinghoffer:* Sheila Nadler; London Opera Chorus

1992 **RIHM** ***Die Eroberung von Mexiko*** Hamburg Philharmonic Orchestra, Ingo Metzmacher (1992; live)
*Cortez:* Richard Salter; *Montezuma:* Renate Behle; *Soprano:* Carmen Fugiss; *Alto:* Susanne Otto; Hamburg State Opera Chorus

1992 **SCHNITTKE** ***Life with an Idiot*** Rotterdam Philharmonic Orchestra, Mstislav Rostropovich (1992; live)
*I:* Dale Duesing, Romain Bischoff; *Wife:* Teresa Ringholz; *Vova:* Howard Haskin; *Guard:* Leonard Zimnenko; *Marcel Proust:* Robin Leggate

# BIBLIOGRAPHY

In assembling the information in the book, I have drawn widely on a variety of sources, including opera programmes, record sleeves and inserts, and issues of *Opera*, as well as books, but the following general works have proved particularly helpful: Alfred Loewenberg's *Annals of Opera* (rev. Harold Rosenthal, London, 1978); Nicole Wild's *Décors et costumes du XIXe siècle* (2 vols, Paris, 1987, 1993); *Dictionnaire chronologique de l'opéra* (Paris, 1994); Winton Dean's *Essays on Opera* (Oxford, 1990); William Weaver's *The Golden Century of Opera* (London, 1980); *The Gramophone Opera Catalogue* (ed. Philippa Bunting, London, 1995); James Camner's *The Great Opera Stars in Historic Photographs* (New York, 1978); *Heritage of Music* (eds Michael Raeburn and Alan Kendall, New York, 1989), particularly the articles by Julian Rushton and William Ashbrook; *Knaurs Grosser Opernführer* (Munich, 1983); *Kobbé's Complete Opera Book* (London, 1954 and 1997); *Larousse de la musique* (Paris, 1982); Rupert Hughes's *Music Lovers' Encyclopedia* (rev. Deems Taylor and Russell Kerr, Garden City, N.Y., 1947); Hellmuth Christian Wolff's *Oper: Szene und Darstellung von 1600 bis 1900* (Leipzig, 1968); John Dizikes's *Opera in America: A Cultural History* (New Haven, 1993); *The Oxford History of Opera* (ed. Roger Parker, Oxford, 1996); *The Penguin Opera Guide* (ed. Amanda Holden, London, 1995); Eric Walter White's *A History of English Opera* (London, 1983); *The Victor Book of Opera* (Camden, N.J., 1915); and Wallace Brockway and Herbert Weinstock's *The World of Opera* (London, 1963). The *New Grove Dictionary of Opera* (ed. Stanley Sadie, London, 1992) has been invaluable, particularly for validation of information obtained from other sources. For information on specific topics or individual composers the following books were also useful: Otto Michtner's *Das alte Burgtheater als Opernbühne* (Vienna, 1970); Humphrey Carpenter's *Benjamin Britten* (London, 1992); *Canto d'Amore: Classicism in Modern Art and Music 1914–1935* (eds G. Boehm, U. Mosch and K. Schmidt, Basel and London, 1996); John Willett's *Caspar Neher Brecht's Designer* (London and New York, 1986); Charles Osborne's *The Complete Operas of Verdi* (London, 1969), and his companion volumes on Wagner and Richard Strauss; Angus Heriot's *The Castrati in Opera* (London, 1956); Richard Buckle's *Diaghilev* (London, 1984); Malcolm Boyd's *Domenico Scarlatti: Master of Music* (London, 1986); Alan Kendall's *Gioacchino Rossini* (London, 1992); Christopher Hogwood's *Handel* (London, 1988); H. C. Robbins Landon's *Haydn at Eszterháza* (London, 1978); *The Memoirs of Hector Berlioz* (ed. and trans. David Cairns, London, 1969); Rupert Christiansen's *Prima Donna* (London, 1995); Georgina Masson's *Queen Christina* (London, 1968); Wayne Koestenbaum's *The Queen's Throat: Opera, Homosexuality and the Mystery of Desire* (London, 1993); *Rimsky-Korsakov* (eds D. B. Kabalevsky et al., 2 vols, Moscow, 1954); John Culshaw's *Ring Resounding* (London, 1967); and Marcel Prawy's *The Vienna Opera* (Vienna, 1969).

To the authors and editors of all these works, and to those of other works I have drawn on for individual items of information, I owe a great debt of gratitude.

# SOURCES OF ILLUSTRATIONS

**a** = above, **b** = below, **c** = centre, **l** = left, **r** = right

BN = Photo Bibliothèque nationale de France, Paris; Costa = © by Giancarlo Costa; ÖNB = Österreichische Nationalbibliothek. Photo: Bildarchiv ÖNB, Vienna; RA = Rainsville Archive.

**1** RA; **2–3** Georg M. Kraus, Singers dressing for *Die Zauberflöte*, 1794. Stiftung Weimarer Klassik Goethe-Nationalmuseum. Schloss Tiefurt. Photo: Sigrid Geske; **6–7** Gabriel de Saint-Aubin, A Performance of *Armide*, 1761. State Hermitage, St Petersburg. Photo: AKG London; **9** Photo Hans Hammarskiöld; **10–11** Museo Teatrale alla Scala, Milan. Costa; **12** RA; **13** Photo Richard M. Feldman; **14–15** © Clive Barda, Performing Arts Library, London; **16–17** Jean Le Pautre, engraving from *Les Divertissements de Versailles*, 1676; **18** Biblioteca Nazionale Centrale, Florence; **19** Marco Ricci, *A Rehearsal of an Opera*, *c.* 1709. Yale Center for British Art, Paul Mellon Collection; **21l** Biblioteca Nazionale Centrale, Florence. Photo Scala; **21r** Deutsches Theatermuseum, Munich; **22a** Devonshire Collection, Chatsworth. Reproduced by permission of the Duke of Devonshire and the Chatsworth Settlement Trustees. Photo Courtauld Institute of Art, London; **22b** Drawing from *Teatro di Tor di Nona del C. Carlo Fontana.* Trustees of Sir John Soane's Museum, London; **23a** Tiroler Landesmuseum Ferdinandeum, Innsbruck; **24** Deutsches Theatermuseum, Munich; **25** Biblioteca di S. Marco, Venice; **27a** Costa; **27b** Bibliothèque de l'Opéra. BN; **29l** Musikbibliothek, Leipzig; **29r** Carlo Vigarani, Théâtre de la Salle des Machines, 1662. Nationalmuseum, Stockholm; **30** Louvre, Paris. Collection Rothschild. © Photo R.M.N.; **31a** By courtesy of the National Portrait Gallery, London; **31b** Herzog Anton Ulrich-Museum, Brunswick; **32** BN; **33a** Etching from Bibiena's *Varie Opere*, 1703–8. Courtauld Institute of Art, London; **33b** Engraving from *Recueil Général des Opéras*, 1703. Musikbibliothek, Leipzig; **34** V&A Picture Library; **35** Engraving from the libretto of *Crösus.* Landesbibliothek, Weimar; **36** Engraving from T.I.'s *Le Théâtre de la Foire ou l'Opéra-comique*, 1721. Musikbibliothek, Weimar; **37al** Kupferstichkabinett, Dresden; **37b** ÖNB; **38** Biblioteca Apostolica Vaticana; **39** Carl Jehling, performance at Dresden court opera, 1719. Kupferstichkabinett, Dresden; **40** The Royal Collection © Her Majesty Queen Elizabeth II; **41l** Private Collection; **41r** The Fotomas Index; **44** BN; **45** Photo: AKG London; **46** RA; **47a** RA; **47b** Nationalmuseum, Stockholm; **48a** Kupferstichkabinett, Dresden; **48b** Bibliothèque de l'Opéra. BN; **49** Pietro D. Olivero and collaborators, The Teatro Regio, Turin. Museo Civico, Turin. Photo Scala; **50** Charles-N. Cochin, Madame de Pompadour in *Acis et Galatée.* Deutsches Theatermuseum, Munich; **51** Bibliothèque nationale de France, Paris. Photo: AKG London; **52a** Musikbibliothek, Leipzig; **52b** Bibliothèque de l'Opéra. BN; **53** National Gallery of Victoria, Melbourne. Felton Bequest, 1949–50; **54** Photo: AKG London; **55a** Bibliothèque de l'Opéra, BN; **55b** V&A Picture Library; **56–7** Staatliche Museen zu Berlin. Bildarchiv preussischer Kulturbesitz; **58** Engraving from Henry Krehbiel, *Chapters of Opera*, 1908; **59** Costa; **60** Bibliothèque nationale de France, Paris. Photo: AKG London; **61** Per Krafft, Gluck and his wife. Museen der Stadt, Vienna; **63l** The Fotomas Index; **63r** Engraving from *Berliner Genealogischer Calendar auf das Jahr 1775.* Kupferstichkabinett, Dresden; **64** Deutsches Theatermuseum, Munich; **65a** ÖNB; **65b** Gesellschaft der Musikfreunde, Vienna; **66l** Engraving from *Theaterkalender auf das Jahr 1776.* Landesbibliothek, Weimar; **66r** Bibliothèque Municipal, Besançon. Photo: AKG London; **67** ÖNB; **68** ÖNB; **69a** RA; **69b** Stadtarchiv Augsburg; **70** Städtsiche Musikbibliothek, Leipzig; **71a** Engraving from *Musik-und Theater-Almanach*, 1786; **72** Historisches Museum der Stadt, Vienna; **74a** BN; **74b** ÖNB; **75** BN; **76a** ÖNB; **76b** Akademie der bildenden Künste, Vienna; **77** Engraving from the libretto of *Die Zauberflöte*; **78al** BN; **78ar** Bayerische Staatsbibliothek, Munich; **78b** Stadt-und Landesbibliothek, Vienna; **79a** ÖNB; **79b** Musée de l'Opéra. BN; **80a** ÖNB; **80b** Akademie der bildenden Künste, Vienna; **81** Bibliothèque de l'Opéra. BN; **82** V&A Picture Library; **83a** Costa; **83b** ÖNB; **84a** Photo: AKG London; **84bl** Museo Teatrale alla Scala, Milan. Photo Scala; **84br** Photo AKG London; **85** Deutsches Theatermuseum, Munich; **86** Museo Teatrale alla Scala, Milan. Costa; **87** Museo Teatrale alla Scala, Milan; **88l** Musée de l'Opéra. BN; **88r** Private Collection; **89l** Musée de l'Opéra. BN; **89r** Staatliche Kunstsammlungen, Weimar. Photo: AKG London; **90a** ÖNB; **90b** Costa; **92** Costa; **93** Bibliothèque de l'Opéra. BN; **94a** Engravings from *Orphea-Taschenbuch*, 1831. Universitätsbibliothek, Leipzig; **94b** Photo: AKG London; **95** Biblioteca Sormani, Milan. Costa; **96** Museo Teatrale alla Scala, Milan. Photo Scala; **97r** V&A Picture Library; **97b** Opera Rara; **98l** Photo: AKG London; **98r** Costa; **99** Museo Teatrale alla Scala, Milan. Costa; **100** Bibliothèque de l'Opéra. BN; **101** Private Collection; **102** Österreichische Nationalbibliothek, Vienna. Photo Fayer; **103l** Opera Rara; **103r** Musée de l'Opéra. BN; **104** Opera Rara; **105** Raccolta Bertarelli, Milan. Costa; **106** Musée de l'Opéra. BN; **107al** Covent Garden Archives; **107ar** Victoria and Albert Museum, London. Photo Eileen Tweedy; **107b** Bibliothèque de l'Opéra, Paris. Photo: AKG London; **108** Bibliothèque de l'Opéra, BN; **109l** BN; **109r** Museo donizettiano, Bergamo; **110** Museo Teatrale alla Scala, Milan. Photo Scala; **111a** Baron von Leyser, *Rienzi*, 1843. Deutsches Theatermuseum, Munich; **111b** Johann K. J. Gerst, Sketch for *Der fliegende Holländer*, 1842. ÖNB; **112a** Lithograph from *Journal de Musique.* BN; **112b** Th. Tischbein, *Tannhäuser.* Stadtgeschichtliches Museum, Leipzig; **113a** Biblioteca Correr, Venice. Costa; **113b** Paul Lormier, design for *L'Enfant prodigue.* Musée de l'Opéra. BN; **114** Victoria and Albert Museum, London. Photo Eileen Tweedy; **115a** Richard Wagner Museum, Bayreuth; **115b** ÖNB; **116–7** A. von Volborth, *Isolde's Death*, 1909. Archiv für Kunst und Geschichte, Berlin. Photo: AKG London; **118** Istituto di studi verdiani, Parma. Costa; **119** RA; **120** & **121b** Costa; **121a** Biblioteca Correr, Venice. Costa; **122l** Private Collection; **122r** RA; **123l** Raccolta Bertarelli, Milan. Costa; **123r** ÖNB; **124** Musée de l'Opéra, Paris. BN; **125l** Collection Viollet; **125r** Musée de l'Opéra. BN; **126l** Costa; **126r** BN; **127** Opera News; **128** Bibliothèque de l'Opéra. BN; **129** Engraving from *Illustrirte Zeitung*, 1865; **130b** Engraving from *l'Illustration*, 24 November 1866. BN; **131** Bibliothèque nationale de France, Paris. Courtesy Opera News; **132** Private Collection; **133** RA; **134** Richard Wagner Museum, Bayreuth; **135a** RA; **135b** Opera News; **136** RA; **137a** Engraving from *L'Illustration*, 13 March 1875. BN; **137b** Costa; **138l** Richard Wagner Museum, Bayreuth; **138r** RA; **139l** Opera News; **139r** RA; **140** Private Collection; **141r** Photo: AKG London; **141b** RA; **142a** V&A Picture Library; **142bl** Musée d'Albi; **143** ÖNB; **145l** Museo Teatrale alla Scala, Milan; **145ar** Museo de Arte di São Paulo, Assis Chateaubriand. Photo Luiz Hossaka; **145br** Musée de l'Opéra. BN; **146** RA; **147** Opera News; **148** Raccolta Bertarelli, Milan. Costa; **149al** Photo: AKG London; **149ar** Musée de l'Opéra. BN; **149b** Costa; **150** Engraving from *l'Illustration*, 8 November 1890. BN; **151a** Bibliothèque de l'Opéra. BN; **151b** Engraving from *Le Journal illustré*, 1889. BN; **152** Costa; **153r** Museo Civico, Treviso. Costa; **153b** Photo: AKG London; **154** ÖNB; **155a** Collection Viollet; **155l** Courtesy The Edward Gordon Craig Estate; **156** Collection of the National Gallery of Victoria, Melbourne, Australia (Purchased by the Art Foundation of Victoria with the assistance of Diana and Henry Krongold, C.B.E., Founder Benefactor); **157r** Los Angeles County Museum of Art; **157l** Victoria and Albert Museum, London. Photo Eileen Tweedy; **158** Opera News; **159a** Opera News; **159b** Ullstein Bilderdienst; **160** Costa; **161r** Österreichisches TheaterMuseum, Vienna; **161b** ÖNB; **162** RA; **163al&ar** RA; **163b** Lithograph from *L'Illustration*, 19 August 1899. BN; **164** Photo: AKG London; **165r** Photo: AKG London; **165l** ÖNB; **166a** Bibliothèque de l'Opéra. BN; **166b** Opera News; **167** Historical Sound Recordings Collection, Yale University; **168** State Russian Museum, St Petersburg. Photo John Massey Stewart; **169r** Photo: AKG London; **169b** ÖNB. Reproduced by Permission of Boosey & Hawkes Music Publishers Ltd; **170–1** BN; **172** Kenneth Green, design for *Peter Grimes.* The Britten-Pears Library, Aldeburgh. Courtesy the Kenneth Green Estate; **173** Photo Siegfried Lauterwasser; **174r** Photo Matzene, Chicago; **174b** BFI Stills, Posters and Designs; **175** RA; **176** Galleria Nazionale d'Arte Moderna, Roma; **177a** Costa; **177b** Metropolitan Opera Archives, New York; **178** Historisches Museum der Stadt Wien. Photo: Bildarchiv ÖNB, Vienna; **179l** RA; **180a** Bibliothèque de l'Opéra. BN. © ADAGP, Paris and DACS, London 1998; **180b** *Opera*; **181a** Theatre Section – Národní Muzeum, Prague; **181b** Arnold Schoenberg Institute, © DACS 1998; **182** Atelier Dietrich, Vienna; **183a** Costa; **183b** Deutsches Theatermuseum, Munich; **184** Photo: AKG London; **185a** Photo: AKG London; **185b** RA; **186ar** Private Collection; **186b** Theatre Section – Národní Muzeum, Prague; **187** Opera News; **188a** Bibliothèque de l'Opéra. BN; **188b** Moravské Muzeum, Brno. Photo: AKG London; **189l** Ullstein Bilderdienst; **189r** Österreichische Nationalbibliothek. Foto Vouk; **191a** Billy Rose Theatre Collection, The New York Public Library for the Performing Arts. Astor, Lenox and Tilden Foundations. Vandamm Collection Photo; **191c** Metropolitan Opera Archives, New York; **191b** Goldsmith's College Library; **192a** Courtesy Glyndebourne Festival Opera; **192b** RA; **193a** Private Collection; **193b** Opera News; **194a** Opernhaus, Zurich; **194b** Reproduced from the Collections of the Library of Congress, Washington D.C.; **195r** Photo Carlo Edwards. Opera News; **195l** Opera News; **196a** BFI Posters, Stills and Designs; **196b** The Britten-Pears Library, Aldeburgh; **197a** Private Collection; **198** The Harvard Theatre Collection, © Angus McBean; **199a** The Britten-Pears Library, Aldeburgh. © Edward Mandinian; **199b** Photo Fayer, Vienna; **200l** Photo David Sim; **200r** Photo Giancolombo, Milan; **201a** Photo Günter Englert, Frankfurt am Main; **201b** Bibliothèque de l'Opéra, Paris. BN. © ADAGP, Paris and DACS, London 1998; **202a** Archivio Storico delle Arti Contemporanee della Biennale di Venezia; **202b** Photo Harry Croner; **203** © Bildarchiv Bayreuther Festspiele Production; **204** Österreichisches TheaterMuseum, Vienna. Foto Vouk; **205l** Photo Denis de Marnay. Hulton Getty; **205r** Photo Houston Rogers. V&A Picture Library; **206** Photo W. E. Baur, Zurich; **207** Deutsches Theatermuseum, Munich; **208a** © Zoe Dominic; **208b** Opera News; **209ar** Copyright ©. BBC, London; **209l** Photo Leone; **209bl** Photo Scottish Tourist Board; **210** Photo: AKG London. © ADAGP, Paris and DACS, London 1998; **211** Photo Colette Masson. Agence Enguerand/Iliade; **212a** Foto Fayer, Vienna; **212b** Decca/Hans Wild; **213** Národní Divadlo, Ostrední Archiv, Prague; **214a** Photo Jochen Clauss/Storypress; **214b** Copyright ©. BBC, London; **215** © 1974 Ron Scherl, Performing Arts Library, London; **216** © Clive Barda, Performing Arts Library, London; **217r** Photo Reg Wilson; **217b** BN; **218** Stockholm National Opera. Photo Enar Merkel Rydberg; **219a** Agence de Presse Photographique Bernard; **219b** Photo Siegfried Lauterwasser; **220** © Babette Mangolte 1976; **221** © Clive Barda. Performing Arts Library, London; **222a** Courtesy Gianni Versace S.p.A.; **222b** Finnish National Opera. Photo Kari Hakli; **223** © Kleinefenn, Paris; **224** Photo Jaap Pieper. Fotoarchieven MAI Amsterdam.

# INDEX

Page numbers in *italics* indicate references in captions

# L



# M

# T

# U



# V